SAM JONES' OWN BOOK

SOUTHERN CLASSICS SERIES

Mark M. Smith and Peggy G. Hargis, Series Editors

SAM JONES' OWN BOOK

A Series of Sermons

Collected and Edited under the Author's
Own Supervision with an Autobiographical Sketch

SAM P. JONES

New Introduction by

RANDALL J. STEPHENS

The University of South Carolina Press
Published in Cooperation with the Institute for
Southern Studies of the University of South Carolina

Cloth edition published by Cranston & Stowe, Cincinnati, Ohio, 1887
Paperback edition published by the University of South Carolina Press,
Columbia, South Carolina 29208

www.sc.edu/uscpress

Manufactured in the United States of America

18 17 16 15 14 13 12 11 10 09 10 9 8 7 6 5 4 3 2 1

Library of Congress Cataloging-in-Publication Data

Jones, Sam P. (Sam Porter), 1847–1906.
[Sermons. Selections. 2009]
Sam Jones' Own book : a series of sermons / Sam P. Jones ; new introduction by Randall J. Stephens.
p. cm. — (Southern classics series)
Originally published: Cincinnati, Ohio : Cranston & Stowe, 1887.
Includes bibliographical references.
ISBN 978-1-57003-827-3 (pbk. : alk. paper)
1. Evangelistic sermons. 2. Methodist Church—Sermons. 3. Sermons, American. I. Title.
BV3797.J85O96 2009
252'.3—dc22

2009009308

This book was printed on Glatfelter Natures, a recycled paper with 30 percent post-consumer waste content.

Publication of the Southern Classics series is made possible in part by the generous support of the Watson-Brown Foundation.

CONTENTS

ILLUSTRATIONS

SERIES EDITORS' PREFACE

Rich in meaning for an understanding of southern religion and culture, *Sam Jones' Own Book* is here reprinted for the first time since its initial publication. As Randall J. Stephens explains in his fascinating new introduction, Jones was a controversial figure, ridiculed by Mark Twain but applauded by Tom Watson, adored by thousands of evangelicals even as he was roundly criticized by suspicious newspaper men, discounted as coarse and unduly simple yet revered as an authentic, genuine messenger of hope. One of the most widely quoted Americans of his day, Sam Jones was listened to and read by millions, his plain style of delivery important for making evangelical religion relevant to broader late-Victorian values. At once a southern and national figure, Sam Jones was a celebrity, and his life and activities tell us a great deal not only about religious sensibilities at the turn of the century but also how evangelical religion functioned locally and nationally, how it served, in the hands of a witty, masterly preacher, to inspire optimism in a country undergoing significant social and cultural changes. *Sam Jones' Own Book* offered tools for counteracting what Jones perceived as the damaging tendencies of a radical new secularism. It inspired a generation of Americans and, in many respects, prefigured later debates concerning the moral trajectory of modern America.

Southern Classics returns to general circulation books of importance dealing with the history and culture of the American South. Sponsored by the Institute for Southern Studies, the series is advised by a board of distinguished scholars who suggest titles and editors of individual volumes to the series editors and help establish priorities in publication.

Chronological age alone does not determine a title's designation as a Southern Classic. The criteria also include significance in contributing to a broad understanding of the region, timeliness in relation to events and moments of peculiar interest to the American South, usefulness in the classroom, and suitability for inclusion in personal and institutional collections on the region.

MARK M. SMITH
PEGGY G. HARGIS
Series Editors

know that dynamite can be used successfully in fishing?" Jones retorted. "Well, if a fool fisherman who doesn't know how to use it blows his head off, is that any reason why a wise man who does know how to use it shouldn't catch his fish that way if he wants to?"[16] It was a pragmatic, simple message, much like that of another towering Methodist of the nineteenth century, Phoebe Palmer. Just as Palmer, from her New York home, had encouraged the faithful to claim holiness or sinless perfection, Jones prodded readers and revival audiences to simply stop sinning. "Quit your meanness," "Quit sin," "Quit the world," "Quit the devil," he exhorted.[17] It was one part Dwight Moody, one part Horatio Alger. Jones was always practical and confident. Like the holiness people with whom he associated—radical Protestants who believed in sanctification, or a second sin-cleansing work of grace—he was not afraid to use modern means to preach an old-time religion. "If I could go through this country with Mrs. Winslow's Soothing Syrup, and get more souls to Christ by having the sinners each take a teaspoonful," he crowed, "I would invest every nickel I have in that syrup."[18]

His simple message enchanted millions. For audiences and readers across the U.S., he vividly recounted the "wickedness" of casinos, theaters, dance halls, and barrooms. He was an entertainer as much as a spellbinding sermonizer. The puritanical, populist themes he crafted would remain central to evangelicalism throughout much of the twentieth century. Jones won ardent followers among holiness folk. Like Georgia's revivalist, they lashed out at backsliding, urbane Protestants and the "sodom-like" luxuries of Victorian Methodism. "The city churches are . . . nice gathering places for the rich and tony crowd who go to spend Sunday in a respectable place and keep up a reputation for general business," but they were spiritually lifeless, commented a bitter holiness stalwart.[19] Alcohol was a chief holiness target. And as prohibitionism remained a major force in American religion and politics, Jones seemed deeply relevant. With others of his generation and region, he was a paternalist. Blacks who opposed prohibition did not deserve the vote, he thought. Like Billy Sunday later in the twentieth century, Jones railed against foreign domination. He also condemned "negro rule" and unrestricted immigration.[20] Sunday shared more than just his predecessor's bigotry. He was also fond of the well-turned aphorism. And Sunday embraced Jones' biblical literalism and staunch defensive posture. "I believe that the whale swallowed Jonah," Jones once quipped. "And the only reason I don't believe that Jonah swallowed the whale is because the Bible don't say so."[21]

In 1886 when he published *Sam Jones' Own Book*—a kind of comfort food for the soul, packed with folk wisdom and down-home observations—Jones was a national icon. Like Billy Graham decades later, Jones proclaimed a simple message that epitomized southern evangelicalism. From the mid-1880s through the 1890s, the southern evangelist was at the pinnacle of his career. He preached in every major city in the United States. In 1886 alone he claimed to have delivered one thousand sermons to three million Americans from coast to coast.[22] One prominent convert in Nashville, Tom Ryman, even built a large structure, Ryman's Union Gospel Tabernacle, for Jones and other evangelists to conduct revivals in. (That edifice would later become the home of the Grand Ole Opry.) Not surprisingly Jones was one of the highest paid ministers in Gilded Age America. He boasted an annual salary of $30,000. Upon his death he left an estate worth $250,000. His lavish Cartersville, Georgia, home, Roselawn, displays that wealth and has become a popular tourist stop for travelers in the region. Today the Roselawn Museum registers approximately six thousand visitors a year.[23]

Oddly enough the evangelist whom Democratic warhorse William Jennings Bryan praised for his "earnestness, his evident sincerity, and his plain, common sense way of putting things" has faded from public memory.[24] And now that colossal figure of southern humor and religious wit is forgotten in most of America outside of Georgia. Besides Kathleen Minnix's exceptional scholarly biography of Jones, *Laughter in the Amen Corner: The Life of Evangelist Sam Jones* (University of Georgia Press, 1993), and a handful of articles written in regional historical journals, Jones is absent largely from southern history and American religious history. His widely read works, nonfiction best sellers in his lifetime, remain hard to find or out of print.[25]

Indeed *Sam Jones' Own Book* has been out of print since it was published roughly 120 years ago. The book ably represents the folksy humorist and moralizing preacher at his cleverest. It contains a collection of his most popular sermons, a selection from his chief preaching associate—Sam Small, a fellow southerner "delivered" from alcohol—and a host of the preacher's rich southern witticisms. (Jones dictated his books from his sermons much as he dictated the articles he "wrote" for the *Atlanta Journal* and religious newspapers.)[26] In addition *Sam Jones' Own Book* contains thirteen illustrations —including images of the massive venues at which he preached and depictions of various ministerial colleagues. A fifty-page autobiography recounts his conversion in 1872, his "victory" over alcohol, his early ministry in North Georgia, and his subsequent fame. The sermons included in the text are those that won him so much acclaim and admiration. Among these are "Personal Consecration: 'Quit Your Meanness,'" "Delighting in the Lord," "The Secret of a Religious Life," and "Sowing and Reaping." In those and other sermons, he bluntly challenges Americans to act on their faith and help reform society. With equal fury he denounces what so many Victorian evangelicals considered the sources of sin: card playing, drinking, and theater attendance. He spices all his jeremiads heavily with humor. The sayings included at the end of each chapter reveal as much while reflecting his "turn or burn" outlook. "Everybody ought to keep good company," Jones declares. "There is not an angel in heaven that would not be corrupted by the company that some of you keep." "Whisky is a good thing in its place," he writes with typical attention-grabbing skill, "and that place is in hell. If I get there I will drink all I can get, but I won't do it here." Elsewhere he jokes, "A man who believes only in what he can see, doesn't believe he has got a backbone."[27] Even Jones' harshest critics recognized that his humor and unbuttoned style drew the crowds.

Like so many others in this uncertain era, Jones believed that a new secularism—evident in the circus, the theater, ballroom, the saloon, and other "dens of iniquity" that could not even be mentioned—posed grave dangers to society. These diversions led to perdition, he warned. In his sermon in the book titled "Sowing and Reaping," he pleads: "Sow cards and reap what? Industrious, hard-working boys? Sow cards and reap farmers? Sow cards and reap first-class mechanics? Sow cards and reap lawyers? No! no! a thousand times no! But sow cards and reap gamblers." Jones thunders, "Men and boys go from the bar-rooms to the gambling hell and from the gambling hell to the shameless houses, just as naturally as a living man breathes."[28]

In 1886, around the time that *Sam Jones' Own Book* hit the shelves, the enormously powerful industrial workers union, the Knights of Labor, claimed seven hundred thousand members. It united skilled and unskilled labor to protest wage cuts and abysmal, unsafe working conditions. A tumultuous year, 1886 began with a wave of strikes, culminating in what was called the Great Upheaval. Railroad workers, miners, and factory laborers brought the economy to a grinding halt. On May 4, 1886, a bomb exploded at a workman's rally in Chicago's Haymarket. Eight died as a result of the blast. The nationwide reaction to new immigrants, laborers, and anarchists was immediate and intense. Other American cities erupted in violence that volatile summer. In the coming decade political protest took the form of third-party politics. Jones lent his support to the breakaway Populist Party, though he later wavered.[29]

Sam Jones and millions of other evangelicals feared that the church had become an overcivilized, overeducated, irrelevant institution. He castigated both elites and "sinners," calling for a "manly" faith that would meet the challenges of the era. In one of the sermons in *Sam Jones' Own Book*, "Purity of Heart," he calls for a masculine army of God to wage war against sin and impish Christianity: "Brethren, we don't want any peace in any sense until we have rid ourselves of those things that are cursing our city and our neighbors. Let us have war, and carry our warfare on our knees through this city."[30] He had been vocal about the failure of earlier ministers. They lacked practical education, he exclaimed. "We have been clamoring for fifty years for an educated ministry," sneered Jones, "and we have got it to-day, and the church is deader than it ever has been in its history." Educated divines, he hooted, were little more than the sum of their degrees, "A.B.'s, Ph.D.'s, D.D.'s, LL.D.'s, and A.S.S.'s."[31] Judging from *Sam Jones' Own Book,* he was deeply distressed by what he perceived as the problems of the church and urban America. Though not a liberal reformer, he called on Americans to aid the poor, care for the sick, and feed the hungry.

That message appealed to his readers. Though there is no clear estimate of the number of copies *Sam Jones' Own Book* sold, it is safe to assume that it went well beyond the ten-thousand mark. As historian Kathleen Minnix notes, Jones' first book, *Sermons and Sayings*—printed by the Southern Methodist Publishing House in Nashville in 1883—sold 30,000 copies in just four months. In terms of America's current population that would amount to 171,000 copies. At that point he was not yet the national celebrity he would be three years later. In the 1880s and 1890s, excerpts from Jones' works were being reprinted in England, Sweden, Australia, and Scotland. The publisher of *Sam Jones' Own Book*, Cranston and Stowe of Cincinnati, Ohio, had established itself as a leading printer of religious biographies—including one of the popular African American preacher Amanda Berry Smith—and theological works—such as the systematic theology of Samuel Wakefield. Cranston and Stowe had been in operation since the 1850s. Jones' book, issued in 1887 as well as 1886, would have been, quite possibly, one of the publisher's best-selling titles. It was an entrepreneurial move for Jones, too. He had suffered some financial loss and embarrassment with the printing of unauthorized, shoddy versions of his sermons and adages. "A firm in Chicago has perpetrated the boldest robbery (on my wife and children)," Jones lamented, "and burnished their deed with the most audacious impudence on record. They have copyrighted my own sermons against myself." Hence the title he chose was meant to indicate that it was his "own" authorized version. The book was subsequently issued in Dunedin, New Zealand, by Malcolm and Grigg; in London, England, by T. Woolmer; and in Toronto, Canada, by William Briggs.[32]

Those who had seen or heard of the "Georgia Wonder" received it favorably. Advertisements in religious and secular newspapers proclaimed, "Everybody wants to see what Sam Jones has to say." In May 1886 an editor at the *Atlanta Constitution* praised the newly published *Sam Jones' Own*

Book: "The admirers of Sam Jones should take notice that this is the only authorized edition of his sermons. The readers of THE CONSTITUTION are already acquainted with the merits of this book. Thousands of them have laughed and wept over his characteristic utterances. The book is selling rapidly."[33] The English *Wesleyan Methodist Magazine* heaped praise on the volume, announcing that "no one who reads the sermons of Sam P. Jones . . . can help feeling that much of their force is due to rough and ready putting of moral and religious truth." He skillfully translated theological subtleties into "the language of the street-corner."

The volume would have likely appealed to middle- and working-class Americans and those countless individuals who had recently moved from the countryside to the cities and suburbs. His books, priced at around one dollar, were not out of reach for those of modest means.[34] He preached and wrote for the plain-folk Methodists not unlike those parodied so mercilessly by the late-nineteenth-century novelist Harold Frederic. In Frederic's *Damnation of Theron Ware* (1896), Brother Pierce admonishes the new young minister of a tiny rural, upstate New York church:

> "We are a plain sort o' folks up in these parts," said Brother Pierce. . . . His voice was as dry and rasping as his cough, and its intonations were those of authority. "We walk here," he went on, eying the minister with a sour regard, "in a meek an' humble spirit, in the straight an' narrow way which leadeth unto life. We ain't gone traipsin' after strange gods, like some people that call themselves Methodists in other places. We stick by the Discipline an' the ways of our fathers in Israel. No new-fangled notions can go down here. Your wife'd better take them flowers out of her bunnit afore next Sunday."
>
> . . . "Another thing: We don't want no book-learnin' or dictionary words in our pulpit," he went on coldly. "Some folks may stomach 'em; we won't."[35]

Jones' readers were probably like those who assembled to hear the southern minister preach. Those who crammed into Boston's Faneuil Hall for Jones' 1887 revival, observed the *Andover Review*, included "workingmen in blue blouses, and marketmen in white frocks, scattered amongst the throng, while in the crowded galleries the bright hats of small groups of ladies gave a dash of gaiety to the spectacle. . . . Here and there was a shabby individual, odorous with the mingled fumes of whiskey and tobacco."[36] Jones' old-time, shouting-Methodist style was favorably received. Holiness as well as Methodist newspapers and journals regularly trumpeted his revivals and publications. His sermons and sayings have much to teach about the values and ideals of Americans in the late Victorian period, and religious historians still consider *Sam Jones' Own Book* a classic example of his preaching style and a valuable window onto an exciting and turbulent age in American history.

Notes

1. On Watson as an orator, see C. Vann Woodward, *Tom Watson: Agrarian Rebel* (1938; repr., New York: Oxford University Press, 1963), 308–9. First Watson quotation in Laura Jones, *The Life and Sayings of Sam P. Jones* (1907; repr., St. John, Ind.: Christian Book Gallery, n.d.), 419. Watson quoted in Harry Malcolm Chalfant, *These Agitators and Their Idea* (Nashville, Tenn.: Cokesbury Press, 1931), 186.

2. For newspapers' criticism of Jones, see Kathleen Minnix, *Laughter in the Amen Corner: The Life of Evangelist Sam Jones* (Athens: University of Georgia Press, 1993), 5, 66, 176–77; "The 'Circus Preachers,'" *Atlanta Constitution*, 28 August 1886, 1; and *Puck*, 17 November 1886, 189.

3. Mark Twain, "A Singular Episode: The Reception of Rev. Sam Jones in Heaven" in *The Bible according to Mark Twain: Writings on Heaven, Eden, and the Flood*, ed. Howard G. Baetzhold and Joseph B. McCullough (Athens: University of Georgia Press, 1995), 199, 200, 201.

4. Sam Jones, *Sam Jones' Own Book* (Cincinnati: Cranston and Stowe, 1887; Columbia: University of South Carolina Press, 2009), 374, 425, 186. Citations hereafter are to the 2009 edition.

5. "Scores Look on Dead Face of Sam Jones," *Atlanta Constitution*, 18 October 1906, 1; "Dead Soldier of the Cross Comes Home," *Atlanta Constitution*, 17 October 1906, 1; Minnix, *Laughter in the Amen Corner*, 240–41.

6. "Sam P. Jones Dies Suddenly on a Train," *New York Times*, 16 October 1906, 9.

7. Minnix, *Laughter in the Amen Corner*, 17–39; Jones, *The Life and Sayings of Sam P. Jones*, 42–49.

8. Jones, *Sam Jones' Own Book*, 14

9. Jones, *The Life and Sayings of Sam P. Jones*, 50–51

10. David B. Parker, "Sam Jones (1847–1906)," *New Georgia Encyclopedia*, http://www.georgiaencyclopedia.org/nge/Article.jsp?id=h-1606&hl=y (accessed 19 June 2008); Walt Holcomb, ed., *Popular Lectures of Sam P. Jones* (New York: Fleming H. Revell Company, 1909), 97.

11. Minnix, *Laughter in the Amen Corner*, 128–29.

12. Quote from "Sam Jones in Iuka," *Atlanta Constitution*, 23 August 1884, 5; Jones, *The Life and Sayings of Sam P. Jones*, 112–13.

13. Quoted in Jones, *The Life and Sayings of Sam P. Jones*, 205–6.

14. Ibid., 133–42; "Elder Sam Jones," *New-Hampshire Sentinel*, 10 June 1885, 1.

15. Quoted in Jones, *The Life and Sayings of Sam P. Jones*, 135. An article from *Our Young Men* quoted in "Religious Press," *Christian Index*, 19 May 1887, 1.

16. "Sam P. Jones Dies Suddenly on a Train," *New York Times*, 16 October 1906, 9.

17. For an excellent analysis of Palmer's pragmatism, see Briane K. Turley, *A Wheel within a Wheel: Southern Methodism and the Georgia Holiness Association* (Macon, Ga.: Mercer University Press, 1999), 51–59, 58. Harold E. Raser, *Phoebe Palmer: Her Life and Thought* (Lewiston, N.Y.: Edwin Mellen Press, 1987), 149–226; George R. Stuart, *Sam P. Jones, the Preacher* (Siloam Springs, Ark.: International Federation Publishing Company, n.d.), 37.

18. "Sam P. Jones," *Wesleyan Methodist Magazine*, April 1887, 273.

19. "The Future of Methodism," *American Outlook*, 15 July 1897, 2. See also L. L. Pickett and M. A. Smith, *The Pickett-Smith Debate on Entire Sanctification, a Second Blessing* (Louisville, Ky.: Pickett Publishing Company, 1897), 101. For other examples of antiurban sentiment, see Timothy L. Smith, *Called unto Holiness: The Story of the Nazarenes,* vol. 1, *The Formative Years* (Kansas City, Mo.: Nazarene Publishing House, 1962), 165; and J. Lawrence Brasher, *The Sanctified South: John Lakin Brasher and the Holiness Movement* (Urbana: University of Illinois Press, 1994), 150.

20. Minnix, *Laughter in the Amen Corner*, 183–85. For Jones' views on lynching, race, and paternalism, see Darren E. Grem, "Sam Jones, Sam Hose, and the Theology of Racial Violence," *Georgia Historical Quarterly* 90 (Spring 2006): 35–61.

21. Quoted in Jones, *The Life and Sayings of Sam P. Jones*, 455.

22. Parker, "Sam Jones (1847–1906)."

23. William G. McLoughlin Jr., *Modern Revivalism: Charles Grandison Finney to Billy Graham* (New York: Ronald Press Company, 1959), 110–16. When challenged about his lavish income, Jones responded that he had given away $275,000 of the $300,000 he had earned. Minnix, *Laughter in the Amen Corner*, 106, 129. See *Puck* magazine's criticism of the minister's "laying up for himself treasures upon earth": "Particular Paragraphs," *Puck*, 23 June 1886, 266. Roselawn Museum Web site, http://roselawnmuseum.com (accessed 19 June 2008).

24. Quoted in Jones, *The Life and Sayings of Sam P. Jones*, 414.

25. Two massive reference works on the American South fail to mention him: David C. Roller and Robert W. Twyman, eds., *The Encyclopedia of Southern History* (Baton Rouge: Louisiana State University Press, 1979); and Charles Reagan Wilson and William Ferris, eds., *The Encyclopedia of Southern Culture* (Chapel Hill: University of North Carolina Press, 1989).

26. Stuart, *Sam P. Jones, the Preacher*, 42; Jones, *The Life and Sayings of Sam P. Jones*, 330–31. Jones described the collection as a compilation of material from his successful Cincinnati revival. Sam P. Jones' letter in "Book Notices," *Herald of Gospel Liberty*, 1 April 1886, 208.

27. Jones, *Sam Jones' Own Book*, 317, 361, 78.

28. Ibid., 249, 248.

29. Nell Irvin Painter, *Standing at Armageddon: The United States, 1877–1919* (New York: W. W. Norton, 1987), 39–53; Minnix, *Laughter in the Amen Corner*, 188–93. For the late-nineteenth-century southern context of Jones' theology, see David B. Parker, "'Quit Your Meanness': Sam Jones's Theology for the New South," *Georgia Historical Quarterly* 77 (Winter 1993): 711–27.

30. Jones, *Sam Jones' Own Book*, 299–300. On masculinity and Sam Jones' preaching, see Chad Gregory, "Sam Jones: Masculine Prophet of God," *Georgia Historical Quarterly* 86 (Summer 2002): 231–52.

31. Holcomb, *Popular Lectures of Sam P. Jones*, 25; Minnix, *Laughter in the Amen Corner*, 119. On Americans' fears of powerlessness in these years, see T. J. Jackson Lears, *No Place of Grace: Antimodernism and the Transformation of American Culture, 1880–1920* (New York: Pantheon Books, 1981), 47; and Gail Bederman, *Manliness and Civilization: A Cultural History of Gender and Race in the United States, 1880–1917* (Chicago: University of Chicago Press, 1995), 14.

32. Jones, *Sam Jones' Own Book*, xxi; Jones, *The Life and Sayings of Sam P. Jones*, 331; and Sam P. Jones' letter in "Book Notices," *Herald of Gospel Liberty*, 1 April 1886, 208.

33. See advertisements in *Zion's Herald*, 12 January 1887, 16; *Christian Advocate*, 24 February 1887, 129; and "Briefs about Books," *Atlanta Constitution*, 15 May 1887, 13.

34. Advertisement, *Literary World; a Monthly Review of Current Literature*, 3 April 1886, 122.

35. Harold Frederic, *Damnation of Theron Ware* (1896; repr., New York: Holt, Rinehart, and Winston, 1960), 28.

36. "Evangelism in Faneuil Hall," *Andover Review*, March 1887, 320.

PUBLISHERS' PREFACE TO THE FIRST EDITION

Mr. Jones has given this book a title which carries the evidence of his direct authorship. It is not likely that the speculators upon Mr. Jones' popularity will presume to ask an intelligent public to purchase their crude and unauthorized versions of the discourses of the great evangelist in preference to his *"Own Book,"* but experience with this class of publishers has shown the need of the most careful precautions on the part of both the author and his chosen agents. It is with our consent that Mr. Wm. Briggs, of Toronto, Ont., publishes Mr. Jones' sermons in Canada; but we still hold the exclusive right under contract entered into early in the year 1886, to handle all Mr. Jones' works published after that date in the United States. We have aimed to produce these sermons in becoming style and at as low price as is consistent with superior workmanship. The present volume excels any other in that it contains through close condensation fourteen more sermons than former books, does not repeat the sermons hitherto presented by us, is more largely illustrated, and to crown all, has Mr. Jones' autobiography. Mr. Sam Small's great sermon, *"Deliverance from Bondage,"* has been also included at the special request of the admirers of this already distinguished convert and helper of Mr. Jones.

Altogether we believe that "Sam Jones' Own Book" will be the favorite volume of the thousands who love the man and admire his genius.

THE PUBLISHERS.

Frontispiece to the 1887 edition

SAM JONES' OWN BOOK

Autobiographical Sketch.

As Mr. Charles G. Finney, one of America's greatest revivalists, said: "It has pleased God, in some measure, to connect my name and labors with an extensive movement of the Church of Christ." The world naturally looks upon these movements. Some men are aroused to bitter criticism, others are brought to Christ by the sweeping tides, while others seem to be indifferent. I suppose the latter class are the ones most to be pitied, for indifference is the most insurmountable obstacle when you would reconcile man to God.

I shall speak of myself in connection with these movements, recognizing the hand of God as the power, and the faithful ministers who have co-operated with me, and the ten thousand prayers of consecrated Christian men and women as the great factors under God that have helped me in doing my work. If I speak honestly of these revivals and my relation to them, I do so simply with the facts as they occur to my mind, without any purpose to use the first personal pronoun, except as it represents the smallest factor in the movement.

I shall give a brief account of my birth, family, etc., as these few pages are autobiographical. I was born in Chambers County, Alabama, on the 16th of October, 1847. My father was Captain John J. Jones, the son of a Methodist preacher; my paternal grandmother was one of the most godly, consecrated women of her day, she being the daughter of Rev. Robert L. Edwards, one of the pioneer preachers of Georgia, and a giant in his day. Four of my father's brothers are now ministers of the Gospel of Christ. We have been Methodists on both sides of the family for several generations. As I have frequently said: I am a Methodist just as I am a Jones, and if it is a sin to be either, it is a sin that is visited upon the children from the parents. Methodists and Joneses are getting to be very common, in that they are very general everywhere.

My mother was a painstaking, sweet-spirited, Christian woman. I remember to have seen her and kissed her the last time, in my father's parlor, as I stooped over her burial case, when

I was nine years of age. She sleeps in the old cemetery of Oak Bowery, Alabama. With one brother older than myself, a sister and brother younger than myself, with a heart-broken father, we left the cemetery for our home, to answer the oft-repeated question: "What is home without a mother?" Eternity can hardly compensate a man for the loss he suffers when he buries his mother. Four years after my mother's death (in the meanwhile my brothers, sister, and myself remained at our grandfather Jones's home) my father married Miss Jennie Skinner, of Cartersville, Georgia, and removed us there in the year 1859, where we lived, controlled and guided not only by a father's advice, but our new mother did all she could in instilling the principles of virtue and right in our young hearts and lives, until our father joined the Army of Virginia in 1861, and by reason of his absence and the disordered state of society and the country, due to the presence of cruel war, I began to drift away from the teachings of my sainted mother and the rules of my home; and when my father returned from the army, before peace was restored, I had so advanced in the company of those who were worldly and wicked in the habits of profanity and *gentlemanly* dram-drinking and other immoralities, that I found it much more easy to proceed in a life so at variance with the right that I drifted on from month to month, until at the age of twenty-one years I was physically wrecked and morally ruined. I am sure many of the excesses of my early life would have never been indulged had it not been for the absence of my father, which gave me liberty to associate with those whose habits and character would certainly ruin those who mingled with them.

From the beginning of my school age up to the time of my mother's death, I had been a little scholar in the excellent school of Professor Slayton, now superintendent of the public schools of Atlanta. I remember at one of his commencements he had written for me a parody on the oft-repeated juvenile oration:

> "You 'd scarce expect one of my age
> To speak in public on the stage."

It was at night, and when the time came for the delivery of my speech, I was asleep in my mother's lap. Professor Slayton came to my mother, awoke me, and carried me in his arms to a table on the stage and stood me there. I delivered the speech, the last two lines of which I remember were these:

> "In thundering peals and Thornton tones,
> The world shall hear of Sam. P. Jones."

I remember that for months after the delivery of this speech I kept my little associates and myself in candy, for whenever and wherever I would repeat it for them, I could name my price in candy.

The faithful tutorship of Professor Slayton was worth much to me, because the ground work of an education had been faithfully laid before I was seven years of age. My studies were grossly neglected when my father was away from home in the army. After he returned and the war was over, I began to prosecute my studies anew in the school of ex-Congressmen Felton and his intelligent wife; farther along under Professor Ronald Johnson, in the High-school of Euharlee, Georgia. There my health completely broke down, and I suffered from the worst form of nervous dyspepsia, and this robbed me of the collegiate course which my father intended for me. With health wrecked, sleepless nights, and restless days, I began to seek relief in the intoxicating cup, with no object in view but to get through the weary day and to seek some plan by which I could sleep an hour at night. Oh, the horrors of nervous dyspepsia! It was in this state of mind and body that I began to read law, and in twelve months I was admitted to the bar, growing more dissipated all the time.

In November, 1869, I was married to Miss Laura McElwain, of Henry County, Kentucky, only one month after my admission to the bar. I started out in the practice of law with rich promise of success, but drink had become a passion with me, and all the ambitions and vital forces of my life were being undermined by this fearful appetite. My wife, with a courage born of despair, and with a faith in God that would laugh at impossibilities, and cry, "It shall be done," in the weakest and darkest hours of our married life, endeavored always to be the crutches under my arms, and to hold me up; and never did she cease her efforts or take her faith from off the promises until she realized at last that God is not slack concerning his promises. While I was frequently moved by her tears and affected by her prayers, yet I persistently maintained a dissipated life until the month of August, 1872, when I was brought to face the fact that my father, my best and truest friend, was bidding earth good-bye forever; and as he said "good-bye," he looked as if he meant forever, but he lingered on this side long enough to extort the promise from me that I would meet him in heaven. Wretched and ruined as I was, I made the promise, and upon my fidelity to that promise I hang my highest hope of heaven. No man could feel as I felt or see what I saw in that death chamber, as father almost literally shouted his way out of this world, without crying out from the depths of his heart,

> "I yield, I yield!
> I can hold out no more;
> I sink, by dying love compelled,
> And own thee Conqueror."

When peace and pardon were given, after days of seeking, I was impressed that I should preach the Gospel. I did not know from whence those impressions came; I thought, as did Gideon Ouseley, "I can not preach, I am not fit to preach, I do not know any thing to preach." I sought the advice and counsel of several faithful preachers, and I believe each of them said the same thing: "You are called to preach. You can go willingly into it, or you will be whipped into it, or you will lose your religion if you refuse." The last point was always the most powerful in the argument. As I stated before, I was born and raised a Methodist. I conferred not with flesh and blood further, but began immediately to preach the Gospel as only a man could preach it who knew but two facts—God is good, and I am happy in his love. Like Ouseley again, I knew the disease and I knew the remedy, and this gives the physician complete control over the patient.

The first sermon I ever preached, I believe, was the week after my conversion, at old New Hope church, two miles from Cartersville—my home. I had gone out with my grandfather Jones to that place. He was then pastor in charge of Barton Circuit, and this was one of his churches. After we had arrived on the ground, about the preaching hour at night, he learned that the Rev. Mr. Sanford, who was to preach on that occasion, would not be there. My grandfather was very hoarse; he could not preach, and he said to me: "My grandson, you must preach for us to-night." I replied, "I thought the call was first to get ready, and secondly to preach the Gospel." He said: "If God is calling you to preach, you can preach;

come on in the pulpit." I did so, with much fear and trembling. The whole congregation knew me—a wild, reckless boy. After the singing and prayer, I read the text: "I am not ashamed of the Gospel of Christ, for it is the power of God unto salvation to every one that believeth, to the Jew first, and also to the Greek." My exegesis and the critical analysis of the text I have forgotten, but, really, I do not think that either the exegesis or analysis came in on that occasion. I think before I had proceeded far into the text I adopted the plan of a good, old Methodist preacher "in the brush" who shut up his Bible and said: "Brethren, I can't preach the text, but I can tell my experience in spite of the devil." And out of a heart gushing full of love to God and to men, I told them of God's gracious dealings with me. Hundreds were melted to tears, and when the invitation was given for penitents to come forward, they thronged the altar, and I believe many were converted. After the service, my grandfather slapped me on the shoulder and said, "Go ahead, my boy! God has called you to the work." Much of my time in those days was given to prayer and reading the Scriptures.

It was still three months until the meeting of the Annual Conference in Atlanta. I began preparations by reading the course of study prescribed by the bishops of our Church for applicants for admission into the annual conference. Rev. George R. Kramer was my pastor and my spiritual instructor; he did much for me; a saintly, good man, now pastor in Brooklyn, New York.

I preached around through the community as opportunity offered until the meeting of the North Georgia Annual Conference. I went to that conference and offered myself, with all my ransomed powers. They accepted me; they gave me a place in the rank of Methodist itinerants, and gave me as my appointment the Van Wert Circuit. No gladder man ever accepted an appointment. My heart leaped for joy, and I said, "Thank God! I now have a place to work for Christ." On my way home from the annual conference, a good preacher said:

"Jones, do you know what your circuit paid its pastor last year?"

I replied: "No, I have not thought of that."

"Well," said he, "it paid the preacher for his year's service sixty-five dollars."

I laughed, and told him I did not care what they paid or did not pay; that I had a field to work in, and I was going to it gladly.

This circuit was in Polk County, only twenty miles from my home—Cartersville, Georgia. I went down, prospecting around, before I moved my family. The brethren were kind, and yet I could see that Burns was right when he said:

> "A man may take a neighbor's part,
> Yet have no cash to spare him."

Of course, I could not see this in comparison with any thing else. I had nothing to discourage me, because the picture drawn in my mind of itinerant life was one of hardships and privations. The brethren told me of a house that I could procure for my family, but did not propose to rent it for me, or even help me in procuring it. I gave my notes, twelve of them, of ten dollars each, payable monthly, for the rent of the house. This sum alone was fifty-five dollars more than the preacher received for his last year's services. In two weeks more I moved my family, consisting of wife and one child, into this house, in the town of old Van Wert. I had sold every thing that would bring money and paid on my debts so far as the money would go, and still I was hundreds of dollars in debt. I entered upon my work with faith in God and in the people, knowing that if I would do my duty I should not want any good thing. I was reappointed to this work until I had spent three happy, successful years on this, my first, circuit; and, if I remember correctly, the salary and perquisites of these three years amounted to over two thousand one hundred dollars, or over seven hundred dollars a year. When I entered upon my work in this circuit, I had three books—the Bible, the fifth volume of Spurgeon's Sermons, and some old volume of skeletons of sermons. Of course, my Bible was the book of all books to me, but I read and reread that volume of Spurgeon's sermons, until my soul and nature was stirred with the spirit of the man. I remember how I have frequently read the text of one of his sermons and then read his sermon; then I would read my text and, say: "If Spurgeon treated his text that way, how shall I treat mine?" And much of the directness of my style I owe to Spurgeon, the grandest preacher of this nineteenth century, if what a man does is a test of what a man is.

My preaching the first few months, and even the first years, was what my brethren called "earnest exhortation," but whether I exhorted or whether I preached, I have always been in earnest. Poor sermons and poor exhortation with the spirit of earnestness behind them will yield richer fruits than the most powerful logic and ornate rhetoric without the spirit of earnestness. Earnestness can not be feigned. It is like the natural and healthful glow on a maiden's cheek compared to the artificial coloring produced by rouge. So earnestness can always be distinguished from emotional gush or bellowing hurrahism. Earnestness is a thing of the eye and the face more than of the voice or of the words. "Let us go and hear that fellow, he seems to be in earnest," is a great compliment to any preacher. Earnestness in the pulpit is born of the experience which conscious pardon and complete deliverance from sin gives to the speaker. In a Gospel which has done so much for him, he sees that which will do as much for others, and he presses the Gospel, with its warning voice and its pleading tones, square upon the consciences of those who hear. There are many who are faithfully preaching the truth, but with earnestness only can they preach the truth efficiently. I have always had an inborn, constitutional hatred for shams, and especially for religious shams. Heaven and hell, one topless and the other bottomless, are real to me. Truth is real. Life is real; and no man can be a sham or a hypocrite without getting out of line with God and truth, and hell itself will make real devils out of religious shams before it will receive them. I have always contended there is no hoof and horn, fang nor poison attached to theoretical infidelity, but practical infidelity has all these things. I had rather be an Ingersoll and disbelieve the Book, than to be a Methodist believing every thing and living just like Ingersoll.

I saw upon the first round on my first circuit that there were either two distinct kinds of Christianity, or else a majority of my people had Christianity and I did not have it, or *vice versa*. They had indifference and carelessness and prayerlessness, and I found no room for any of these in my religious life. O, how many hours I spent as a youthful pastor trying to solve the problem and to know my duty towards my people. It was more than three years before my courage was screwed up to the sticking point, where I could preach the truth in such a pointed way as to leave no one to doubt that I meant him. In other words, in the fourth year of my ministry I began to preach to my people just as I thought about my people. I may preach the truth as it is in Christ, but a dissertation on truth is one thing, and the application of truth to the lives of men is another. A dissertation on mustard, where it grows, how it grows, and how it is prepared for the market, is one thing, and that one thing does not help the colic, but it is the spreading of the mustard upon a thin cloth and applying it to the stomach that relieves the aches and pains of the agonizing patient. Abstract truth may influence the mind to some extent and bring out the brain sweat, but consecrated truth, vigorously applied to the conscience, arouses the mind, produces conviction—and all upward movement is from conviction, from first to last. The bootmaker who makes the best fit gets the most customers. The preacher who fits the most consciences will get the most hearers. I have known for a long time that men knew better than they did. It is not in the pointing out of new paths, but it is the power to make them walk in the old paths; therefore, my preaching has been at the conscience. The intellects of men, when taken in the whole, vary in altitude like mountains and valleys; but the consciences of men form a vast plain, without an undulation from shore to shore, and he who stands on a level like this will move not only the peasant and laborer, but the intellectual giants of earth alike, for the conscience of a Webster is on the same plane and level with the conscience of a brakesman or any other common laborer.

In preaching at conscience there are three essential requisites: first, clearness; secondly, concentration; thirdly, directness. He who conceives truth clearly will express it clearly. Show a man all sides of the truth and then open it out and bathe it in a sea of light; then take a whole lead mine and run it into one bullet, and then aim where you want to hit, and your work is done. When you arouse the conscience, amid its ferocious lashings, the only alternative left is a better life or complete abandonment. Very few men will choose the latter. I remember this incident, which illustrates the point. In —— City, one of the leading merchants sent for the pastor, at whose church the union services were held. I was preaching directly at conscience. When the pastor went to his counting-room, the merchant excitedly said:

"I do n't like this preacher you have."

"Why?" said the pastor.

"Why, he makes men's wives jealous of them."

Said the pastor, "My wife has been in regular attendance, and she has not grown jealous of me."

"Well, mine has with me," said he. "Last night, as I rolled upon my pillow, wife saw I could not sleep, and she asked me what was the matter. I told her, nothing. She replied, 'I believe something that preacher said has taken hold upon you.' Of course, I said, 'No, no, nothing he said affected me;' but," said the man, "I am miserable because my wife is jealous of me, and d—— such a preacher."

"Well," said the pastor, "may be she has reason to be jealous."

"Ah," said the man, "that 's the trouble. My mistress is boarding at a first-class hotel, and I have sent for you, sir, to know what I must do."

"Well," said the faithful pastor, "abandon your adulterous life, and confess it to your wife."

The man replied, as the great drops of sweat gathered on his face: "Such a confession would be death to the happiness of my home, and I am in mortal agony."

Not twenty-four hours after this conversation, this man was an humble, earnest penitent at the altar, as his wife knelt at his side; and I trust he was among the number of converts of that meeting. I touched his conscience that night with the one allusion that when Christ came down from the mountain side, the multitude thronged him, and a leper walked up, and the multitude fell back and gave the leper plenty of room; and I said, "If some of your wives knew you as God knows you, they would give you the whole house to yourself." Perhaps this man was only one of the many whose consciences were stirred by that remark.

Whenever I take off at a tangent like that, I generally find fish up that stream. When a minister earnestly preaches and applies the truth, he may rest assured that he has the consciences of men on his side. While they rebel with their wills and curse him with their tongues, yet their consciences are on the side of the preacher and the truth. Applying the truth to every phase of life is the general work of the preacher. Let him get this truth either from the oldest Testament or the Old, the newest or the New. All truth is God's truth; all that is false is frustrated and driven in confusion before the truth. When Nathan told David the truth, David replied: "The man that hath done this thing shall surely die." But when Nathan dropped his finger on David and said, "Thou art the man," the next we heard of David, he was on his knees uttering the words of the fifty-first Psalm in the most abject penitence and thorough conviction. It is the "thou art the man," that brings humanity to its knees.

Thus, for thirteen years, I have not only tried to preach the truth, but so to apply the truth to the consciences of men, that there could be no mistake as to whom I meant, and amid all the harsh and seemingly unamiable expressions by which I have reached the consciences, my heart has always looked in sympathy and love upon the man whose life I laid bare by truth. I do believe where love expresses itself in sympathy, the subject will submit to any treatment at your hands; where love exposes guilt, the man falls out with himself, grows angry with himself, and loves the one that discovered it to his own eyes; and you have done a bad man a good service when you make him despise himself. The object of all true Gospel preaching is to make sin odious and holiness attractive; to make goodness as beautiful and as fragrant as a rose, and sin and hell inexpressibly horrible. O, the hideous deformities of sin, and the symmetry and beauty of righteousness!

The first three years of my ministry, as before stated, were spent on the Van Wert Circuit. They were three joyous years, and by God's help and grace they were successful years, a gracious revival of religion at each Church (there were five Churches forming the circuit). I believe the aggregate increase of membership in the circuit was not less than two hundred a year, while all my Churches were quickened into new life and spiritual growth. From there I was moved, and placed in charge of De Soto Circuit, in Floyd County, Georgia, with seven Churches forming the circuit. I had two happy, successful years on this circuit. Hundreds were converted to God and all the Churches quickened. These were the years that I was fortunately placed under Rev. Simon Peter Richardson as my presiding elder. At that time he was the most powerful, and at all times the most entertaining, guest I ever saw. The great nuggets of truth thrown out by him in pulpit and parlor, were food to me. He saw some great truths more clearly than any man I ever heard talk; he was a father and brother and teacher to me. I learned more from him than all other preachers I have ever come in contact with. I first learned from him that the pulpit was not a prison, but a throne; that instead of bars and walls and boundary lines, I might have wings and space as my heritage. I can recollect as well when my involuntary confinement ended and liberty began, as any fact in my history, and for years I have enjoyed this liberty and never consulted the theological landmarks or visited the orthodox prison. To think the thoughts of God is a freeman's right, with as little reverence for the Nicene Creed as for the resolutions of the General Conference or the Baptist Convention on the prohibition question, assured of the human origin of both alike. To stand on some mount of freedom and see that God is love and see that Christ is the manifestation of that love,—how transforming the vision! How unlike the picture we have looked on so often—God angry with a world, and with the weapons of his anger drawn, he poured his wrath and anger upon the victim on the cross! To see in Christ a Savior loving a sinner and saving a sinner, rather than a victim scarred by divine vengeance and abandoned by divine sovereignty; to see that the pierced side was an open doorway; to see in his hands, prints made by the cruel nails, the marks of his sympathy; and in his cross, my death to sin; and in his resurrection, my hope of eternal life; and realize that in all his works and sufferings and death, there is to me power given to begin, and grace given to continue, and help and weapons with which to conquer, and crowns and harps for my reward!

From the last named circuit I was moved to Newberne Circuit, in Newton County, Georgia. There I had two more pleasant, delightful years, with greater success, perhaps, than any two years previous, in building up my Churches and adding to the Church hundreds of souls. At the end of my second year in the Newberne Circuit, I was moved to Monticello Circuit, Jasper County, and there I had a remarkable year among the noblest people in my State. Thus, eight years of my ministry were given to four different circuits in my conference. In the eight years, I suppose not less than two thousand members were taken into my Churches in these circuits, and I did a great deal of revival work in other circuits and stations. In some of those revivals there were near five hundred conversions. In scarcely any of them did the conversions aggregate less than one hundred. I suppose that I might safely put the figures of the first eight years of my life as a pastor, of those who professed conversion under my ministry, at not less than five thousand altogether. I say these things, not because I am proud of them especially, for I believe with the appliances which God affords to us as his ministers, that five thousand souls in eight years is a very poor work. It seems to me, as I look back over those years, that I did my best, and yet I am sorry that more was not accomplished. I think last year alone I saw more souls than that brought to Christ in our various meetings. I am trusting and believing I shall live to see the day that I shall see a thousand souls born to God at one service, and I pray that God may make me the instrumentality of bringing fifty thousand souls to him in one year. If St. Peter, with the meager appliances, especially on the human side, could win three thousand souls in an hour with all Jerusalem against him, why might not a consecrated minister, with a hungry world and almost a despairing world of sinners about him, take them by the hand and lead ten thousand a day to Christ? I verily believe that I have seen five hundred souls converted at a service; there were three thousand praying Christian people present; there were a hundred consecrated preachers present; there were in the aggregate ten thousand people present; God was present; a thousand penitents were present; then doubt the statement, if you will, that five hundred of those who stood up accepted Christ and were converted.

When I began to preach, I was brought face to face with this fact, that to succeed as a preacher, one must be a great thinker or a great worker. Affinities made me choose the latter. I had serious doubts as to whether I could think above the plane where the masses stood. I knew I could work under God, and be a constant, persistent, and indefatigable laborer. I started out, determined that I would do my best.

I suppose, during the eight years of my

life as a pastor, I preached not less than four hundred sermons a year; and I have preached four times a day for weeks and weeks; and when my good friends would tell me I was working myself to death, I would laugh them off by telling them what Whitefield said when a physician told him he must stop working so much, that he must not preach but four hours every day and six hours on Sunday, and he rebelliously asked, "Doctor, do you want me to rust to death?" No doubt, I would have preached better sermons if I had preached fewer sermons, but a square or an oblong bullet will do as much execution as a polished, round one.

I have never made theology a study. The great doctrines of depravity and repentance and justification and regeneration and of the judgment and final award, I have preached with all the clearness of my mind and all the unction of my heart. I have never tried to show a congregation the difference between evangelical and legal repentance. I have never discussed whether depravity was total or partial, or simply developed. I have never tried to prove there was a God, or that Christ was divine, or that there was a heaven or a hell.

I have made these things, not an objective point, but a starting point. They have furnished the basis for all I have said, and they are either the inspirations of my hopes, or the ground-works of my fears. I have left the proof of the inspiration of the Bible, the demonstration of the fact that there is a God, the settlement of the question as to heaven and hell, to those who make a specter of such things and then speculate upon them, to the "muddy physicians." My idea has always been that Christ meant what he said when he said, "Preach the Gospel," not defend it; "Preach the Word," not try to prove the Word is true.

A very laughable, and yet forcible, incident occurred during the revival at Memphis, Tennessee, in Court Street Cumberland Presbyterian Church one morning. The services had been going on for nearly three weeks with great power; hundreds had been converted and Churches awakened. The meeting was a union meeting; thirteen pastors and congregations, representing five different denominations, were united in the fight, and on this occasion we had what we called a talking-meeting. The pastor of the First Methodist Church made a short, pointed talk, in which he told how the meetings had been a blessing to him. Other pastors followed, and when the pastor of the First Baptist Church told how he and all his Church had been blessed, he continued his talk by saying that he had learned something also about how to preach. He said that in the three weeks' preaching of Mr. Jones in that city, he had not heard a single attempt on the part of the preacher to prove that there was a God, or that Christ was divine; there had been no hair-splitting on theology, or an effort to prove that heaven was real or hell existing, and so on. After he sat down, old Uncle Ben, the faithful, old colored sexton of the First Methodist Church, stood up in the rear of the Church and said: "Brethren, you all know me. I have been trying to serve God from my childhood, and I have been greatly exercised in the last few years for the salvation of the perishing souls of Memphis. On my knees I have begged God to send just such a preacher as this to Memphis, though I did n't know who he was or where he was. Now he has come, thank God for him. He preaches the Gospel so that every one can understand it; he feeds me, he feeds the old and the young, the learned and the unlearned. Our pastors have been putting the fodder too high. I remember when Brother Mahon was our pastor last year, I looked into his study one morning, and he had five books lying open around him on the table, and I said, 'Brother Mahon, if you get one sermon out of five different books, you are going to put your fodder up Sunday morning where I can't reach it, for,' I said, 'I've gone to Church hungry on Sunday morning and come away hungry; fodder too high for me.' But this man of God scatters the fodder on the ground, and we can all reach it, and we also relish it." And so Uncle Ben went on in his rambling talk until he made as fine an argument on homiletics as many of the preachers said they had ever listened to.

The finest compliment I have ever had was in the second year of my ministry, when a little son of one of my members said:

"Father, will Mr. Jones be returned to this circuit next year?"

The father replied he hoped so, and asked his son, "Why?"

"Well," said the boy, "I want him to come back, because he is the only preacher I ever listened to that I can understand every thing he says."

I believe it is possible to preach our best thoughts and highest conceptions of God and truth so that children may understand us. The fact that they do not understand us is better proof that we are "muddy" than that we are high, for truth is like the water of the River of Life—clear as crystal.

Of course, in all these years of my life as a pastor, I was the object of a great deal of criticism. If no truth furnished others material with which they could assault, there was no lie that earth or hell could concoct that they would not take and circulate against me—some very ridiculous lies, some venomous lies, some very lying lies. O, how I have looked at my wife sometimes and seen resentment written upon every feature of her face; for instance, when she read the well-credited story of how I had abandoned my "first wife," and of how I was unkind to my "second wife." They have reported me drunk on a hundred different occasions; they have reported me as a wife-beater; and rumors that I afterwards thought the devil himself must have felt ashamed of, they have circulated time and again on me. I found out, after all, this world does not give a man the right of way, and the devil has rights, he thinks, that even preachers must respect; and frequently, after you have procured the right of way, the change of a switch, a wash-out, a cross-tie on the track, and sometimes an innocent cow, plays sad havoc. The faster you run, the more dust you raise; the more noise you will make, and the more stock you will kill; and yet it is wonderfully true, the more passengers you will haul. All other railroad men, who can not make the same schedule time, will talk of danger and disaster that must overtake those who patronize the lightning express, and thus help advertise to the world that there is a lightning express—and thus keep its cars packed. Still, the slow schedule trains get a great many passengers. Some people like to ride all day for a dollar and still pay the just fare of three cents a mile; just as a gentleman remarked of the Rome railroad in Georgia, sixteen miles long. He said it was the cheapest road he ever saw, the fare being one dollar from Kingston to Rome, and he could ride all day for that amount, as it took a day to make the trip. But these are, after all, the days of the telegraph and the locomotive engine and rushing commerce. Every thing has quickened its pace, except the Church. The world and the devil can run a mile before the Church can tie its shoes.

I believe in progressive theology, in aggressive effort, in agitation, in conflict, in conquest, and in crowns. It was God who said, "Fight, and I will help you; conquer, and I will crown you." David saw four thousand years ago that he ought to make haste. Jesus said, "What thou doest, do quickly." St. Paul said, "I run and press towards the mark." What if some men live only two-score years and die in the prime of life, after accomplishing much, how much better is it than to run the Christian race of sixty years, and die before they reach the first mile-post towards the kingdom of God?

There can be no movement without friction, no battle without an issue, no issue without the drawing of lines. When the line is drawn then comes the tug of war.

The world and the Church walk together, because in many things they are agreed; but when, like Joshua of old, we draw the line, and say, "Those who are on God's side come over here," then it is that they are separated; and as surely as Mason and Dixon's line was drawn and the South separated from the North by the acts of secession and war begun, just so surely when a faithful preacher draws the line, the issue is made and the good fight of faith begun. The devil has rights in this world, but they are the rights of conquest; and only by that right does he hold it, and never will he surrender an inch of his dominion until it is covered with blood. I have never seen the lines drawn any where, that those who were loyal to God did not take a stand for truth and right; and God fought with them, and through him they did valiantly, for he said himself, "one can chase a thousand, and two can put ten thousand to flight."

The greatest triumphs of the cross I have ever witnessed have been when the roar of the cannon and rattle of the musketry and smoke of the guns almost drowned the voice of God and hid his face; and yet when the din and smoke of the battle blew away, we saw God was with us, and the angels had pitched their tents about us. The Bible has much to say of warfare, and we sing much of "soldiers of the cross." This is truly a warfare, and while victory means crowns, and palms, and harps, it also means scars, and hardships, and fears, and tremblings, and at times defeats;

but the command is, "Fight the good fight of faith, and lay hold on eternal life."

I believe it is possible to preach the Gospel and live in peace with the devil, with an armistice unbroken, but "woe be to the preacher when all men speak well of him."

Rowland Hill was a target for men and devils; they scoffed, they called him a mountebank, they derided him as a flippant wag, and declared he brought the pulpit into disrepute. I have laughed as men of to-day would eulogize Rowland Hill and then call me the same things that Rowland Hill's generation applied to him.

Charles G. Finney, the most omnipotent preacher of this nineteenth century in America, seemed to be the worst slandered and worst traduced man in America. Read his autobiography, and see what the dignitaries of the Church and hypocrites said of him. He was tried, he was condemned, he was excluded from the pulpits of his own Church.

"Nothing succeeds like success," and it succeeds in projecting its favorites on a stormy sea of abuse and criticism. Where is there a successful man in any calling of life who has not been either swallowed by a whale or nibbled almost to death by minnows? I sometimes envied Jonah. Criticisms, when wisely administered, are helpful; but I never could endure these little spelling-book critics, who were utterly incapable of appreciating a thought or catching an idea, yet they could see and recognize a grammatical error or a rhetorical blunder in the distance. It has been the source of much pleasure to me to see with what avidity they would pounce upon a disjointed sentence, and how their eyes glistened and gleamed as they caught it, and silently said, "We have got something to talk about now."

I have been interested in the reading of natural history, and especially as it treats of the habits of some animals and what they feed upon. My knowledge of natural history has frequently helped me in the right understanding of human nature. I have been called vulgar by barkeepers, obscene by women who loved the German in the ball-room, and a religious jester by those whose only stock in trade was a solemn countenance and a diseased liver. When a child suffers you can generally locate the pain, because the child puts its hand where it hurts. I have seen the hands fly to a thousand different places on the moral body, and I knew where each man was hurt by where he put his hand.

There is a great deal in taking aim, and yet, as Brother Richardson used to say, "there is nothing like holding the gun all over the tree." As with the old palsied father who went out with his son squirrel hunting, the old man's part was to shake the bush, and he had but to take hold of the bush and it would shake, without any effort. On one occasion when he was to shake the bush and turn the squirrel, after he had turned the squirrel for four or five different shots for his son, all of which failed of their mark, the old man said: "Give me the gun and you shake the bush." The boy gave up the gun and shook the bush and turned the squirrel. The old man held up the gun in his palsied hands, and as it "wobbled" all over the tree, "bang," went the gun and down came the game. At which the old man remarked, joyfully, "I told you I'd git him." The boy replied, "Any body could kill a squirrel up a tree who would hold a gun all over it, as you did."

Of course in all these years, as I have tried faithfully and persistently to preach the truth to others, I have never forgotten a single day that I had a soul in my own body, to be saved or lost, and I have prayed earnestly for God's help so to live the truth I preach, that I shall never be among that number who shall say, "Lord! Lord! have I not prophesied in thy name, and done many wonderful works in thy name?" and then have him say to me, "Depart, ye accursed, I never knew you."

I have been sorely tempted and fearfully tried; I have fought the battles of temptation and the devil, that left me covered with blood. God has put me in the fire at times until the sparks flew all around me, and I thought he would burn me up soul and body, but I found, as he took me back into his arms, that the flying sparks, which the fire caused to fly off me in its intense heat, was but the burning off of a fungus growth.

Frequently as the great congregations have waited on my ministry, I have been warned to keep humble—not to take the "big head," and so on. Thank God, I have never forgotten "the pit from which I was dug," and my only reply has been, "If you knew how many things I have to give me the 'little head," you never would be uneasy about my taking the 'big head.'" They have talked about my heights, and of my falling from those heights. To the top of Calvary is not very high, and lying down at the foot of the cross is not a very dizzy altitude. The overwhelming responsibility, that there are ten thousand immortal souls now listening to your words, to be faithful to those souls and to God precludes all possibility of being puffed up. The checks and balances work in all phases of life, and the responsibility is commensurate with the altitude; really "Love vaunteth not itself, and is not puffed up." Wherever love predominates, the man is safe—love to God and love to man.

I am frequently asked the question, "How long have you been an evangelist?" I am not an evangelist, except in the sense that every Methodist preacher is an evangelist. There is no order of evangelists in the Methodist Church. I have been doing revival work, however, since the second or third year of my ministry—I mean outside of my own charge, as pastor.

I was always in my younger ministerial life diffident and very much embarrassed when I tried to preach outside of my own pulpits, and not until the fifth or sixth year of my ministry could I preach in another's pulpit with any ease or liberty.

The first revival work I did that gave me any notoriety in my own State, was in 1879 and 1880; then the calls to work in revival meetings multiplied upon me, and I soon found that I was giving half of my time to outside work. In the Fall of 1881, I was appointed Agent of Decatur Orphans' Home, the property of the North Georgia Conference. I accepted this appointment, mainly because it gave me more tether line, and from then until now I have been almost constantly in revival work. Atlanta, Griffin, Macon, Columbus, and Savannah, Georgia, including many of the towns, which I will not mention, furnished a field for my work in 1881 and 1882.

In the First Methodist Church, Atlanta, I have repeatedly worked in gracious meetings. That Church has many of the most consecrated men and women I have ever known. My first revival work there was when General Evans was pastor, and again, when Howell H. Parks was the pastor.

Trinity Church, Atlanta, has been a field where I have also worked repeatedly during the pastorate of Dr. T. R. Kendall, a faithful man of God, who loves Christ with all his heart, and loves humanity with all his soul.

I have seen many conversions in these two old Methodist Churches in Atlanta.

At St. Luke's, in Columbus, Georgia, when Rev. J. O. Cook was pastor, we had a glorious meeting. For three weeks great crowds gathered at this church, and many were brought to Christ. At old St. John's Church, Augusta, Georgia, during the pastorate of W. H. La Prade and Warren A. Candler, the Lord was gracious to us. In Trinity and Monumental Methodist Churches of Savannah, Georgia, God blessed me in my work. In Mulberry Church, Macon, Georgia, Dr. Key, pastor, we had a gracious revival; and so in a score or more of leading Methodist Churches in Georgia I have worked, under the blessings of God, and many of the dear brethren of those Churches have borne me on their faith to the throne of God, and in answer to their prayers for me in my work God has greatly blessed me since.

The first revival I ever held which gave me newspaper notoriety, was in Memphis, Tennessee, in January, 1883; since then I have worked in more than twenty different States with marked success, including the cities of Brooklyn, St. Louis, Cincinnati, Chicago, Baltimore, Washington, D. C., Indianapolis, St.

Joseph, Mo.; Waco, Texas; Mobile; Nashville, and Knoxville, Tenn., and in other cities, and in no place where I have ever preached has the building or tent been sufficient to hold the multitude who attempted to get in. I have repeatedly preached to ten thousand people at one time who sat under the sound of my voice. At Plattsburg, Mo., there were at least twenty thousand who were trying to hear.

Parties who were capable of estimating the numbers, said that in Cincinnati there were not less than three hundred thousand people who sat or stood under the sound of my voice in the five weeks of our meeting there. In Chicago there were, perhaps, an equal number.

I regard the meeting at Nashville, Tenn., as one of the most remarkable in my life as a preacher. Some of the papers, and many of the people of that city, had persecuted and denounced me with a persistency such as I had never seen, and wherever I have been most persecuted and denounced, I have been most successful in winning souls to Christ. In looking over the past twenty-four months of my ministry, I dare believe that in these months not less than twenty thousand souls have been brought to Christ. The converts

COTTAGE HOME OF REV. SAM P. JONES,

CARTERSVILLE, GA.

were not only among those who heard the Gospel from my lips. Even the newspapers that denounced me editorially, printed my sermons in full in their columns.

Take the work in Chicago, for instance. In the *Inter-Ocean* and *Tribune*, the Cincinnati *Commercial-Gazette* and *Enquirer*, and the St. Louis *Globe-Democrat*, all of them with an aggregated circulation of three hundred thousand, and with the reasonable circulation of five readers to a copy circulated, I enjoyed the privilege of preaching to a million and a half of persons a day—a wonderful congregation for one preacher, and a privilege, I dare say, that no other man in the history of the Church has ever enjoyed. Think of it, nine thousand words each night, as they flashed out on eighteen different telegraph wires to the cities of St. Louis and Cincinnati, while they were being set in type by the papers of Chicago! Thus at the breakfast table the next morning, in these three cities, I was greeted by three hundred thousand readers, and before the sun went down that day a million and a half more had read the words. From the statement of newspaper men, I suppose that is a reasonable estimate. The secular papers are so much more alive and aggressive than the religious papers, that when they fall into line with a good work they are a power we scarcely know how to estimate.

To the newspapers I owe much. They have been kind to me in their reportorial columns, and I can cheerfully overlook any criticisms in the editorial columns. After all, criticisms of a man and his work only go with him up to the edge of the tomb. Every man will have his hands full "toting his own skillet" beyond that point; but, I suppose, the strongest temptation of a man's life, a temptation like that which a boy feels when he stands with rock in hand and sees the dog as he jumps the fence—I repeat it, the strongest temptation of my life, and to it I have frequently yielded, is to hit back and criticise some of the critics, and especially as some of them "set so fair," that to keep from "hitting back" requires an immense effort, yet I am sure it is best not to do so. If it is the truth they tell, we should amend. If it is a lie, we should let the lie run on and run out of breath and die. After all there has been more good said of me than evil, and as long as that is true the balance sheet shows something in my favor.

My correspondence for the past several years has furnished me data, out of which I have gotten a great deal—letters from those who have been brought to Christ through my ministry, telling of their happy experiences, and their consecrated purposes. These letters have been a source of great thanksgiving and joy to my heart. A wife thus writes: "Our home has been an Eden since you were here." Children would write, "What a change there has been in papa!" Letters like these have a thousand times gathered me up and carried me back, in memory, to the home of my dissipated days, cheerless, starless, rayless—the sad face of wife, disappointed ambition, and a hopeless future—and then how Christ transformed my life, thereby transforming my home; and, O! what a change was there; and as memory looks upon the picture, how dark, and then how bright. What a privilege to

"Tell to sinners around,
What a dear Savior I have found."

What a field of this description is open for the work of an earnest preacher; how many thousands of ruined homes, made desolate by the presence of sin and the absence of Christ, and how blessed to know that when the strong man is come, he binds the wicked one and casts him out forever. How many broken hearts and disappointed lives and wretched homes, and worse than widowed wives and orphaned children are calling to-day for Him, of whom Moses, in the law and the prophets, did write. Not only is he in himself the "chiefest among ten thousand and the one altogether lovely," but he is the comfort of ruined hearts, and can make a home like himself, "altogether lovely."

Blessed fact; he is seeking open doors. O, that the world might open the door to him and bid the heavenly guest come in; and how sweet the reflection, Jesus himself said to all true disciples, "Behold, I am with you alway, even unto the end of the world." By virtue of that fact, in going upon errands of mercy, Christ goes upon those errands with you, and he goes to cheer, to comfort, to bless, so full of sympathy and love and tenderness is he. He it was who told us when he found the lost and hungry sheep, tired and ready to die, how there was no room for clubs and kicks, but he gathered the tired and hungry sheep upon his own shoulders and brought him back to the fold. The gladness of his presence cheers myriads of hearts and millions of homes.

"Jesus, the name that charms our fears,
That bids our sorrows cease,
'T is music to the sinner's ears,
'T is life, and health, and peace.

Dear name, the rock on which I build
My shield and hiding-place,
My never-failing treasure, filled
With boundless stores of grace."

There is music in his name, a charm in his presence, and life in his touch. And amid the throes and agonies of a world steeped in guilt, but for the cross of Christ the great heart of the world would break. My most lonely hours are when he is absent, and my happiest days are spent in company with him.

"Happy, if with my latest breath,
I may but gasp His name;
Preach him to all, and cry in death,
Behold, behold the Lamb!

The object of all my preaching, of its harshness and denunciation of sin, and its exposure of sham, has been simply to make men fully realize the truth that "all the fitness Christ requireth is" that we feel our need of him; or, in other words, it has been the object of my life, as a preacher, to make sin hideous and righteousness attractive, and I have but shown sin up in all its deformity, that I might better show righteousness up in all its beauty, and drive men from the former, and attract them unto the heights and beauties of the latter.

SERMONS.

SERMON I.

PERSONAL CONSECRATION: "QUIT YOUR MEANNESS."

"Rejoice evermore; pray without ceasing; in every thing give thanks. For this is the will of God in Christ Jesus concerning you."—1 THESS. v. 16–18.

A MAN who understands practically what those three verses teach is not only a Christian, but a philosopher. There 's a great deal of philosophy in Christianity, and the best philosophers make the best Christians. This term "rejoice" is a very different word from "happy," or "happiness." Our word "happy" comes from the same word that "happening" comes from, and my happiness depends largely on my happenings; but joy is very different in its meaning, and different in its effects on the human heart. Joy, when we analyze it, is a sort of trinity in unity: 1. I am satisfied with the past. 2. I am contented with the present. 3. I am hopeful for the future. If you will combine these three elements in a human life, I will show you a man who rejoices evermore.

"I am satisfied, first, with the past." How many

persons can look back over the past and say: "I have done my best since the day I started in on a religious life?" Let me say right here, brethren, that heaven is just the other side of where a man has done his best; and sanctification, when you bring it down to where you can get hold of it, is nothing more nor less than doing the best you can under the circumstances.* That 's practical sanctification, and, really, I do n't care much about any other sort. I want a practical religion.

"I am satisfied with the past." That 's the grandest thing a man ever said—"I have done my best." I was talking some time ago with a grand old man in our State—one of the noblest men I ever knew—and he said, "Jones, I do n't know what people talk so much about a second blessing for. I got all that was necessary in the first place." "Well," said I, "what do you mean?" The old man replied, "Jones, when I got religion I told the truth, and I have stuck to it ever since. When I told God I was going to quit my meanness, I quit it; I meant what I said." I asked him, "Do you mean to say you never repeated a sin you repented of?" and he said to me, "Certainly not, sir; never." Right here, brethren, I bring in this point: I have said that if we would only quit our lying we would get nine-tenths of our difficulties out of the road. Mr. Finney relates an incident that occurred at one of his revival services. One of the elders in the Presbyterian Church received an overwhelming

* Mr. Jones would insist that divine grace is a circumstance not to be left out.

baptism of the Holy Spirit, and that day there came in from an adjoining town an elder from another Church. At the dinner-table this elder discovered the traces and movements of divine power in the very face of his host. Finney says he himself was sitting at the table. This visiting elder looked at his host and said: "Tell me how you have received such heavenly baptism? How did you get it?" The host looked at him and answered: "I fell down on my knees and said to God, 'I have told my last lie. I will never tell thee another while I live;' and the Holy Ghost descended on me, and I have been so gloriously filled since that time I scarcely know whether I am in the body or out." This elder to whom the host was speaking then jumped up from the table, and ran into a sitting-room near by, and fell down on his knees and prayed: "My God, I have told my last lie. I will never tell another on my knees or off my knees in my life," and when they arose and walked from the dinner-table the holy blessing fairly beamed. He had received the baptism, and went on his way rejoicing.

Brethren, that 's our trouble. We have been promising God all our life that we would quit our meanness and get to doing right, but we never have done it. If I were to stop at this point and ask every Christian in the house who never told God a lie to stand up, how many do you suppose could stand up and say: "I told God the truth at the beginning, and have stuck to it to this hour. I said I would quit my meanness, and I did it. I said I would do right, and I have done it."

I want to tell you that every man's condemnation is bottomed on this one word, neglect. Take the best citizen in this town, and let him be every thing else you want him to be, and yet let him neglect to pay his debts, and there isn't a tramp on your streets who would have any respect for him. Isn't that a fact? My duty is my debt to God, and if I neglect to pay my debts to God, there isn't an angel in heaven who would respect me, even if I had sneaked in there unnoticed.

Duty! "I am satisfied with the past, with myself as a father. I have set a good example, and have led a Christian life before my children." "I am satisfied with myself as a mother; I have done my duty to my children." "I am satisfied with myself as a member of the Church. I have kept my vows to it." Brethren, here's a source of joy—"I have done my best from the time I started until this hour." Can you say that? Brethren, did you ever, when your innocent children played about in your lap, say: "I am the purest father God ever blessed with children?" Did you ever say that? Mother, have you looked at your innocent children, as they threw their soft, white arms around your neck, and said: "I am the purest mother God ever blessed with children?" What is your home life? "I am satisfied. I have done my duty." Sister, you may be satisfied with some things in your home to-night, but you'll be be very much dissatisfied later along. You card-playing fathers and mothers! Playing cards with your children! You may think that's very nice now, but when you turn out on the streets of this city three more gamblers from your so-called Christian home, you are going to get very much dissatisfied with the way you have made things at your house.

I think statistics will bear me out when I assert that nine out of every ten gamblers in this country were raised in Christian—so-called Christian—homes. They are refined, educated, and well raised men—many of them—and they come from the homes where mother and father have dedicated them to God, and, it may be, had them baptized in the name of the Trinity.

I want to say another thing. People say, "Jones, you hit a little thing as hard as you hit a big thing." Yes, I do, brethren. The Church is paralyzed in this country. It has n't the power, and we may just as well acknowledge it. Hear me! It is not lying that is hurting the Church, nor stealing, nor drink. It is not this kind of meanness that is hurting the Church. Every body knows that Church members who do these things are vagabonds, and pays no attention to them. Hear me. If you want to know what is demoralizing the Church, and paralyzing the Church, I 'll tell you. It is this tide of worldliness that is sweeping over the Christian homes of this country. That 's it! O, my sister, the day you entered society you laid down your piety, and you know it as well as I do, and you have learned that when a woman gives up her consecrated life to enter society, she begins a life of misery that hardly a damned spirit can exceed in bitterness.

Now, when you can say, "I am satisfied with the past, with the way I have lived before my family, my Church, my community, satisfied with my example in all respects," you are laying the foundation for Scriptural joy.

Then the next point is, "I am contented with the present." When a man looks back with the consciousness that he has done his best, and is contented with the present, he is rich, and rich enough. St. Paul said: "I have learned, in whatsoever state I am, therewith to be content." He said another thing on that line: "Godliness with contentment is a great gain." Brother, contentment is one of the elements of real Scriptural joy in this life. When a man builds on God's pattern, and is contented with his lot, and is hopeful for the future, that man is happy anywhere and everywhere.

Hear me, brethren. Hope, as it shines out of a consecrated past and a contented present, is like the mile-posts on the way to God, telling us how far we have come, and how much further we have to go. Thank God for hope in the Christian life, and we sing:

"O, what a blessed hope is ours
While here on earth we stay!"

Satisfied with the past, contented with the present, hopeful for the future—a joyous Christian—you will find the secret right along in there.

Now, brethren, what are you going to do? Thank God, you can do something; thank God, there is only one thing necessary to be done.

Quit your meanness. Go to God in honest penitence and tell him: "My Lord, this night I burn up the cards; this night I turn out the wines and entertainments; this night I draw the line, and I come over to God's side. Good Lord, forgive me for the way I have lived as a professor of religion." Then comes in the pardon.

O, mothers, fathers, let 's call a halt; let us bring these matters to an understanding at our homes, and say, "We are done." Let us call a halt, and, on our knees before God, repent of these things.

I want to live before God and my family, so that when I come to die I can say to my children, "Go and live just as your father has lived, and do just as he has done, and as certain as Christ died for sinners, some of these days we will all meet in heaven."

Satisfied with the past, content with the present, and hopeful for the future! This gives me the attitude and the altitude where I can rejoice evermore.

Then we take the next verse, "Pray without ceasing." You say, "I can see how a fellow can act when he can rejoice evermore, but to talk about praying without ceasing—that is all foolishness. A man has got to work; he has got to do other things. A man can 't pray all the time. That won't do at all." I heard of a fellow once who had so much work to do on a certain day that he had to lay all down and stop and pray three hours in order to get through with it. Well, you say, "That is the biggest foolishness I ever heard of in my life." Do you see that engine stopping yonder? The schedule of that passenger train is forty-five miles an hour, and that train has stopped still. I look at it and I say: "What does this all mean? The engineer has stopped, and he is on schedule time. Why does n't he go on? What has he stopped for? He has stopped one minute, two minutes, three minutes, five minutes. O, why does n't he go on?" I look a little closer, and I see he is taking on coal and letting water into the tender. He has spent six minutes at the station, and has secured a supply of coal and water, and now he says to himself: "I have lost six minutes, but I have got steam power enough to carry me along sixty miles an hour if I want to go that fast; but if I had run by that coal station I would have got stalled on the first grade. But now I have power enough to carry me through." I will tell you, brethren, when you run up to God Almighty's coal and water station, you must take on enough for your needs. That is it. That is the way to get steam to make the trip. That is the meaning of prayer.

I will say a thing now, and I would say it loud enough for all the earth to hear me. We have got men that won't pray in public and won't pray in their families. Do you want to know why that is? It is because they do n't pray anywhere. Hear me. I want to be understood now, if you do n't understand any thing else to-night. The man who really prays anywhere, will pray everywhere. The man who maintains secret prayer will pray everywhere in God's world that you call on him. You say the reason you do n't pray in your family is just because you are timid. That is a lie. It is because you are mean, and you know it. Talk about a great big fellow, with whiskers six inches long, who will go down town on 'Change and talk bigger than any man in the pit, and he won't go home and pray with his children. "You know I would do it," he says, "if I were not so timid." Look here. If a man does n't pray in his family there is but one reason for it, and that is because he does n't live right before his family. I know what I am talking about. I recollect once since I was converted I got up one morning out of humor, and I said some things I had no business to say. I had the dyspepsia they said. It was meanness. Every time a fellow gets his meanness off, it is dyspepsia. Do you hear that, wife? As I said, I was talking right smart around that morning, and directly, just before the breakfast bell rang, wife got down the Bible. I looked at it, and I would have given fifty dollars that morning if I had had some preacher there to have prayer in the family for me. O, how I hated to get down after talking that way. Brother, when you get to living right before your family, it is just as easy to pray before them as it is to sit down and eat before them. If I did n't have sense enough to pray in my family, I 'll tell you what I would do. I would go and hire me an old colored man that wife and children had confidence in, and I would pay him by the month to come and hold family prayer for me. I would.

Talk about a man being religious who does not

pray in his family! Ridiculous! I found out long ago that religion is a good thing to have, and a father who becomes religious wants his wife and children to have all the good things in the world; and the next thing you hear from him he will be leading in prayer and demonstrating his religion in his family, and they will fall into line with him. Brother, if you don't pray in your family, go home and begin to-night. Do you hear that? Begin to-night.

"Pray without ceasing." How many people in this house hold family prayer and go to the theater? How many people in this house that pray in their families, play cards in their families? How many people in this house who give wine suppers pray at night and morning with the children? Ah, brother, those things won't mix, and you needn't tell me they will. They won't. Pray in your families. I like family prayer, and I can't get along without it at my house.

I want to get God's old family prayer elevator down into my house every night, and let wife and children get into it and all go to heaven for a few minutes, and then come back and go to bed. And then in the morning before the breakfast bell rings, down comes God's old family prayer elevator, and we will all get into it for a few minutes and go to heaven, and come back and get our breakfast and go to work. If I can just get wife and children to heaven that way a few years, they will be such children that when they come to die, they will go to heaven as naturally as they breathe. The Lord save my home. If there is one thought that my mind dwells upon in restful, peaceful moments, it is when I am looking ahead to that happy time when I shall dwell with my wife and loved ones in heaven. Mother, children, all of us at home in heaven forever! Then will I have received pay for every lick I have ever struck for God and right on this side of the grave. God bless and save you, brethren.

SAYINGS.

I USED to think when a man mistreated me, Why does n't the Lord let me jump on him and beat him? The reason is the Lord does n't want to protect that rascal; he wants to protect me.

YOU will hear people say: "Let us Christianize America, and then let us go across the waters. I do n't believe in sending the Gospel to China while we have so many heathen at home." But the Christianity of Jesus Christ makes the heathen Chinese my next door neighbor. A Christianity that sweeps around the world—that is the sort of Christianity we want; a Christianity that locks its arms around the world.

INFIDELITY.—The infidelity that is hurting the Church in this nineteenth century is not theoretical infidelity; the infidelity that is demoralizing the Church and the world is practical infidelity: the fellow that believes the Bible and won't do one thing. Now you have got a fool and a rascal mixed in one compound. It is the most awful compound that Christ ever tackled. He believes in prayer-meetings, but he has not been to one this year; he believes in the missionary cause, but he gets out with the least he can give. He believes in family prayer, but you can't prove it by his wife and children. He goes on the principle that he that believeth not shall be damned, and he believes in every thing.

THE GERMAN AND THE BALL.—If there is a thing in this world that I have a contempt for and can't express it, it is the german. I suppose some of you people through the country don't have germans. It is about all this city can do to rig out enough spiderlegs for a german. To see any average little town try to put on airs! If I were you, sister, I would call it a ball; and a ball-room is so indecent that I would not let my cook go into one of them. This is enough to hurt your feelings, isn't it? Your feelings! The less sense a girl has the more feeling she has. The checks and balances must operate. What you lack in sense you make up in feeling. I wish some of you ball-room girls could hear the boys talk after the thing is over. Did you ever hear of a ball in the day-time? Did you ever hear of a lot of men getting together and having a man's german? There isn't a boy in this town who would cross the street to hug another boy. As sure as you are born, these things are based upon the consciousness of sex.

SERMON II.

THE BLESSEDNESS OF RELIGION.

"Blessed is the man that walketh not in the counsel of the ungodly, nor standeth in the way of sinners, nor sitteth in the seat of the scornful; but his delight is in the law of the Lord, and in his law doth he meditate day and night."—PSA. I: 1, 2.

THE Psalms are an interesting study for any man. I like to read Dickens and Thackeray and Bulwer and Shakspeare, because they evince such a deep insight into human nature. A man may study the pages of such books as these to advantage, but there is more for me in these one hundred and fifty psalms than in the writings of all these masters. The authors I have named give me human nature as we might see it if we were standing on the streets or in your stores. But David gives us human nature as it is acted upon or influenced by the Divine Spirit. I never have much to say against human nature. I have very little abuse for a man in his normal state.

It is perverted human nature I fight. It is the perversion of hand and foot and tongue and mind that I am ready always and forever to denounce. David gives me human nature as it is acted upon and influenced in the best way. I love to read David, because, in the first place, David knew what he was talking about. I love to hear a man talk who seems to know what he is talking about. I 've heard men trying to explain a great many things they did n't understand. I love to read David, because he experienced what he was talking about. No man before him knew more of God and more of humanity than David, and the best preacher that ever planted his foot in this city is the preacher who knows the most about God and the most about humanity. He stands between the two, and hence he ought to know God, and lay his hands on the shoulder of his living Father in heaven, and then put the other arm around the race, and try to lift humanity up to God. This David could do.

Now this man who had studied life in all its phases, a man who seemed to understand God as no man before him and very few after him, a man who seemed to understand himself and understand human nature—gives us the conclusion he had reached in these words, "Blessed is the man that walketh not in the counsel of the ungodly," as much as if to say, "If you want to be a happy man"—and all men want to be happy—"if you really are in search of happiness, listen to this prescription: 'Blessed and happy you will be, if you walk not in the counsel of the ungodly.'" An ungodly man may be a very moral man; an ungodly man need not swear, nor drink, nor violate the Sabbath, nor commit any of the flagrant sins which men are so often guilty of. An ungodly man means simply an ungodlike man. Ungodliness and ungodlikeness are synonymous—they mean the same thing. What does ungodly mean? It signifies not acquainted with God, and God's ways. Every man who knows God loves God, and every man who does not know God, does n't love him. It is just as natural for a soul that knows God to love God, as it is for a mother to love her babe, or as it is for a father to love his son. An ungodly man is a man who cares nothing about God. I 'll tell you the distinguishing characteristic of that sort of men. They love to talk. They scoff at the idea that any body ever died for them, but they are all right, and they can give more advice, and practice less of it than any tribe in creation.

The way to tell an ungodly man is that he is always talking about what harm is there in this, that, or the other thing, and the way to tell a godly man is, he is always hunting around for something with good in it, and not going about trying to find something that people can see no harm in, as they say. If there is no harm in cards, why I have n't the time to play cards, and I 'm sorry for the man and woman that have time to dance. I tell you, brethren, when I look around me and see a sinking world and humanity drifting off from God, and so many sick-beds to visit, and see so many that are poor and need sympathy and help, I have no time to spare for these things; and you would n't have either if you were of any account. You can put that down!

"Blessed is the man that walketh not in the counsel of the ungodly." In other words, if you want to be happy in this life do n't take counsel or advice from ungodly men. Do n't do that! When you are lost as to any moral problem go to the best man or the best woman you know in the world for good advice, for they 're the only ones capable of advising you. I want a man first to practice what he preaches, and show me it is good to do it, and then tell me how he did it, and then I want to do just like him. An ungodly man! As I said before, you can hardly pick a flaw in him; he never goes far enough to be dubbed immoral. What 's the difference between an immoral sinner and a moral sinner? Why, it 's just the difference between the typhoid fever and the small-pox. That 's the only difference at all. One 's internal and the other is external, but both will kill nine times in ten. An ungodly man "can 't see any harm in any thing." He is like an old Irishman down in our town, who was a devout member of his Church. He was very profane, and a man said to him one day, "Jack, how can you be called a devout member of your Church and swear and curse as you do?" And Jack replied, "Faith, sir, and there 's no harm in cursing unless you make harm out of it." Do you get the idea, brethren? I am not hunting those things that have no harm in them, but I 'm hunting the things that have good in them, and so are all good men under all circumstances. They ain't inquiring whether there is much or little harm in this, that, and the other thing. If you want to be happy, brethren, do n't take the advice or counsel of the ungodly, or of those men who run on that line of things. They 'll get you into trouble sooner or later, sure.

Take the question of theater-going, and nine-tenths of these ungodly people in the Church and out you'll find go to the theaters. Let's raise that question a little while here. A preacher in St. Louis told me that during his pastorate in Chicago there was a young lady, teacher in one of the schools, who came to him during a revival. Her conscience was stirred, and she walked up to him and said, "I want to be a Christian. I want to join your Church, but you object to theater-going, and I can't see any harm in that at all." The pastor said to her, "Sister, give your heart to God, join the Church, and go to the theater as much as you please." She joined the Church, and after that went to the theater. Next Summer the revival started again, and the young lady came into the church, and took a class in the Sunday-school, and tried to live right. One day during the revival one of the young lady's pupils, who had become penitent, came to her and said, "Miss So-and-so, do you go to the theater?" And she answered, "Yes; I go occasionally." The pupil then asked, "Do you think it is right as a Christian to go to the theater?" "Well," said the teacher, "I do n't know." And the pupil asked again, "Miss So-and-So, if you can go as a Christian, can I go as a penitent?" And the young lady told her pastor, "I looked that sweet girl in the face, and said, 'Darling, I'll never put my foot inside another theater, God helping me, as long as I live.' My liberty as a Christian was costing that girl her soul, and I said to myself, 'My liberty shall never do that,' and I gave up the thing that was leading a soul off from God."

That's the way a Christian will settle that question every time. My liberty and license in these things shall never cost a human being his soul. Lord cure us of this abominable way of asking, "What harm is there in this?" But nobody has ever asked me, "Is there any harm in family prayer?" They never asked me if I thought there was any harm in reading the Bible! Do you want to know why? Because they knew there was no harm in it! Why did they ask me the other question? Because they knew there was harm in it, and that settles the whole question.

"Blessed is the man that walketh not in the counsel of the ungodly." When a man gets to listening to bad advice the next thing he's going to do is to stand in the way of sinners. That means, keeping the company of sinners; and a man is n't going to listen to bad advice long before he'll be with sinners. I do n't care whose boy, or wife, or child you are, you can not stand the pressure of bad company.

We need to inform ourselves in this question of company. There is n't an angel in heaven that can keep the company some of you do and be pure. Above every thing in the universe, a man ought to be choice about his company and about his books. If you will show me the company you keep, I will write your biography ten years ahead of your death, and I will not miss the mark one time in ten. "Birds of a feather flock together."

I will tell you another thing. There is but one safe rule in this line. Do n't you ever go with any body that will say things you won't, that will do things you won't do. You won't run with them long until you will be doing those things and saying those things yourself. Always hunt better company than you are, for when some of us get up to ourselves we are with the biggest rascal in town right then. And that gets things in a bad shape, does n't it? I am sorry for a fellow when, every time he goes off by himself, he is in the worst company he was ever in in his life. I will illustrate that for you. There was a very stingy man I once heard of down in our country. His wife was a Methodist, and he would go with his wife to Church, but he never would pay a dime toward the support of the Church. One summer he professed religion and joined the Church himself. Well, shortly after he joined the Church the stewards went over to his house and spoke to him kindly and told him: "Our preacher is now in need of provisions, and I came over to see if I could get some meat from you for him." He had a smoke-house full, and he thought a minute: "Why," said he, "certainly, I will give the preacher some meat." He went out to his smoke-house while the steward sat at the window. He walked up to the smoke-house, unlocked the door, took down a big, fine ham, brought it about half-way to the house, stopped and laid it down. He looked at it a while, and turned around and walked back to the smoke-house, got another and came and laid it down also. Then he stood and looked at it a minute, turned back to the smoke-house and brought another. The steward was watching him, and he looked down at the three hams. He heard him say: "If you don't shut your mouth, you old stingy devil, I will go and give him all the meat there is in the smoke-house." The devil was in him, and told him every time: "Are you going to give away that ham?" And the devil kept after him, and he tried to hush his mouth by putting down one ham at a time, but finally he silenced him when he said: "If you don't hush your mouth I will give him every ham in the smoke-house." And then the devil hushed. So a man can be in bad company when he is by himself. "Bad company will ruin you."

Above all things we ought to be careful about the associations of our children. If that neighbor of yours is worth fifty, or seventy-five, or a hundred thousand dollars, he may have the worst children in the town, and yet you will let those children of his come over there and ruin yours because he has got a little money. Did you ever notice that streak of human nature? If that neighbor's son of yours drives a fine horse and buggy in the streets of this city and belongs to one of the fashionable clubs, that is all I want to know about him or any other man. It is only a question of time when he will be drowned in debauchery and ruin if he is a member of a city club. I don't care if you are as pious as Job, if you will join one of those clubs and begin to run with them I would swap your chances of heaven for those of Judas Iscariot.

I am determined to be understood, you see, and

you all can disagree with me if you want to; but you shan't run away from here and say: "I declare, I did n't understand that fellow." You shan't say that. I want to make you see what I am talking about.

"Nor standeth in the way of sinners." O, mothers, look to the company of your children. Fathers, look to the company of your sons. And I say to you to-night, whenever it becomes a known fact that my daughters keep company with dissipated young men and my sons have gone out into bad company, I shall lose all hope for the future of my children. O, stand by your children and protect them.

Boys, listen to me. You never can get higher than the company you keep. If you would be noble and true, seek the best atmosphere of earth, and live in it forever. Stand not in the way of sinners.

In this verse, David adds, "Nor sitteth in the seat of the scornful." Now, brethren, we notice first he is walking along, in the counsel of the ungodly. Well, when a man is walking in this way he can turn to the right or turn to the left by the movements of one set of muscles; but you let him stand right still and he has got to move every muscle in his body to get off; and then let him sit down, and nine times in ten he is there to stay. While walking along in your youthful days, God's minister used to come and impress you and move you and turn you, but by and by you got to standing, and then the thunders of worlds could not shake you or turn you. Some of you have reached the last stage, the ante-room to hell, and that is sitting in the seat of the scornful. God pity a poor wretch that has gone through bad counsel into bad company until finally he is sitting down in the seat of the scornful, where he can laugh at the preacher and make fun of God and scorn the Bible.

"Nor sitteth in the seat of the scornful." A man never gets over the fact that he has taken such an attitude toward God. "But his delight is in the law of the Lord." I tell you, brother, when you get to where you will like this Book, and read this Book, you are laying a foundation then. Young boys, take this Book; let your delight be in the counsel, in the law of the Lord. I never think of what this Bible is to a man but I think of a little boy. He was the good boy in the town, and all the boys recognized him as a good, upright boy. And they laid their traps to get him drunk. They sent one of the shrewdest of the bad boys to him, and he met him on the street, and he said, "Johnny, come into the grocery and let us have a mint julep." Johnny says, "O, no, I can 't go in there." "Well, why?" "Well, my Book says, 'Look not upon the wine when it is red,' much less drink it." "O," he says, "I know the Book says that, but come in and take one drink." "Well," he says, "I can 't do it." "Well, why?" "Because my Book says, 'At the last it biteth like a serpent and stingeth like an adder.'" "O," he says, "I know the Bible says that, but come in and take one drink." "No," he says, "my Bible says, 'When sinners entice thee, consent thou not.' " And the bad boy turned off and left him, and went over to his companions, and they said, "Did you see him?" "Yes." "Did you get him to drink?" "No, I could n't get him in the grocery." "Well, why?" He said, "That boy was just as chuck full of Bible as he could be, and I could n't do a thing with him." Ah, brother, "his delight is in the law of the Lord."

Now, let me give you the germ of happiness that may spring up and be a tree under which you can sit in its shade and eat its fruits. Listen: these texts, these two verses, furnish the secret of a happy life. I beg you, do n't walk in the counsel of the ungodly! Do n't stand in the way of sinners! Do n't sit in the seat of the scornful, but take the Book of God, make it your counsel, give yourself to the right, and live and die for God.

SAYINGS.

THE roar of commerce, the click of the telegraph, and the whistle of the engine have well-nigh drowned out the voice of God.

WE little preachers think that we are doing first-rate if we take a text and announce about three propositions, and discuss them for an hour. But do you know that Christ, in his sermon on the mount, announced and discussed one hundred and twenty different propositions in the compass of half an hour?

A MAN who believes only in what he can see, does n't believe he has got a backbone. I am not running on understanding. I could not get to my front gate on understanding, but I could get from earth to heaven on believing.

GOING to Church is like going shopping: you generally get what you go for—no more and no less. A woman will go into a store with a hundred thousand dollars' worth of goods all around her, buy a paper of pins, and walk out; that is all she came for. I have seen the store-house of God's grace packed from cellar to ceiling, and I have seen men go in and gather up an expression of the preacher and go home.

IF any man does n't love God, it is because he does n't know him. To know him is to love him, and to love him is to serve him. And if any man on the face of the earth does not love God, it is because he has not seen him in all his characteristics. If any man does not love God at all, it is because he has not seen him at all. "Blessed are the pure in heart, for they shall see God." I have evidence of God's presence all around me; but when I want to see God I will go and talk with him, and put my arm in his, and walk step by step at his side. Just take the path of Christian duty, and all along the line you will find God at every step.

SERMON III.

THE RIGHTEOUS AND THE WICKED.

"The righteous shall flourish like the palm-tree; he shall grow like a cedar in Lebanon."—PSA. xcii, 12.

"I have seen the wicked in great power, and spreading himself like a green bay-tree."—PSA. xxxvii, 35.

WE narrow these two expressions which I have just read down to this: "The righteous are like the palm-tree, the wicked like a bay-tree." First let us stop and ask, "What is a palm-tree? What is that thing which I am or ought to be like?' The Eastern people boast of the fact that the palm-tree is good for three hundred and seventy-six different things. They say, "We live upon its fruits; of its sap we make wine for medicinal purposes; its wood we use for various manufacturing purposes; its bark and its roots we use for this and that;" and they have summed up all the different things that the palm-tree is good for. They say that from its topmost sprig to the last fiber of its roots it is of use. There is not a particle of the palm-tree that is not useful, and all over, through and through, first to last, it is good for three hundred and seventy-six different things. "The righteous are," or ought to be, "like the palm-tree," good for many different things, good from top to bottom, through and through, with not a particle of soul, body, or spirit that is not good in the service of God.

My Bible here, brethren, looks upon me as a sort of trinity in unity—a body, a mind, and a spirit. Now, a man who takes good care of his body, and eats when he ought to eat, and does so with special reference to the great purpose of his existence, is physically religious. Then contemplate the mind. A man who reads the right books, and only the right books, and who improves his mind and grasps at those thoughts which are ennobling and elevate him, is intellectually religious. A man who looks after the spirit—a man who lives in a spiritual atmosphere, and who abides in eternal life, and has eternal life abiding in him here and now—that man is spiritually religious; and, brethren, I like a religion that permeates a man from the top of his head to the sole of his foot. I like a religion, a Bible, a Gospel, a system that looks after me as I am now—mind, body, spirit.

A man who eats too much, drinks too much, sleeps too much, or sleeps too little, is a physical sinner, and he will suffer for it, too. I do n't know how much he 'll suffer for it in the next world, but he 'll catch it in this—no avoiding that! A man who punishes his mind sins against it. It has its life just as the body has, and needs nourishment, too. There 's many a starved mind in this country, brethren. If I were simply to feed my body upon husks that had no nutriment, how could I perpetuate physical life? If I do not sit down and eat those things that tend to produce strength and perpetuate life, in so far am I sinning against my body. I wonder what those people are doing that spend their intellectual hours playing cards? How much mental food is there in that? One evening, where I was preaching, I denounced social card-playing and progressive euchre. Let me tell you, too, if you play progressive euchre—and I do n't care whose son, whose wife, whose husband you are—you are a gambler as much as any blackleg in this city. You can't play progressive euchre without the "Booby prize," and you can't play for a Booby prize without putting up the stakes; and if you win or lose, you are a gambler in the sight of God just as much as is the worst blackleg that ever cursed this city. Well, one of the society women who heard me, a member of the Church, said: "Why, I'm disgusted with that preacher. I have a contempt for him. How in the world could I interest my husband at night if I did n't play cards with him? It's the only way I have of amusing my husband." If I were you, sister, I'd send my husband to a lunatic asylum, where they have cards for the inmates in all the rooms. The Lord pity the woman who has married such an intellectual starveling that she has to sit down and debauch her mind to interest her husband.

Intellectually religious! Thank God for a system of religion that from foot to scalp makes one a holy man all over. I like that sort! The religion of Jesus Christ makes me eat just as the engineer fires his engine—to get strength to go on! Nothing more, nothing less! My intellectual nature calls for things that bring out the brain sweat, and fill the brain with thoughts like those which God thinks, and the brightest man in this world is the man who thinks the thoughts of God.

I can see how the righteous are like the palm tree, for they are good all over, good for many different things. Brother, how many are you good for? Sister, get out your pencil and a little piece of paper, and let's run the rule of addition over your life. Now, how many things are you good for? I mean how many things are you good for religiously? You can run a world of things outside of your religious duty, but I am talking about the thing religiously. Now how many of these things are you good for? That sister yonder says, "Wait a minute, and I'll tell you. I'm good for—I'm good—I'm—I'm—I'—I—um;" and, brethren, that's just where she'll get to. That brother yonder has been in the Church for ten years, and he is idle to-day, and God speaks every day in his hearing, "Go work in my vineyard," and he stands there with his hands in his pockets, and says, "I would go to work in a minute if I only knew any thing in the world to go to work at." Whenever you hear a man talk that way he's a fool or a rascal, one, inevitably; and sometimes he's a compound of both, and then you get him in bad shape indeed! Standing here idle with his hands in his pockets, and there are thirteen hundred and fifty millions of sinners in this universe! He's standing around idle, with a world sinking, sinking down to hell, and he says, "I can't find a thing to do!" Brother, when you talk that way, you show mentally you are a blank. If you are intellectual at all, then you are intellectually false, and you misrepresent yourself when you say, "I can't find a thing to do in the world."

There's work for you. Every sinner in this town is a good subject for you to work on. If I had my home here I wouldn't say, "I can't find a thing in the world to do;" and you'd better not go to the judgment and talk that sort of foolishness, for God will say, "Didn't you live in such and such a city?" Good anywhere—good everywhere! O, brethren, the Lord gave us the sort of religion that doesn't stand on the banks of the river and shudder and shake with dread, and shrink; but the Lord gave us the sort of religion that runs and leaps into the current that is lined from source to mouth with human wretches. God help us to bring them over. The Lord give us the sort of Christianity that doesn't sit around with folded hands waiting for something to turn up, but give us the sort of Christianity that will pitch in and pound the iron until it gets red-hot, and then we can shape it as God wants it shaped. It will get warm under the blows of an honest, earnest heart! God everywhere, and God all over! I want the Christianity that makes every deed of my life and every word of my life a maxim for universal application, and as I apply the maxim the world grows better.

Good for three hundred and seventy-six different things! I have heard some brethren in the Church say, "You're all loading me too heavy. I must help myself some. I'm going to quit being deacon. You're all putting every thing on me." Look here, brother, get down on your knees and count out the three hundred and seventy-six different things you are good for and busy at, and then when you come out get the measure of the palm tree, and then you 'll let them put any thing on you. There 's something wrong with the man that lies down on the ground with his cross on top of him.

I am disgusted with the Christianity that thus breaks down. I look back about eighteen hundred years ago, and I see what the disciples of Jesus Christ went through in order to make their way to God, and to make themselves the ministers of God's grace, and I am ashamed of every officer of religion we have upon the face of the earth. Why, brethren, then they took them out of their homes and stripped them and misrepresented them, and persecuted them, inflicting stripes and imprisonment, and crucified them. And yet people are no better now than they used to be. I wonder if the difference is in the preachers, and not with the people? I have been hunting for a martyr for thirteen years. I want to find a martyr; a fellow that died for the truth. If I could get him, I would have a text that I could make things hum with. But I have been hunting one for thirteen years, and I have never found a martyr yet. O, for a Christian that goes out to battle red-hot, and makes it so warm for those who sin that this world would surrender, or put that man out of the way. You can get it in that shape if you want it. God forbid that I should bring a railing and a scoffing against any preacher.

I would not strike a blow at you that I would not be willing myself to receive.

But what is the matter with us? We want a Christianity that walks right out. A liquor paper in Georgia denounces Sam Jones as a firebrand. God grant that if ever I have my name changed from Sam Jones to "Firebrand," I may go forth a firebrand in the name of Jesus Christ. Jesus said: "I am come to send fire on this earth." We need an issue, brethren—a clearly defined issue, and we must have it, brethren, if we ever get this city for Christ. The devil now possesses it, and the only road we have to take in order to get it from him is the road of Christ.

The Lord help every preacher in this city next Sunday morning to turn his guns on sin, and if you will bombard sinners in the right way, they will run up their white flag within thirty days from to-day. Let the pulpit be sure that it is right, and then go to hitting hard, and "carry the war into Africa." Rush it right on. How your enemies will howl, and kick, and rear, and pitch, and talk about vulgarity and vulgar witticisms, and slang, and all that sort of thing. But I tell you, brethren, one thing, that you will get at the meanness of them if you will get at them in the right way. Meanness is always cowardly. One good Christian can chase away a thousand, and two good ones put ten thousand to flight if you will get God with you. I hope that every newspaper in this city, and every pulpit in this city will get square up on the Ten Commandments. They are good for anything and every thing; good everywhere, and good at all circumstances. They are good at prayer-meetings. They are good at family prayer. They are good at visiting the sick. They are good at serving the needy. They are good at helping the weak. They are good anywhere and everywhere.

O, my, how I do like to see a Christian that knows his rights, let you talk to him and abuse him as you will. How many in this house can say, "I am the Lord's with reserved rights in the world?" Christianity is like the man when he found the pearl of great price. He sold out every thing and put it all into the pearl of great price. Brother and sister, have you a reserved right in Christian life? Turn it all over to God. Then he will use you for his glory and your eternal good. A reserved right! Some people promise to enter a Church if the preacher will not ask them to pray or to speak in public. He takes them in as a sort of honorary members. And do n't you honor the Church with a vengeance, you honorary member! A fellow told me one night, "I am going out to the Church to-night, but I want you to promise me that you will not call on me to pray." "I won't make any promise," I said. "Then I won't go," he replied. I said, "I would fight you from now to daylight before I would promise not to call on you to do your duty. How are you to give us an example if you do n't pray?" The freest man is the one who is ready at all times for any thing that God or the Church calls upon him to do. Brother, I would rather be a whole Christian and do my whole Christian duty fifty times over than shirk a duty, as you do, once a week. God knows it is easier. He who does otherwise is always dodging. He never gets clear from fear. He 's afraid somebody will shadow him when he walks out, and proclaim all he sees. You want to be good in three hundred and seventy-six things, like the palm-tree. Add up your good things until you build up a palm-tree in heaven. A good Christian will grow anywhere, like the palm-tree, which will grow anywhere in its latitude—in the bottoms, in the marsh, among the rocks, on the hillside.

Some people say, "I can not be good and keep house." But there is more religion in the kitchen than in the parlor. "I can not be good and be a merchant." "I can not be good and be a lawyer." A palm tree grows everywhere; and some of the best people that I ever knew were hotel-keepers, were lawyers, were merchants. And every good hotel-keeper and every good merchant, every good lawyer is a demonstration of the fact that all of them could be good if they wanted to be. All can be good anywhere, no matter what their business may be.

Another thing about the palm-tree. If you plant it in the Desert of Sahara, you will notice that it takes root and shoots out and other palms grow up around it, and these draw moisture, and by and by a palm-tree grove is spread around the spring that is formed in this oasis in the desert, where the weary traveler can stop and slake his thirst. A good Christian is like a palm-tree in this respect. When you find one, another one will grow up around him. His roots are like those of the palm-tree. They just spring up all around him, and their moisture is the river of life, and these form the oasis in the desert of life, where the weary traveler can slake his thirst in the shadow of the tree of life.

Then there is another thing about the palm-tree. You can take it and bend it over and press it right down to the earth, but it shoots itself up again toward heaven. Poor Job said when he was smashed down in the ash bank, and his wife put additional pressure on his fall by telling him his breath was a stench and his body corrupt, and told him to curse God and die, "Shall we receive good at the hand of God, and shall we not receive evil?" "Though he slay me, yet will I trust in him." Glory be to God that we can be like a palm-tree. Let us be like the palm-tree—good everywhere and through every day in the week from head to foot; good anywhere you hitch. I like that sort of Christianity.

But the wicked are like a bay-tree. Do you know what a bay-tree is? Now you will find your latitude, some of you. If you have studied yourself for hours you will know. A bay-tree is good for nothing in the universe, that we know of. God may see good in it, but we can not. In the first place, a bay-tree will come out and blossom as prettily as any tree in the land, but it never has any fruit. Then another thing about the bay-tree. If I were going out for a load of wood I would drive five miles further rather than try to split up a bay-tree, it is so hard. And another thing about a bay-tree. It not only has no fruit upon it, and not only is it not fit for wood, because it is so hard to cut, but it will only grow down in a marsh bottom, and is fit for nothing but shade, and it casts its shade just right where the sun ought to shine.

The wicked are like the bay-tree. O, brethren, what is a wicked mother worth to her children? O, sister, what are you worth? You will bear and blossom out beautifully in your worldly life, but you have no fruits of righteousness. You flower best in the marshy bottoms of sin; and you are fit for nothing but to shade, and you shade the light of heaven from your precious children. God forgive us. Brother, is it true that you are a bay-tree? In any heavenly sense, are you good for any thing? Good for yourself, or any good for the next world? O, brother, you flourish best in the swamp of sin, and do nothing but shade, and you shade the light of heaven from the precious ones in your home.

Mother and sister, let us go to our homes this evening and ask ourselves, "Am I like the palm-tree, or am I like the bay-tree?"

I might talk an hour about this subject, but we have got enough to think about. I want to get you down to bottom rock. I want to get you down to the roots. We want to shuffle off the incrustations of evil until we can plant our feet on the "Rock of ages," and then we will stand secure when the last storm has swept over us. I know I am not up, but I am down, and the way up is down. If you want to go up start down. He that humbleth himself shall be exalted. If you go down deep enough you will never break off the stem. Go down and down. David said he was brought low, and the Lord helped him. Good Lord, help me to go down.

And, brethren, God will help us to see eye to eye. Some of you do n't understand me, and, perhaps, I do n't understand you. But God will help to bring us to where we can see each other face to face; mark what I tell you. There are as good people in this house as any that live on this earth. I have never said otherwise. I will tell you another thing. You talk about living out of the Church. It is all I can do to live in the Church. It is the only house that Christians have got; and if they turned me out of one I would join the next I came to, and be ready for the next opening of the door; and if they turned me out I would go again. A colored man was noticed joining a Church every time he could get a chance. He was asked, "What makes you do that way?" He answered, "O, it did me so much good the first time that I joined that I want to keep on joining every time you open the door." Thank God for his grand Church.

God bless you and help you to see that the Church of Jesus Christ is the only hope of this world. If that is the truth, then let us make the Church what God wants it to be.

SERMON IV.

THINK ON THESE THINGS.

"Finally, brethren, whatsoever things are true, whatsoever things are honest, whatsoever things are just, whatsoever things are pure, whatsoever things are lovely, whatsoever things are of good report; if there be any virtue, and if there be any praise, think on these things."—PHIL. IV, 8.

WE have been misled, perhaps, some of us, as to what Christianity is. We have heard much on the subject of the terms of discipleship; we have heard a great deal about repentence for sins committed; we have read and heard a good deal about pardon; we have heard a thousand sermons, more or less, on the subject of faith, and many on the subject of regeneration and sanctification, but here is a clear, sensible, philosophical statement as to what Christianity is.

St. Paul begins this verse with this word "finally,"—"finally! brethren;" as much as if to say, "I have written many things previous to this, I have said many things in your hearing, but, brethren, you may forget all I have said and take your eye from off all I have written; yet if you will just fix your mind and memory on what I am going to say now (for I will now give you the whole thing in a nut-shell), you can get hold of this, it is brought to you clearly and plainly."

As a man thinks, so he is. What I think to-day will determine what I may be doing to-morrow. The actions of this day are the embodied thoughts of yesterday. Let me know what you are thinking about to-day, and I will tell you what you will be doing to-morrow. A man partakes of the nature of the thing he is looking at with his mind and eye. In the presence of the dead, I turn my thoughts to the object before me, and become saturated from head to foot with solemnity. You may bring in a beautiful bouquet of flowers, and I put my mind and eye intently upon that bouquet, and the first thing I know my whole nature is filled with the aroma and beauty of the flowers. I partake of the nature of the thing I look at, hence God tells us he will keep him in perfect peace whose mind and heart is in him.

And, brethren, we have something to do with creation around us. We partake largely, morally I mean, of the world in which we live. He who thinks and sees only goodness, mercy, glory, and blessings with his own eye, shall live and die in a perfect atmosphere of heaven. Brethren, let's have some more of it down here now. Let's not talk so much about hereafter. I need it here. This old world needs heaven, your city needs heaven, needs it implanted right down in every street, in every home, and in every heart in the community. And I say unto you, if you will, under God, make your city what God intended it to be, it will be a suburb of the city of the New Jerusalem.

Think on these things. And, after all, what is a thought? I am no metaphysician, and I'm no kin to one, but we'll say for the sake of the argument, as the lawyers say, that thought is the result of an impression upon one of the five senses. Now we won't go into the discussion of intuitional thought, that's a matter too deep for me, but we'll take things as we see them. We say all thought, below the strata of the intuitional, is the result of an impression upon one of the five senses. I know God has come into my soul, but when I touch intuitional thought God gets in without entering through one of the five senses, for I do not hear him come in, I do not see the door open as he comes in, nor do I see it close as he goes out, and yet I know God has been in there and talking to me.

I see something that puts me to thinking; I touch something, and it brings up a thought; I taste something, and it sets me to thinking, and so all the way through. The sense of perception then looks upon the scene, and the sense of conception then carries me back into my room and shows to me again, even with my eyes closed, the picture I have just perceived. Then judgment will measure and weigh the picture for me, and by and by I turn it to the faculty of imagination, and I see her poise on her wings, and then go up, up, and up, until she goes above the moon and the stars, and I find myself looking down on towering spires, jasper walls, and pearly gates of the city of God.

Thought! Well, if what I see opens my mind to thought, I had better be careful what I look at. If what I touch opens my mind to thought, I ought to be careful what comes in contact with my hands. If what I taste brings forth thought, then I ought to be careful what I taste. Brother, be careful of what you hear, touch, taste, feel; be careful of your five senses. Think on these things. Well, we say, thought is an emotion arising from something we see, something we hear, something around us. A developed thought is ready for the hand, is ready for the tongue, is ready for the foot; that's the idea of developed thought—thought gotten into shape for the tongue, for the hand, and for the foot. A thought will develop into purpose. You had better look out there, there's danger all along that line. A man can't help evil thoughts coming in, but he can prevent them from developing into a purpose. Wesley said: "I can't help evil thoughts from coming into my mind any more than I can help birds flying over my head; but I can help the birds from building their nests on my head and there hatching their young." Always keep the back door of your mind open whenever you open the front door, and make these evil thoughts pass along, and say to them: "You can't stay until you are developed into an idea." I can't help a tramp knocking at my front door, but I can prevent myself from asking him into my parlor and telling him to make himself at home. Ten thousand evil thoughts may come in unawares, but I say, You can't stay here and make yourself at home and develop into an idea. Bad ideas are like the devil; he tries to make your acquaintance and be with you; but he is too much of a gentleman to stay where he is not wanted. I'll tell you another thing, if the devil comes and stays with you it is because you make him at home and treat him well and are kind to him.

"Think on these things." Now, brother, St. Paul said, if you would be what the honest aspirations of an honest soul would make you, put your mind and thought entirely upon the truth. Now, just as with the pictures of the bouquet and the corpse I stirred my nature up, then just so, by thinking of God, I can put myself in an attitude, and keep there, until my whole nature is stirred with religion and truth, and when I speak I speak the truth just as naturally as I breathe. Truth is always uppermost in the normal state of man, and no man who is a man of integrity will tell a lie until he rams back the truth first. Men tell the truth naturally, but it is unnatural to tell a lie; and now, if I come up those steps and a man shakes my hand and bids me God-speed, it is perfectly natural for me to say that he shook my hand and bade me God-speed; but it is perfectly unnatural for me to say that the man cursed me and kicked me down the stairs. It 's natural to tell the truth; it 's unnatural to tell a lie. Whenever a man is a cordial liar he has perverted his nature from head to foot. A liar is a consolidated, concentrated lump of falsehood, and when he talks he tells lies just as easily as he lives in that atmosphere. I despise a liar. I have seen some men who thought on evil so much that they could n't tell the truth at all. The man who thinks on the truth, who reads the truth, and fills his heart with the truth, will speak the truth: for out of the abundance of the heart the mouth speaketh.

A man can tell lies and never open his lips; he

can tell lies with his hands, and he can tell lies with his feet; he can tell lies with his eye, with an expression of his face. O, brother, be so loyal to truth that it will be impossible for you to tell a lie or act a lie. And, brother, you can never be right unless you are saturated with truth and on the true side of every thing.

God give us truth if we have any thing else or not. We need it all over this country. We want men we can bank on. If every body in this city and State will not tell another lie for ten years it will starve the lawyers to death and put them to plowing; no doubt about that. Now, I do n't say that men of this profession live upon the falsehood of the world. They may have to defend truth. It is not always a lawyer's duty in his practice to assail the opposite client, but it is the noble duty of a great lawyer to defend a good man against the onslaughts of unjust men. God give us lawyers who scorn the wicked side and stand up for justice and truth. Truth—I think in truth; I saturate mind and heart with truth, and then I can speak nothing but the truth. It ought to be the normal state of every man. "Whatsoever things are true!" Brother, let 's avoid evils of every kind; let 's look out for the things that would lead a man into telling a lie. Let our utterances be truthful, and let us die before we tell a lie.

"Whatsoever things are honest!" When I say "honest" I do n't mean simply a man who pays all his just debts, as we call it. I have heard of a man walking all across the town to pay a nickel he owed; but I would n't trust that man in my room when I was asleep if I had a quarter in my pocket. Bless your soul, he is often paying that nickel to get some hold for an imposition upon the community. When you let me define that word, "honesty," it is a man who lives up to his convictions, and will die by his convictions. That's what I mean by being an honest man. Many a man who has paid every dollar he owed in this world may be put in hell at last for being a thief. You say that is a mighty strong expression; but theft is the unlawful taking of the property of another without his knowledge and consent. You can steal from a man when he is looking at you as well as you can when he is asleep if you just cover up some fact in the trade, and thereby carry your point; but may be you would have seen the covered point if you yourself had not been working your tricks to gouge him.

Dishonesty! Down in my State I had my mind directed, two or three times, to a man of whom every one said: "There goes an honest man." I thought, a time or two, I'd walk out and take his hand and ask him if he did n't feel lonesome in this country. He was a cotton buyer, and he would pay to the most ignorant negro as much for his cotton as to the shrewdest white farmer. An honest man going around by himself in broad daylight!

I was in a store, in a circuit I was on once, when a farmer came in to get some plow-points. He had just moved into the settlement, and it was the first or second time he had been to town. He came into the store and he asked the proprietor: "Are these plow-points tempered hard enough?" "No," said he; "I think not. I tried some of them, and they are soft." When the farmer had gone out I said to the proprietor, "Why did n't you tell that man that the plow-points were well tempered and hard, and would do the work he required of them? Why, you told him the naked truth, and missed a sale; you 're a strange man." But I tell you one thing: just as long as I staid in that community that man had a customer who would spend his last dollar with him.

Tell the naked truth—the naked truth that makes a man honest. Do you know where we get that expression, "the naked truth?" The old story is that Truth and Error, a long time ago, went in bathing together. It is n't told what Truth was doing, but, while bathing, Error ran out of the water and put on Truth's clothes, and ran off with them on; and when Truth saw that Error had taken all of her clothes, she said: "I have nothing left to put on but the clothes Error has left; but before I will put those on I will go naked the balance of my life." Since that time we have had the plain naked truth, and I never want any clothes on it.

"Whatsoever things are just"—I like a just man. Brother, you hear people say, "You had better be just before you are generous." It 's a great deal harder to be just than it is to be generous. I could pull out ten dollars and give it to a poor woman, and I do n't miss it, and it does n't bother me. But to be just to all mankind, that 's another thing. I tell you what it is: it is a great deal easier to give fifty dollars to an orphans' home than it is to be just. I hurt my little boy's feelings, and take little Bobbie in my lap, precious little fellow, and say, "Son, forgive your father for hurting your feelings." It's a great deal easier to be generous than it is to beg your little boy's pardon for your harshness and meanness.

Justice! It is very easy for a man to be generous, but, brother, have you the justice in you to implore the forgiveness of a wife for an unkind word uttered? If I infringe on the rights or feelings of others, then I will go to them and do right by them.

"Whatsoever things are pure"—pure in word, pure in your life, pure in all manner of conversation, in every thing. Observe it—purity! purity! purity!

We want purity! purity! I tell you, my brother, if a man lives pure and acts pure and is pure, he is good in the best sense—in the most refined sense. Purity is like the little ermine, with its hair and skin as white as the driven snow; and when its capture is sought, its path to its home is made dirty and muddy, and when the little animal reaches the mud and dirt it lies down and subjects itself to capture and death before it will besmirch one of its beautiful white hairs. I want to say to the Christian world, rather let us lie down and subject ourselves to capture or to death than besmirch our character as Christians by any contact with the sins of the world. God make us pure on earth. God bless you and take you under his care, and God help you to live so that if you put your head under the block and it is severed from your body, God will be there to pick it up and put a crown of everlasting life on it.

SAYINGS.

THE fellow who believes only what he can understand does n't believe there is a muley-headed cow in the universe. I revere him, but I will not imitate him.

IF I had a "creed," I would sell it to a museum. Creed shows itself in the wars of the last few hundred years. It was over creed that men fought, and not over Christ. Orthodoxies are what have ruined this world.

I ONCE made this proposition: If there is a man in this house who feels in his heart that nobody prays for him, I want him to give me his hand, and leave here with the assurance that *one* prays for him. It is something to know that some one prays for me. The most lonely feeling that overtakes an immortal spirit on its pilgrimage to eternity is the feeling that nobody prays for him.

SERMON V.

REST IN CHRIST.

"Come unto me, all ye that labor and are heavy laden, and I will give you rest. Take my yoke upon you and learn of me; for I am meek and lowly in heart, and ye shall find rest unto your souls. For my yoke is easy and my burden is light."—MATT. xi, 28-30.

THE first clause of this portion of Scripture which we read is an invitation. "Come unto me." Christ was not only a divine Savior, but he was as truly a divine philosopher. Christ was not only a physician in the sense that he had remedies for the race, but he was a philosopher in the sense that he understood the condition of the race. He not only knows the remedies for man's ills, but he knows what your ills are in every sense of the word. There is a great deal, brethren, in a physician having the case thoroughly in hand. In sickness in my own home I have sent for our old family physician. I have great confidence in his medical skill and ability. And when I see that my child is very sick, I watch the doctor as closely as I do the child. I never feel satisfied about my little one until I can see an expression of confidence on the doctor's face. And I will tell you when that expression of confidence comes. It is the very instant when the doctor sees he has the case thoroughly in hand, that he understands the nature of the disease afflicting the child.

All physicians will tell you that the greatest trouble in their practice is with little children. If you ask them why—as it is a fact that the system of a child will respond to treatment much more readily than those of grown people and old people—they will say: "The great trouble in the management of a child is in the diagnosis—to find out what is the matter with the little fellow. If I know just exactly what his trouble is, I know what to do with him." And there is where the skill comes in. Right at that point a good doctor will beat a sorry one in finding out what is the matter. The sorriest doctor knows exactly what to do if he knows what is the matter. What is the trouble? Locate it, and when the trouble is located and named, then any physician knows exactly what the remedy is.

Now, brethren, I thank God there is a great Physician that diseased humanity can apply to, and apply to with the most unbounded confidence. He not only knows the remedies, what the "balm in Gilead" is, but he knows just exactly what is the matter with every one of us. He can put his finger on the spot that hurts you to-night, and he knows what it is as well as you know your name. There, you poor, broken-down wagon of humanity. He knows what part is broken. He knows whether it is axle or tongue; he knows whether it is spoke or hub. The Lord Jesus Christ knows just exactly where you have broken down; and that is not all. He has in the great store-house of his remedies the very thing at hand to supply you and make you every whit whole.

And now, brother, you can go and apply, or answer to the call of this great Physician. We generally call our doctor when we are ill, but in this case, blessed be Christ, he calls us, "Come unto me, all ye that labor and are heavy laden, and I will give you rest." He does not say, "Go to that Church," or "this priest," or "that rector," or "this pastor," but "Come to me." These are the words of the Lord Jesus. "Come unto me." I am so glad it is a call from a person to a person. There is not much theory about this. And after all, brethren, when you come to weigh this question aright it is not creeds and dogmas that saves men. It is the name of Christ, and he is the only name and the only power in the universe that can save a man.

"The great Physician now is near,
The sympathizing Jesus,"

and he bids you come to him. He knows you. He knows what your trouble is and where your pain is, and he has the remedy at hand. "Come unto me, all ye that labor and are heavy laden."

Well, that invitation takes us all in. There are but two classes in the world. The first class are the decent, respectable, law-abiding, clever folks that want to do right, and do their best to get to heaven. Well, now Christ says to them, "Come." And then there is another class that are very heavy laden. Their cry is, "I have sinned and done wrong, I am guilty before God and man. I lay no claims to righteousness. I break down under the law." Now, Jesus looks at them and says, "Come to me."

And after all, brethren, we need a sovereign remedy, every one of us.

Now "come to me, and I will give you rest." It is peace to come. It is yours to come, and it is his to give the rest. "Come unto me, ye that labor and are heavy laden, and I will give you rest." What does this world want anyhow? Years and years I struggled and toiled and suffered, and I did n't know what I wanted. If you had asked me I could n't have told you to save my life. But I will say this, when the Lord Jesus Christ took me in his arms and gave me rest, then I said, "Glory to God, this is the thing I wanted. I did n't know what I wanted, but if this is rest, then it is rest I wanted exactly." Poor, tired, ruined wretch! Rest I wanted! Rest! And I will tell you, brethren, about all the rest from the cares and the troubles in this life is when you pillow your head on the blessed Christ.

That is where rest is. I recollect when I went to Corinth, Mississippi, I was broken down in strength and I had only a week to stay. I told the brethren I would have to preach four times a day in order to get through with my work. It was midsummer. I had been working incessantly and preaching four times a day, and preaching right along, and about the first day I said to my wife, jogging on to the Church, "I believe I will ask them to let me sit down and preach to-night. I can 't stand up; I have n't strength." She said she would ask them; they would n't care. I went on to Church and got up and read my hymn, and we sung and prayed, and I got up and took my text and preached longer than sixty minutes, and the Lord bathed my soul and body in a perfect sea of heavenly rest. And I preached an hour, and ran about all over that immense building that night until about eleven o'clock, and then went to the house where we were stopping, and pillowed my head, and in five minutes I was sound asleep. The next morning, after sleeping eight hours on a stretch, I woke up and turned to my wife and said I did n't feel as if I had struck a lick in six months, and I believe it was weeks and weeks after that before I had a conscious sense of tiredness upon me. And I tell you, my brethren, this blessed rest will come to a man. In the tiredest moments of my life I have gone home to my room sometimes and lain down, and I said, "I am so tired I can 't sleep to-night. O, how truly tired I am." And I would lie there a few moments, and directly the restful praises of heaven would begin to play all over my soul. I would lie still so far as I might as they passed over me backward and forward, and I said to myself, "I wish this night was a thousand hours long and I could n't sleep a wink. God give me this kind of rest." Bathed in that bliss I woke up the next morning, and it was the same delightful sensation playing all over my soul. Brethren, I tell you the Lord Jesus Christ has the keys to the great storehouse of rest, and can rest the soul in the sweetest and divinest rest.

"I will *give* you rest." Well, that is what we all want. That is what you want, friends. That is just what you need. You have known all the time you needed something, but you did n't know what it was. But if you ever get rest you will realize that this is the thing you wanted. Rest! "I will *give* you rest." And what more does he say? "Take my yoke upon you and learn of me, for I am meek and lowly in heart; and ye shall *find* rest." There is a *given* rest and there is a *found* rest.

There is a difference between rest and resting. First the Lord gives us resting. You see a man who comes in from his field after plowing all day, and sits down quiet in his cabin home with his arms folded. I ask, "What are you doing?" He says, "I am resting." "Then, what are you going to do?" "I am going to get up and eat my supper, and do something." Just as soon as a man is rested he begins then his activity again.

A man that is resting must be quiet. The Lord Jesus *gives* us rest from guilt and soul-quiet. When we are rested, then the natural instinct is to get up and go at something. Take the yoke and *find* rest. The grandest rest in this universe is the *found* rest; the rest in activity, the rest in movement, the rest in doing something; that 's it. I have sat in my own State, as well as other States, on a grand engine, with twelve or fourteen passenger coaches attached, and heard its exhaust noise, and felt its powerful influence as it moved the train along. It looks as if it do n't need any rest at all. It has been pulling us two hundred miles, and it rolls on as grandly as it did when it first started. "Ah, Mr. Jones," says the engineer, "she takes her rest better when she 's flying on the track trying to make her destination on time." I tell you, my brother, the soul goes on its way to God, and takes its greatest rest when it is bringing other souls to God with it.

Praise the Lord! What are you good for? A great many people think, "Well, I will just look after myself, and I will take care of myself," and the Lord knows that that is the biggest job a fellow can undertake—to look after himself. I would rather try to run this city than try to run myself—to sit up with myself. What is a man worth that won't do any thing but look after himself? Suppose the president of the grand trunk railroad had an engine that could run by itself sixty miles an hour, and would run as smooth as a die, but would n't pull any thing else; how long do you reckon he would keep that engine? How much would he value it at? He would n't value it any more than a scorpion. He would just tell the master machinist: "You just take that engine to pieces and throw it into the scrap-pile." Just show me a man that can not run any thing but himself, and I 'll show you humanity not fit for any thing but the devil's scrap-pile.

Brothers, go out and do something for God and humanity, and find the grandest rest that ever stirred a mortal soul. Go out and go to work if you want to find rest. You see that little brooklet as it flows along, winding its way through fields and villages, and turning around mountains, until finally the little streamlet says: "I am so tired; I have been rolling and running, and leaping and jumping ever since I was born into this world, and I am so tired." A kind friend throws an obstruction across its bosom, and makes a dam across it. And it stops still to pile its placid waters up, and I see it resting as quietly as a forest on a summer's afternoon. Then I see the water piling higher and higher, and the little streamlet is sleeping so nicely, and it sleeps on and on, and by and by it breeds miasma, mosquitoes, and frogs, and a great many things; and it says: "I have slept too long; turn me loose and let me go again." And they open the dam and the brook rushes on and turns the factory wheels, and runs on and on, doing its work and making music as it goes.

Brother, a few years ago I was so tired, I had run so long, and had been a sinner so long, when the Lord Jesus Christ laid his hand lovingly upon me and said: "Have rest!" And soon my soul was bathed in the sea of heavenly rest, under the powerful influence of his love. He removed all obstructions, and turned me loose to preach the Gospel to every creature, "that he that believeth on the Lord Jesus Christ may be saved." Thank God, he bids us go on our way rejoicing every day.

"Take my yoke upon you, for my yoke is easy." The yoke is an emblem of subordination, of servitude. See that wild ox roaming out in the forest. He comes when he pleases, and he goes when he pleases and where he pleases. He eats and drinks when he wants to. But go out there and bring that ox in, and let man control him; then, when his master says go he has to go, and when he says stop he has to stop; and he permits him to eat and drink when he thinks it proper to do so. When his master bids him to lie down he lies down. Look here! that ox has changed his whole nature. He is now submissive under the yoke. Look at that man. He won't work; he will do as he pleases; but now he takes the yoke of Christ upon him, and says: "Speak, Lord, thy servant heareth."

There is the difference between the Christian and a sinner. "Take my yoke upon you and learn of me, for I am meek and lowly in heart, and ye shall find rest for your soul; for my yoke is easy and my burden is light." Thank God that there are so many to testify to that!

Religion! If I were young, or if I were old; if I were rich, or if I were poor; if I were living, or if I were dying; if I were in heaven, or if I were on earth, I would want religion. Religion is the best thing on earth, and there is nothing in heaven that will surpass religion. Let's have it now, and let's have it every day, and work our way to the better world. Religion is like a beautiful casket. A man takes one home to his wife, and she puts it on the center-table in the parlor, and friends come in, and she shows it to every one, and they say, "O, how beautiful it is!" But one day the woman picks it up and touches a secret spring, and when the lid flies open for the first time she sees that it is not the inlaid casket on the outside, but the gem inside, that makes it lovely. Religion, with love, joy, peace, long-suffering, is like so many diamonds inclosed in this old, wretched nature of ours. It is beautiful to the world in its outer appearance; but, when Christ touches the hidden spring, then heaven itself opens up in all of its glory to the eyes of the faithful. Glory to God for it! May God give it to you, and may he bless every one in this house.

SAYINGS.

HE has either a mighty long head or a mighty short creed who believes only what he understands.

MANY a fellow is praying for rain with his tub the wrong side up. God can not fill a tub when it is wrong side up without inverting the law of gravity. God is holding up his clouds for you while you are holding your tubs the wrong side up. Turn them up and push them under the eaves if you want them to be filled, for the shower is coming.

LIFE, with its three-score years and ten, is said to be like a tale that is told; like grass that groweth up in the morning, and is cut down and withereth. Life is but one step from the cradle to manhood, but one step from manhood to old age, and but one step from old age to the grave. The few moments spent here to-night are but a few moments we spend on our way to the bar of God.

SERMON VI.

GOD'S GRACE SUFFICIENT.

"And lest I should be exalted above measure through the abundance of the revelations, there was given to me a thorn in the flesh, the messenger of Satan to buffet me, lest I should be exalted above measure. For this thing I besought the Lord thrice, that it might depart from me. And he said unto me, My grace is sufficient for thee: for my strength is made perfect in weakness."—2 COR. XII, 7–9.

WE ask your attention, especially to these words: "My grace is sufficient for thee." The devil is a cunning and an artful adversary. His first effort on humanity is to make us believe that we are strong enough and that we are good enough without any religion, that we are all right, and we need n't give ourselves any trouble; we 're as good as any body; a first-class fellow; but by and by we become possessed with an idea that we are not so strong, and not so good, and not so pure. The fact of the business is that when we reach the conclusion of a sensible and wise man, we say, "I am not good at all—I am not strong at all," and then the devil takes that fact and works on it and says: "You 're too mean and too weak to travel and to talk about being good."

How many thousand men who walk the streets of this city have been possessed of one of these ideas to their ruin and to others' ruin! The first thing a man so possessed says, is: "I 'm all right—I do n't need any help—I don't want any Christ to die for me. I don't ask odds of any body. And the next thing you see, the poor fellow has jumped clear over on the proposition, and says, "Now, there isn't any use of my trying; I'm the meanest man in the world, the wickedest and of the least account. If I just thought there was any chance for me I wouldn't mind starting. The fact is, I'm so low down, and so weak, there's no chance for me at all."

Now, I want to say to you, brother, that of the two cases I prefer the latter. There is no hope at all for a fellow who believes he is all right, when he isn't. That man is hopelessly lost while in that condition, but I have great hopes for a fellow that has touched bottom on the other side, and who feels, "I am not right, I'm not pure, nor good, and I haven't strength to be so, though I want to be right."

I sat this morning a half-hour talking to an honest man. I believe he was an honest and a true man. He said, "Mr. Jones, I have indulged in sin and been so depraved that I have lost my will power. I want to be good. I want to be a Christian and to abandon my sins. I want to live right and get to heaven. But, Mr. Jones, my will power is gone." I wish every Christian in this house and all these preachers could say, "I have lost my will power." Their case is mighty hopeful then. They can then say, "All my will is swallowed up in Thy will. Now I will consult the will of God and bid good-bye to my will and accept the will of God and the truth of God." I wish the whole universe would lose its will and have its will swallowed up in the will of God.

Now, here, we have a case before us to-day. Paul was largely like some of us, in that he once felt, "I am all right now; I am blameless; I never did contrary to right; I live on the straight edge;" but the time came, when in hopeless despair he fell; and when he arose he said: "Though I am a Pharisee of the Pharisees, of the tribe of Benjamin, I count all these as nothing compared to the excellency of the knowledge of Christ Jesus, my Lord."

Paul seemed to have been in need of this subdued condition of his will. He had been exalted to the third heaven, and had heard the unspeakable words which it is not lawful for a man to utter; his ears had been touched with the music of heaven; but at last he came down from these towering heights. Like Paul, the deeper down you go the more Artesian power will be added to the current of your life. There are many little shallow wells in this country, with a great many wiggle-tails in them. You all do n't know exactly what that means. We do in South Georgia. In some places down there they keep a long-handled gourd—they do n't need any bucket or rope for a man can dip his water out of the well—but in one place in South Georgia there is a long-handled gourd and a pine knot at the well. The pine knot is very much worn. The first thing they do when they want to get water out of the well, is to knock against the wooden sides with the pine knot to make the wiggle-tails sink, so that they can dip the water up, free from them. And there are many preachers in this country that have to use the pine knot.

O, brother, we will go into the deepest depth, and go up into the highest heights, but there are depths and heights in piety I know nothing about. There are heights in divine life I never have reached. There are beauties in Christian experience that you and I know nothing about. O, brother, let's go down in humility, in contrition, in honest confession before God.

Now, when you find a fellow away down, remember David said, "I was brought low and the Lord helped me." The Lord fishes on the bottom, and if you want to get to his bait and hook, you've got to get right on the bottom, brother. "I was brought low and the Lord helped me." Now, St. Paul had been high and he had been low. We find him here on a very low plain. "There was given to me a thorn in the flesh, the messenger of Satan to buffet me."

What was that thorn, do you know? I am glad I do not know. I am glad no human being knows just what that thorn was. Some of the wise men say the thorn in St. Paul's flesh was the fact that his eyesight was defective. For you know when he fell under the convicting power of God, he was blind three days and nights, and they tell us his eyesight was never entirely restored, and that that was the thorn in his flesh. Perhaps as he walked the streets the people said, "There goes old half-blind Paul, trying to teach people the way to heaven. Just look at him!" This was trying to a sensitive nature such as his. Others have said that the thorn in St. Paul's flesh was a defect in one of his legs, by reason of which he had to limp as he went through the world, carrying the Gospel, and then perhaps they would say as they saw him, "Watch old Paul now, hobbling along, trying to show the people how to get to glory. He is a nice fellow trying to teach people." The fact that he was lame was indeed a sore trial to him, and then to be scoffed at on account of his infirmity was indeed sad. Another wise man tells us that he thinks the thorn in St. Paul's flesh was the continued suppression of the ambition of his nature. Paul was eminently a great man. God never made a greater man, intellectually, morally, or spiritually than St. Paul. I measure his head and his heart, and I don't know which is the bigger. If you will find me a man who has a great deal of brains and no heart, I will find you a stolid, sound, solid, decent, dogmatic doctor of divinity that has not won a soul to Christ in twenty years; but there is one thing he will do,—he will "contend for the faith once delivered." And he is giving a falsehood to his own proposition, "contending for the faith once delivered." It ought to be for the faith delivered ten thousand times.

Brother, I reckon we need these men in the world. I have never been wise enough to know why these men go all to head. There is a woman, they say, in the show who is nearly all gone to feet, but it's a sad sight to see a fellow gone altogether to head. He would wear a number thirty hat, I suppose, and his head would weigh fifty pounds and his body forty. That's out of proportion. Brother, it 's the head and the heart together that we are to look at, and this grand man had both.

And now to curb the ambition of his nature, St. Paul—the Saul of Tarsus, with a world stretched out before him, with powers to succeed in any direction, with qualifications equal to the grandest accomplishments in life—is chained in the eyes of the world to the humble and despised Nazarene and his truths.

I do not think it was the defect in his eyesight; I do not think it was his lameness. I do not think it was suppressed ambition or subdued ambition. You ask me what it was—this thorn in his flesh. I say I do not know. Look here. If suppressed ambition were all my trouble, I could get along finely. If it were only lameness, I could hobble along. If it were defect in my eyesight, I could put up with that. But I tell you, brother, every man in this world has some supreme thorn in his flesh, and he can cherish the blessed thought, "May be this was the very thing that crushed St. Paul's spirit, and brought him so low to the mercy-seat."

Now, what your thorn is I do not know, but there is not a person here to-day without a thorn. You know there is something you never talk about, never mention to any human being on the face of the earth. Did you ever notice that? You may talk a great deal, yet there is something you keep to yourself. There are some moments when God alone can take our arm and walk with us, or we would not go right.

Paul did not tell what his thorn was. He might

have said, "I am suffering more than angels can bear." What is your case? "I can not tell you about it; I want your sympathy and prayers." Where is the man who has not carried a thorn in his flesh of which he has never spoken? I know that I have gotten a great deal of consolation in my distressed moments in the thought that "Well, after all, may be this thing that pressed so sorely on the life and character of this great man—may be I am to bear that."

Now, brother, St. Paul carried this thorn in his flesh, the messenger of Satan, to buffet him. He carried it until he felt in his heart, "I can carry it no longer." Have n't you been right there? Have you not felt that you must be relieved, or you would die? St. Paul reached that point. What did he do? St. Paul looked at this whole trouble, and then, when the world and his friends had turned their backs upon him, he fell on his knees and prayed, "O, Lord, I beseech thee, let this depart from me; I am overloaded." He got up off his knees and said: "I get no relief in prayer. If angels do n't help, humanity won't. My friends turn their backs on me. What must I do?" And he dropped on his knees the second time, and said, "O, Lord, do have mercy upon me." And he prayed earnestly, and got off his knees the second time, and there was the thorn still in his flesh, with all of its unspeakable pain. He looked at the world; his friends turned back from him; and at the angels, and there was a moment, perhaps, when he said, "O, what can I do?" And St. Paul dropped the third time on his knees. And there is a charm in this third prayer, brother; and imagine the third prayer of St. Paul, and the blessed Christ, as he stood at the Father's side and said: "Father, something must be done. I recollect the third time I prayed in the garden of Gethsemane. I remember when I had prayed once and got up, I found my disciples all asleep, and I awoke them, and when I went into the garden a second time, and came back, I found them asleep again, and I went all alone and almost hopeless into the garden, and kneeled down the third time, and the bloody sweat burst from my body, and how I prayed that the cup might pass from me, and that I might be fanned with the wings of thy love. O, Father, I recollect that. Something must now be done." And I imagine the great God stood up in the presence of the angels, and looked over the parapets of heaven, reached down and put his thumb on the thorn in St. Paul's flesh, and drove it up, and said, "My grace is sufficient for thee." And St. Paul stood up, and has never said a word about that thorn from that day to this. Thank God!

"My grace is sufficient for thee." That 's it, brother; that 's it.

I tell you, my brother, to-day, whatever your supreme trouble is, whatever may be the thorn you are carrying, go to God with it. If God does not pluck it out, he may drive it to the very head, but he will say, "My grace is sufficient for thee." When we go to God, and he puts his hand on that thorn, and drives it up, and says, "My grace is sufficient for thee," trust him and he will give you strength. When you are weak you are going to be strengthened under him.

Thank God, I say, that there are weak moments in our lives. Then God shows his power and love. May God help you to trust in him, and help you to see that whatever your thorn is he will take care of it for you.

SAYINGS.

REPENTANCE is the first conscious movement of the soul from sin toward God.

CHRIST always lives where there is room for him. If there is room in your heart for Christ, he lives there; if there is room in a law-office for Christ, he lives there; if there is room in your store for Christ, he lives there; if there is room on a locomotive engine, he will be there; if there is room in your baggage-car, he will be there. Everywhere there is room for him; he will come into our homes, and into our stores, and into our shops, and on our engines, and in our cars—that is, if we will provide room for him.

SERMON VII.

WHAT WAIT I FOR?

"And now, Lord, what wait I for? My hope is in thee."—PSA. XXXIX, 7.

"WHAT wait I for?" Here is a very practical question, and a very wise conclusion; and we notice, first, that it is a personal question. It is not, What is this city waiting for? not, What is my neighbor waiting for? not, What is my wife waiting for, or my children waiting for, but "What wait I for?" It is a personal matter at last; nobody can believe for you; nobody can repent for you; nobody can join the Church for you; nobody can be baptized for you; nobody can shoulder the cross for you; nobody can die for you; nobody can stand before the judgment throne for you; nobody can be bound hand and foot and cast out for you; nobody but you can wear the starry crown that may be yours. O, if we could just get men to think personally about this question:

"As soon as I from earth shall go
What will become of me?
Eternal happiness or woe
Must then my portion be."

O, how can a man be religious without making it a personal matter? How can a man write a religious epistle, as St. Paul did, without putting a great deal of the first person singular in it? If a

M. J. MAXWELL.

CHORISTER FOR REV. SAM P. JONES.

man talks out of his heart he appears egotistical. If a man sits down and writes out of his heart he appears egotistical. Somehow or other, though, if you take that "I" out of your head you'll be egotistical; but when the "I," and the "my," and the "me" come out of the heart there is really no egotism in it.

"What wait I for?" "Well," that man sitting back there says: "I'll tell you what I'm waiting for: I'm waiting for time to consider this great question. It is a momentous question. I do n't believe a man ought to hurry into a thing of this sort; and I believe if there is any thing that ought to demand the most painstaking care and coolest thought and meditation it is this great step. This is an important point to me, and I tell you I'm waiting for time to consider this question." Consider what? Look here! Do you want any time to consider whether it is better to live right than to live wrong? Do you want any time on a proposition like that? Do you want any time to consider this proposition: "Is it better to live and be a good man than it is to be a bad man?" How much time do you want to consider that question in? Why, there is not a sensible man forty years old that did n't settle the question twenty-five years ago that right is right, and he ought to do it; that wrong is wrong, and he ought not to do it; that it is better to be good than it is to be bad; that it is better to go to heaven than it is to go to hell; and yet some one says: "I want time." Look here, brother: is that wise? is that sensible? When I look at the infinite goodness of God and his numberless calls to men to lead a better life, and I look at what an infinite cheat the devil is, and always has been, that is the most ridiculous proposition that a mortal man ever made in his life. Want time to consider this great question!

"What wait I for?" "Well," says another, "I 'm waiting for better terms. You preachers and the Bible are too hard on us poor fellows. I 'm waiting until the day comes when I can drink whisky, and tell lies, and dance, and play cards, and do as I please, and be a Christian man at the same time. Whenever that time comes around you can put my name on the roll." Now, brother, if you want an easy religion, some of the Churches in this town will accommodate you. That is, they will accommodate you as far as they run their train. There 's a great deal in that. There 's many a little short branch road in this country, and they 're trying to advertise them as grand trunk lines to Glory. But, brother, there 's only one grand trunk line to Glory, and the only terminus of that grand trunk line is Conviction and Repentance. The next station along the route, as you move up the line, is Conversion. That 's a beautiful city. I stopped there, and found grand accommodations. The next station on that line is Obedience. You never spent a day in a happier, brighter town than that. A little further along the line is Brotherly Love, and this line just runs through the garden spot of the universe. When you step aboard that train once you step aboard with a through ticket, and your baggage checked, and do n't get off anywhere. I believe the Methodist train on this route stops occasionally and lets off passengers that do n't want to go through. But I pray God, if the Methodists of the city ever get going again fifty miles an hour they will never stop any more, and if a fellow is fool enough to jump off you let him go!

O, how I wish every man here to-night could see that the terms of Christianity, the terms of apostleship, are just about these: Quit every thing that ever degraded a mortal man, or ever led a soul astray, and then do the thing that will help humanity and bless the world. The terms of discipleship are about these: "Cease to do evil; learn to do well," and I, for one, am glad that the Lord won't take a man until he agrees to do the clean thing. I am so glad God told me, "You have got to quit drinking." If the Lord had said, "I will take you in, but you can drink on," I should to-night, it may be, have been in a drunkard's grave and in a drunkard's hell. I am so glad the Lord imposes conditions that must be agreed to if a man wants to be religious.

Another says: "I 'll tell you what I am waiting for: I 'm waiting for the Church of God to get right." Yes, and you 'll be in hell a thousand years before that thing ever happens. You can put that down. It never has been right. When Jesus called his twelve apostles aside aud consecrated them to the work of their discipleship, one of them had a devil; and I think we 're getting on first-rate if we have twelve hundred members and have but a hundred devils in the whole number.

If there 's any thing in the world that disgusts me, it is to see an old sinner walk into the Church and take out the lamest, shortest, crookedest, triflingest old member we have got, and measure with him. Why does n't he pull out a first-class member, and measure with him? He would n't go within a mile of him. If he were to lie down by his side, he 'd look like a little rat terrier lying by an elephant. I say, in the name of sense, brother, what do you want to bother with the hypocrites in the Church for? Listen to me. Those mean members in the Church are cast into hell, to live with the wicked forever. Come into the Church and live with the hypocrites, anyhow, for twenty or thirty years here, and go on to heaven and be rid of them forever. That 's my doctrine. Hypocrites ain't in my way. I have put them all behind me. Nothing can be in my way unless it 's ahead of me. I 'll tell you, whenever you hear a man talking about hypocrites being in his way, it 's because he 's in the rear of the hypocrites, and that 's mighty low ground, is n't it?

"I want the Church to get right." Brother, let 's you and I tote our own skillets, and let every body else alone. What do you say? When it comes to working, and striving, and toiling with other men, I want to do what I can to help every man to be good, but you can 't talk the meanness out of some men, because they take their meanness as a reason why they 're mean. Talking about hypocrites as being in your road, you 're mighty far back if that 's the case. "Waiting for the Church to get right." Stop all such talk as that. There are enough good people in the Church to form fellowship with you, and help you to God if you want to go, thank God.

Another man says: "Well, I 'm not waiting for the Church; I 've got through that. The Churches ain't bothering me. I used to talk a heap about them, but since I have got a good look at myself I have never been bothered much about other folks' meanness." And there is a good deal in that, too. An old member of the Church said to me one day, "Jones, my trouble is this—I can 't love my neighbor as I do myself." Said I, "You can 't?" He answered, "No, I can 't." "Well," said I, "I have never had any trouble on that score." "How did you work it?" he asked. "Well," said I, "I got a good look at myself thirteen years ago, and I have n't met a man since that I did n't think more of than I did of Sam Jones." Why, I am getting along finely on that line. O, me, if you ever get a good look at yourself, then you are going to think more of every body you meet than you do of yourself. You let all other people alone. Every tub must stand on its own bottom. I am responsible to God at last for myself, and for no other being in the universe.

"But," says another, "I am waiting for feeling. If I ever get feeling, then I am going to start." Look here! The dog is running on feeling. When he feels like running rabbits he will run them, and when he does n't he won't. If I were you, and had made up my mind to run on feeling, I would run rabbits the balance of my life. I think I would make that my business.

A man waiting for feeling is like a fellow sitting down by the big oak tree in the morning. It is a frosty, cold, crisp morning. He is sitting there by the tree, with an ax leaned up against his knee. I ask him, "Friend, what are you going to do?" "I am going to cut down this tree and maul it into rails." "You are?" "Yes." "Well, why do n't you get up and go at it?" "I am waiting to sweat." "Well, if you will get up and go to cutting, you will sweat." "I—I ain't going to cut a lick until I sweat," and he just sits there until he freezes to death. Now, what are you going to do with a fellow like that?

Feeling is the result of religious exercise, just as perspiration is the result of physical exercise. But I can prescribe feeling for you now, if you are honest about it.

You stir around and begin to right the wrongs you have done in this city. Go and try to bring character back to the one that you have robbed of her character. Go and take that money that you have defrauded another man out of, and count it out, and say: "Sir, I got this wrongfully. I am sorry for it. Here is your money." You will have feeling.

Look here, what do you mean by feeling, anyhow? Listen; if you mean serious thought, then I say you are right. Have n't you got serious thought, and have n't you had it for several days, on the subject of religion? Then, brother, that is all the feeling that a sensible man wants — serious thought.

Another says, "Well, I am not waiting for feeling; I am waiting until I know I can get through." Now, we get to the serious part of this question. Brethren, I always had an infinite horror of starting to be a Christian and then stopping. I preferred waiting until I got religion enough to take me clear through before I started. Now let me illustrate that for you. Once I was going out of Atlanta. Just before the engine backed down to couple on the passenger train, I was walking out around the engine. I wanted to look at the magnificent locomotive that would pull us out toward my home. The engineer was oiling it up. Directly he looked up in the cab and said to the fireman, "Have you got steam enough to start?" The fireman answered, "Yes." I walked back and peeped around at the steam gauge and I saw he had about seventy or eighty pounds of steam, and about three minutes later he rolled his engine back and coupled on to the passenger train and rung his bell and moved out. When I got on that train, I thought, "Well, it is strange; it is one hundred and thirty-eight miles to Chattanooga, and a great deal of it up grade, and that engine carries one hundred and sixty pounds of steam, and he left here with eighty pounds. I wonder what in the world is the matter with those men? What do they mean?" Well, then I got to thinking. The engineer never asked if he had enough steam to run to Marietta, twenty miles, nor enough to run to Cartersville, fifty miles, nor enough to run to Chattanooga, one hundred and thirty-eight miles, but he asked, "Have you got enough to start with?" Then the fireman said yes, and off he started. And Chattahoochee River was sixty-seven miles from Atlanta, and just before we got to the river the engine turned around the curve, and why, she was blowing off; she had more steam than she wanted; she had more than one hundred and sixty pounds. Then I got to thinking this way: Suppose that engineer had stopped and waited in Atlanta until he had steam enough to run to Chattanooga. That would have blown the engine into ten thousand pieces; she could n't have held it to save the world, do n't you see. And there is a little fellow out there who is waiting for enough religion to take him to glory, but before he could turn a wheel, if he could get that much into his little soul, it would blow it into ten thousand pieces.

Do n't wait to get enough religion to take you to heaven. Do n't wait to get enough to take you half-way to heaven, or ten years on the way to heaven; but, brother, have you got enough to start with? That's it. Well, how much is enough? Wrong is wrong; I will quit. Right is right; I will go at it. That is steam enough to start with. If you will pull your throttle wide open, and move out, you will be blowing off before you get half-way to heaven.

But now let us step back on the right side of this question. "What I wait for? My hope is in God." Well, brother, here is the great soul-stirring thought of the whole thing. When I first started out they could have said to me, "Jones, you are as weak as a bruised reed;" but I would have told them, "O, I know that, but my hope is in God." If they had said to me, "Jones, you will have ten thousand temptations," I would have said, "O, I know that, but my hope is in God." They could have said to me, "O, Jones, I tell you, you have undertaken a task that is a great one indeed;" but I would have told them, "I know that, but my hope is in God." "Jones, you will fail a thousand times." "Well, I may, but I want you to know that my hope is in God, in God." If my hope had been in money, I could not have bought a hope. I had nothing to buy it with. If my hope had been in my wife—and she has been all the world to me; she has been like a crutch under each one of my arms, carrying me along for seventeen years—I might have had to bury her, and then my hope would have been buried forever. Suppose my hope had been in my children, the time might have come when I would bury the last one of them, and then my hope would have perished with them. Suppose my hope had been in the preachers, the time might have come when they would all turn their back on me, and then my hope would be departed. Suppose my hope had been in the Church, the time might have come when the Church would drive me away from her presence, and then I would be driven away from my hope. But hear me, brother, my hope is not in wife, dear as she is; nor in children, precious as they are; nor in the Church, as blessed in her influence as she is to me; nor in the preachers, whom I love more than all other men in the world; but thanks be unto God, my hope is in him, and I want to announce the truth that ought to inspire every heart here to-night. Brethren, I am as strong as the thing I commit myself to and no stronger. If I start across the Atlantic Ocean in a paper box, just as soon as my paper box gets wet, it goes down, and I go down with it. I am no stronger than the box I have committed myself to. If I step on board of that grand ocean steamer and start out over the ocean, then all the strength in her hull and all the power in her boiler and all the comfort of her cabin are mine, and I will never go down until she goes down. If I commit myself to the arm of flesh, I am no stronger than the arm I commit myself to, and when the arm of flesh fails, I fail with it. But blessed be God, if I commit myself to God, I will never go down until God goes down. He is my hope and my strength and my portion forever. Blessed be his holy name. I give him my hand and my heart. Let your hope be in God, and there is no power in earth or hell that can wreck you or ruin you. Start out, friends, with that hope to-night. If you will just start, then God will carry you through.

SERMON VIII.

HOW TO BE SAVED.

"What must I do to be saved? And they said, Believe on the Lord Jesus Christ, and thou shalt be saved and thy house."—ACTS XVI, 30, 31.

THIS is the language of the Philippian jailer to St. Paul, and Paul's answer. As a minister of the Gospel of Jesus Christ, I have no right to advise a man to do any thing that he may not die doing and die saved. I might advise a man to join the Church—I know that is helpful and good advice, and I wish every man was a member of the Church of Jesus Christ, and was living up to the precepts of his blessed religion; and yet I see how a man may join the Church, and live in the Church and die in the Church, and yet be lost at last. And that's the saddest reflection of a human soul—gone from the heights of profession down to the depths of damnation. I might advise a man to read good books, and I wish there were no bad books in the universe. I am sorry that a bad book was ever published. I am sorry that any bad book ever had an entrance into your home, brother. I am sorry that one of your children, or one of you, ever sat down and worse than threw away your time reading bad books. I wish there were only good books, and that men would read them, and when I advise a man to read good books I am giving him good advice; but I see how men may go from the best libraries of earth down to hell at last. I might advise a man to be baptized in the name of the Trinity, and, brethren, this is a rite commanded of God; yet a man who has been baptized may go down to hell, unsaved at last.

I might advise a man to take the sacrament of the Lord's-supper. This is one of the sacraments of the Church of God, and I am sorry for any man who lies down to die with the consciousness, "These hands have never handled the cup of my Lord, and have never tasted of the bread which is emblematic of the broken body of the Son of God." Yet I see how a man may take communion regularly, may partake of the sacrament once a month, and die and be lost at last.

I might advise a man to keep good company, and I wish all men were good, so that there would be no bad company, for nothing can be more injurious than bad company, and nothing more helpful than good company; and yet I see how it is possible for a man to keep good company all his life and die unsaved. These things are all good. I would not, I say, underestimate a single one of these efficient means to take us to God; but there is only one sufficiency, and that is faith in the Lord Jesus Christ. And he who has this faith with works of love, and purifies his heart and overcomes the world shall be among that blood-washed number that shall shout and shine forever in heaven.

"What must I do to be saved?" The question is given, the question is answered, and I have often thought how good God is to us. He asks us questions and there on the pages of that book six thousand years old, some of them four thousand, some two thousand years, are the answers. But now here's a trembling, ruined man who cries out, "What must I do to be saved?" And the answer in the twinkling of an eye comes ringing down through his soul: "Believe on the Lord Jesus Christ and thou shalt be saved." Thank God for an answer as quick as heaven can give it to all who ask in sincerity and truth what they must do to be saved.

We might stop profitably to-night on the question itself, "What must I do to be saved?" Now, this term, "saved," "salvation," is not a song; it is not a sentiment; it is not a tear; it is not a shout; it is not feeling happy; but in its broadest, highest sense it means simply this—deliverance from sin; deliverance from all that God despises.

Brethren, we may leave this city for the city of refuge. Every step that takes me away from it is carrying me towards the city of refuge. Every step from sin is bringing me a step closer to the right. And conversion means being turned from the wrong and turned to the right. It is being brought into such relations to God, and into such harmony with God that I naturally love the right, and abhor the wrong. Behold all old things have passed away, and all things have become new. Now I find that what I once hated I love, and what I once loved I hate. Whenever I realize in my soul that I abhor sin and love the right, I have passed from death into life, because passing from death into life is always presupposed by the fact that I loved the wrong and did the wrong, and eschewed the right and would not do the right. But now, when one steps out into the realm where he hates the wrong and loves the right, if there has n't been a mortal change in the nature of that man, what in the universe could have produced such a state of things with him?

"What must I do to be saved?" Now we have had a great deal to say about getting religion. There is no such a phrase as "getting religion" in the Bible. Brother, let your religion get such a grip on you that you love the right and eschew the wrong the rest of your days.

Religion is not the love of the beautiful and æsthetic, but it is the grand principle underlying every stratum of life, guiding me and directing me in the path of truth and of righteousness. A good many men are looking for some mysterious transformation, some sudden, unexpected, serious, radical transformation. The best men I have ever met in my life did n't know the day nor the hour when they were born to God. The best man in my State told me from his own lips: "Brother Jones, I have loved Jesus ever since I commenced loving my mother, and my mother and Christ have always been associated together in my mind." Brother, I never ask a man what sort of experience he had to begin with, but, "Brother, are you loyal to God now? Do you love the right, do you hate the wrong?" That is the question.

Well, a great many say, "If I ever get religion as you say, why, I will know it by certain signs."

Do you know that has been the curse of the world, crying for signs? Do you know that religion does not come by signs, but it comes by faith? It comes by faith. Listen to me. If a man believes any thing after he gets religion that he didn't believe before he got it, I have never had any religion. I never saw the day in my intelligent life since I have been old enough to read my Bible that I didn't believe every thing that I believe to-night. If there is a drop of blood of the infidelity of my people for four generations back, I have been unable to trace it up. My grandfather and his father, and my own father and myself, have never doubted the truth of the word of God. I was as well satisfied up to twenty-four years of age that Jesus Christ died to save sinners, and that I was a sinner, and that he was able to save unto the uttermost, as I am to-night. I believed in Jesus Christ twenty-four years, and lived just as if I didn't believe a word of it. But for thirteen years I have believed it, and I have lived the best I could, God being my helper.

The mistakes of my life have been many. I am not what I want to be. I am not as far along as I hoped to be, but if I ever get through the pearly gates at all, it won't be for any good thing I have done. I am so glad that at the last day my salvation will not depend upon my works of righteousness.

If I ever get to heaven and my precious mother throws her arms around my neck and begins to congratulate me about getting through safely, I will say, "Hush mother. You go and show me the Lord Jesus, and I will show you the grand Being that put me on his shoulder and brought me all the way. I never could have come unless he had brought me safe." I do n't believe good works ever took any body to heaven, but, brother, I can 't see how I can get there without them.

What must I do to be saved?—saved from the wrong and saved to the right? Brother, I used to want religion to keep me out of hell. I used to say, "I must be religious, I do n't want to go to hell." Then at times I would say, "I want religion because I want to go to heaven." But as I view this whole question to-night, heaven and hell are both secondary in my mind. I want the religion of Jesus Christ to make a man out of me. I do n't believe any thing in the universe of God can make a true man except the religion of Jesus Christ shed abroad in his heart.

Now, what must I do to be saved?—saved from all that will harm me, and all that will offend God; saved to a good life, to a noble life and to a pure life? The answer comes from God. Let us take God at his word. "Believe on the Lord Jesus Christ and thou shalt be saved;" and thank God for those other three words, "and thy house." Now faith is the principle upon which omnipotence slumbers. You touch that principle, and you wake God up and wake angels up, and they rush to your help and your succor. Now we frequently hear, "Well, as soon as God gives me faith, then I am going to believe and be saved." Well, brother, faith is the gift of God; that is true. Eyesight is the gift of God. Hearing is the gift of God. God gives me the power to see, but he never sees for me. God gives me the power to hear, but he does not go to Church and hear for me. I say the power to believe is the gift of God, but believing is the act of man. Suppose God had said to you, "You are born blind. You are blind and I know it, and sight is the gift of God, and I never gave you sight; and now your salvation depends upon your seeing." You could have gone to judgment with your sightless eyes and turned them toward the great white throne and heard your condemnation: "Bind him hand and foot and cast him into outer darkness, because he did not see." You could go down to perdition and ride the crested waves of damnation and cry, "Unjust! unjust!" so loud that your cries would penetrate heaven itself.

You say, "I can 't believe." A man goes into a store and says, "I want credit for a thousand dollars." The owner says: "I can 't trust you." What does he mean? Simply, "I won't do it." He could trust him for every dollar in that house if he wanted to. But when he says, "I can 't trust you," he means in plain English, "I won't trust you." When you hear a man say, "I can 't trust God," he means in plain English, "I won't trust him." I know what is the matter; men won't believe. That is the way this world presents itself. Suppose I say, "There is a light over there, and if you see that light, you will be saved."

You say, "I do n't believe there is any light there." "Well, come on and I will show you." "I ain't going." I catch the fellow and pull him up on the top of the hill where he can see the light; then he puts his hands over his eyes. I jerk them down and he turns his head off from it. I push his head back around and he shuts his eyes. "I just do n't intend to see it; that is all." Many a man in this world does n't intend to believe, and therefore he can 't believe. But the man who intends to believe is like the man who intends to see. He will see if the way is open.

I say I can 't believe. I put my hand over my eyes and say, "I can't see that light." Why? Because I do n't comply with the conditions of sight. Take my hand down, and I can 't help seeing. Why? Because I comply with the conditions of sight. So, when I comply with the conditions of faith, I can 't help believing. When I do n't comply I can 't believe. Now, let us see what it means. What are the conditions of faith? Repentance. Now, what is repentance? Repentance is the gathering up of all the sins in your life in one common pile and throwing them down, and then walking off from them. When you walk off far enough from your sins, and walk up close enough to God for the warming rays of his life to begin to cause the doors of your heart to fly open, God comes in. Faith is the condition of receptivity. It gets up under God and says, "Lord, let love drop and I will catch it, and it shall be mine forever."

God is all around you in every direction, and you are walking right up to God; and when you walk far enough from sin, and close enough to God, the doors of your heart fly wide open, and you say, "My Lord and my God."

Is n't it strange that God will come to a poor fellow when he gets down to where there is no chance at all? Every other hope is gone. In your lost estate God begins to whisper to the soul, "The word of faith is nigh thee, even in thy mouth and in thy heart." There is the life, there is the hope, there is the blessedness, and there is the heaven in following the Lord Jesus Christ. That is it. Believe on the Lord Jesus Christ. When Matthew was sitting at the seat of customs, Christ came along and looked at him with his tax-books, and said, "Follow me." Matthew closed up his tax-books, and went right after Christ. When he got up and commenced to put one foot after another right down in Christ's tracks, if that is not religion, what do you call it? Listen: It is not the sentiment of faith, but it is the actual stepping out; it is the actual committal of your soul to the care of Christ. Believe. Now, a great many men say, I believe. Well, the mere believing that Christ died to save sinners does n't amount to much. You must believe with the heart, and believe unto the Lord Jesus Christ. Let your heart take hold upon him, and then follow him, "and thou shalt be saved and thy house." That is the sweetest thought. Not only thyself, but wife and children, and the servants of thy home, shall be saved. I do n't believe we care enough, brethren, for our women-folks. How many of us hold a love-feast, as the Methodists say, with our wives? "Wife, how are you getting along now?" "Husband, how are you getting along now?" I want my wife not to come and follow along behind me, but I want my wife to take hold of my arm and keep right along with me. I recollect once I had been off for three or four weeks, and I came home and found my wife in bed sick. I sat there the next day with her, and she turned to me, with tears running out of her eyes, and said: "Husband, have n't you got more religion than you ever had in your life?" I said, "I do n't know." She said, "You have either got more or I have got less, one or the other. If you have got more than I have, I want you to pray God Almighty to bring me up right side by side with you." I tell you, brethren, we do n't care enough for wife, and we do n't care enough for the children. The people of the world are more interested in the fashion of the world than we are interested in the good of our children.

"Believe on the Lord Jesus Christ and thou shalt be saved, and thy house." Thank God. The brightest sight I ever looked upon was a wife taking her husband's arm, and then the oldest child coming right along, and then the next, and the next, on down to the youngest, the whole family, marching right into the kingdom of God. The saddest sight mortals ever looked upon is to see a husband taking his wife's hand, and the wife the oldest child's hand, and the oldest child the next, on down to the smallest one, and to see that husband leading them right along down to the very brink of the river of death, and then making the final leap, and bringing them into that awful gulf with himself, wife, and the children. O, what a sight it must be to see an earnest and good wife loving and serving God, and trying to train her children right, while her husband, in his influence and life, is carrying the children off in another direction! If there is a deeper, more fearful place in hell for one than for the rest of humanity, it must be for the man with a good wife, trying to train her children right, who is leading them to death and hell. O, stop a moment to-night, and think what is the character of your lives at home!

Sayings.

God implanted in every woman's nature an inveterate hatred of the devil; and your success for both worlds depends on how you live out that principle. Die fighting him.

It is customary in Georgia to build storm-pits to protect the people from the fury of storms. I would not give one honest prayer for all the storm-pits in Georgia. I heard of a lady who, when she thought a storm was coming, started down to the storm-pit, and fell and broke her neck, and they never had any storm.

SERMON IX.

RELIGION A REASONABLE SERVICE.

"I beseech you, therefore, brethren, by the mercies of God, that ye present your bodies a living sacrifice, holy, acceptable unto God, which is your reasonable service."—ROM. XII, 1.

THERE is nothing more reasonable than religion and the conditions upon which we may become Christians. It is reasonable, right, and wise to become a Christian, and we are besought to do so by the mercies of God. The great question in this nineteenth century is not whether a man ought to be religious, but how can he be? We have in our text a lesson: "Present your bodies a living sacrifice, holy, acceptable unto God." That 's it.

What do you mean by that? I mean simply this: There is but one road in the moral universe of God; heaven 's at one end of it and hell 's at the other, and this text simply says: "Keep your back on hell and your face on heaven." In this road, and there 's only one, if you turn your back on heaven, hell would be before you. A man does n't have to take a week's journey through the wilderness, across the mountains of God, to be in the road to heaven; all he has got to do is just to turn around, and he is just as much on the road to heaven as any body. There 's only one road. Which direction are you taking? Up or down? Hellward or heavenward? This text turns a man around, and turns his face toward heaven, and turns his back upon all that 's bad. If I turn my back on the good, then I 'm bound to go to the bad. If the train I am on is going forty miles an hour southward to Chattanooga, I can 't come to Cincinnati. Its momentum, its speed, its power, all carry me in the other direction.

"Present your bodies a living sacrifice, holy, acceptable unto God." No man ever was or ever will be religious until he settles the question somewhere along the line of life that he will have religion. The Spirit of God, the Gospel of Christ, the Sabbath-school, with its training, a mother with her prayers, never made any man religious. When a man once decides the question of his destination all the resources of God help him along. How are you going to make a farmer out of your boy when he does n't want to farm? How are you going to make a lawyer out of your boy when he does n't want to study law? If you want to help him how are you going to help him? How can God Almighty help a man to be religious when a man has n't made up his mind to be religious? That 's the question. This text involves the idea of choice. Do you know what choice means? It means I 'll take this in preference to that. It means I 'll give up that and take this.

There is a great difference between a desire to be religious and a choice to be religious. A man may die desiring to be a Christian and yet he may go to hell, for he dies without religion; but no man ever did make a choice to be a Christian and die without religion. Choice means, I 'll give this up and take that. Choice means, I will sell out all I have and invest in this. I will be religious. A man must come to an agreement with his Maker. O, happy man that has reached this point in his experience, where he can look into the face of his Maker and say, "Father, God, from this moment I will be loyal to thee; I will do right, I will quit wrong!"

"Fear God and keep his commandments." Let a man come to the point in his understanding with his Maker, and say, "In thy name and with thy blessing I will quit all that 's wrong and do all that 's right," he is a happy man. There 's no doubt about that; there 's something sensible in that. It 's astonishing how we know right from wrong and wrong from right. It 's astonishing how many people know all about these two things! There 's something practical about this. Quit what 's wrong and get to doing what 's right. That 's it! Just as certainly as any railroad leads into or out of this city, just so certainly a man who will quit wrong and take to doing right will find his way to God.

There are a great many little side issues I might bring, to be specially orthodox; but the question is not whether you are orthodox, but is your life consecrated to Christ, and are you doing your duty? That 's my religion. I like the good old practical religion that will make a fellow tell the truth whenever he opens his mouth; that will make him pay his debts, and love his neighbor, and be good to his wife and pleasant to his children. I do n't care what your professions are, if you have that kind—if you 're not a hypocrite—you are on the right road. A man who is snappish, and cross and mean to his wife and his children, and won't pay his debts, no matter what he professes, is a hypocrite.

If a man has assumed a right attitude towards God, then the next question comes, "What are you going to do about this world?" This world is a multitudinous affair, and the apostolic injunction is, "Be not conformed to this world, but be ye transformed by the renewing of your mind."

Do you know what 's the matter in this city? Is it the drunkenness, lying, thieving, licentiousness and outbreaking wickedness of the Church members? No, sir! But, if you want to know what 's paralyzing the Church and destroying its heart power, I 'll tell you: It 's the tide of worldliness that 's sweeping over your homes and dragging families down to hell. It 's dancing with this world, and going to theaters with this world, and drinking with this world, until we have only about one more thing to do, and that 's to go to hell with the world!

A great many of us are doing that very same thing, too. I like to see a Christian put himself in a right attitude towards the world. This world has no right to furnish a fashion for us to be governed by. Fashion! Custom! I declare it has reached that point now where some of our Churches increase their membership by dragging the Church to see new families moving in the neighborhood, and saying to them: "If you want to get into society you 'll have to join our Church." I am glad of every social feature in this universe, but you know what I mean by "society." These dinners, where you 're considered stingy, may be impolite, if you do n't have wine on your table, and cards in your home, and germans in your house; that 's the society I mean. It is a heartless cannibal, feeding upon soul and body. "But every one has cards, or social dances and germans!" Every body! It 's a lie! They do n't, and I 'm glad of it.

My house is consecrated to God, just like this church, and nobody comes there to dance or engage in a wine supper, or a ball, or a game of cards. They all know that house is God's house. I will protect my home. I never shall let this tide of worldliness sweep over my children. I see what it has done for others. I see how others are cursed and blighted. A Catholic priest in New York said that nineteen women out of twenty who had lost their character, and came to the confessional, told him they got their downfall in a ball-room.

I know a man who opposes the world will be called a fanatic, and worse things than that. You Christians need to be looked after. If these sinners want to dance and drink and carouse about you I can safely plead with them; but, when a man professing to be a Christian goes into these things, I will denounce him as Jesus Christ denounced whited sepulchers eighteen hundred years ago. What 's the use talking to sinners when the deacons and leaders of the churches, and stewards, rent their houses to women of ill-fame, and their property for bar-rooms and whisky-shops, and gambling hells, and worse? You will have to sweep before your own doors before you can reach Jesus' heart.

Lord Jesus, give us men who say, "I have settled some questions with God. I am going to settle it now that I won't drink, nor play cards, nor run with this world, nor do any thing for or have any thing to do with it any further, if Jesus Christ will be with me.

One of the governors of Georgia removed to the capital of our State. His wife, a good woman, accompanied him. After they had moved into the city of Milledgeville she sent her children to school, and one afternoon they came home and said to their mother, "Mamma, if you do n't take these red flannels off of us we 'll quit school." "What 's the matter?" said the mother. "Well," said her children, "all the other children laugh about wearing red flannels, as they 're out of fashion." The old governor's wife said, "Now, look here, children, you must n't come here and complain about the fashions, because I set the fashions here, myself, for the other folks." Let 's look this old world in the face, and set the fashion of what is right and keep it.

"Be not conformed to this world." Do right under all circumstances, and everywhere. Suppose you starve to death, do right anyhow. Come to a good understanding with the world, but do not follow or love it. I do not know that I have been any more lucky than other people, but I tell you this, brethren, when I gave my heart to God, and my life to the service of God, this old world, somehow or another, thought I was in earnest. From that day to this no man has ever asked me to take a drink of whisky; no man has ever invited me to a ball; no one has ever invited me to a german, or to play a game of cards. I heard a trifling old Methodist in my town say once, "Our candidates are grand boys; they 've asked me seven times to drink this morning." A candidate knows whom to offer drinks to. God help me so to keep my life ever before people that they may never dare ask me to do an unholy thing. It is an insult to a good man to be asked to do any thing a Christian should not do.

The truth! the truth! Be not conformed to this world. I love to see a man or woman in the right attitude toward this world. Brother, you 'll never feel religious until you settle some questions with this world, and say, "I will not drink, or dance, or frolic, or go to theaters, or do any thing that 's wrong—I won't do it." Now, let us see how good we can be.

SAYINGS.

WHAT is salvation? Every theological book I look into tells me that salvation is deliverance—first, from the guilt of sin; second, from the love of sin; and, third, from the dominion of sin. That is what the books say salvation means; but if I were to answer out of the Word of God, and out of Christian experience, I would say that it is the loving of every thing that God loves, and the hating of every thing that God hates.

SERMON X.

WORKS OF FAITH AND LOVE.

"Remembering without ceasing your work of faith and labor of love and patience of hope in our Lord Jesus Christ, in the sight of God and our Father."—1 THESS. I, 3.

THESE are the three elements of a Christian Church in its active life: works of faith, labors of love, and patience of hope in our Lord Jesus Christ. The Thessalonian Church, my brethren, did have favor with God and great influence among men. I believe in primitive Christianity. I will take apostolic Christianity with all its Puritanism and with all its transcendentalism before I will take nineteenth-century Christianity, with all its adulterations and all its finery.

Apostolic Christianity; first-century Christianity! Well, that involves a great many things, brethren. A man gave up all then, and received all. A man is filled with the fullness of God just in proportion as he empties himself of the fullness of the earth. No two substances can occupy the same space at the same time. The more of this world we have in us, the less of God we have in us. In the very nature of the case this must be so. And if any man loves the world the love of God is not in him. We have made a great many improvements in other things, but when have we made any improvement on apostolic Christianity? Paul said to this Church of the Thessalonians, "Remembering your works of faith." What is a work of faith? What is faith? Faith is taking something that is offered us from God, and giving something to God that he asks for. That is all. There is a sense in which I receive from God by faith. There is a grander sense in which I give to God by faith. It is more blessed to be where you can give than where you have to receive. Now, there is a faith that receives, and I like that sort of faith. "Every good gift and every perfect gift comes from God." O, brother! God did not say, "Stand still and receive salvation," but, "Work out your salvation with fear and trembling." Works of faith! Now, I say that faith—simple faith—either takes something or gives something every time you offer it an opportunity for so doing. It is doing the one thing or the other all the time.

Whenever God offers you something—and he is always offering you every thing when you have got hungry—take it of God and be thankful for it. But there is a giving faith also, and that is shown in works. I know what is the work of sight. There is a farmer there plowing all along between the rows of his corn in his field. The corn waves on both sides of him, like a sea of green, and he plows along between the rows of his corn, and the man almost hears the joints of the corn crack in its covering, it is growing so fast. That is a work of sight. What is a work of knowledge? I will give you an illustration. I see a colored man walking along the street. I talk to him and he tells me, "I likes to work for So-and-so." "Why?" "Because I knows that jes' as soon as the work 's done there 's the money." You see there is the work of knowledge. But what is a work of faith? An old colored man hit it the best. He said, "If God would tell me to jump through a rock wall ten feet thick I would jump at it. Going through it belongs to God, but jumping at it belongs to me." That is pure, clean-out, naked faith—God's faith. In other words, a work of faith speaks out, as Joshua did at Jericho, and says, "The Lord hath delivered this city into our hands," when there is not a crack in the wall.

I will tell you another thing about faith. There is a past faith and there is a present faith, and there is a future faith. Faith ought to be like the Hebrew verbs. They are all of one tense, and that a present tense. You see sometimes our faith coming ahead of us, and we say that we are going to have a good meeting, and then it runs on for a while, and they say, "We should have had a good meeting, a splendid meeting, if we had done so and so." Now, it is the tense gone back and dropped behind. Whatsoever faith we have let us have it now. That is what we want. It is a faith that appropriates now the blessings God proposes to give us.

Present faith! A work of faith! It is getting right straight along and doing what the Lord tells you to do, and asking no questions about it. A work of faith is manifested by obedience to the will and the word of God. The best reason that I have for knowing that my children have faith in me and faith in my love and devotion to them, is that they never question me a moment when I tell them to do any thing. I would hate to have them to stop and question me about every thing that I tell them to do. If I told my little boy to bring me a drink of water, and had to explain to him for ten minutes why I wanted a drink of water, I would sooner get it myself and have done with it. If the Lord had to spend all his time in explaining why he wanted us to do this thing and that for him, why, he would not do it, for he can and would come down to do it himself. When you understand what the Lord wants, go on and do what he tells you.

Well, then, the next thing we take up is the labor of love. What is the difference between a work of faith, and a work of love? There is no difference in kind, but there is a difference in degree. Let us illustrate again. The day I joined the Church I sat up at night and talked with my wife. She was a happy woman, too, you can believe. A new day and a new life had dawned upon our home. And before she retired that night she took down the Bible, and said "Let us begin right," and gave the Bible to me. I took the Bible in my hand, and I commenced reading, but the words seemed to run all together, but I managed to get through some chapter, but I never remembered what chapter it was, or a word in it, and I have never remembered a single utterance. But this much I do remember, and that is that I read this Bible, and that I prayed, and that big drops of sweat covered my face when I had got all through.

O, how hard it was. It was a work of faith. But I have kept at family prayer every night and morning ever since, and the most blessed moments—the sweetest moments I have at home are passed when I am reading the Bible. It was a work of faith then, but it turned into a labor of love, and now it is one of the sweetest duties in my home.

Labor of love! Get so as to love to do right. I recollect the first sermon that I ever preached. O! the agony I felt while I stood up before the people and tried to preach. O! brethren, I went right along, straight ahead, preaching the Gospel of the Son of God; and this evening, I would rather be a preacher than be a king. I would not swap places with the President of the United States. I would much rather be an humble minister of Christ Jesus than be the king of England or the czar of Russia. I will make it look as if I meant what I say if I show what I am talking about. I never told a bigger truth than that, and if God helps me to do my part well, and in the kingdom of God, I shall outshine every man who has been President of the United States, every thing else being equal.

And labor of love! I am sorry for the Christians that have been long in the heavenly race and have not yet got so that they love to run. We have been cursed with people who have only talked about duty and done no running. What we want is love of labor. We want to be God's willing agent. We want to consider it a privilege to do what God wants us to do. I tell you I use family prayer, and trusting prayer, and seeking the needy, and giving to the poor. I use all of these things as a bird does its wings, to carry me to where I am going to; and when I get to the kingdom of God I will cut off my wings and throw them away. I shall have no further use for them. But while I am going there I want wings just as a car wants wheels to roll on. I want visiting the sick, I want prayer, I want prayer-meetings, I want reading the Bible, because I use these things as the engine uses its wheels—to roll on. Take the wheels away from under an engine and what is it without them? It is nothing but an old stationary affair and good for nothing but to run a saw-mill in the back-woods to saw fuel for the devil. And there is many a fellow in the Church who is good for nothing but to serve as a stationary engine back in pine woods cutting out lumber for the work of the devil.

Labor of love! I like a Gospel that gives a man a delightful feeling every step he takes on the way to the better world. Labor of love! I recollect when I was visiting Brother Prade in Rome. I was then a preacher at De Soto. Brother Prade was at the First Church. I was standing on my side of the river in a cabinet shop, and a lady stepped up on the front step and said, "Gentlemen, we have a gracious meeting in our church. Won't you come and enjoy it with us?" And they said, "Yes, ma'am;" and I walked to the door to see who the lady was, and recognized her as the wife of Colonel ——, who was confined to her room six months in the year with sickness, and yet I saw that woman halting and tottering along the sidewalk, pale and trembling, doing a labor of love. And if I ever saw an angel of mercy on her mission of love and kindness to the human race, she was one. That is the sort of Christians we want. That is the labor of love we want. Those are the people who want to work for God, and you can not help them out of it.

Let us take hold of these things we have been talking about, and get some good out of them. There is a rich, delightful territory higher up the stream to talk about. Brethren, there is nothing like leaning upon God's promises, and waiting upon God for his own good time.

SAYINGS.

IF you will tell me what you love, I will tell you what you are. A man's likes and dislikes determine his character. The difference between the Lord Jesus Christ and the enemy of souls is in their likes and dislikes. A man's affinities determine who he is and what he is.

I AM no metaphysician, but I can see a hole through a ladder if there is any light on the other side. I will tell you there was very little metaphysics when the jailer stood up there trembling and asked, "What must I do to be saved?" And there is not much metaphysics in the answer: "Believe on the Lord Jesus Christ, and thou shalt be saved." There is not much metaphysics about that.

SERMON XI.

WHY WILL YE DIE?

"Say unto them, As I live, saith the Lord God, I have no pleasure in the death of the wicked; but that the wicked turn from his way and live; turn ye, turn ye from your evil ways; for why will ye die, O house of Israel?"—EZEK. XXXIII, 11.

GOD has said frequently to his children, "Come, let us reason together." He is a reasonable God, and you are reasonable men in many things, and he challenges you into his presence, and says, "Let us reason together about this. I have no pleasure in the death of the wicked." In other words, "I have nothing to do with the death of the wicked." I say there is nothing in the grace of God, and nothing in the blood of Jesus Christ, to save an impenitent man.

These are clear, honest statements of Scriptural truths. There is nothing in the Pacific Railroad's movement of its trains to make you ship your goods over that road if you do n't want to ship them that way. There is nothing in the management of the Pacific road that can compel a man to travel over its lines if the man does n't want to go over them; and we say honestly and emphatically that there is nothing in the atonement of Jesus Christ to save any but the lost; and no man is saved, in a Gospel sense, until he first sees and feels he is lost. When a man feels that he is lost in this sense, thank God he is getting to be found! Your salvation depends on your patient continuance in well-doing.

What is the judgment at last? "Well done, thou good and faithful servant." It is n't, Well commenced. I have known people to begin a great many things well. It is n't, Well carried on. I 've known a great many people to carry on an enterprise for years, and then break down. It is n't, Well begun or well carried on, but it is "Well done, well finished, well rounded up, thou good and faithful servant." And now, brother, listen: If you are an earnest, humble Christian, your salvation does not depend so much on what happened in the past, may be, as on what are you going to do from now on? "If a righteous man forsake his righteousness and commit iniquity, the righteousness he hath done shall be forgotten, and he shall die in his sin." God says to the wicked, "If you forsake your wickedness and do right, you shall live. I have no pleasure in the death of the wicked."

I know the question is asked, "If God is omnipotent and is love, then why should any man perish?" Brother, we have what we call human will in this world, and that will determines for you where you will go. If you go to hell, it is a matter of choice with you; if you go to heaven, it is likewise a matter of choice. Say, why did God endow man with will, then? Look here, there are some things that are inherent in the nature of the thing. How cometh that engine on the track yonder? Its gauge indicates one hundred and fifty pounds pressure of steam. What do they want with the steam?

Why, to pull the train behind the engine. But it may burst the boiler into ten thousand pieces! Yes, but that 's the inherent nature of the steam. When you sit in the train you always feel the powerful pulsations of the majestic engine in front, and that engine has power enough in its nature to blow the boiler into ten thousand pieces.

The powers that God has given you to direct you and move you, these same powers may destroy you for time and eternity. Righteousness is the right use of God's given thing, and sin is the wrong use of God's given thing. If you use a thing wrongly, God is not responsible if you are blown up by it; and the power to do right or wrong is inherent in the nature of man. I suppose they could have made an engine so that its boiler would n't burst; but if they did, they 'd have to make some other sort of an engine than a steam engine. I 've seen caloric engines, but they never get anywhere.

Hear me. God has no pleasure in the death of him that dies! My mother loved me because she had some of the nature of God in her own heart; my wife loves me because some of the nature of God has been poured into her heart. God is love, and the great store-house of God's love is his heart, and we all draw from that store-house; and all the love my wife and my mother and my children have for me has been drawn from the great store-house of the love of God. Did my wife's love save me? Did my mother's love save me from a wicked life? No, sir! No, sir! In that sense God's love can 't save any man, and it never did save any man.

If God's mercy, and God's love, and God's goodness could save a man, then God was guilty of cruelty to send his only begotten Son to suffer on the cross that he might wash away with his blood our sin. There is no means by which we can be saved except in the name of the only begotten Son of God. The Father sent his Son into the world not to condemn the world, but that through him the world might be saved. He bridges the chasm between a sinking world and the God that made it; and he was sent not to break down and crush and ruin humanity, but that we might cross over in safety on his atonement into the kingdom of God.

I declare it to be as true as that I read my Bible that there is not a man here to-night but who may be in heaven within a hundred years from to-day. There is n't a man here to-night but who, if he makes the choice, can be in hell a hundred years years from to-day. Those ten decades will soon be gone, brethren. O, how the time flies! Let 's you and I settle it to-night. "By the grace of God, if that be true, I 'll be in heaven a hundred years from now." We may be there in ten years; it may be in ten months; it may be in ten days; it may be in ten hours;—we will be in the one place or the other.

To the righteous I say, "Keep on; plow your furrow out; go on through;" but to the wicked I say, "Stop! there 's danger and death ahead of you." There 's a message for you both to-night! Christian people, hear me, and go on in your way; but, sinners, just stop long enough in your mad, onward rush to hear these truths. "Turn ye, turn ye, why will you die." The turning spoken of here means an actual, business-like turning away from sin, not a mock turning. There 's no farce about this thing; it 's an actual turning away from sin.

Here 's a merchant that 's been merchandising ten years, and he 's been losing money right along, and now he 's almost near to bankruptcy, and he resolves he 'll close out his stock on hand, and quit the business and go to farming. There 's a business turn about that thing. He does n't want to go on losing money; he sees he 's sinking every year, and he resolves to quit merchandising and go to farming. Turning away from sin is just as actual as is that man turning from merchandising.

It seems to me sometimes that we 've got religion diluted down to a sentiment or to a song; but it 's an outrage on the glittering, glorious Gospel of the Son of God. It is not a sentiment—it 's a sanctified business. It 's a business contract binding on you. You do what God tells you to do, and then if God does n't do what he said he would do, you have an issue that will bankrupt heaven in a minute.

A great many people in this world want their pay before they do the job. There are two bad paymasters—one who pays before the job is done, and the one who never pays at all; and the one that never pays at all is the best one, because if he pays humanity before they do the job, they will tell a thousand lies to get out of it, and never do it at all. Listen! Some of you people want the pay before you do the work! That's your trouble. You say, "If God will bless me, I will do so and so." I guess you will. Who are you that want to dictate the terms to him, and receive all the benefit yourself? God says, "You do so and so and I will do so and so." Do your duty; that's the way. If you will do your duty, you will be religious, and you will be religious if you do your duty. Some people are always troubled to know what the Lord will do for them. Turn and you will be saved, said the Lord. The turning is your duty, and the saving is God's. If you turn and God does n't save you, then you will have an issue that will overturn the pillars of justice. The turn must be business-like, however. You do n't want other people to pay you before you do your duty, and why do you want the Lord to do it? A man does n't want to pay for a bill of goods until he orders and receives them. You do n't want to pay the blacksmith until he shoes your horse. Let's be decent and sensible in our turning to God.

What's the use in forswearing ball-rooms, and then wanting to go back to them? What's the use in giving up cards, and still you're nearly dead to play cards again? I believe in Christian liberty, in a fellow getting religion and doing right. But whenever you get to rubbing up against ball-rooms and card-rooms and theaters, and such, you make a mistake—you have n't given up any thing. I loved to dance and do a hundred things that are wrong, but I have had as much desire to go to hell as to a ball-room since I got religion. I believe in a religion that sets us at liberty, and makes us do the things we love to do, and makes us love the things we ought to do. You can 't turn away heartily to heaven, and yet long for the fleshpots of Egypt. I 've got into Canaan now, where the grapes and the pomegranates and the figs cluster thick above my head, and I can eat and rejoice. I have had enough of the leeks and onions. It is all choice. I take God's love to my heart, and put it on, and follow his directions.

Now, from every thing that is wrong I take my heart, and put it on these things which are right. And a man is never converted until he is converted from the wrong and converted to the right.

God pity you, my brother! Let us go out on one side or the other. Let us take a stand. If it is right to do wrong, let us go on boldly; and if it is right to do right, and stick to God and live for heaven, let us go over on that side.

I heard of a gambler in Louisville who gave himself to God, and joined the Church; and then he went on the streets next day, and when he met his former companions, he said to them, "Good-bye, boys; I will never do those things again; and unless you come into the Church and take a stand with me, I will cut your acquaintance to-day, and cut it forever." That is what I call taking a stand! And if you want to be religious, take a stand. May the good Lord give these poor sinners grip. That is what we want; the nerve to come up and assert our manhood, and take sides in this great moral issue.

Turn—an actual, hearty turning away from sin.

And not only that, but let it be an immediate turning. Be not among these everlasting dilly-dally men, putting off, and putting off.

You can 't be in too big a hurry in this great question of preparing for eternity. And, thank God, when a man prepares to die, then he is prepared to live; he is prepared for every good work and word. It is an immediate turning away from sin that is necessary. O, brother, that heart that beats in your bosom is but a muffled drum beating your funeral dirge to the tomb, and you know not when that heart will stop beating. Brother, you have no time to lose—you have no more time to throw away. Whatever else may happen, if you will put in your best licks from this hour until you die, you will find out you just barely made your way safely to the good world.

An immediate turning away from sin! And not only must it be an immediate turning away, but a thorough turning. Brother, there is no use in talking about giving up part. One sin in your life is like one leak in a ship; it will sink your soul before it reaches the other shore; and it is a question not of how many sins have you given up, whether twenty or fifty or a thousand, the one question for eternity is, have you given them all up; and have you emptied them down to-night so that you can say, "There is the last sin of my life, it is given up forever?" Will you do that? O, brother, you can not swim the ocean of time with any sin resting upon you; you can not do it. And you can just as well give your sins up now and give them all up. I know what human nature is. I recollect how I tried to scatter my sins along and give up those I felt I could get along best without. But, brother,I never made any headway until I emptied them all down, and said, 'Lord, I will never do another thing that displeases thee." And I said, "If I am damned at last it will be for those sins already committed. I will never commit another."

And it must not only be a thorough giving up, but, brother, hear me once more—it must be an eternal giving up of sin. When General Lee, under the apple tree at Appomattox, handed his sword to General Grant, he said with his whole heart, and said it for his whole army, "We will never take up arms against the old flag again."

I tell you, my fellow-citizens, when a poor sinner goes to the cross and surrenders, let him surrender with the understanding that he lays down his old weapons of rebellion. Let him say: "I do not lay them down for a week, or a month, or a year, but so help me God I will never, never fire that old gun again. I will never handle it any more. God helping me, I will be true to the flag of the cross from this day until the minute I die."

Now you say, "What is the necessity of my turning?" Do you know, brother, that this nineteenth century is wicked, and more wicked perhaps than the century that preceded it, and that the more wicked and depraved men get the more they fight this idea of hell? And did you ever see a man that did n't believe in an eternal hell, but that when he came to die he would go there? There is many a fellow in this country who says, "There is no hell," and mark the expression, he won't be in hell more than ten minutes before he jumps up and cries out, "O, what a mistake I made in my doctrine. I did n't have any hell in it, and now I am in hell forever."

Hear me, my brother. Let us open the pages of this Book, and we will see that for the wickedness of man God drowned this old world. We turn over a little further, and see the burning hail falling on Sodom and Gomorrah. And we turn over a little further, and there are Pharoah and his hosts, horses, chariots, all drowned in the Red Sea. We turn over page after page, and we find a little further along Ananias and Sapphira as they dropped dead in their tracks for lying. We turn over and over until the end, and find that God has been punishing sin for four thousand years.

As I look an all merciful God and loving Father in the face to-night, then I look at myself and say, O, God, if thou hast destroyed armies and drowned the world, and sent the burning hail upon cities and destroyed them, and caused the earth to burst open and swallow the wicked; I look at all this and then I ask myself the question, if God will drown worlds and burn cities and destroy armies as he has done in the past, then will God let me go unpunished in the future? And the man who says that God will not punish sin must fly in the face of the record and of the history of this universe.

And, now, the means of turning. What are the means? "Lord, here I am to-night, a poor sinner. I give up and surrender to the cross. I take the line of duty thou hast marked out for me. I give myself to thee from this time on." Brother, sister, won't you turn to-night?

> "Sinners, turn! why will you die?
> God, your Savior, asks you why?"

Won't you turn to-night and be saved forever? Turn! turn!

SAYINGS.

IF there is any thing in this world I admire it is a man with a big soul—a soul big enough for God to come in and live with him, and for the angels to come in and sit down and be at home forever. God give us a soul on fire, and growing and developing in divine light! Brother, is your soul growing every day?

LET your light so shine that every one will see your good works. A great many people, with what little religion they have, will run out in the corner and sit down and say, "God save me and my wife, and my son John and his wife, us four and no more!" That is the sort of religion that is cursing the world. The true principle of a good man is, the more he gets the more he wants; and the more he gets the more he wants others to have.

SERMON XII.

THE WAYS OF PLEASANTNESS.

"Her ways are ways of pleasantness, and all her paths are peace."—PROV. III, 17.

THE Christian life is often spoken of in the Scriptures as a "way," and our walking in that way makes what we call a Christian pilgrimage. This is a world of traveling. *Here* we are on our journey; *there* we will be at our journey's end. There is no such thing as stopping. The vast surging masses behind us push us along in life's pathway, and as earth is filling up daily with its thousands, it is gradually, yet persistently and continually pushing others into the grave. We are all on one grand solemn march from the cradle to the grave. We are all marching day after day, hour after hour, in the great journey of life. We are all in the same broad illimitable thoroughfare, some going in one direction, some in the other. Now, there is a way, and its ways are pleasantness and all its paths are peace. It is to this that I want to direct your attention briefly to-night.

There are many things to make a journey pleasant. We will mention a few of them. The first thing that contributes to the pleasantness of a Christian's journey is that he goes upon a good errand. When a man starts out on a good errand, he starts out with a good heart and a light step, and it makes but little difference to him whether ragged rocks line his pathway, or whether the flowers blossom all along. I imagine that when God summoned an angel to his side and said to him, "Strike dead to-night the first-born of Egypt," or, "I want you to go down and with the blast of your wing drive Cendebeus's army from the earth," the angel lingered about the throne and waited, with a hope that the order might be countermanded. He looked at the Father's face and at the destination before him, and lingered about the throne, loath to go on such an errand, and when at last he leaped over the parapet and poised his wings for flight, he came slowly to earth, wishing that a countermand would come, but on he comes, slowly, to his mission of death and destruction; but I imagine that when God summoned that angel into his presence and said, "I want you to go to earth and cry out in the ears of the people that now it is peace on earth and good will to men," that angel stayed scarcely long enough in the presence to hear the message, before he was winging his way, swift as the morning light, and in the twinkling of an eye he had reached earth and shouted it out to earth's furthermost limits, "Peace on earth and good will to men."

Another thing that helps to make a journey pleasant is to know that you 'll have the strength and ability to make the whole journey. Down in my section, frequently from these Northern States come in the wintry months of December and January the invalid and the consumptive, seeking the balmy climate of Florida, and on the journey some stop at Atlanta, and can go no further, and die; some die on the train; some get as far as Macon; but, brethren, thank God to-night I know not whether I will have strength and ability to get to my home, four hundred miles to the south, but thank God for the assurance that I will have strength and ability to go all the length of the celestial road, and make my way to God. "As thy days, so shall thy strength be;" and in thy weakness shall thy strength be developed in all its beauty and grace. I care not how feeble you are, or how lame you may be, or whether you are unfit for the journey physically; thank God, if you start you have the assurance from the God that made you of strength and ability to travel all the length of the celestial journey.

Again, it helps to make the journey pleasant to know that we shall have all needful accommodations on the way. Sometimes we dread a journey because the accommodations—the hotel fare, and one thing and another—are so bad. Trains miss connection, we miss meals for a whole day; and O, what dreadful times we sometimes have *en route;* but God Almighty has promised to see that we have all needful accommodations on this heavenly road. The heavenly road is one on which you never miss connections, and never pass an eating-house without having full time for dinner; and the fare on this road is love to God and love to one another. It 's a feast of love, day after day. You shall have love for supper, love for dinner, love for breakfast, and you shall have a big bed of love to lie down and sleep in all the way to the good world. Thank God, on this journey you shall want for nothing good but it will be supplied to you. Do n't forget that.

Then it helps to make the journey pleasant to have a good guide along with you. It makes the way through the wilderness less devious. The finger-boards, the sign-boards, all along this route, read, "To the world of bliss;" and every man can read and rejoice that he is in the path that leads to heaven, where, Jesus said, "I will be with you always."

Another thing that will help to make it glorious and blessed, is to have some one along with us to guard and protect us. God says the angels will pitch their tents about us, and watch over us, and that the sun shall not smite us by day, nor the moon by night, and he promises us protection in every hour of danger. I used to think what a grand thing it would be to have Samson for a friend. If I had lived in Samson's time, and had Samson for my friend, to go round with me, I used to think I would n't be afraid of man or devil. But, brother, I have n't got Samson for a friend, but I have Samson's God for my friend, walking with me side by side, ready to protect me in every time of danger. Blessed be God for the guide that goes along with me to show me the way, and for the guard that protects me if any danger should overtake me. Live right up to the truth, love the truth, and God Almighty will take you through safely in this world of cares and troubles.

And then it helps to make a journey pleasant, brethren, to know that the way lies through green pastures and beside the still waters. Thank God for every green pasture along our pathway, and the still waters of grace that gladden our hearts.

Then it helps to make a journey pleasant to know that there are the footprints of good men and women that have gone on before. O, how blessed it is marching through the paths of life to see the footprints of my precious father, and I know he went right. This is his footprint. And to see the footprint of my precious mother, marching to a better world. What a blesssd thing it is to know these are the footsteps of Jesus himself, and that I am putting my tracks in his tracks as I am marching along to glory and to God. It is worth a great deal to a man to know that his pathway is marked by the footprints of all the good that have gone on before, and those that follow shall see their footprints and take courage and press their way along.

Then it helps to make a journey pleasant to have good company all the way. O, me, what a pleasant thing good company is. I have sat in the train sometimes until one or two o'clock in the day, and I was just utterly worn out; and directly some good man would come in and sit down by me, and we would sit and talk three or four hours, and suddenly the engine would whistle and the train would come to a stop, and I would turn to the brakeman and say, "Where are we?" and he would say, "So many miles from So-and-so." "Why," I would say, "the last time I took notice we were one hundred miles from there, now we are going right into the city." Brother, it helps to make a journey pleasant to fall into good company; and then, glory be to God, it helps to make a journey pleasant to sing on the way. Thank God for the old songs of Zion. I love to hear a grand congregation rise up and sing,

> "Praise God, from whom all blessings flow."

I like that good old song—

> "Happy day, happy day,
> When Jesus washed my sins away."

It brings up pleasant memories. And I like that grand old song, that will never die in earth or in heaven,

> "Amazing grace, how sweet the sound,
> That saved a wretch like me;
> I once was lost, but now I 'm found,
> Was blind, but now I see."

And then, brother, the grand old harmonies of the Gospel in melodies and music, breaking out upon the ears of the people—O, how they cheer our hearts. I like good singing, and thank God for the consecrated singers. Brother, the angels of God listened to that organ to-night. It has got religion. That old organ sounded as if it were one of the converts of the meetings. It has heard enough sermons, and I believe there has been enough power in these meetings to convert even an organ. O, brother, I want that old organ to have the chance to sing it out—

> "Praise God, from whom all blessings flow,
> Praise him all creatures here below."

God bless every instrument in the world that makes music and melody in the ears of the people. And I have been mad for fifteen years because the "fiddle," that grandest instrument that man ever made, and which gives the sweetest music I have ever listened to in my life, has been stolen by the devil and taken away from me. Let us get it back and have it reconverted; let us have it and keep it.

Then, it also helps to make a journey pleasant to know that we have been instrumental in bringing others along the way towards the good world. I have led some men and boys off into mischief; but I thank God I don't know of one that associated with me in my wicked days that I have not, through God and other means used upon him, brought to Christ, and they are members of the Church to-day. I don't believe there is a soul on earth or in hell that can say I was instrumental in damning it. Thank God for that. And I hope some day to be able in heaven to rejoice in the fact that I have been instrumental in the salvation of some poor soul.

Lastly, brethren, it helps to make a journey pleasant to know that it is going to end well. I just sit down sometimes, hours at a time, when I am too tired to do any thing else, and think about the journey's ending. O, grand time ahead! I have thought of the glorious world up yonder. And do you want to know what I am going to do for the first thousand years—if there is any such thing as years in heaven? I am going to spend them at the pearly gates, if that is possible, just watching the flow of souls sweeping in one at a time, sainted forever. O, what a grand time that will be! Do n't you reckon I will be glad when wife comes in with the speed of the archangel, and alights at my side and says, "Glory to God, safe here with you forever." And we will stand at the gates and see all our precious loved ones coming in. Glory be to God for the world where our journey is at an end, and we can just look back at the others coming in, saved forever. What a grand sight that will be!

I love to think of the journey all over now, when soul and body shall be reunited. I have often thought about the resurrection. What a sight that will be! What a sight—the earth giving up its dead! But the grandest sight of all will be to go up a little higher and see the arm of Jesus Christ that is lifting the world up and passing it into heaven forever.

May God start you upon this journey and guide you up safely into the kingdom of God.

SAYINGS.

SOME people say they do n't believe in woman's work. There is an old preacher down in Georgia who preaches against woman's work, and that preacher has not had a conversion since the war.

SERMON XIII.

TENDENCIES OF RIGHTEOUSNESS AND OF SIN.

"As righteousness tendeth to life, so he that pursueth evil pursueth it to his own death."—PROV. XI, 19.

WHEN a good man dies, as we say, he goes to heaven, drawn thither by the natural forces of spiritual gravity, by the approval, not only of God and angels, but by the common consent of every intelligent being in the universe. When a bad man dies he goes to hell not only by the approval of God and the angels, but of every other man in the world.

Did you ever attend the funeral of a good man? Have you, when the minister had pointed down to his body and said, "The spirit of this good man has gone home to God," walked away from the Church and heard the comments of both saints and sinners? Each one said alike, "Yes, that good man has gone home to God. He is in heaven now. That preacher told the truth." Then, again, have n't you attended the funeral of a bad man—a doubtful character, even though he was a member of the Church, and have n't you heard the minister say, "This is the body of our brother, but his spirit has gone home to heaven?" And have n't you, in walking away from the Church heard such comments as these?—"That preacher outraged every principle of truth. I never will hear that man preach again.

That dead man's spirit is not in heaven. That preacher knows it, we know it, God knows it, and every body knows it." O, brother, the common conviction of humanity—I mean the common impression made on the common-sense of the world—is this, that when a good man dies he goes to heaven, and when a bad man dies he goes to hell.

"As righteousness tendeth to life, so he that pursueth evil pursueth it to his own death." A good man goes to heaven because he is a good man, and because heaven is the center of gravitation for all that is good; and a bad man goes to hell, not because God binds him hand and foot and sends a convoy of angels to carry him to the lost world, but because he is bad; and that's the end of logic on this question of heaven and hell. May the Lord God show us by his word and truth that righteousness tendeth to life, and only righteousness, and he that pursueth evil pursueth it to his own death. Just as naturally and logically as one goeth to life, so the other goeth to death.

Now we have witnesses to the truth of this Scripture: "The path of the just is as a shining light, shining more and more unto the perfect day;" and of this: "Godliness is profitable unto all things, having the promise of the life that now is, and of the life which is to come."

Just as truly as virtue and sobriety and temperance and goodness and love and mercy and justice are better for you here, and you live in those things, just so certainly will vice and intemperance and wickedness of all description prove the death of your soul. Just as naturally as the good go on more and more in the path unto the perfect day, just so he that commences life in sin tends to more and more wickedness, and every day but brings him one day closer to death and hell. Every good man in this house is one day nearer to heaven than yesterday, and every bad man in the house is twenty-four hours further along on the journey to death and hell. There 's no such thing as standing still, as jerking up and stopping in this great current that is sweeping us along. I am to-day nearer my grave, nearer the judgment, nearer the final sentence than I was this time last night. Theologians differ as to what evil is, or rather as to the origin of evil, and as to the nature of evil; and we might stop and spend an hour on that point; but, brethren, there 's no good in that discussion to us. I have said it again and again on this question of depravity; you may say it 's partial, it 's total, it 's developed, but whatever you may say of it, this fact faces us in our consciousness to-night, that every man of us has enough corruption in us to damn us.

"He that pursueth evil, pursueth it to his own death." Brethren, this race is diseased. As soon as I draw my infant breath, the seeds of sin spring up for evil.

> "The law demands a perfect heart,
> But I 'm defiled in every part."

The tendency of human nature is downward and hellward, and you may trace its source, its origin where you may. Sin is in me, evil is in me. Some months ago I picked up a secular paper, and saw an account of one of our Senators from Georgia, Ben Hill, who had some trouble on the side of his tongue. His friends made light of it, and said it was caused by a fractured tooth. The next I read of Ben Hill, he was under the knife of a surgeon at Philadelphia, and they took out about one-third of his tongue, and then they said he would be well in a few days. But the next I read of his case he was back under the knife of the surgeon at Philadelphia, and they had taken out all the glands in one side of his face and neck, and when the operation was finished, young Ben Hill said to the doctors, "Now, doctors, is there any chance for my father's life?" And the doctors said, "Yes, sir. If we have extracted all the virus of cancer from his system he will certainly get well, but if the least particle has strayed out into some other gland of his system, he will certainly die." The next I saw he was at the famous mineral springs in the West. A few days later I walked down to the depot at my home, and the passenger train came rolling down and trembled under its air-brakes and stopped, and I thought I saw in one of the coaches the outlines of Senator Hill's face. When I walked out toward the car window, the window was up. He pushed his bony hand out of the window and took mine, and I looked in his face and thought, "O, my soul, is this all that is left of Senator Hill, the man that Georgia is most proud of?" Then a few days afterward I picked up the Atlanta *Constitution*, and read where it said, "The grandest procession that ever marched through Georgia marched to the cemetery yesterday and buried the remains of Senator Hill out of sight forever." Brethren, just as certainly as the virus of cancer killed Senator Hill's body, just so certainly will the virus of sin kill your soul at last. It is only a question of time.

Brother, we are diseased unto death, and I praise God to-night that eighteen hundred years ago, before my mother sung the lullabys of the cradle to me, that there was a fountain opened in the house of David for sin and uncleanness. I thank God that eighteen hundred years ago, before I saw the light of this glorious country, Jesus Christ the Son of God, found a balm in Gilead, and he has successfully treated millions of patients, and they have passed into the blood-washed throng that surrounds the throne of God to-night.

The question is not, "Have you quit drinking?" "Have you quit swearing?" "Have you quit gambling?" or "Have you joined the Church; have you been baptized?" But the question of all questions in time and eternity is, "Have you been down under the blood, and have you had this sin in your nature washed away, and do you rejoice to-night that there is cleansing power in the fountain, and that the drop of blood can purify you and make you clean, and rid your nature of all disease that could destroy you in time or eternity?" That's the question! Will you face it to-night? O, my soul, it is not a question of morals, or outward right-living. God knows I put as much stress on that as any man in the world, but I hang my hope, not on the fact that I keep the commandments, not on the fact that

I live by the Sermon on the Mount, but my precious experience dates from the day, from the moment that I went down on my knees under the blood, and realized that the blood of Jesus is the only thing that cleanseth. That is the key-note of the Gospel of the Son of God.

"He that pursueth evil"—the evil tendencies, the innate tendencies of his nature—pursueth it unto death. To be practical now, let us say, first, "He that pursueth evil pursueth it to the death of his conscience." Sin does its work gradually and almost imperceptibly on man. I read, some months ago, how an insidious, subtle, venomous serpent in the East fastened its poisonous fangs in the toe of a native, and how he sent for the doctor, and the doctor walked up and said to him, "There is no remedy for the bite of that serpent." And I read, further along, how the poor victim said: "Doctor, my foot is now dead up to my ankle." A few minutes later the poor fellow said again: "Doctor, my leg is now dead up to my knee." And soon he said again: "Doctor, my leg is dead all the way up to my body." Then again he said: "Doctor, I feel this deadening sensation creeping all over my body; my right arm has now lost its power—it is dead." Then he said: "I can not move my left foot. My left arm is growing powerless." Later he again said: "Doctor, it is gathering near my heart, and now," he said, "I feel the deadness in my heart;" and in a few moments he was in a sitting posture, perfectly dead. The subtle poison had crawled over his body inch after inch.

Now, brother, sin does its work the same way. Its first work is with the conscience. Every deliberate sin of your life is a stab, and a stab of death, at your conscience. I might stop here and say the great trouble in America to-day is that conscience is dead. Church members live in sin because their conscience is dead. Worldlings sin all day and gloat and rejoice in sin, because conscience is dead. The world is running rampant into wickedness to-day because conscience is dead. Brother, listen: To-day, this nineteenth century, is wicked, far more wicked, and far more outrageous in its flagrant sins, than the century behind us, but we feel it less, because conscience has been stabbed and murdered; and to-day a man can walk your streets with head erect that is guilty of sin that would have made him skulk and hide a century ago. What 's the matter with humanity? O, brother, we are wicked beyond description, but we hold our heads up and march erect because conscience is dead. O, conscience! Conscience outraged! Conscience stabbed! Conscience dead! Conscience buried! Conscience with its tombstone erected! O, sir, what is the condition of your conscience to-night?

He that pursueth evil pursueth it to the death of his own powers of resistance. Every sin in a man's life is a sin against his powers of resistance. The greatest power of this nineteenth century is the throttle of the locomotive engine. It represents the power to start, the power to move, the rate of speed of the engine! Next to that grand invention, the throttle, comes the air-brake—the power to stop. I was sitting, some months ago, with a locomotive engineer in his cab. The engine was sweeping along at the rate of fifty miles an hour around curves, and pushing its way on rapidly to its destination. I threw my eyes ahead, and said to the engineer: "See those cattle!" In an instant his hand flew to the air-brakes, and he turned them on, and pulled open the whistle valve, and with the noise of the whistle the cattle scampered from the track, and I said to myself: "If we had no brakes we might have run into those cattle, and perhaps been ditched and killed on the spot." Thank God for air-brakes on the trains running across this country at such speed!

And then, he that pursueth evil pursueth it to the death of his reason. Now, man sins against God, and sins against himself, and sins against his reason, till—I dare assert it—a man can sin against his reason so that his mind, at last, will reach a point where he can not grasp a Scriptural truth to save the world. In my own State there is a prominent lawyer; whenever I get to his town I see him in the congregation, and then I meet him some time the next day on the street. He says: "I go to hear you preach; I believe you are honest in what you assert. But, Jones, the Gospel itself is all nonsense and foolishness to me; there is nothing in it." And I have looked at the poor fellow many a time and said: "That poor man has sinned until he has been given over to a delusion that he may believe a lie and be damned." O, sir, what a fearful thought: to tamper with a man's mind and abuse it to where the truth is a lie and a lie the truth! O, God save us from this mental prostitution! Save us from this mental degradation that paralyzes the mind and ruins the soul! The Lord help us to stop at this point to-night!

Next we say, he that pursueth evil pursueth it to the death of his sensibilities. I believe it is the natural tendency of sin to dry up the fountains of a man's nature to where he has no sensibility at all; he can not feel. Why, I have had men to boast to me, "I have no religious feeling!" and, whenever I hear a man say, "I can not feel," I look at him and think, "I would as soon shake hands with a dead man as to shake hands with you." You are dead to all that is noble and true; dead to all that is loving and gentle, and all good report. You are as virtually dead as you will ever be.

Thank God for the preservation of sensibility! I have seen the time when I would n't go to church in twelve months; I would stay out of church and let my good wife go by herself. God forgive me for the way I treated my wife. I have begged her pardon a thousand times, and I will never be satisfied until I have begged her pardon in the presence of the angels of God. I want to tell every man in this house, every wicked man, you owe your wife a debt you will never pay her, until you pay it at the cross of Jesus Christ. You mark that expression. I say, sometimes I would not go to church in twelve months; but I can tell this and say the truth, I never went to church in my life and heard an honest sermon that it did not stir me from head to foot. I would n't have let my wife know how much I felt. God knows I have gone off by myself and buried my head in my hands and said: "O, how I suffer! how I suffer!" Brother, have you reached the point where truth makes no impression upon you? And then, lastly, he that pursueth evil pursueth it until the death of his soul.

Now, I see conscience is dead, and I see powers of resistance are gone, and I see that reason has been dethroned; I see now that sensibilities have been destroyed. There is but one thing left for sin to do. O, sir, what is that? The death of the soul! Somebody has said eternal death is death prolonged forever. I know what natural physical death is. I have seen that. But couple that on to this, the word eternal, death eternal. These are the most fearful words in human language. Death eternal! Eternal death! Each word rendered ten thousand times more awful by its association with the other! I have walked up to the bedside of my friend, and I have looked at him as death was doing its work, and I have said: "O, death, how hard thou art upon my friend." I have stood and looked at the glare of his eye, at the heave of his bosom and the jerk of his muscles, and the twitch of his nerve, and then I have walked off and said: "O, death, how terrible thou art!" And then I have walked back and put my eyes on the scene, and there was the same heave of the bosom, the same glare of the eye, the same jerk of the muscles, the same twitch of the nerves, and I have walked off and said: "O, death, what is eternal death? If that is death, then what is eternal death?" And then I said: "O, God, is eternal death the everlasting glare of the eye? Is it the everlasting heave of the bosom? Is it the everlasting jerk of the muscles? Is it the everlasting twitch of the nerves? Is this to die forever?" And yet I can never die. O, sir, may God impress upon every man to-night this tremendous thought:

> "Nothing is worth a thought beneath
> But how I may escape the death
> That never, never dies;
> How make my own election sure,
> And when I fail on earth secure
> A mansion in the skies."

Thank God, whosoever liveth and believeth on the Son of God shall never die! Thank God for the Gospel!

Here is death to my friend; here I am a sinner dying; here I am bound in physical infirmity and death; I can not move hand or foot, and there the venomous reptile of eternal death is approaching. It comes nearer and nearer. I shrink from its presence, but I can not move. It comes up closer, and coils around my limbs and my body, and in the cold embraces of this reptile I am fastened; and then it draws back its head and opens its mouth and exposes the fangs and poison of eternal death. I look in this mouth a moment with terror, and then it makes the fatal plunge of the fangs and injects the poison of eternal death in my veins, and I die forever and forever.

O, to the Christian what is death? I see that reptile approaching! Here I am a Christian, and can not get out of its way, but just before it reaches me a kind friend steps down and takes the reptile back of its head, pries its mouth open, extracts the fang, takes out the poison, turns him loose right before my eyes. He coils around my body and around my limbs. It makes me shudder to be in the embraces of this cold serpent—and then when the snake brings back its head for the final bite and opens its mouth, I look it in the face and say, "O, Death! where is thy sting? O, grave! where is thy victory?" and leap out of the coils of the serpent into the arms of God to live forever. God give us the Christian's hope of life, and the Christian's grace of death, and in God to live on forever. O, brother, friend, to-night let me beg you, shun that death that never, never dies.

SAYINGS.

THE woman that never helped the Lord never got much help from the Lord. The best way to help yourself is to help somebody else.

A WOMAN is naturally a very sharp trader, and very few women have any conscience when it comes to a trade. They will sell an old pair of trousers for more than their husband gave for them when new, and then brag about it.

SERMON XIV.

THE CHRISTIAN'S COMMISSION.

"Delivering thee from the people and from the Gentiles, unto whom I now send thee, to open their eyes, and to turn them from darkness to light, and from the power of Satan unto God, that they may receive forgiveness of sins, and inheritance among them which are sanctified by faith that is in me."—ACTS XXVI, 17, 18.

THIS is what we might call St. Paul's credentials; this is his parchment; this is his instruction from head-quarters; this is what God said to him when he wanted him to go forth as a preacher.

You remember in this chapter, St. Paul is standing in the presence of Agrippa, and perhaps the finest piece of oratory extant in the whole universe to-day is his defense before that monarch; and now he gives us these words as those which he heard when he had fallen down before the light, and the conversation had been carried on between him and his Christ. "And I said, Who art thou, Lord? And he said, I am Jesus, whom thou persecutest. But arise, and stand upon thy feet, for I have appeared unto thee for this purpose to make thee a minister and a witness, both of these things thou hast seen, and of those things in the which I will appear unto thee."

"Arise—stand upon your feet," or in plain English, take a stand. There's a good deal in that. Take a stand! What's the matter all over this country? No man is fit to be a Christian, no man will ever succeed as a Christian; no man is fit to be a preacher, no man will ever succeed as a preacher, until he takes a stand.

I tell you, my brethren, to-day, the Church of God is at fault right there. The ministry of Christ, with some glorious exceptions, always, is at fault right there. They have n't taken a stand. Well, there is a reason why we have n't done all we ought to have done, but is there any reason why we have n't taken a stand?

I know one pastor in Chattanooga, Tenn., who took a stand, and he took it on high ground, and he commenced shelling the words over the people, and the newspapers commenced shelling back, and his cowardly, pusillanimous members began to take to the woods, and it was n't three weeks until perhaps one-half of that man's Church had taken to the woods and the other half put him on the shelf and told him he had better go slow. Well, the preacher, poor fellow, said: "Brethren, have I been preaching a lie?" They said "No." "Have I been preaching any thing but the truth?" "No," they said. "Well," said he, "you want me to go slow on the truth?" "Yes, you'll have to do it. If you do n't things will be ruined."

Ruined! Ah, my brother, if I had but one prayer to offer up that prayer would be, God help every preacher, God help every professed Christian to take a stand, take a stand—one way or the other, either for or against.

There was a newspaper man after me to-day on the subject of amusements. Said he: "Mr. Jones, please give us the amusements that Christian people can go into. You've named a great many that they can not." "I won't do it," I said. "I can point out to a man the amusements that are not sinful, but just as soon as I point them out every body will run them into a common meeting ground for the world, the flesh, and the devil, and it would n't be six months before they would be the dirtiest things in the country, and I do n't want to do that."

Rise, stand on your feet, take a stand, that's it. O, how I wish we could be brought to our feet, and brought to take a stand on every moral question. Brother, if I can get you to take a stand for God and right, for piety and spirituality, you will never go into the Stock Exchange and Produce Exchange any more. You have taken a stand, and that means, "I have done with it." You know that. You can find out why you do n't take a stand if you look around you. Well, brother, let's take a stand and hold our ground if we starve to death for it; if we do, it will only be a nigh cut to heaven. I told them down in my State, when they threatened to send me up between the flashes of dynamite into the other world; "Well," said I, "the roaring of the thing won't die out before I'll be in heaven. You ain't doing me any harm; you'll just start me by a nigh cut to glory." If you are a man take a stand and let the world do its worst on you. If they starve you to death you'll just get to heaven a few minutes ahead of time.

Take a stand. Rise, stand on your feet. If you

are a Christian, be a Christian; if you are a Methodist, be a Methodist; if you are a man, be a man—all over, from head to foot. Do n't be a little dwindling fool. Nowhere and under no circumstances be any thing else but what you are. I had rather be a first-class sinner than a tenth-rate Methodist, and when you get a Methodist down to about a tenth-rate Methodist you are getting him down pretty low, for a first-class one is n't up very high. Rise—stand upon your feet. O, brother, if we would just come out on the Lord's side. I know Paul did. He arose, he stood on his feet and fought for the right, and when the battle had ended he said, "I have fought a good fight, I have finished my course, I have kept the faith."

Ah me; if we could get people to take sides. Sinners! Men of the world! God says to you, "Choose ye whom ye will serve." If you want to be on God's side come over here. You have got just as much right as any body, just as much right as I have; the only difference is that you love sin and fight for it, and I love holiness and fight for that. We are men alike, with the same characteristics. Brother, come over on the Lord's side, lay down that old musket and take up the flag of the cross and fight with the weapons God gives you. That 's it. Take a stand. Ah me; if I could get every man who professes to be converted to take a stand—but they are doubtful about it, hesitating, uncertain. I say to one: "Brother, are you going to pray in your family?" "I do n't know. I have n't decided yet. I 'll see about it." Go to another and ask him: "Brother, are you going to the theater?" "I do n't know. I dunno whether I will or not; sometimes I think I will and then again I think I won't." "Are you going to keep on playing cards?" "I dunno; I came mighty near burning up my cards the other day, but I did n't do it, though." "Going to have any wine suppers?" "Sometimes I think I will and then again sometimes I think I won't."

And now, what can God do with that sort of a tribe? And that 's the truth about it. You know, brethren of the ministry, as well as you know your names, you can 't bank on a man like that. You do n't know whether he will be playing cards or at prayer-meeting next Wednesday night, except you know pretty well that he 'll be playing cards. "Rise, stand upon thy feet." Take a stand one way or the other. If it 's right to play cards, stand up to it, and tell your preacher it 's right to do it, and defy earth and hell. If it 's right to go to the theater, just stand by it like a man, and tell your preacher, "If you do n't like theater-going Christians, turn me out." Be a man. Then take a stand on one side or the other. I like a man that will do that.

"Rise, stand on your feet." When a man says, "I 'll take my stand," ask him, "Are you going to pray in your family?" "I 'm going to pray in my family every night and morning." "How are you on prayer-meetings?" "I am going to prayer-meetings every chance I get, and if I stay away I'll send the preacher a doctor's certificate that I am sick in bed and can 't go." "Well, how are you about visiting the sick?" "I refer you to the five blocks around my house. There is n't a family with sickness in it that I do n't look after if I hear there is any sickness there." "How are you about giving for missions?" "I refer you to the trustee. I can show you his receipt for foreign missions every year." Ah, me, brother, that fellow means business; there is no doubt about that. Then take a stand.

How much are you going to be a man this year? "I do—do—n't know. I do n't know what I 'll do." Brethren, what can we do with your sort anyhow? You are like a fellow's piece of timber that I heard of, that was so tough and crooked that when he wanted to plane it and smooth it, he tried it both ways, but could not plane it from either end. He would dig in both ways.

"Arise. Take a stand!" Brethren, if we be Christians, let us be so out and out. If we be sinners, let us be sinners out and out. O, in the name of all that is true and good, and all that is worthy, if we are not going to take a stand for the right, let us go out of the Church; but if we are willing to take a stand, let us go into the Church and do its work and stay there till we die. Now, if these old sinners want to play cards, and go to the theater, and run after the devil, I am perfectly willing that they should do so, if that is their line. I never said a word about an old goat going into the devil's pastures, for that is just where they belong. But if I am a Christian, let me stand up and fight the devil every time he sticks up his head. That is business. O, I wish that we had that sort of religion, every one of us. I wish we would all fight it out on that line.

Well, I will tell you another thing. When you take a start so that you have got to fight, you can not back. You have got to fight. I will tell you, you will reach that point when you see that blessed moment when men shall revile you for His name. Christ tells you of it when he says: "Blessed are ye, when men shall revile you, and persecute you, and shall say all manner of evil against you falsely for my sake." You will find out what that means. They will call you vulgar, and they will call you a blackguard and a mountebank. I am much obliged to them for it. Pile those names on me and I will bear them to the judgment and throw them down at the feet of Jesus, and tell God what they did to me when I tried to get them to live right. Just look! Take a stand. O, I wish I could get every body here to take a stand on one side or the other. If we think it is right to be a Christian let us be one soul and body, and every day in the week and every minute in the day, and every breath we take let each of us be one sure enough.

There is many a fellow in this country riding his little religion around, as he calls it. This religion reminds me of the time when I used to get on a stick, astride of it, you know, and I would lope it and pace it and trot it. In fact, it could go all the paces; I called it a horse, and I used to ride it up to the bucket and water it, and take it to the trough and feed it, though it was only a little stick horse. And if any body had told me that it was n't a horse, I would have been mad enough to fight. And I rode and drove and watered and fed him, and all that. And it was only a stick. But when I got on a sure-enough horse, and felt his great muscles under me, I looked back upon my little stick-horse with the greatest disgust. And, I tell you, there is many a Christian in the country to-day riding a stick. I say, brother, they do n't like to be told that they have stick religion. It makes them mad as can be to tell them that. They do n't like it. They say it is a genuine horse. O, take it to Christ every Sunday morning, and water it and have it baptized, and make it take communion. Do n't you see this is religion. O, but brother, if you ever get to be mouuted on the grand principles of the Gospel of Christ, as St. Paul was, and feel every fiber of your being stirred as it is driven by the impulse of this divine life, you will look back on such a life as you are living now with the greatest disgust in the world.

Now, brethren, here is where Paul's life started. The first was he took the stand; and then Jesus said: "Now, Paul, go forth and preach to the people, and open their eyes. I want you to say to every people in this world, 'Open your eyes.'" A man, or a woman, or a Church, or a city, or a country will never be what each ought to be until you show them what they are. Hence, open their eyes that they see themselves and see what they are.

Do you know what that quarrel was which God

had with his ancient Church. They would not consider. Consider? Do you know what the etymological definition of the term "consider" is? I am not much on syntax, they say. I have been doing a good deal with sin-tax, and have been taxing sin since I have been in the city. But I am some on etymology. Consider—look at a thing until you see it. Now, brethren, if you will make people look at themselves in this way, you have taken the first step toward their reformation. A man can never reform his life until he sees what his life really is. He can never reform until he can say to himself, "I see wherein I am slack; where I have done this, and where I have neglected doing that." Brother, will you open your eyes to know yourself as you are; to know how you look in the sight of God?

Paul's first duty was to open the eyes of the people, and, when he had opened their eyes, to lead them from darkness to light. This term darkness means simply sin. Darkness and sin mean about the same thing. Light and righteousness mean about the same thing. Lead them from sin into righteousness, Paul was told. Now, brother, show me where I stand. Look at the Prodigal son! He came to himself. He was without food. He was hungry and naked and far away from home, and disreputable among men and disgraced before God; and he then got to thinking and thinking about himself, and what he was, and he saw. He came to himself. And when he saw himself he thought about home. And then he said: "What am I here for?" And then he said, "I will arise and go to my father."

Open their eyes and show them what they are, and then let them come out from that city of sin. Let them come from sin unto righteousness. Brothers, it is the duty of every preacher to go after you and tell you what you are; to show you what you are; but that is dangerous business. Many a preacher has got a cursing for doing just such work as that. That is a fact. And I suspect many a preacher has got a whipping for it; and I know that the one I am talking about now got his head cut off just for nothing in the world but showing people what they were, and for telling them how they lived. There ain't any preachers' heads cut off in these days, though; and the saddest commentary on the world to-day is that none of them have got their heads cut off. I do n't want mine cut off; but—but I wish I could see a martyr!

Show them what they are, and, when you have done that, take them by the hand and lead them out into a better state of life. Open their eyes; show them their sins and their sinful life; and lead them from that vile and wicked life. What does that mean? If you open your eyes you see your life, and you know what is right and what is wrong in it. Then comes the next thing, the next question: Is there any thing better? If there is, show me it, and tell me how to get it. Lead me into a better state of things. Lead me from the power of Satan into the power of God. That is the plain thing about it. Now, brother, where you are now you are in the power of Satan, in the power of sin; in the dominion of the devil. You have made a thousand efforts to reform. You make good resolutions. You have said a thousand times that you would be a better man; but a man can never be a good man while he is under the dominion of the devil. First come out of that dominion, and then say to yourself: "By the grace of God I am out from under his feet, and I will put myself under the power of the good Spirit of God." You know what the Bible says: Come "to the help of the Lord against the mighty." Does it mean that God wants you to help him in the reformation of human sin? No; it means, Come up where I am, and I will protect you. There was no power to protect the Union man from the bullets of the rebels if he stayed in the ranks of the rebels. I will tell you that, if a young man was just standing with both armies in front of him, his own friends will be just as likely to kill him as his enemies. If God wants to protect you, and turns the guns loose upon your enemies, and you are among them, you may be the first one that will fall. And now he wants you to take a stand on his side, so that the evil can not touch you, and he will not mistake you for one of his enemies. He says: "I will protect you then, and look after you, and save you; but there is no power to save you while you are in the ranks of sin. Come over to this side." Come from under the power of Satan, and be under the power of God, that you may have remission of your sins.

Now, here is the point: When I quit sin I quit

all that is bad, all that is wrong. I come over to the Lord's side, and it is his business to save you. God will condone your sins if you will come over to his side. By doing so you get remission of your sins. Lay down any thing that is bad and take a stand for the right, and if the Lord does n't save you it is not your fault. And I will tell you, if a man will quit all his meanness, and take the side with the Lord's people, and that man is unregenerated and not pardoned—I will say this to you, and that is, the Lord will have to make another world for him. He can not take him into heaven if he is not regenerated, and he will have to make another world and stop the machinery of the universe in order to do so, for he can not take any body into heaven who has not been born again. But you will never find such a case as this.

Lead them from the power of Satan to the power of God, that they may have a remission of sins and an inheritance. If I go from Satan to the side of God I am saved, and have an inheritance here and hereafter among the people of God. I am glad that the Church is mine, and that I am the Church's. I am glad for the home for Christian people in this world.

And I want to say another thing: You may live right and go to heaven outside of the Church, but it is all I can expect to do to get up there from inside the Church. I thank God for this inheritance among the people of God. And I trust that this night every one of you will say: "I am done with my sins. My eyes are opened. I am done with my sins. I come out from the devil's side to the right side, to the Lord's side. And now, what I want is a remission of sins and an inheritance among the people who love the Lord, and then an inheritance in heaven." That is what we want.

And, brethren, if we will come from the other side and take a stand, and get our friends to see these things, then we can lead them from the power of the devil into the power of God, and then to a remission of their sins, and then take them to their inheritance, and then to everlasting life in the world to come. Can not we do that? Can you make any thing plainer than that? Is not that your duty? Down with your meanness first, and take a stand for the right, and then pray God for a remission of your sins, and for an inheritance in heaven.

SAYINGS.

WHEN a poor sinner falls on his knees and says, "God, be merciful to me, a sinner," there is always some angel near by to gather up the prayer and carry the news, "Behold, he prayeth!"

A MAN is never free until love abounds in his heart toward God and man. The freest man is the man who loves God most and loves his neighbor as himself. There is no law in heaven or earth that fetters or proscribes a character like that.

SERMON XV.

GOD'S DOCTRINE, AND HOW TO KNOW IT.

"If any man will do His will, he shall know of the doctrine, whether it be of God, or whether I speak of myself."—JOHN VII, 17.

AT the time Jesus uttered these words, he was surrounded by the sharp, cunning Pharisees; by the shrewd, calculating Sadducees, and the lawyers of the day. They were probing, and dissecting, and looking, and wondering, and questioning, and Jesus looked at them, and threw the gauntlet down on the' ground at their feet, right in their faces.

It is wonderful, but strangely true, that all the scholars in this world's history have met with opposers. They have met with scoffers, and perhaps a large majority of them with contempt and scorn. You know that when Galileo discovered that this world rotated on its axis, the stupid monks arraigned him immediately, and they tried him as a heretic and a humbug. And they convicted him, and made him retract. But the wise old man, as he walked out, whispered to himself, "And still the world moves." When Harvey discovered that the blood circulated from the heart to the extremities and back again, the medical world arraigned him as propounding a false theory, and argued against it. When Watt discovered that steam, a bland vapor, had

MUSIC HALL, CINCINNATI, O.,

WHERE THE GREAT REVIVAL MEETINGS WERE HELD.

power almost omnipotent, the scientists of his day arraigned him, and demanded the proofs. When Morse discovered that you might chain electricity to a wire, and that one man could sit a thousand miles from another, and hold a conversation with him, the world arraigned him, and doubted his discovery. No wonder, then, that when Jesus Christ discovered "a balm in Gilead," a remedy for sin, this world arraigned as an impostor, and tried and convicted him. I do n't see how the discovery that the world rotates on its axis breaks into a fellow's program much. I do n't see how the fact that steam, a bland vapor, is omnipotent, could interfere with a man's system of living. The fact that the circulation of the blood is a great discovery does not make a fellow quit lying, or stealing, or any thing of that sort. And when it is a demonstrated fact that a man can sit down to-night, anywhere in America, and hold a friendly conversation with a man in Liverpool, that does not make him pray or quit his meanness.

It is no wonder that men oppose the science of Christ crucified. All other sciences have had their opposers. No man to-day, excepting the famous preacher of Richmond, doubts the fact that the world turns on its axis. I believe he still sticks to it, that "the sun do move." No one to-day doubts that steam is an almost omnipotent power. I have only to look on those iron horses as they move over the country, with their giant power, in order to tell the world that steam is power. The moment that a physician walks into my room, and tells by the accelerated movement of my pulse my condition, I can not doubt as to the circulation of the blood. No one can doubt the fact that we may sit in this city and talk with a friend in London to-night. Brother, these grand discoverers met with opposers, and yet the world does honor the first four to-day, but still the majority of the world to-day despise the last one—the blessed Christ—the greatest discoverer of the ages. Do you know why that is? The greatest discovery ever declared to man is the fact that God can be just, and the justifier of the ungodly. The greatest fact in the universe made known to men is, that a poor man may have his sins forgiven, and may make his peace with God, and die in faith, and go home to heaven. And yet while the opposition, which these other great discoverers met, has died out, still to-day, after the blood-washed throngs of earth have been marching home to God for eighteen hundred years; after our precious mothers and our pious fathers have marched into heaven under this gracious banner, and after all that his blessed scheme of redemption has done for our race, there are thousands and millions of men who despise Jesus Christ and reject him as a grand discoverer, with all the power of their nature.

O, strange beings that we are! Wonderfully strange! And when you go breaking into a fellow's program, he gets his heart full of doubts immediately. Did you ever notice that? There can be but one objection to the Lord Jesus Christ among men, and that is, when they bring their life up and place it beside his life, there is an overwhelming sense of guilt and shame.

Brethren, it is a good deal owing to circumstances as to what you are. When I hear you sit in judgment on the spotless character of Christ, I do n't want to hear a word from your lips. I want to hear what your life is, and then I will know what your comment on the character of Jesus Christ will be. If your life is confirmed to Jesus Christ, then is the Christ the Son of the living God to you. But if your life is disreputable and dishonest, you see in him nothing but the son of a harlot and an impostor. Is not that strange?

A man's moral condition determines for him what the Gospel and Christ and the truth are to him. O, blessed Christ! When I look over this world toward thee, all is mystery, all is confusion, all is desolation! O, brethren, there is but one place in this universe, from which I can look, and see as God sees, and that is when I reach right up to the point where Christ is, and look out upon this world as Christ looks upon it; and look at truth as Christ looks at it; and look at God as Christ does. Look from a Christ-like point, and you will see a thousand things you never saw before.

"If any man will do his will, he shall know of the doctrine, whether it be of God, or whether it be of myself." I want to say, in the first place, that if any man has a peculiarity in his case, I want to know what it is. Now, you make out as if you had something peculiar to yourself; you say that there is something special about you; that you see very well how others should do such things, but not yourself. Brother, I look at it simply as the devil's work to persuade a man to follow him by saying, "Now, if your case were just like that of any body else, it would be all right to do that; but yours is a peculiar case." That is what you say to yourself. Poor fellow! I wonder if you think the Lord never made any one else like you. I do n't know, but I think that if he did n't the world has n't lost much. But at the same time, brother, that is just what is the matter with the world. There are so many like you. There are plenty of peculiar cases. I have seen mental, and social, and phenomenal peculiarities. Brother, God does n't care any thing about your peculiarities, he wants you!

A genuine, thoroughly trained musician can play on any thing in the universe, from a jew's-harp up to the grandest instrument. Well, brother, the Lord Jesus Christ can take a man up and down every grade of his spiritual nature in the twinkling of an eye, and make music that would charm an angel's ear. Your trouble is, that you are trying to fix up, and tune up your own instrument. But you have no tuning fork; you do n't know the lick it is done with. That is the trouble with you. I do n't care how old you are, or how young you are; I do n't care how learned you are, or how ignorant you are; I do n't care what your difficulties are, or what your peculiarities are; if any man will do the will of God, he shall know of the doctrine. There is no hobby, now, in that. It is simply, "Have you faith?"

Now, I want to say that Christianity is something that may be tested like any thing else. Now, here is a man who comes up to me and says, "Brother Jones, the science of mathematics is a grand science, and it is true." "Well," I say, "demonstrate the truth of mathematics." He says, "Well, twice two are four." "But I don't want any silly talk like that; demonstrate it to me." "Well," says he, "five times six are thirty." "Go along with your school-boy talk; demonstrate to me that the great science of mathematics is true." He says to me, "We will demonstrate the thing; I will demonstrate every problem; I will work it out by that rule that two and two make four. The two governments of France and Switzerland proposed to tunnel the Alps, and desired to begin the tunnel on both sides of that immense mountain range at the same time. So the engineers took their instruments to the mountains, and located the route, and the miners and sappers toiled for days and weeks, and thousands and hundred of thousands of dollars were spent in the work. And the two gangs labored and wrought towards each other, while all the world stood gazing on. Finally, one day while France's side were sitting down to dinner, Switzerland's side got up and went to work, and the thuds of the pick were heard through the thin partition, and then France's side jumped up and gathered their tools and commenced digging away. In five minutes' time the middle wall of partition fell out, and their lines met each other to the hundreth part of an inch. There is an everlasting demonstration of the truth of mathematics."

Now, I say Christianity may be tested just as the science of mathematics is tested. "Well," you say, "give me a demonstration." Thirteen years ago I looked to God and prayed, and he saved me, and I have been happy ever since. "Ah, me," you say, "do n't talk that sickly sentimentalism to me. I have heard that all my life. There is n't any proof in that." Well, my mother told me that at the age of thirteen, Jesus saved her, and she lived happy in his love, and died happy and went home to heaven. "O, well, I do n't want any old woman's story about the thing. If you can demonstrate the truth of the religion of Christ crucified, I wish you would do it."

Well, look here. Take the case of the man that was born blind. As he walked up, groping in darkness, he said, "Lord Jesus, that I may receive my sight," and Jesus stepped down and spat on the ground, and made clay of the spittle and rubbed it on his eyes and said, "Go wash in yonder pool." I suppose if some of you scientific gentlemen had been there you would have told that poor blind fellow, "Look here, science has demonstrated that there are curative powers in dry dirt, but He has gone and spit on the dirt and wet it, and taken all the curative powers out of it, and in addition to that he tells you to go and wash in that pool, where you have bathed a hundred times. Just look, now, he is playing his pranks on you. But the poor blind fellow had more sense than that. He said, "Whether the clay has curative powers in it before or after it is wet I don't know; and about that pool, I have washed in it many a time; but this man says if I will go now and wash this dirt off my eyes in that pool, I will have my eye-sight. That is what I am after, and I am going to do his will; I am going to put him to the test." And I see the poor blind fellow groping off in darkness, until he reaches the edge of the pool, and he steps down and lifts the water to his eyes, and washes off the clay and spittle, and then he looks up and sees rocks and rivers and mountains that his eyes had never looked on before. That crowd got around him and said, "Well, now look here, give God the glory. This man has a devil." "Well," said he, "whether he has a devil or not, I know not, but one thing I know, that whereas I was blind, now I see." There is demonstration.

Well, let us take another instance—the ten cases of leprosy. Here is the most fearful disease man ever had. The lepers came up and said, "Master, look. We are diseased from head to foot with this fearful disease, leprosy, for which there is no cure"—and no cure to this day has ever been discovered. "Now, Master, that we may be made whole." Jesus just looked at the lepers and said, "Go show yourselves to the priest." Now the scientific gentleman I suppose, if he had been present, would have said, "Listen to that. Doesn't he know the priests won't let those fellows come about them, as they have banished them from the congregation of the people? And they have to spend their lives in old waste places, and every time any body approaches them they must raise up their hands and cry, 'Unclean!' O, how wicked in him to tell those men to go to the priests when the priests won't let them approach." But those poor lepers said, "Master, we will do thy will; we will do what thou sayest." And I see just ten men start off, and they walk but a short distance until one looks at another and says, "The scales are all gone and I am sound from head to foot;" and one runs back and praises God for the wonderful cure of the whole. Brother, do you believe that?

I have often wondered what a life Christ must have had among men. I picture to myself, brethren, as the news went abroad, how he gave sight to the blind, and how he healed the sick, and how he raised the dead, that they pressed him on all sides; and when all along his pathway he scattered blessings in the hearts of men, I wonder that any man to-day by his life and character, should fight such a being as the Lord Jesus Christ.

Demonstrate this truth. Now, sir, I feel just this way about it. I was preaching down in one of the towns in our State. An old colonel—a clever old man—sat in the congregation. He was wicked and godless. He was an old citizen of my town. I was a boy there, grew up there. This old citizen had been away for several years. I went down to his town in Georgia, and stood up and preached to the people, "Repent and come to God." Well, hen I walked out of church that day this old gray-headed man was standing at the gate of the yard in front of the church, and he took my hand, and the big tears ran down his eyes. Said he, "Are you the same wicked, daring, godless, drunken boy that used to curse Cartersville so?" Said I, "I am the very one." "Well," said he, "no matter what my doubts have been about the power of God to save a sinner, I yield them now, and pray God Almighty to save me just as he saved you." Demonstration? I don't reckon there is a man or woman or child in Cartersville that doubts there is power in Christianity to save a sinner, not one.

Now, brother, "if any man will do the will of God, he shall know of the doctrine"—know for himself. And what does God want us all to do? "Cease to do evil, learn to do well." "Let the wicked forsake his way, and the unrighteous man his thoughts, and let him return unto the Lord." It is the will of God that we repent. It is the will of God that we accept salvation on his terms. Doctrine is a good thing and fear is a good thing; but one fact stops a man; he can't get over it, nor under it, nor around it, nor through it. There it is, and he must do something with it. Now, I will tell you—one man became the grandest Christian in our State, and his plan just opens the way for every man. God is no respecter of persons. Now, listen to this. If you really want to be religious, I will tell you how. This man lived in middle Georgia. I was afterward the pastor of his wife, and pastor of the Church in which he lived and died. For forty odd years he labored in the Church of God.

I will tell you how he started. Shortly after he was married, perhaps a year or two—I do n't know exactly—the Church that he and his wife attended was in the country; they lived in the country. He was a farmer. On a certain Sunday his wife did n't go to Church with him. The preacher came around once a month, and it was the regular preaching service there on that Sabbath. In his sermon the preacher made this remark: "If a man will do before he gets religion just as he thinks he would do after he gets it, he will get it." Now, do you get that point? Well, this fellow was a sensible man, and he took it in in all of its bearings. So that day, when the preacher was through preaching, he opened the door of the church. This man walked right up and gave his hand to the preacher, and joined the Church. He got home, and his wife said, "What sort of meeting did you have?" "Well," said he, "we had a good meeting, I think. Mr. So-and-so preached a good sermon, and I joined the Church." "You joined the Church?" "Yes." "Have you got religion?" "No." "Well, what in the world did you join the Church for without religion?" "Well, the preacher said if I would do before I got religion as I thought I would do after I got it, I would get it; and I know I would join if I had it, and I am going to do before I get it just what I think I would do after I get it." "Well, well, well," she said, "that beats any thing I ever heard." That night, just before time to retire, he said, "Wife, get the Bible, please, and a candle." "What are you going to do?" "I am going to read a chapter in the Word of God, and hold family prayers." "Hold family prayers and got no religion?" "Yes." "Why, what are you going to do that for?" "Well, the preacher said if I would do before I got religion as I thought I would do afterward, I would get it; and I know I would pray in my family if I had religion." He read his chapter and got down and led in family prayer. The next morning, when the breakfast bell rang, he said, "Hold on to that breakfast, wife! I am going to read another chapter and pray here." "Are you going to pray on here every day, and have n't got religion?" "Yes," he said. "Well, and what are you going to do that for?" "Well," he said, "the preacher said if I would do before I got it as I would do after I got it, I would get it; and I know I would pray every night and morning the Lord sent, if I had it." And Wednesday night they went out to the week's prayer-meeting, and the leader of the meeting called on him to pray, and he got down and prayed the very best he could, and his wife, as soon as they came out of the church, caught his arm, and she said, "What in the world do you pray in public, and have no religion, for?" "Well," he said, "wife, the preacher said if I would do before I got it just as I thought I would do afterward, I would get it; and I know I would pray in public if I had religion." And he just plowed his furrow along that way for about two weeks, and got the biggest case of religion that any man ever heard of. Now, that is the whole thing in a nut-shell. The means of grace will take a man to God.

"If any man will do the will of God, he shall know of the doctrine." Do as God wants you to do, and he will bless you as certain as you are a man. Yes, but you say, "Mr. Jones, that won't do, because I joined the Church once, and I finally told them to take my name off. I would n't be a hypocrite, and there is n't any thing in joining the Church." No, there is n't; but there is a heap in what sort of fellow joins, I tell you that.

Yes, but you say: "Now, I like what you say, but, Mr. Jones, I ain't fit." I declare I never want to go into the family that ain't fit to join the Church; ain't fit to do any thing. They are the hardest cases that I ever struck—these "ain't-fit" fellows. I will tell you, you may take the most ignorant man in this city, colored or white, to-morrow, and you may meet him on the street—say he is a colored man—and say to him: "Tom, are you a member of the Church?" "No, sir." "Why?" "Because I ain't fitten." That is just what he will say. Then you meet the most intelligent lawyer on the next block, and say, "Colonel, are you a member of the Church?" "No, sir." "Why?" "Well, to tell you the truth, I ain't fit." And he talks just like that poor ignorant fellow that does n't know a letter in the book. The fact of the business is, that is the only thing that is the matter with them. I will tell you just where all such as that stand to-day. Here is a fellow out here that has n't had a bite to eat in a week; he is starved nearly to death, and he says: "I never was so hungry in my life." "Well, here is a table loaded with food.

Come up and eat." He says, "Ugh, ugh!" I say, "Why?" He says, "My hands ain't fitten." "Well," I reply, "there is soap and water and a towel. Wash your hands." "Ugh, ugh! I ain't fitten to wash." So he just stands there and starves to death. Now, is n't that so? What are you going to do with him? There you are, friend. Give yourself to God and his Church. "Ugh, ugh!" "Why?" "I ain't fitten." Well, come up here and seek to be saved and seek to be made fit. "Ugh, ugh! I ain't fitten to get fitten." And there he sits and there he dies. Now, what are you going to do with a case like that? He says he is n't fitten, and when you want him to get fitten he says he is n't fitten to get fitten. And what to do with a case like that is the profoundest mystery of the world to me.

Brethren, let us learn some real good hard sense on this thing, and say this: The only fact that ever commended me to God was the fact that I was n't fit. Jesus came to seek and save the lost, and all the fitness he requireth is to feel my need of him. I feel my need; you feel your need. If you were fit, then I have no word to say to you. Jesus came to call not the righteous, but sinners, to repentance, and these poor fellows that ain't fit—you are the very ones. If your hands are dirty you are the man that ought to wash your hands; and if your soul is dirty by sin you ought to seek the fountain that washes away all sin and uncleanness from your soul. Won't you do that to-night?

"If a man will do the will of God he shall know

of the doctrine." And I want to tell you to-night, if I were you, standing where you are, I would walk up and say, "My brother, put me down on God's side from this day until I die." God says, "Choose ye this day whom you will serve." Now, will you listen to-night, and will you not, as an honest man who knows he ought to be good and give himself to the right—will you not in love and kindness say, "God being my helper, I start a better life to-night? I start on God's plan, eschewing the evil, taking up the right, and the balance of my days I give to the service of God." And when the battle is over God will say, "Now you are crowned," and then the palm, and then everlasting life.

SAYINGS.

THE first and lowest expression of love is the love of trust. This we see manifested in the conduct of the child toward its mother. There is a sort of love that we call the love of admiration, which admires the true, the noble, and the good, and makes us aspire to it. That is a higher order of love. Of all love that is the most sublime which you see illustrated when the bride and bridegroom walk up to the altar. He gives himself to her, and she gives herself to him. There they are, and if they are married according to God's ordinances, he does n't consult his own wishes—he just wants to know what his wife wants; and she does n't consult her own wishes—she just wants to know what will please her husband.

SERMON XVI.

THE SECRET OF A RELIGIOUS LIFE.

"I beseech you, therefore, brethren, by the mercies of God, that ye present your bodies a living sacrifice, holy, acceptable, unto God, which is your reasonable service."—ROMANS XII, 1.

WE have down South what we call the intensive system of farming. That means, enrich your soil, cultivate it more thoroughly, and you can make more cotton and corn on ten acres with less work than you now make on forty acres; and, after all, the question is not how many acres you cultivate, but how many wagon loads of corn you gather, and how many bales of cotton you have for the market. That's the test at last of farming.

The intensive system of farming is to get the most possible out of the parcel in hand. I would like to see the same system universally tried in religion—to get the most possible out of the facilities afforded. I have always heard it said, there is more in the man than there is in the land, and I have found out in this country, as I have opened my eyes and looked around me, there is more in the character of the man who joins the Church than there is in the Church which he joins.

You will excuse me, I hope, if I say there are some pieces of hickory the Lord himself can't make an ax-handle out of. That's not exactly orthodox, but it's a fact. He can polish it up, and make it of the same shape and same size and the same polish as any other ax-handle, but it will break off the first time you throw the ax into a log. You've seen this sort? Hickory that has been subjected to certain influences and despoiled by certain atmospheres, brother, is n't the sort that is good for the purpose you want to use it. I want to tell you that there are men and women all over this country that have subjected themselves to so many injurious influences and despoiled their character and undermined their foundation with so much that is wrong, that there must be, in the very nature of the case, a new creation to make them of any account. That's true of a great many men. Now, I want you all to-day to get down to the bed-rock facts, and let us talk about them. I like the rock idea. A rock is the foundation stone; a rock supplies the great shadow in a weary land. Now we strike this bed-rock on this text: "I beseech you, therefore, brethren, by the mercies of God, that ye present your bodies," first, a living; second, a holy; and third, an acceptable sacrifice. Now these three words are not put there to round up the rhetoric in this sentence. They are put before that term "sacrifice," but each word is a pillar holding up the great truth expressed in it.

"A living sacrifice." The Lord wants fifty million Christians. I believe there are that many professed Christians—fifty million people—in this world, who love God with all their heart, and love their neighbors as themselves. He wants fifty million soldiers of the cross that ain't afraid of any thing but sin, that love the right, and that dare to do the right.

We are willing to give our proportion of hospital rats and ambulance drivers, and so on, but I tell you when we get three-fourths of that kind into the front we ain't in much fix to fight. We know, though, there are plenty in the rear to take care of our wounded if any fellow happens to get wounded. We can do that. The finest hospital facilities in the universe are found in the Church of God. Is n't that true? Brother, Christianity in earnest, the intensive system of living right, means simply this: "Lord God, here I am, just as I am, with every passion of my soul, every faculty of my mind, and every power of my body. Here I am; if you want to use my hand, use it; if you want to use my foot, use it; if you want to use my tongue, use it; if you want to use my brain, use it; if you want to use my eyes, use them. Lord God, here I am, all over, through and through, from head to foot, I give myself to thee." A living sacrifice in fact—that's what we want in this country. I will tell you how we can have heart religion, brother, unintentionally. We have heard some old friend get up and talk, "I have religion in here. I know I have it in here." Well, if you have got it at all it is in there. "O, I believe in heart religion" you hear folks say. "That's my sort of religion." Well, I believe in heart religion, too, but I believe in finger religion as strongly as I believe in heart religion. I'll tell you another thing. If I could n't have it in but one place I want it in this hand here, and make it go out and do something for somebody. Your heart religion is n't worth a thing in the world by itself, because your heart never comes out; and if it did and any thing would come in contact with it you 'd be gone. If any thing touches it, even the point of a cambric needle, you 're dead. You 've got religion as you 've got your heart—if you expose it, if any thing touches the receptacle of your religion you 're gone. I 'm sorry for you if you have only heart religion. I want head religion, hand religion, foot religion as well as heart religion. I want every square inch in me, and about me, all over, head to foot religious. Get a man religious all over, and if the Lord wants him to work his head and feet he will visit the sick; if his head and tongue, he 'll talk to him; if he wants to put intelligent thought into his heart his ear is open to hear.

What we want in this country is the sacrifice that is willing to do right and live right and whole in every respect—a whole sacrifice. Now, some of you here are thinking men, and some of you are thinking about going up a little higher, getting dissatisfied with your latitude, and with your altitude, to say the least of it. Let 's see what we can do. A man said to me about six months ago, and he was an intelligent Christian, "Mr. Jones, we have got men in our Church worth one hundred thousand dollars, and some worth two hundred thousand dollars. They have been in the Church twenty-five years, some of them, and some of them pay our pastor two hundred dollars a year; they pay about twenty dollars for missions, and for all purposes they pay about three hundred dollars. Mr. Jones, I 've been in the Church only six years. I 'm not worth more than twenty thousand dollars, but I tell you I had to settle that money question some time ago. The Lord just brought me up to where that question had to be settled, 'What are you going to do about money?' and the least amount I can get off with to save my life is one thousand five hundred dollars, and sometimes I have to overhaul the thing or I feel bad about it, and still I do n't think I 'm doing right toward God." A whole sacrifice—a man that will tote fair with God in his money! There is n't one in a thousand that will do it. Did you ever notice how still a crowd becomes when you get to talking about money? O, my friends, hear me to-day; if you intend to give yourselves a living, whole, sacrifice, you 've got to settle this money question. Your money has to do with your religion just as every thing else. A man's money will help him to heaven just as it will help him to New York. "O," you say, "you 're preaching a moneyed gospel now." Well, now, let 's talk a little sense along with it as we go and see how the thing works. I can get to New York without a cent if I foot it all the way and beg my bread. Can 't I? It is n't necessary to have a cent to go to New York just as surely as it is n't necessary that you must have a nickel to go to heaven; and that old sister that sang "I 'm glad salvation is free," said, "I 've been in the Church forty years, and it never cost me but twenty-five cents." The old soul spent her quarter at last, but I do n't believe she ever got up there to enjoy it. Here a man's money will help him to heaven, or it will help him to hell, whichever route he wants to go. A man can take his money and go up with it or down with it, or run on a dead level with it—either way.

"Let 's hear you explain that." Well, I 'll illustrate it for you. Here 's a mechanic that has worked a couple of days for a man, and has earned two dollars a day, we will say; the man has n't the money, but he says, "I 'll pay you in four bushels of corn, if that will suit you." "Yes, that will do." Now, I 've got four bushels of corn. I want to run on a dead level with it. How am I to do it? I 'll take that corn out here in this field and plant it, and next fall I have five hundred bushels; but I have n't any thing but corn.

I started with corn, and I ended with corn. You see that 's a dead-level, dog-trot line. There 's many a fellow in this country, if you were to analyze him and show him how much genuine dog he had in him, he would be ashamed of himself the balance of his life. A fellow has got one hundred thousand dollars, and he says, "I 'm going to make this one hundred thousand dollars earn me another one hundred thousand dollars." He has money. He started with money, and he ended with money. You put it in two piles, and when death turns his lantern on one pile and then on the other you would n't turn around for it.

I want to go down with my corn now. How am I going to do it? Why, I 'll take it up to the still-house and have eight gallons of whisky made out of it, and then every thing I touch is going downward and hellward. Do n't you see? I want to go up with it. How am I going to do it? I 'll take my four bushels of corn to the mill and have it ground, and put it on a dray-wagon, and get up on the sacks myself, and drive down this street and turn up this alley, and stop in front of the house of a poor widow, and I 'll take those four bushels of meal out of that wagon and carry it into the house and lay it on the floor, and tell that poor widow and her children, "In the name of Jesus, my precious Savior, I will give you these four bushels of meal;" and at the last day, when the man walks up to the pearly gates, Jesus will say, "Open wide the everlasting gates and let him in," and the angels say, "Why, Master, on what grounds do you admit him?" and Jesus will say, "I was hungry and he fed me. I was naked and he clothed me. I was sick and he visited me." Jesus points at the little cabin in the alley, and says, "Even as ye did it unto the least of these, my brethren, you did it unto me. Enter thou into the joys of thy Lord."

Now hear me. What about my money? Have I consecrated myself to God? I will say one thing, and I mean it with all my heart. If I had as much money as some of you have got who look me in the face, and if I did n't do more for God and humanity than you do with your money, the devil would get me as certain as my name is Sam Jones, and he 'll get you, too, unless you make out a clear case of idiocy.

If you do that you may slip through. If you go up there as a sensible man, and show no better dividends in righteousness than you now show, my candid judgment is the sentence will be, "Depart, ye accursed. I trusted you and you robbed me." Your money—you 've got to straighten that out somehow. Many a man is appreciative. A fellow in Cincinnati said, "I would n't have missed that sermon for two hundred dollars," but when they passed around the hat he slipped in a copper cent. He was just one hundred and ninety-nine dollars and ninety-nine cents meaner in his pocket than he was in his mouth. That fellow's mouth was all right, but his pocket was all wrong. I said once, "Brethren, pitch in and give every thing you have to God," and a brother tackled me after dinner and said, "Look here, Jones, you told these people to give every thing they had to God. Do you mean it?" "No," I said, "I just put it strong that way and told them to give their all, and by the time it works down to their pocket-books it will be just about ten cents." We have got to start mighty strong to get there at all. Money! Religion is the cheapest thing in the world. There is n't an entertainment on earth as cheap as a religious entertainment, if you won't put it on any other basis in the world. I recollect going down the street of my town one day and I passed a squad of men, who were standing on the sidwalk, and heard one man say, "Every time I go to Church its money, money, money." I have heard that, have n't you? I 'll tell you another thing. Have you not noticed that whenever a pocket-book flies shut a man's mouth flies open, and he 'll talk; but whenever his pocket-book flies open his mouth flies shut? The fellows that never give a cent are the fellows that are running around talking money, money, money all the time. You watch the next tonguey chap that 's going about talking money and he 's the very fellow that has n't invested a quarter since these meetings started. Did you ever notice that. "Barking dogs never bite." I have heard that all my life; and the man that growls about money is the man that never pays any thing.

Listen. I was walking along the street when one of these men said to the others: "It 's just money, money, money the year round." I stopped, and there it was the steward of the Methodist Church talking that way. I looked at him and said, "What did you say?" and he said: "Sam, I did n't see you, or I do n't reckon I 'd have said that." Said I, "What did you say?" He said: "I declared it a shame how people are going about talking about money. Every time you go to Church they take a collection, and they stick the contribution-box under your nose now every time you go to Church." I said, "Look here; talking about money, I 'll tell you what I 'll do. You pick out six of the leading Methodists or Baptists in the Church, the most liberal ones, and I 'll agree to pay every dollar of what these six pay in a year, every cent, to the preacher and to Church missions, with less money than it takes to run one old red-nosed drunkard. Now, what do you say? Why, one old red-nosed drunkard pays more for his whisky and his devilment every year than the six leading Christians of the town pay for the privilege of serving God and doing right and going to heaven. Brother, I'd just shut my little mouth and never open it again on that subject if I were you. It's better to be poor than to be drunk; it's better to be a good man than a bad man; you better shut your mouth and go along and say nothing about money."

If I were on any thing else than money, you'd all cheer like forty, but I do n't expect much cheering on the line I'm on. It is as the old colored preacher says, "Talk about money and you throw a dampness over the meetin'." I'm not preaching for my pocket, brethren, I'm preaching for souls. Do you hear that?

Brother, tote fair with God; do right towards God your Maker, and wherever there is a demand on your head or heart or hand or feet or pocket-book, in the name of sense meet it as an honest man ought to meet a thing. That's religion—a holy sacrifice. Well, we take it for granted you have given God your heart and pocket-book, and your hands and feet, but now how about your time? Have you ever settled any thing about your time, whether any of it belongs to God, and if so, how much of it belongs to God? Did you ever sit down and make an honest division with God of your time—I will give God so much every week? John Wesley, a grander man than whom never lived, sat down and divided the twenty-four hours of the day into three equal parts, and said, "Eight hours a day I give to sleep and recreation; eight hours I give to my business, and eight hours I give to

God." When I look at Wesley's life, and see how many sermons he preached, I'm astonished that he had any time to travel; and when I look at the number of miles he traveled on horseback, I'm astonished that he had time to preach; and when I look at the number of books he left behind him I say, "Well, well, how did Wesley have time for writing and preaching?" and the whole life of that great man, the most laborious life almost of any century, was made successful and extensive because he divided up rightly with God.

How many weeks in the year do you give to God? How many hours a day do you give to God? That's the way to talk it. How many days in the week, how many hours in the day do you give to God? Many a fellow goes crying around a big meeting and asks people to pray for him, but, brother, you don't want to go where God is. He is all around here. I tell you you can find God all over this city, and there's many a place I'd rather go to find God than to this hall. "What do you mean?" I mean this: I heard of a backslidden Methodist once who was making money pretty fast—and that's a pretty good way to find a blackslider. It's a fellow in the Church making money rapidly. "He's preaching against riches," you say. Well, if were I would preach against Abraham, and I never will preach against Abraham. That grand old saint could have come to this city and bought out the whole town before breakfast, and it would n't have interfered with his other transactions of the day. You show me a man that says I am preaching against Abraham, and I 'll show you a man that 's not growing in grace.

This man went to a Methodist preacher, and said he, "I wish you would tell me where and what heaven is;" and the preacher said, "I can tell you where it is." "Where is it?" Said he, "Last year you made forty thousand dollars on one lot of cotton; now you are rich, and there 's one of your sisters in Christ who is a member of the Church, and she 's lying up on the hill yonder and she 's down with the typhoid fever and her children have the chills, and that poor woman has n't a cook or a nurse or any one to look after her wants. Now, if you will just go down town and buy fifty dollars' worth of nice provisions and take them up there—and she has seen better days—and get a cook and nurse to take care of her so that she 'll never want for any thing, and then get down the Bible and read the twenty-third Psalm, "The Lord is my Shepherd, I shall not want," and pray God's blessing on the poor widow and her children; if you do n't see heaven before I see you again I 'll foot the bill." The next day as he was walking down the street along came this man, and with the tears running down his face he said, "I did as you told me. I bought fifty dollars' worth of provisions and put them in a wagon and drove up to her house, and I got her a cook and a nurse, and I told her she should not want again, as I was her brother; and I read the twenty-third Psalm, and got down to pray, and God and angels came down and filled that room, and I was the happiest man I have ever been in my life."

The charity that will simply pitch a ten-dollar piece into a poor widow's lap, is not charity. The charity that hunts up and sympathizes with and puts its arm around and helps a brother—that's the charity that takes us close to heaven.

SAYINGS.

THANK God, this old world has never seen the time when it did not take its hat off and make a decent bow to a good woman!

THIS world is the fruit-bearing world. Up yonder we will eat and rejoice forever over the fruit we have matured here below. Between the bud and the blossom and the ripe fruit of love there are many difficulties. There are the cold winds of neglect, and the biting frosts of temptation; there are a thousand intervening difficulties between the blossom and the ripe fruit.

As soon as a man quits doing wrong toward God he begins to see how good God is. I had a friend in Cartersville who was mad with another member of the Church; and I said: "If you will go and pay that man all that you owe him, I venture to say that it will be all right." I got the man to pay his debts, and there are no better friends in the town than those two men. If you will pay your debts to God, none will be better friends.

SERMON XVII.

PRISONERS OF HOPE.

"Turn you to the stronghold, ye prisoners of hope; even to-day do I declare that I will render double unto thee."—ZECH. IX, 12.

GOD is in earnest about the salvation of men. As I read this book I close it ever and anon, and say to myself, the all-absorbing theme with God and angels and good men is the salvation of the living—not the salvation of men who lived a hundred or a thousand years ago. They have had their privileges, enjoyed their opportunities, and destiny is fixed with them. Their cases have ceased to engage the mind and heart of God in the sense in which our cases engage his mind and heart.

It is not in the salvation of men that shall live a hundred years hence; they have yet to be born, and yet to enjoy their privileges and opportunities. But it is the salvation of men and women who live and walk and talk upon the face of the earth now. Is it not strange that this question should so engage the mind of Deity, and so interest the great heart of the Church and angels, and that you, for whom all this sympathy is poured out, and all these manifestations are given, should be the only being in the universe disinterested in this great question?

Now, locate yourself somewhere in one of these classes to-night. I do not purpose to draw upon my imagination, but we will stick to the record. If you believe the Bible, give me your attention. If you do n't believe in the Bible, the discussion to-night will have very little to do with your case. When a man has found something better than the Bible, something more promising than the Gospel, something more inviting than heaven, he is not the man to whom I preach the Gospel, or would plead with to lead a better life. But, if you have found nothing better than the Gospel, nothing truer than the Bible, and nothing sweeter than heaven, give me your attention; we will stick to the record. I shall talk about things we all know about.

The first class of prisoners with hope we mention are the good men and women, the best characters in all the Churches of earth. I have never yet been pastor of a Church that did n't have consecrated men and women, who loved God with all their hearts and their neighbors as themselves. I am ready to say that every good man I have ever met was a member of some Christian Church. I have never yet found a man out of the Church that talked like a Christian in the deeper and better things of a spiritual life. Now, I have heard people say, "My father was a good man, and he did n't belong to the Church;" and "My mother was a good woman, and she did n't belong to the Church." Well, in the name of common sense, do n't take me to the graveyards to find good folks. Every body out there is good, if you will read their epitaphs and what is written on their tombstones. Every body is good after they die, but I want you all to rack me out a living, kicking fellow in this world that does n't belong to the Church. He's the one I'm hunting for. Where is he?

I say all the good people I have ever known were members of some Christian Church. If you have a man in this city that's a good Christian and does n't belong to any Church I want to see him. I want to get his photograph to take around with me, and say, "Here's one Christian that has had an opportunity to join the Church, but would n't join." When a man gets religion, brethren, he breaks right away for the Church of God, just as a young duck does for the pond, precisely. I do n't care how he was hatched out, it's his nature to go to the pond. I used myself to talk that way—"I can live as well out of the Church as in. There's no use in joining the Church at all." But, as soon as I gave my heart to God, if the door of the Church had not been opened to me I would have broken it down and got in anyhow. I must get in.

I'll tell you another thing: When a man stands up and preaches the Gospel to me I want to know that he's a member of the Church, and I do n't want him to be ashamed to tell what Church he belongs to, either. If you ever expect to be a Christian, the fact that you gave your heart to God involves the fact that you gave your hand to the Church. Some people, when they get religion, sit up and say, "To save my life I can't determine what Church to join. I do n't think any of them suits me." Perhaps yours is a peculiar case, and I reckon the Lord will have to send his angels down just to organize a Church to suit you. Lord, have mercy on some people in this world. They are like a class of fighting men we had during the war: There were Union men and Southern men who would n't join any regiment, and they were what we called a "bushwhacker;" and a bushwhacker would kill a Union man as quick as he would a rebel, because he was after what the fellow had in his pocket. God deliver me from these religious bushwhackers that do n't belong to any command, but are just after the spoils.

You give your heart to God, and do n't let a Sabbath pass without going to some of these Christian Churches, and say: "Brethren, take me in, and lift me." And do n't come in to be a little baby to be nursed; but say, "Brother, I will lift you; I will measure arms with any body. I never come in to be fed on soothing syrup and the bottle; but I 'm going to be some one, God being my helper." Brother, we do n't want any more babies. It 's a heap of trouble to run a church full of babies. Now, the prisoners with hope are the first class we mention—faithful men and women who belong to the great Church of God in some of its branches, and are working out their salvation with fear and trembling. They have denied themselves and taken up their cross to follow after Christ. Every good man in this town who is striving to please God and do good is a prisoner with hope; but he 's a prisoner still, hemmed in with the environments of earth, and with the temptations of earth thrown all around him, with nothing certain except heaven to him, if he is faithful unto the end. Now he's a prisoner with hope.

> "O, what a blessed hope is ours,
> While here on earth we stay;
> We more than taste the heavenly powers,
> And antedate that day."

Hope to the Christian is the anchor of his soul which entereth into that within the veil. When hope, the anchor, is pitched out into the great deep of life, the winds may beat and the storms may blow, but, blessed be God, it will hold me fast.

A prisoner, but a prisoner with hope! My precious mother was a prisoner with hope once, but twenty-eight years ago her spirit went home to God, and she has ever since been roaming Elysian fields, one of God's freemen in heaven. Thank God, they are freemen up yonder, with no environments, no imprisonments, but everlasting freedom in the presence of God. My father was a prisoner of hope thirteen years ago, but death cut the last ligament, and his liberated spirit went home to God, and he has been walking the golden streets for thirteen years—a freeman in God's great world. Every good man and every good woman is a prisoner with hope here, but there they are God's freemen.

I have sat down often and buried my face in my hands, and wondered if I will ever get to heaven. It will be a glad moment to my spirit when I have fought my last battle, when I have overcome my last temptation, when I have kneeled down and said my prayers for the last time, when I have kissed my wife and children good night, and started home to heaven like a little school-boy going home from school, and when my feet shall strike the pavements of the golden streets of God, and I shall at last, blessed be God, be at home, and free forever.

There is another class of prisoners with hope, and they are the men and women who are not members of the Church, nor professors of religion, but they are seeking it; they are penitent sinners. After all, there are but two classes of sinners in this world of people—the penitent and the impenitent. All penitent sinners are saved, and all impenitent sinners are lost. Every penitent, heart-broken, and contrite mortal in this house is a prisoner of hope. If a man is honestly seeking grace in the pardon and salvation of his soul, that man is as much on the road to heaven, as far as he has gone, as any man here. Thank God, he never lets a penitent die until his penitence has issued into pardon and peace. If you are an honest penitent, and will keep your traces tight going in that direction, you can never die until you are pardoned. An honest and persistent penitent never yet was damned. Are you an honest penitent? Do you mean business? Are you honestly sorry about the way you have been doing? Have you honestly made up your mind to give your heart to God and be religious? If you have, my brethren, you are prisoners with hope. There is a chance for you to get to heaven, and I say to you this, that is all I want to know to-night or any time in my future life in this world: Is there a chance for me to get to the good world? If there is, count me in.

I 'll tell you another thing. I 'm going to take every chance for the good world. I was at a meeting once, and the preacher said: "All of you that are not doing your whole duty come up here." And I felt that I ought to be the first one to go. "All of you that want more religion," said the preacher, "come up." And I said to myself, "That means me." "All of you that feel in your heart," continued the preacher, "that you are unworthy, come up." And I thought, "I am the most unworthy man in the world. That means me." And then the preacher said, "All of you that want to consecrate life and soul and body to God, come up here and kneel down.' And I ought to be the first fellow there, I thought. "And all of you who love God and trust in him, come up," said the preacher again, and then I thought, "Well, I ought to go right along with the first, for I do love him and trust him every day." I 'm going to take every chance for the good world, and if there 's any good in the Methodist mourners' bench, I 'm going to get it; and if there 's any thing in the Presbyterian inquiry chair, I 'm going to take that chair; and if there 's any good in those rooms, I 'm going in there. I 'm going to take every chance I can get for a better life. I shall never dodge a duty or shirk a responsibility. Now, here, if we are prisoners of hope, then let us take the chances that we have to-night, and let us fight it out, fight the world, the flesh, and the devil, until we are no longer prisoners of hope, but enjoy the freedom of God's children in heaven.

There is another class of prisoners with hope. There is that man out there, who does n't know what to do, hardly. He has very nearly made up his mind to-night: "It is right to do right, and it is wrong to do wrong, and I believe I will fall in with this movement." Thousands came for curiosity, or for the fun there is in it, and he among the number. He said to himself, "I will have more fun to-night than I ever had in my life. I am going to have lots of fun." But watch him, and the first thing you know the man sits uneasily in his chair. The spirit of God has convicted him, and before the service is over he will look just as if the devil had a mortgage upon him. He is a prisoner with hope. Every man here, anxious and earnest for the salvation of his soul, no matter whether he has taken the step or not, is a prisoner with hope. Thank God, I would that every man in this house to-night might take his chance for heaven and work it out until it should end in a grand result. Look at Garfield, shot down by the assassin's bullet. We see the doctor probing the wound, and Garfield turns to him and says: "Doctor, what are the chances? Do not hesitate to tell me the worst, because you know I am not afraid to die." The doctor looks at him and replies, "There is only one chance in a hundred for your life." "Then," says Garfield, "I will take that chance." He did grapple with death for ninety days as scarcely any man ever did. Now, brother, there is a chance for you to be saved. Will you just say, "By the grace of God I will take that chance, and grapple with sin and the devil until God shall say, 'It is enough; come up higher?'" That is what we want.

Now, turn, you prisoners of hope; I dare assert that every man here is a prisoner of hope. There is a chance for you to be saved, and come to God and have your sins pardoned. There is a chance for each and a chance for all. Now, let us to-night say: "Whatever others may do or not do, by the grace of God I will take that chance, and will work out this great problem by the direction of the good Spirit, and make my way to heaven."

"Turn you to the stronghold, ye prisoners of hope." Then what is the promise? "Even to-day"—to-day, says the Lord, not to-morrow nor next week, but to-day—"I will render double unto thee." I never read that promise that I do n't think of an incident that one of our old preachers told me. He said, in one of his revivals, there was a young man who was very much interested in the meeting. He came up and was earnest and prayed and yet he was not converted. He walked out of the door with the young man one day, and turned to him and said, "My young friend, you seem to be in earnest, and seem to be honest. What is the matter with you? You are not converted yet." "Well," said the young man, "I am in earnest. No man was ever more in earnest than I am, but I tell you, whenever I go up to the altar and begin to pray, I think of the business I am in. I am employed as a clerk in a grocery store where they sell provisions in one room and liquor in another by the quart, and I frequently have to go into the liquor part and draw whisky and sell to customers. Every time I kneel down at the altar and pray God to save my soul, that part of my work comes up, and I can 't pray to save my life."

Do you hear that? A man can 't get religion and clerk where whisky is sold, much less can he keep it and rent a house for others to sell it in, or sell it himself after he is converted. No, sir; no, sir. A man that will rent his house to a bar-keeper and call himself a Christian, is a hypocrite of the deepest dye, and he does not find quarters in my Church where I am pastor.

That boy could n't get religion and sell whisky, and the preacher said to him: "My young friend, it is not a question at all. If it is in your way, give it up. Give up your employment and give your heart to God." "Well," said the boy, "you know my widowed mother and my three orphaned sisters are depending upon me for every bite they eat; and," said he, "if I give up my employment, my mother and sisters will starve; and if I do n't give it up, my soul is lost. I am in a strait." The preacher said, "Now, listen to me. God never asked a man to do any thing that would damage him in either world. Now, if it is your duty to give up that job, you do it." The young man went right down to the store and saw the head employer, and told him, "I have been seeking religion three days and nights, and I can 't get it. Every time I go to the altar and try to pray, that whisky part of your business comes up before me, and I can 't get religion and sell whisky." "Well," said the senior partner of the firm, "I am sorry to have you leave. You have been a dutiful, faithful boy, and I am sorry to give you up. We are paying you good wages, fifty dollars a month, and you are poor; but if you say quit, we can't say a word." The young man replied, "I am obliged to quit for conscience' sake." His employer settled up with him that afternoon, and the boy went back to the Church at night and was converted to God. The next morning after breakfast he received a note, and opened it, and it was a note from his old employer, saying, "Come down to our store this afternoon." After dinner the boy walked down to the store and into the office room, and his employer met him and shook hands with him, and said, "I am glad to see you back, sir. Now, walk into this room." He took him into the liquor-room, and every barrel had been rolled out. He said, "Now, you see we have quit that business, and I will give you a hundred dollars a month if you will come back and clerk again."

"Even to-day!" In twenty-four hours after the time that boy gave up his business for Christ's sake and for conscience' sake, God doubled his salary and put the whisky out, and put him back. Thank God, no man loses any thing by doing right for God and conscience' sake. "Even to-day do I declare that I will render double unto thee."

"Well," you say, "I don't believe that story is true." Well, sir, I know it is true. And what I am going to say now is true, and it is a story a hundred times bigger than the one I have just told, too. You say,

"What is that?" Well, sir, when I was a poor sinner, they used to tell me that "if any man will forsake houses, and lands, and wife and children, and home, and friends, and be my disciple, I will give him a hundred fold more in this life, and life everlasting in the world to come." Thirteen years ago, brethren—listen to me—I left one little cottage home in Cartersville to follow Christ, and, glory to his name, he has given me a thousand homes as good as any man ever had. Thirteen years ago I bid farewell to a few friends in my town to follow Christ, and he has given me a thousand friends for every one I left on that day. Thirteen years ago I left one mother—a step-mother, but kind and good to me—to follow Christ; and I want to say to you that everywhere I have gone, God has ever given me a hundred mothers just as good and kind to me as my own mother could be. And I want to say to you brethren, that God has given me a hundredfold more in this life. I left two brothers at home to follow Christ, and God has given me a hundred thousand brethren who are just as good to me as my own brothers could be. I stand here to-night to testify to the fact that God gives a hundredfold more in this life, and his precious promise of everlasting life in the world to come. Half of the promise is true, and I just know that God is going to fulfill the whole promise.

Brother, turn to the stronghold to-night. Your Savior, Christ, is the stronghold, and God himself has promised, "Even to-day do I declare that I will render double unto thee."

SERMON XVIII.

SOWING AND REAPING.

"Be not deceived; God is not mocked; for whatsoever a man soweth, that shall he also reap. He that soweth to his flesh shall of the flesh reap corruption; but he that soweth to the Spirit shall of the Spirit reap life everlasting."—GAL. VI, 7, 8.

WE say there are three absolute impossibilities in this life. There may be many, but we know of three. First, it is an absolute impossibility for a man continuously and successfully to practice a fraud upon his own immortality. If you are a good man you know it. I care not how much you may bring to bear—your self-pride and the flattery of your friends—if you are not what you ought to be there are periods in your history when God wakes you up and shows you what you are, and who you are, and whither you are tending. I am so glad God won't let a man lie down and sleep his way to hell. In spite of dissipation, in spite of gayeties, in spite of temporal pleasures, there are moments when God arrests you and shows you what you are, and who you are, and where you are going. I imagine that every thing in the universe has its purpose. There is not an agency but what is working to an end. I think that bar-rooms, and ball-rooms, and card-tables, and a thousand things I might mention, are but so many influences to keep a man's mind off of himself. A man infatuated with the game of progressive euchre never thinks who he is, or what he is, or where he is going. A man looking at the gay jim-jams, you might say, on the stage at the theater, is attracted by the sight, and never sees himself. A man steeped in and stupefied by whisky loses sight of himself; and these are agencies employed by the devil, and by devilish men, to make you shut your eyes to yourself; but sooner or later, ever and anon, God makes you stop, wakes you up and shows you what you are. And now, brother, if you are a good man, you know you are a good man; if you are not a good man, you know you are not a good man, and that 's the end of logic on this question.

We say, in the second place, it is absolutely impossible for a man continuously and successfully to practice a fraud upon his neighbor. Now, your neighbor knows you, and a great many things he has never told you. Somehow or other if there 's any good about you, your neighbors will find it out, and if there 's any thing bad about you they 'll find it out, too.

If you were to dress up in disguise to-morrow night and go to your neighbor's house and get him to talk about you, and spend an hour with him on this subject, you 'd leave that house with your face buried in your hands, and you 'd say: "Well, well, well, I had no idea in the world that that man knows me as well as he does." You 'd be astonished along on that line. O, how much we know about each other, and how false we are toward each other. There 's many a person in this world that will fawn around you and flatter you to get your money, or influence, or something; but they can look clear through you, and they know you; and when the day comes they'll tell it, too. You mark what I say.

Do you know that the worst enemies you have in the world are those who were once your best friends? They ran with you until they found you out, and, my, my, what a contempt they have for you now! You can't practice a fraud on your neighbor. This estimate of a man is pretty fair at last; and I want to say to you if your neighbors all concur in the fact that you won't do, I'll take their word; if they concur in the fact that you are upright, and generous and noble, I'll take their word. Mark you, you are known in this community as you are. That's a sad revelation to some of you. You'd be astonished to know how many people have seen you going into certain places at doubtful hours, too; doubtful places where a decent man can't go. You'd be astonished to know how many could write your life and history. You are practicing a fraud upon nobody.

Then we say, in the next place, it is absolutely impossible for a man to practice a fraud upon God Almighty. He knows you through and through. He knows where you live, what your name is, how old you are, and the very hairs of your head are numbered. He not only hears every word you say, but he knows the motives of your life. This is the meaning of the expression here: "Be not deceived; God is not mocked." You know yourself; your neighbor knows you; God knows you. This is one text that the world assents to whether you be Jew or Gentile, whether you be atheist or deist, Christian or infidel. Do you know that all humanity gathers on .it as a common platform, and all agree to the truth of this proposition that, "whatsoever a man soweth, that shall he also reap?"

This text is not true simply because I find it in the Bible; but it would be as true if Hume, the historian, or if Bacon were its author as it is true when God is its author. Really, brethren, leaving out the question of God, we know this text is true.

"Whatsoever a man soweth, that shall he also reap." This world around us, brethren, is but the photograph, a counterpart of the immortal world. Now we know this text is true in physical things, for whatsoever I sow as a farmer I reap. Like begets like. If I go out in my garden and sow a row of lettuce, I do n't expect any thing but lettuce from the time the seed drops from my hand until it is gathered for the table. I go into my garden and plant a row of potatoes, and I do n't expect any thing but potatoes. If I go into my field and plant corn, from the time the seed is covered up in the furrow until the ear is gathered for the barn, I do n't expect any thing but corn, If I go out into my field and sow wheat, I do n't expect any thing but wheat. Whatsoever I sow, that I reap. I want to call your attention to another fact along here. Like not only begets like, but multiplied productions follow. I plant one grain of corn and I gather eight hundred grains. Some years ago one of our leading pastors in our State told me himself that there sprouted in his garden a seed of oats. He let it grow on and spread, and mature; and he said, "I pulled up that bunch of oats all growing from one seed, and carried it to my back veranda, and sat down and counted the grains, and there were eight thousand seven hundred of them. They all came from that one single grain." I believe it is a true, plain, literal fact which he stated.

You take that eight thousand seven hundred grains of oats and sow it; next summer you have forty bushels. Take that forty bushels and sow it, and you have one thousand six hundred. Take the one thousand six hundred, and then begin to multiply in this way, if such a thing were possible, and you would have this world a hundred feet deep in oats in two or three decades.

Now, brother, listen. Like not only begets like, but look at the multiplying, increasing nature of every thing you sow. Back yonder in the Garden of Eden, six thousand years ago, Adam dropped one little seed of sin in the garden, and now to-day this world is foul with sin and full of woe.

Now, there is a sense in which we are immortally sowing. Every man is going through this world with a basket of immortal spiritual seed on his arm, and every step he takes in life his hand goes down into the basket, and he scatters the seed to the right and to the left, not out on your prairie lands, or down on the red hills of Georgia, but in human hearts, and they grow up and mature, and there is a harvest from the sowing that has been done in the preceding months and years. O, brother, as I look at this city to-day, and see it reeking with iniquity, I say, "O, my God, what a sowing! O, what a harvest there is in this city to sadden the heart of God and make angels weep!"

Every word of my mouth is a seed; every act of my life is a seed, and it falls in ground that will produce and reproduce, and we are sowing and reaping, and sowing and reaping until by and by comes the harvest; and then the time of weeping, or the time of rejoicing, when we shall bring in our sheaves.

When a Catholic woman went to her devout priest in confessional, and said to him, "I have talked between my neighbors, and I have got the community in a perfect uproar; neighbor is mad with neighbor, and it is caused by what I said," the priest listened through, and said, "Now I have heard your confession. I give as a penance now that you go and gather a basket of thistle-seed and go between each house and houses in the community, and scatter the thistle-seed to the right and to the left along your pathway." Next morning she came back and said, "I have done as you told me. I pray for absolution." "No," the priest said. "Before I absolve you I want you first to go and gather up all this seed you have scattered by the wayside, and put it in a basket and bring it back to me." "O," said the despairing woman, "I can never do that." "Neither," said the priest, "can you ever undo the mischief you have done in your community by scattering your bad talk and communications among those neighbors."

O, brother, it's mighty easy to scatter, but O, how hard it is to pluck up and bring back again.

Can you take back that oath you swore yesterday? It dropped in the ears of a little boy, and that boy will scatter oaths for fifty years to come. You might afford to be wicked and sow evil seed if you were shut up in some lonely island all by yourself, but in this community, where every man touches another man, where little children play around you as you walk along the streets, where your examples are seen and felt by all men, I warn you, brother, you sin with a vengeance when you do wrong in this city of many thousands of people.

"Whatsoever a man soweth, that shall he also reap." There is a very general sense in which this is true. Now, I want you to answer one question for me. If I sow bar-rooms and whisky, what will I reap? Will you answer it in the halting, staggering gait of every drunkard that curses this city to-night? If I sow whisky I shall reap drunkards. Do you doubt it? Is there a man here to-night that says, "That logic won't do?" Is there one? I don't care whether you sow whisky at your wine suppers, or whether you sow beer for your health; I care not what your excuse may be; every glass drunk by yourself, and passed to others, is sowing a seed that shall produce a harvest of drunkards that will curse this country when you are dead and gone.

Do you know that every bar-room means ten steady drinkers? I am told that there are in this city thirty-three hundred bar-rooms. If you can put out two or three hundred bar-rooms, or five or six hundred, or a thousand bar-rooms with high license, I want to tell you how you can put them all out, and put them out forever—and that is with prohibition.

Now, I ask every intelligent man, if you have ten steady drinkers for each of these bar-rooms, ten men who have crossed the line and will die drunk as certain as those bar-rooms stay in your city, will you not have thirty-five thousand human beings that to-night are marching into drunkards' graves? I verily believe, and I utter it with the conviction of my soul, that in less than fifty years from to-day our children will look back on us for licensing whisky as the most blatant barbarians that ever cursed the world.

Talk about civilization, prate about liberty, boast about intelligence! God Almighty let our children live and die idiots, if you call the present outgrowth of things the product of intelligence, and liberty, and freedom!

Sow whisky, reap drunkards. They have reaped your husband, may be, sister. They have reaped your boy, may be, mother. They have reaped your neighbor, may be, friend. Call me a fanatic; say, "There is a religious enthusiast;" then go and shoulder your drunkards and bear them to the judgment-bar of God.

Sow whisky, reap drunkards. Do you deny it? Can you, my brother, be a party to the sowing of the seed that will produce drunkards when God himself has said, "No drunkard shall enter the kingdom of heaven?" Will you tie your own brother, hand and foot, and cast him out of the reach of the arm of God? Can you do that? Every license to every bar-room in this city is furnishing the tether by which your brother is bound hand and foot and cast where God's arm can never reach him. I 'll tell you another thing. We have lain low and said nothing, until to-night the strongest power in America is the whisky power. The Congress of the United States just stands and trembles in its presence. The legislatures of three-fourths of these States stand and tremble in its presence, and the pulpits of this country say, "I do n't want to preach politics." What 's the matter with them? The liquor question is no more a political question than is "Thou shalt not steal" a political question.

Sow whisky, reap drunkards. My most earnest prayer, my greatest longing, is to live to see the day in this grand country of ours when there is nothing to break a mother's heart or to make a wife weep her life away; when there is nothing in America that will make a man stagger, and make an honest man steal and a sensible man a fool. Every lewd house in this city is bottomed on your bar-rooms; every gambling hell in this town is bottomed on your bar-rooms; and when you put whisky out of America you will put out of it the gambling hells and lewd houses, and those are the three biggest guns of hell turned loose upon our country. They fire often enough to kill more of our race than all other guns put together. Men and boys go from the bar-rooms to the gambling hell, and from the gambling hell to the shameless houses, just as naturally as a living man breathes.

But we go on. Sow cards and reap what? Industrious, hard-working boys? Sow cards and reap farmers? Sow cards and reap first-class mechanics? Sow cards and reap lawyers? No! no! a thousand times no! But sow cards and reap gamblers. Corn never grew from corn and wheat never grew from wheat more legitimately than the sowing of cards in your household will produce a harvest of gamblers. "I can 't see any harm in the world in a social game of cards," you say. I repeat what I have said frequently, that nine gamblers out of every ten that I have ever met were from the homes of so-called Christian people. That is a fact. What does that teach us? It teaches us this: that in the boyhood of your sons you teach them a passion for games and gambling that in their after-life they can never overcome. God pity a man that can 't run his home without a deck of cards! Some of you say, "I must have amusement for my children; I shall bring cards to my house; and I am going to put a billiard-table in there, too." A billiard table in a private house! As God is my judge, in all my relations of life I never have seen a first-class billiard player that was worth the powder and lead that it would take to kill him. Now, what do you say? "O, I believe in having a billiard table, and cards, and wine, and all that sort of things." You say, "Why, give these to the children, and let them have them now, and they won't care any thing about them after a while." Just give your hogs some good slop every morning for a week, and on the same principle they will just get so they won't care any thing about slop at all! Why, they won't look at it!

Sow cards, reap gamblers. O, what a life you project upon this world when you train a boy up who has no respect for God, and his greatest passion is to sit down with a deck of cards before him! And Paul hit on this point, brethren, when he said, "I would have you wise unto that which is good and simple concerning evil." What did he mean? Blessed are they that do n't know how to do any sort of meanness. Their parents have never taught them how, and they have never learned.

Then, again, we say, sow profanity and reap blackguards. I can put up with any other sort of a case better than I can with one of those cursing, swearing men. He is to me the most contemptible animal that walks this earth — a cursing man, a man that can 't talk business, can 't talk any thing without injecting his oaths, the most venomous, into his conversation. I have thought many a time that every swearing man ought to command some lonely island to himself—get off like Robinson Crusoe, and curse it out among the goats.

Sow whisky, reap drunkards; sow cards, reap gamblers; sow profanity, and reap a debauched race. Then, again, we say—and we are following this logic out, and it is as resistless as the tide, and as clear as the mind of God—sow parties and reap balls; sow balls and reap germans; sow germans and reap spider-legged dudes; and sow a spider-legged dude and reap a thimbleful of calves'-foot jelly. I tell you, my congregation, to-night, that certain roads lead to certain places, and I ask you to mark the assertion.

Whatsoever a man soweth, that shall he also reap. Listen to me, brethren. Of all the creation of God, the greatest moral, mental, physical monstrosity in the universe is the natural product of fashionable society, the dude and the dudine; and you never catch a dude and a dudine marrying one another. They will spoil two houses in spite of creation. I have never known them to take to one another, have you?

Sow whisky, reap drunkards. Sow social evils and social amusements, and the natural product is a lot of young people in the community that are shiftless and helpless and powerless, and that will be a dishonor to their parents all the days of their lives.

Now, follow this line out. If I sow to the flesh, I shall of the flesh reap corruption. This is inevitable. If I sow to the Spirit, I shall of the Spirit reap life everlasting. Now, we can not undo what we have done by any power in the world except to change the sowing. That is it. The only process that will overcome the evil that you have done is to change the sowing. Mother, if you have been teaching your daughter worldliness, teach Christ, and peace, and heaven to her from this time on. Father, if you have been playing cards with your boys, change the sowing, and go to reading the Bible and praying with your boys. Mother, if you have been taking your girl off into amusement, change the sowing, and take your girl to prayer-meeting and to the Church and to God.

In my town, when I was growing up, I was a sort of leader among the boys. I reckon I led many a boy off from right. But I will say this much: As soon as I was converted I commenced changing the sowing; I commenced sowing good. I have preached in my town in the churches; I have preached on the streets; I have preached under bush-arbors and under tents; and last year, at our bush-arbor meeting, God gave me the last friend of my boyhood days to join the Church and go to heaven with me. Thank God, there is n't a being in this world that I ever led astray but whom I have, under God, been instrumental in turning around and bringing back to Christ. I am prouder of that than of any fact in my life to-night, except Christ's pardon of my own sins.

Sow to the Spirit and you shall of the Spirit reap life everlasting. Now, if you will pardon me, I will make a little personal allusion here. I want you to think about it when you go home to-night, and I want every mother and every father to take this incident home with them. It is a little family history that I want to give you all.

A few years ago, five or six years ago now, just a little earlier than this in the year, wife and I received a letter from old Grandfather Jones. He is now living and praying for me, and no doubt does so every day in my town, Cartersville. That old man summoned us all down to his double log cabin in our county, for he is a poor man now and has always been a poor hard-working man, to celebrate his golden wedding. At first I did n't think much about it, but the day before the wedding I said: "Wife, let us get in the buggy and go down to old grandfather's golden wedding." We went down there, a family gathering of children, grandchildren and great grandchildren, and we all gathered after dinner in the big room, as it was called. The large room was twenty-four feet square, I believe, or near that. And after dinner the old grandfather and grandmother sat in the center of the room, and all the children and grandchildren and great-grandchildren gathered around them in a double circle, and the old man said: "Now, children, I do n't know how much longer I will be with you, but I want to give you a little history and some statistics. We have been married, your mother and grandmother and myself, fifty years to-day, and we have lived all this time in holy, happy wedlock. When I was a twelve-year old boy my mother and father both died, and I was bound out until I was twenty-one years old. When I was sixteen years old the Methodists started a protracted meeting in the settlement, and I went out, and God converted my soul, and I joined the Church. In a year or two they made a class-leader out of me, and in another year they made me an exhorter, and before I was twenty-one years old they made a Methodist preacher out of me, and I have been a local Methodist preacher now for nearly fifty years. When I was twenty-one I married this, my wife, and we have lived happily together for fifty years. The night we moved into our humble home, the first night after our marriage, I got down the old

Bible and read a chapter and started family prayers, and I have prayed night and morning in my home for fifty years. Nothing ever kept me from this duty. I have preached the Gospel in my poor way for nearly fifty years. I have been tempted many a time to give it up and quit. I have been tempted that I was doing no good; but I have prayed on and praised on, and now," he said, "here are these statistics: There are fifty-two of us in all, children, grandchildren, and great-grandchildren. Twenty-two of that number have crossed over to the other side, and sixteen of the twenty-two were children, infants, and have gone safe. Six were adults, and they all died happy and went home to heaven." And one of that number he was talking about, I had the honor to call my father. O, I saw him literally shout his way out of this world. "Now," said the old man, "twenty-two of them are safe in heaven. There are thirty left, and every one of the thirty left who are old enough to know right from wrong, have been converted and have joined Church except one." O, how I have prayed, and wrestled, and prayed, and had my heart bleed about that poor fellow, until at last God has saved him, and he is a preacher of the Gospel now himself. The old man said, "Now, I don't care much whether I go on up and live with them or stay here with you all. I am ready whenever God shall call."

Precious old grandmother, she has joined the hosts up yonder. I went off from there and said to my wife: "Wife, grandfather said every one that died had gone to heaven, and those that were here were all on the way but one. I have been wanting to go to heaven all my life, and, God helping me now, I can not afford to miss heaven."

Now, that poor old man is in Cartersville to-night, a hopeless cripple the balance of his life from a fall a few weeks ago. He was very low when I was preaching at Nashville, and when I got back to Cartersville and walked over to his humble home, he took my hand and said, "God bless you, my grandson; I did n't believe God would let me die until I saw you again." They write me now from my home, "Grandfather says he is praying for you every day." Thank God Almighty for such an ancestor as he is. Four of that old man's boys, my uncles, are preaching the Gospel to-day. I have two brothers; they are both preachers, and I want to teach my children, if God shall call them to preach, to go on. And if all of us together can gather a million sheaves, we will put them all in that old grandfather's crown and tell him, "Grandfather, you are the blessed one that taught us the way to God, and passed religion down to four generations."

Thank God for such a home as my old grandfather's was and is. Thank God that I belong to a religious family. Brethren, if I had lived in some families, nothing on earth could have saved me. But my grandmother prayed for me, my mother did, my father did, and my grandfather did, and when I was breaking away from every band that could hold me to God and rushing headlong to hell, God threw my precious father in my pathway and let me bid him good-bye, and then I turned around and said, "God being my helper, I am going to heaven with all who are going in that direction of the family to which I belong."

God help you mothers and fathers to begin a religious home. God help you to settle it now and forever. I intend to live a Christian life and set a good example to my children, because God has said if I sow to the Spirit, I shall of the Spirit reap everlasting life.

SAYINGS.

LET me say to you: If you can't help but one family in town, let that be the family which needs the help. I have got a profound contempt for folks who are always helping those that don't need any help.

I BELIEVE the greatest moral monstrosity in the universe is an impious woman. I can understand how men can be wicked; I can understand how men can be wicked and turn their backs on God, and live in sin; but the greatest moral monstrosity is a woman with the tender arms of her children around her, their eyes looking up into her eyes with innocence and love, and that mother despising God in her heart.

INTERIOR VIEW OF MUSIC HALL, CINCINNATI, O.

SERMON XIX.

PARTAKERS OF THE DIVINE NATURE.

"According as his divine power hath given unto us all things that pertain unto life and godliness, through the knowledge of him that hath called us to glory and virtue; whereby are given unto us exceeding great and precious promises; that by these ye might be partakers of the divine nature, having escaped the corruption that is in the world through lust."—2 PETER I, 3, 4.

THE first thing we notice in these verses is that according unto the divine power God hath given unto us all things that pertain to life and godliness. God is the source of all life, physical, intellectual, and spiritual. He is not only the source, but the preserver of all life. I am not only redeemed by grace, but I live by grace. I was born by grace, and I have lived up to this hour by grace, and I shall ultimately be saved in heaven by grace. Unto God be all praise, and all glory, because he is the source of all life, and he is the benefactor who preserves all life.

But I might say at this point that there are conditions upon which I may live physically, and if I meet them I live. There are conditions upon which I perpetuate intellectual life, and if I meet those conditions I live intellectually. There are conditions upon which I live spiritually, and if I meet those conditions I live spiritually. Peter says we become "partakers of the divine nature." What are we to understand by this expression? I may discuss more intelligently, and perhaps more satisfactorily, the results of a converted or renewed life; I may consider more widely the manifestations of a renewed heart than I can discuss the nature of these renewals—the how, the why, and the wherefore. O, how deep this water becomes when you get out in it! Whenever I reach the point of this text I say, "Father, take my hand; lead me; I do not know the way, but thou knowest the way. Lead me unto the way of everlasting life."

Brethren, there are some things we know, and some things we do not know, and some things we never will know here. But I thank God I won't have much to do in the other world but to learn, and have facilities that Harvard and Yale never give any man. I am going to practice what I do understand in this world, and study what I don't understand in the next. I am satisfied that's the best way we can dispose of these things we can't understand. Let's practice the Ten Commandments, and live upon a level with the Sermon on the Mount here, and then hereafter we will study the mysteries with the Teacher who understands and who can explain them. We may have the capacity for learning, but there's no one here who can teach these things. Science proposes to tell us some things; science has to deal with the past and present; but when I get to talking with scientists about the future, they don't know any more about it than I do. Science, after she burrows five thousand feet down deep into the earth, does not know what is beyond that point, because she has not been there, and after science has gone up in the air two and a half miles she does not know what is up beyond there, because she has never been up there; and when it comes to the great questions of eternity, heaven, and hell, science knows as little about them as any six-weeks-old babe in this city.

It is well enough for us, brethren, to take in hand and practice what we understand; and, after all, it is not the mysteries of the Book that disturb me; but I will tell you, the part of the Book that troubles me is the Ten Commandments and the Sermon on the Mount. O, how hard it is for me to live upon a level with them; and I never will be satisfied with myself in time or eternity until I can live upon a dead level with the Ten Commandments and the Sermon on the Mount.

When a man comes to me and tries to draw me out on the mysteries of the Bible, I say to him, "Sir, how are you on the Ten Commandments?" My friends, let us get straight with them, and let 's go on up. Let 's not try to get in the senior class at college until, at least, we have studied awhile in the freshman. That 's a good idea! Let 's not try to explain the mysteries until we understand and practice the plain things of the Book.

Do you enforce the command, "Thou shalt not steal?" If you do n't, you ought to do as the preacher did in Maine, where the business of the community was to get out and market logs, and where the great sin of the community was stealing logs. This preacher preached about it, but without success, until at last he found he must fit his text to the settlement in which he lived, and so he said: "Brethren, my text to-day reads, 'Thou shalt not steal—logs.'" Good Lord, help us to make the practical things of Christianity clear and plain, then the Lord help us all to live up to those things, for if I would be a scholar, I must be a practical worker of righteousness in time.

"Partakers of the divine nature." Brethren, let's talk sensibly. I grant you this much, brethren, that when you get on to this question of regeneration and of renewed nature, being born again, you are in the very whirlpool of the mysterious in Christianity. I do not think Jesus, when he preached his own Gospel among men for three years, ever mentioned the doctrine of regeneration more than once; and he did it then at midnight to one man, and that man the most intelligent of his day; and when Jesus mentioned it to him he staggered back and said, "How can these things be?" Jesus told him, "The wind bloweth where it listeth. Thou hearest the sound thereof, but canst not tell whence it cometh nor whither it goeth." My brethren, if this thing could be explained to men, Jesus would never have let Nicodemus walk off without a full explanation of the whole question; but, instead of explaining it, Christ seemed to push him off with the simple illustration. Now, why should I get on to the divine side of the question, and try to explain it to you? Christ himself did not do it, and why should you as a preacher, or I as a preacher, attempt to do the thing that Christ himself did not attempt to do?

"Partakers." When Christ announced the doctrine of the new birth to Nicodemus, he did it for all the world and for all ages. But be careful how you broach that subject, brethren, and do n't confuse men with it. That 's the point I 'm driving at. I like the way Peter touches on that question here, when he says, "Partakers of the divine nature." Being born again means simply born from heaven, or lifted up. I say that a man, until he is born from above, can no more live a life in the spirit of Christ Jesus than a rock can live the life of a plant, or a plant can live the life of an ox, or an ox can live the life of a man. That which is born of flesh is flesh. If you ever get to the spirit you will have to be lifted up. That 's the idea. A man can 't catch hold of his boot-straps and lift himself up, that 's a settled proposition; and the only hope of the race is the extended hands of God that lift us up, and I 'm not troubled about the Lord being able to lift me up, or being willing to lift me up, but my great concern is, will I ever push my hands up to God, that he may take me and lift me up? That 's the question.

"Partakers of the divine nature." Let us suppose a case, and let us suppose a sensible man, forty years old, if you please. He is a sensible merchant, a sensible citizen, a sensible father—in fact, a sensible man altogether. Now, it matters not what was the primal cause of his spiritual concern, whether it was the death of a good wife or the burial of one of his children, or the pungent words of an earnest preacher, or one of the sweet songs of Zion, or the kind words of a little girl. But all at once that man says in his soul, "I am wrong. I am out of harmony with myself. I am out of harmony with God. My life has not been right. I am sorry for it. I wish I were right. I would give the world if I were what I ought to be." He is pondering now. He is thinking. Somehow or another, just as soon as he gets alone, this question recurs again. It goes to bed with him and gets up with him; it goes to the breakfast-table with him, and goes to his business with him, and he thinks and thinks, and the more he thinks the more utterly he is displeased with himself, until by and by he begins to conceal himself somewhere, and reads the Bible. Suppose he is a lawyer; a Bible has been lying on the table in his office for ten years, and he never endeavored to conceal it from the gaze of those who came to his office, but he conceals the book now. He hears a knock at the office door, and he hastily conceals the Bible under the pile of books on the table before the client enters, and covers it up with his Greenleaf and Blackstone and other law-books. As long as he was a mean sinner he did n't care who saw the Bible in his office, but now when any one comes in he wants that Bible hid. What 's the matter with him? I 'll tell you. Every time any man comes into the room the Bible turns with its index finger to him and says, "Look at this rascal here! What a scoundrel he is!" And he wants it out of the way; he does n't want to be seen reading it; he does n't want it to be seen in his office, and if he prays at all, he will go off into some secret place. If he goes out into the solitude of the woods to pray, the least cracking of a stick or a twig in the woods will make him jump up; he would n't be seen praying for any thing in the world. Poor fellow! But he prays, and angels could not see a gladder thing in heaven than to look down on a fellow and say, "Behold, he prayeth." He has got so far along that he prays now. He goes on in this way for a day or two, growing more and more dissatisfied with himself, until finally he addresses a note to the preacher. May be it's the very preacher of whom he said, "I'll never listen to that man again." The preacher comes around to see him, and he says: "Sir, there's something wrong with me. I do n't know what it is. I'm out of harmony with myself, and I'm growing more and more heartily dissatisfied with myself every day. I do n't know what's the matter with me at all." The preacher talks with him and encourages him. He goes to Church, and now he is at the altar, perhaps, to be prayed for; and, may be, six weeks pass, but all at once he turns loose all earthly hope and all earthly plans, and falls into the arms of Omnipotent love, and realizes "I am a saved man."

Now you ask, "When was he saved? When did he become partaker of the divine nature?" Was it when he looked up and said, "Glory to God?" Was it when he wrote that note to the preacher? Was it when he was hiding the Bible that day? Was it when he was down on his knees praying? Was it when he went to bed and could n't go to sleep that night? No. That man was made a partaker of the Divine nature when he said that first day, "I am wrong, I wish I were right. I would give all the world if I could get right with God." The Divine nature touched his heart and the dead man lived again, and it could never die again until it struggled into life and joy and peace in the Holy Ghost.

Brother, do you see that? Is there a man here that never had a touch of the Divine nature in his dead soul? Have n't you felt dissatisfied with yourself? Listen, brother! The sin against the Holy Ghost is said by some to be, when touched and moved by the Divine nature, willfully to drive from your heart the only thing that can perpetuate your life and carry you to joy; and he who stabs the only influence that can save him, is a man who commits suicide upon his own mortality. Brethren, if you have it, cherish it for all time; give heed to it and foster it. Take care of every divine touch on your soul, and let it live on until it is like a rose, blossoming out into beauty and perfection.

Now, let us escape "the corruption that is in the world through lust." God has given us his great blessing; and, brother, do n't you trouble yourself about the Lord's readiness, and willingness, and ability, for all you need to do in the universe is to trouble yourself about whether you will cooperate with God in this great matter. Here, I see a man as he ascends the narrow, rocky, difficult pathway up the Alps; on and on he goes, until at last I see he reaches a point in the pathway that is impassable; he is on this narrow cliff and he can no more pass that point than he can fly. And that man's personal means, in so far as the reaching of the top of the mountain is concerned, are exhausted. He can't get any further. But he has a guide along, and his guide says to him, "Now you can pass that rock," and the guide lies down on the rocky path and pushes out his brawny arm and hand, and says, "Step on this hand here and I will pass you up and around that rock, and you can step safely on the other side," and the guide pushes his sleeves back, and the man steps on the brawny arm and hand of the guide, and passes safely round, and presses on his journey to the mountain top. There is a point, brother, in every man's experience that he reaches before he goes to heaven, where human power gives way; but blessed be God, the divine Savior lies down and tells you, "Step on this hand, and I will pass you safely round, and you can pursue your way to glory."

Did you ever step in the Savior's hand, brethren? If you have n't, you have to do it before you can get to glory. Put that down! I will tell you; Christ passed me around that rocky place, but I had to go to it before Christ could help me to get around it; and before that I had to press the balance of my way alone, stepping on the pavement as I walked. Christ helps a man only where he can not help himself. I never pray for any thing but that I do my best to answer my own prayer, and right where I get out of breath, that's where God comes and finishes up the job for me. It's all foolishness to pray God to do something for a man that he can do for himself.

I wish I could see five hundred stalwart men and women here to-day rise up and say, "God has touched my heart, and it shall blossom into eternal life. I have the resolution, the purpose, the desire to be good, and, God helping me, I start out on that line to-day." Well, some of us say, "How is it that some men get along easier than others? See here! Here's a man, and it's no trouble for him to live right. He can get along without trouble in the world, but I have the hardest time of it of any poor fellow on earth." Brother, I'll tell you. Largely your trouble is owing to the fact that you never started in, and you never meant any thing when you did start. Look! See that engineer on his engine. At the movement of one muscle of his arm on the throttle, that engine rolls along sixty miles an hour. He shuts off the throttle, turns the air-brakes' lever, and the engine slacks up and trembles and stops. "What an easy thing it is to run an engine," you say; "why it's the easiest thing I ever saw in my life." But you'll have to go behind the throttle, brethren, before you'll get the secret of that rapidly running and easily controlled engine. If you will get up here I'll show you. A few years ago you could see hordes of hard-working men digging and tunneling those mighty hills yonder, and filling up the valleys, and cutting mighty trees down and hewing cross-ties from them; you could see miners far below the ground digging the iron ore; you could see brawny men at the furnaces dumping and smelting that ore; you could see the poor fellows working at the puddling furnaces, almost burning up with the intolerable heat; and again down in the bowels of the earth you could see myriads of colliers busily digging the coal that is to fill that engine tender, and, brethren, if you will only go behind that engine, you'll not think it's so easy to run one. You say Christian people get along easy; but you go behind their lives, go underground, I might say, and see how they pray and strive; and how much they give, and how much they have suffered. If you will go behind and see their conscience, you won't think it's such an easy task to live right after all. You must get behind the throttle to get at the secret of how easy it is to run an engine, and you must get at the inside of a Christian life to see how it moves to the good world!

I'll tell you, if you'll start out to-day and do as the best man in this Church does for the next six months, you'll be as good as he is when the six months are passed. No man can be religious without living religion, and no man can live religion without being religious. The rule works both ways. If the means of grace won't take a man to God, then what's the use of the means of grace? If family prayer, secret prayer, that Bible, joining the Church, baptism, taking the sacrament—if all those things won't take a man to God, what are they for? That's the way to talk it! If that street out yonder does not lead on down town to the bridge across the river, if it isn't a highway to reach a destination, then what's it fit for? What do you want with a street if you ain't going where that street leads? What do you want with means of grace if it is n't to take you where you want to go?

When Matthew made the trip to the good world, where did he start from? He was what we would term down South after the war, a "scalawag." You know what a scalawag is, do n't you? Well, scalawag was the term we applied to a Southern man who held office under the Federal Government. Matthew was a Jew holding office under the Roman Government. I reckon Matthew was considered then a scalawag. Christ came along when Matthew was sitting at the seat of customs—he was a sort of tax-gatherer—and Christ said to Matthew, "Follow me." Now, brother, if, when Matthew shut up his tax-book and took after Christ, he did n't have religion what did he have? He had it as sure as you live; and when a man quits his meanness and gets to doing right, what 's the matter with him if it is n't religion? Did you ever know an old sinner to do that? Some say, "Well, I know he 's religious because he shouted." Yes, and I 've known men to shout a mile high in August and be drunk before the first day in October. Here are two fellows who join the Church to-day; one of them shouts, "Glory to God," and the other is as mum as can be. Next Sunday, when the preacher takes up a missionary collection, the mum fellow gives him five hundred dollars, and the shouting fellow a nickel. Which has the best religion?

"Partakers of the divine nature, having escaped the corruption that is in the world through lust. And besides this giving all diligence." Be busy in your religious life; be faithful to your vows. Start to-day and say, "In heaven I shall rejoice because I started in earnest, I carried it on in earnest; and, therefore, God will say, 'Well done, thou good and faithful servant; enter thou into the joys of thy Lord.'" God bless you all, brethren, and help you to get started in the way of everlasting life. God never saw a minute since you were born when he was more willing to save you than now. You will never see a minute in your future when he is more ready than now and more willing than now. Come, for all things are now ready. The Lord help you to come to-day and give yourself to him, and say, "The question is settled now for time and eternity."

SAYINGS.

RELIGION is like measles; if it goes in on you, it will kill you. The trouble with a great many Christians in this city is, religion has gone in on them. Keep it broke out on hands, feet, and tongue.

WE may give ourselves to the Church—that is helpful; we may give ourselves to good associations—that is helpful; but there is no self-dedication that is worth much in this world, except that self-dedication that gives the life to God.

SERMON XX.

THE GRACE OF GOD.

"For the grace of God that bringeth salvation hath appeared to all men."—TITUS II, 11.

I LIKE this term "grace." There is a fullness of meaning about it that ties me to it. The grace of God! Thank God for that word. Grace, in the plainest, commonest sense among men, gives us about this idea—kindness unmerited, undeserved favor, and goodness. We are not only redeemed by grace, but something more; we are born by grace, we are preserved by grace, we shall be raised from the dead by grace, and we shall be introduced into the kingdom everlasting by grace. It is grace that laid the foundation of our salvation, and grace is the cap-stone. It is grace that started me upward, and grace has brought me safe thus far, and grace will take me home to God. I appreciate very much the old hero who said, when his wife walked into his room and saw him gathering up the covers from his bed into a bundle and taking it into his hand, "O, precious husband, what are you doing? Are you distrait?" "No, wife, I am gathering up all my good works in one bundle and casting them from me, and lashing myself only to the plank of free grace, and I will swim to glory on it." That is the only good route after all—free grace.

Now, this free grace is from a gracious Father. It is not only what I receive for nothing, but what I can take for the asking. How gracious is Christ when we can but just see the hand that dispenses, and the gracious heart that pours forth, like the gush of a river. My Father, your Father, that Father who has called me and you; who went out to look after me, and who, when he found me, brought me back, has promised to be with me to the end.

While I was in my house, some time ago, this little incident stirred my heart very much. The nurse came in to breakfast. She was only sixteen years old. She was not just the kind of nurse that my wife wanted, but she was a good-natured creature. After breakfast I was there in the room, reading, and my wife said to her, "You can go home and tell your mother that I do n't want you any longer, and tell her to come over and I will pay her the balance of your wages." I did not hear her retreating footsteps until I looked up and saw the tears running down the face of the girl as she turned toward my wife and said, "Mrs. Jones, please ma'am, do n't turn me away. I know I am the poorest servant that you ever had, but please let me stay. I will do the best I can."

I said, "Wife, look at those tears. Do help the poor thing if you can." And then I fell to thinking in this way: "Look at me! I have been the poorest servant that Jesus Christ ever had; and if Christ should say to me, 'You can go; I do n't want you any longer, I discharge you from my service,' I would fall down at his feet and say to him, 'Blessed

Master, I am the worst servant that you ever had; but O, Lord, do n't turn me off. Do n't drive me away!'"

O, blessed Lord, blessed be the name of Christ, he never does discharge a loving servant who offers to do the best he can. Let us die in his service. O, the glory of living and the grandeur of doing in his service! This Christ is our Father. The Fatherhood of God and the common paternity of men explain a great many things to us in this world. O, what a blessed Father. It is a glorious thing for the entire family of men to look up into a Father's face and listen to a Father's loving words. God, my Father! Can there be any thing sweeter than this thought? Can there be any thing more inspiring? Yet there is something sweeter still. There is something more inspiring still. The Bible represents God as our Brother. O, elder Brother, with all thy goodness and perfection, with all thy warning voice and with all thy advisory commands, blessed Son of man, I adore thee. But God, my Mother! Let me hurry to put my arms around thee and fold my heart to thy great loving heart. God, my Mother, the Mother of us all! And all these came from the grace of God. Your Father, your Brother, your Mother, your best Friend—this grace of God that bringeth salvation! Blessed be God for that grace that bringeth salvation.

Now, let us take the text. There is no metaphysics in it. Let us talk on its practical, plain, common-sense teachings, and its words will be worth remembering—this "grace of God that bringeth salvation," this grace coming from a loving Lord, this grace coming through the Son of God, to fallen men. Grace! I can not estimate what this grace is worth to the human race. I can estimate any thing in this city. I can estimate how much its real estate is worth. I can estimate how much its bonds are worth. I can estimate how much its railroad stock is worth. I can estimate their worth by their market value. But I can not estimate the worth of this grace of God by what it costs, but only by what it brings. Brothers, we are not redeemed by corruptible things, by silver and gold; but by the precious blood of the Son of God; that blood which has never failed us from the time the bloody sweat burst from Christ's brow in Gethsemane, and it will never fail us until the recording angel dips his pen for the final record. He has said to us, "Peace on earth and good will to men." That blood was shed, brother, that grace might abound to us all in all its fullness; for God loved us so much that he gave Christ to us to redeem us. He nothing extorts from us, but bestows kindness upon us. God loved me with all the depths of his heart, and because God loved me, Christ died for me. And that is the idea. That is the record. This grace comes through the all-blessed Son of God. It comes to me, and it comes to you; and it comes not to bring any one short of salvation.

Now, the grace of God makes me first feel myself a sinner. That is great grace. That is wonderful grace. It is the grace of God that gives me a right to stand among the people of God. But listen. The grace of God bringeth salvation in all its incomprehensible sense to you and to all men. Thank God for that glorious expression; now we have what we seek. It is for all mankind. How gracious this sympathy. It knows no political division. The African sun may turn the Ethiopian black; the Mexican sun may turn the Indian yellow, but before God they stand disenthralled through the universal efficacy of the atonement of Jesus Christ. That grace brings salvation to all men, in all ages, who believe in Him. Thank God I can be recorded on the book of everlasting life, if I say that I believe that Jesus died for me. I thank God I can believe that he died to save not only me, but my wife and my children. He died for you and your wife and children, and for all of us.

Blessed be God for a Gospel that comes to save the race and all the race. And I fully believe, my brothers, that if in the vast universe of God to-day there was one man who could not be saved otherwise, Christ would come back here again and go up to Calvary and shed his blood once more to redeem that man's soul. But I can not believe that Jesus Christ came to this world and shed his precious blood to redeem some of us and refused to die for some others. No, that is not compatible with the loving heart of God, much less with the word and the justice of God. I believe in the elect and the non-elect, but I believe that the elect here are those who seek God, and that the non-elect are those who won't seek God. And it is for you to look out for election, and not God's business.

"The grace of God that bringeth salvation hath appeared unto all men." I believe that if we are lost, at least we shall walk through the halo of the rainbow of God's mercy gilding our vision, and the waters of salvation purling in our ears. I believe, too, that there will, at the last, be a crown in heaven, a palm of victory, that will no head cover, around no brows be wreathed. I believe that there will be, for each lost soul, a golden harp from heaven whose strings no fingers shall ever touch. If I am lost at last I can charge it to no other source in the universe except that I would not be saved.

"The grace of God that bringeth salvation hath appeared unto all men." Now God created man on a common platform, and when he redeemed me he redeemed all upon a common platform. And if one man falls within it all fall within it, and when God lifts up one man—blessed be his holy name—all men are lifted up. I used to hear the old hard-shell preaching about the covenant of God with Christ, to save some and to doom the rest. If there is any covenant of that kind between the Father and Son, I have read my Bible through in vain. It is "grace of God that bringeth salvation to *all* men." And you will never bring on any millennium that is not based on that. You can not bring it on any other plane than a Gospel that will save the whole race of man. It will save one just as certainly as another. I sometimes think that Christ seems to glory in getting hold of one of those hard cases we see sometimes, and showing how God can make him into one of the nicest, cleverest, and most delightful fellows in the whole country. I like that kind of grace, and that sort of Gospel. Now, do you want that kind of a Gospel in this city? Do you want such a Gospel here as that which the grace of God brings to men? Do you want a Gospel that will start you right? Do you want a Gospel that will make you lead a sober life? Do you want a Gospel that will make men pay their debts and tell the truth? The Gospel of Jesus Christ does that, and all that; yes, and a thousand times more than that. Do you want such a Gospel? If you do, then brace up, take hold of it, and pitch into the work of getting it with all your might. You have a chance to get it now. Whosoever wills can do it. Every one will have to tote around his own load. Every one will have to fight his own battle. Do n't try to do as other people do. Will you act regardless of what your set does? Will you help to save sinners? You can never save a man until you can show him his need of being saved, until you can show him that he is a sinner. And the only way is to just show him that he is a sinner, and show him how to go to God, and then men will go to God. May God gird your loins for the fight, for to God will belong the victory.

SERMON XXI.

LIVING SOBERLY, RIGHTEOUSLY, AND GODLY.

"Teaching us that, denying ungodliness and worldly lusts, we should live soberly, righteously, and godly in this present world."—TITUS II, 12.

BETWEEN the first lesson in grace and eternal glorification hereafter there are a good many lessons to be learned, and a great many duties to be performed. Grace does not come gathering us all up into a huddle, and then, by some omnipotent force, catching us around and carrying us into glory, just as we are. Jesus Christ said: "I go to prepare a place for you." Blessed Christ! I will leave that all to thine own taste and thine own wisdom. This much I feel sure of: If I get there at all it will be a grand place prepared for us. My only concern now is whether I am ready for such a home as Christ is going to prepare for me. That's the point. And, after all, heaven is a prepared place for the prepared, and the only question with us is, Can I ever be suited for such a place?

Brother, will you give earnest attention, prayerful attention, to this question of preparation? "Teaching us!" Ah, what a teacher Christ was! He taught us things that Socrates never dreamed of and Plato never thought about. O, what a teacher he is! Go sit at his feet and learn things that shall make you wise unto eternal life. This

Christ came teaching us this. What is the matter with the world? It won't listen; it won't be taught. The great trouble in this nineteenth century is not the inculcation of truth so much as it is the extraction of error. The great trouble is not that the truth is not preached, but there is no room for the truth. Why, the head of every man, woman, and child in this country is already chock full of errors—brimming full, as we say sometimes—and it is a philosophical statement that no two substances can occupy the same space at the same time; and in a man with his head full of error there is no room for truth. Every man in these latter days is full of his own notions.

That brother out there says: "It is my opinion that there is no harm in a social game of cards: it is a scientific game." Another says: "It is my opinion there is no harm in a social dram, and there is n't any harm in club life." Now, one of the wisest men and most prudent men in this city told me of your leading club: "That institution is manufacturing drunkards every day;" and no harm in club life! Well, if you defend that proposition, brother—and I call you brother, and you are as much my brother as any Methodist in this town, and I like you, too—I have got nothing against you; I am just after that devilment you are carrying on, and that is all. If I can strip you of that I would as soon run with you as any other man in this town; but I am not going to run with you until you do shut off some things. If I did I would be no better than you are. Why, my brother, you must have mighty little sense left if you think there is no harm in an institution that has a bar-room in it. Now, what do you say? You will have to go out of the English language and the realms of rhetoric, and the finest-spun theories of earth, and beyond all the climaxes of rhetoric, ever to defend any thing that has that hellish institution in it—a bar-room. How are you going to defend a thing that has a bar-room in it? How can I defend myself in the moral government of my home? Now, for instance, my neighbor has a bar-room in his house, and I say to him, "This is demoralizing to your children." He says, "O, but I have the prettiest pictures in my home you ever saw, and we have the nicest suppers there, and we have the nicest social times." "Well, your pictures and your suppers are all right, but how about your bar-room?" "O, well, I tell you the truth: nobody goes in there except those that want to." And then the dear things—the clubs have entertainments for ladies! They lock up all those places—the nicest, you know—and carry the ladies all through it, and the ladies are charmed with it. "Why, this is one of the nicest places I ever saw." O, the gullibility of a woman! Well, I would as soon be gulled a little as to be as miserable as some of you would be if you knew the fact. Sister, just be gulled on. It is more pleasant.

Then some say, "It is my opinion that I can be as good out of the Church as I can in the Church, and it is my opinion that there is no harm in a dram. There is no harm in a social dance, and I can stay at home and read my Bible and be as good as if I go to Church; and my opinion is this, that, and the other;" and so it goes on until every one of us in this country is full of his own opinions. You have n't got a thinking man in this city; but every man in town is full of opinions. One or two great minds do the thinking for Europe; one or two great minds do the thinking for this continent; and yet all humanity is chock full of opinions, and we become encased in these opinions, and we can 't be reached. To show you how it is, see that old farmer sitting yonder in his cabin, smoking his pipe quietly and honestly; and you see that electric cloud passing over his house, and it deposits the bolt down with crushing power upon the cabin, and it strikes the lightning-rod, and runs up the chimney and runs down and throws itself off into the earth. And the old farmer sits and smokes his pipe just as if nothing had happened. You see the Gospel of Jesus Christ flashing in its beauty and power above the heads of the multitude, and it descends in soul-saving power and strikes this outside encasement of your opinion, and runs down and throws itself off into the earth, and you stick your thumbs in your vest-holes, and you go out and say, "That preacher has his opinion, and I have mine." You are not touched any more than a stump or a log. That is the truth about it.

"My opinion! My opinion!" Where did you get your opinions? You got them from some old colonel or some old judge, that just loves to sit around corners and give his opinions about so and so. "That is my opinion," and the old colonel has just got that fresh from hell. Then that young buck goes out on the street, and he says, "My opinion." He has just got that from the old colonel, you know. When he says that he tells a lie. They are not his opinions. Where did you get your opinions? Folks like you were coming to this country fifty years ago saying, "It is my opinion there is no harm in a dance; in my opinion there is no harm in a social game of cards, and in my opinion there is no harm in a dram." There is less originality about your sort than any class of people on the face of the earth. You are not only wicked and mean, but you have got no originality about you. I have often wondered why sinners in this country did n't get up something new. They always quarrel with us preachers about originality. We have got nothing new, they say. I wish you would rack out a few new views on your side. Have you got any? I will tell you what, if you will just turn your opinions around on the back track, and put the dogs after them, the dogs will tree them in hell. That is right where they come from. I will tell you another thing. They are going back there some of these days, and they are going to take you with them if you do n't learn. That is their business up here—to go for your sort and take you back to perdition with them. Where did you get your opinion about no harm in a dram? I know you never got it out of the Bible, for it says, "Look not on it," much less drink it. Where did you get your opinion that there is no harm in a social game of cards? Did you get that from the wrecked and ruined lives of thousands of men who to-night have wasted their lives and are ready for the last step to perdition? Where did you get your ideas about a social dance? O, I beg you to look upon the virtue of thousands of women that has been danced away in the history of America, and then tell me there is no harm in the social dance? Will you look at these questions? Will you? "No harm in this," and "no harm in that!"

Now, I am going to drop back on a proposition that I will stand on in time and in eternity: No man and no woman has a right to an opinion on a moral question. Now, I do n't say he has no right to an opinion on a geological question, or an astronomical question, or a doctrinal question, but I say on a moral question. Look here! The only way to tell whether a thing is crooked or straight is to put the straight edge to it, and not be guessing at it. And God's blessed Book speaks in unmistakable terms, and tells me what is right and what is wrong, and I am making worse than an idiot of myself sitting down and giving my opinion upon any moral question. Brother, you take the straight edge and that will determine the straightness or crookedness of any proposition in the universe! What is your opinion worth after all? Let us see what opinions are worth, anyhow. It is my opinion that this glass, which I now lift in my hand, is a gold tumbler. Does my opinion of this tumbler change it the least particle in the world? The tumbler speaks for itself. It is glass, "and that fellow standing behind it is a fool if he thinks it is gold," do n't you say so? My opinion of a thing does n't change it one way or the other. A thing is true or false in itself, and my opinion does n't change it. Now, if a thing is right it is right; if it is wrong it is wrong, whatever may be my opinion.

"Ah," but says another, "I am honest in my opinion." Well, let 's try it again. "Honest in my opinion!" I am honest in my opinion that that is a gold tumbler. The tumbler says, "I speak for myself. I am glass, and there is an honest fool behind me talking about it." You see, do n't you, I am very honest about it. Well, I will show you how far a man's honesty will take him. In Macon, Ga., one of the prominent physicians of that town had a patient very low, and at twelve o'clock at night he visited the patient and left a prescription to send immediately to the druggist. When the prescription was filled, the attendant was to give it according to direction. The next morning the doctor returned early and saw the patient was worse. "Did you send for that prescription?" he says. "Yes." "Did you give it to her?" "No." "Why?" They walked to the mantel and took a note accompanying the prescription, in which the druggist said, "I fill this prescription and send it to you, but it would be certain and sudden death for any one to take it." The doctor read it, and he says, "This is an insult. Bring me some water, and I will show you whether it would kill or not." He drank the prescription down, and I think it was only thirty minutes until he was dead and past all recovery. He was just as honest about it as a man ever was about any thing in the world, but that poison in there did n't care whether he was an honest fool or a dishonest one, you see. It did its work all the same.

And now all this talk about "honesty in this, or in that opinion" is n't worth a cent in the world. The question, brother, is, have you gone to the straight edge and had this determined? That is it. Now, this grace comes, "teaching us that denying ungodliness and worldly lusts"—the first lesson grace ever teaches the poor sinner is this, that you are wrong, and you ought to get right. I can recollect it just as well, thirteen years ago, that this grace came like a mighty influence to my heart. I saw in all the depths of my nature that I was not right. I saw that my life was all wrong, that my character was wrong, and that all the tendency of my being was wrong. That is the main point in a man's life, to see that he is wrong—and then, blessed be God, there is but one more thing, and that is to see how to get right, and then, with the will of a consecrated man behind it, heaven will be at the end of your journey.

"Denying ungodliness and worldly lusts." Real Christianity has two forces—rather it is negative and positive. Christianity in the best sense of the word is negative goodness and positive righteousness. If negative goodness is religion, then let 's get some blocks of wood for our members, and defy earth to bring a charge against them. But negative goodness and positive righteousness are like the two poles in an electric battery; you must get the positive and the negative together before there is power.

Honest principle and honest practice are what we want in this country. Righteousness! What 's a man's Presbyterianism or Methodism worth here now on the market? How much can a Presbyterian hypothecate his religion for in this town, and how much can he draw on it here? That 's the way to talk it! Hear me! You go down town to-morrow and go to a banker and say, "Mr. So-and-so, I want to borrow five thousand dollars." "Yes. Can you give any nickel-plate security for it?" "No. I have none at all, but I 'm a Presbyterian." "You are, eh?" "Yes, I 'm a Presbyterian." "Well, sir, you can 't borrow any money on that around here." That 's the way it will be! Well, here 's another man that wants to borrow money, and he goes down town to the banker and says, "I 'm a Methodist, sir, and I want to borrow so much." "Well, sir," the banker will say, "you can 't borrow on that sort of a commodity around here, sir." Brother, try to get a merchant to credit you on your religion. "You 're a member of the Church, are you?" he 'll say. "Yes, sir." "Well, I can 't let you have any money on your Methodism; it 's not worth a cent in this town."

Talk about Bob Ingersoll. He has n't been in my way of getting men to Christ any more than a broom straw! Bob does n't get in the way, but these thousands of members of the Church do. There 's hardly a sinner out of the Church that some member of the Church has n't acted the dog with, and every time you preach Christ to that old sinner, he racks out a carcass of some member of the Church, and says, "You make him settle his honest debts with me, and I'll be religious." That's where the rub comes in, brethren. It's not Bob Ingersoll, its dishonesty between man and man in the Church and out of the Church. That's it!

You want to get a religion in this country that is running on a "straight edge." Do what we say we'll do! If there's any thing I like it's for a fellow to strike a gait to heaven, keeping it up all the way, never slacking up, but, if any thing, rather quickening it a little. If you start out in a trot, God bless you, don't drop back into a walk. If you start in a walk, hold that pace, or else go in a double-quick.

There's many a fellow who'll go to New York city and do things he wouldn't do here at home for any amount of money. A man who will act in that way is like a fellow I heard of down in Paulding County, Georgia. One day the preacher asked him to come up and give his soul to God, and the fellow said, "I guess you're mistaken in the man. I don't live in this county. I live in another county." There's a great deal of that sort of characters in this world, brethren. A man that is just as good in one place as he is in another under all circumstances, everywhere, is a sober-minded man! He lives soberly. We don't mean a man who does not drink whisky. Any fool in this town knows he can't be religious and drink whisky.

Red liquor and Christianity, as I have said many a time, won't stay in the same hide at the same time. As one goes down the other's coming out, sure! I know that! "But," you say, "I drink it for my health." Yes, and the devil would as soon have you ruin yourself in that way as in any other, all he wants is to get you! Talk about a Christian drinking whisky! If I were a sinner I 'd never drink whisky, much less drink it being a member of the Church. Whenever I see a member of the Church going into bar-rooms and frequenting beer-gardens and beer-saloons, I expect soon to see him have the sign of it on his nose. I 'm so glad liquor paints its own sign. A Christian drinking whisky! "Soberly" has no reference in the world to liquor—it does not get down that low, but it refers to a man going on his way rejoicing; the same man, every day in the week, and everywhere, and as religious abroad as he is at home—that is what we call a sober-minded man, a man who takes the broad view of life, and regulates his life every day by the precepts of the Lord. Job was a sober-minded man. Look at him there as he goes into this, that and the other difficulty. He goes along through them all a straight cut all the way. Sober-mindedness to a Christian is what governors are to a stationary engine. See that sixty-inch saw out there in the woods; it 's going to run through a big log; and as it moves along, the little governor lifts up and feeds more steam to the piston-head, and the saw wades through that log and runs out at the other end, and the little governor lets down, and the saw runs the same revolution to the minute whether it 's in the log or out. That 's what we call sober-mindedness, and Job, when he had lost all of his worldly property and lost all of his children, lost his health—all was gone; I see him run out of every difficulty, saying, "Though He slay me, yet will I trust him," and he 's running the same number of revolutions to the minute as he was in wealth, and health, and prosperity, and blessedness in the Lord.

That 's what we want in this country—sobriety. I will bear a bit, and hope a bit, and endure a bit unto the end. We want a Christianity that can go to the dungeon, and take the stripes and the imprisonments, and take crucifixion even, like Peter. Look at him, how they brought him to the cross; and when they were nailing him to it, he said, "Do n't crucify me with my head upward, but crucify me with my head hanging downward, for I am not worthy to die like unto my Lord;" and it is said he hung with his head downward and preached the Gospel for two days and nights. There 's sobriety in the grandest sense of the word! I wish we could all get saved and die sober in this sense.

The next thing is righteousness!—Soberly as to myself, righteously toward my neighbor. Brother, I believe in a religion that straightens me out all right and makes me straight with the world! Righteousness means—what? It means straightedness, right-mindedness! I 've seen a mechanic turn a great long sixteen-foot plank on edge and run his joiner and smoother over it a time or two and shave off a strip as fine as tissue paper from one end to the other. That 's straight now! When you get your life in such shape that God can run his smoothing-plane over it and cut a shaving as thin as tissue paper from one end to the other of it you 're getting right then.

I want to see the Church of God Almighty get honest! I 'd like to see a good many of these deacons and elders get to disgorging some of this ill-gotten money they 've got piled up in this town!

This city strikes the key-note for the price of every thing, nearly—meat, and all that the poor African in the South and the poor white man in the North must perpetuate the lives of himself and his family with. If you 're a member of the Church I want to peel some of the bark off you to-night. I mean the Christian men who are gambling on the bread and the meat of the poor negroes and white people. God bless you, your Stock Exchange is going to throw out enough wood to feed the communistic fires of damnation in this country. Mark what I tell you! You keep on speculating on the meat and bread of the poor people, and you 'll catch it some of these days! I know the sentiment I 'm talking now will be called communistic. But it is not so. I never uttered a communistic sentence in my life! I 'm down on it, and I 'm doing my level best to keep you from piling up the fuel that will burn you, every thing you have, some of these days. What right have you to speculate on the commodities on which we live in this country? I do n't want any of that sort of money piled up for my children. You may pile it up for your children, but it 'll ruin them, sure, after you 're dead and gone. I do n't want to live in a house and raise my children on money procured by any such influences—influences which to say the least, are questionable from a Christian standpoint.

I tell you, my congregation, let 's have some righteousness running through this country. The Church has gravitated down until we 've got so low now you can 't ditch the Church off to save your life. We 're backing water on it. It 's a fact! Getting down too low! Honesty! Honesty! I 'll tell you what I want. I want every man who professes to be a Christian to get his money honestly, and I 'd rather have an honest dollar bill than to have a questionable—to say the least—million-dollar bond.

"Teaching us that denying ungodliness and worldly lusts, we should live soberly, righteously, and godly in this present world." That presents to us two plain propositions—quit wrong and do right. Then let 's say, after these two questions are settled, we will start out to-night to live soberly, righteously, and godly in this present world. Soberly! I like a sober-minded Christian, one that goes on his way smoothly, persistently.

I 'll tell you what you want in this city, and in every other place in America, too: we want a revival of honesty—not a revival of shouting or singing, but of honesty! I 'm down on homestead laws, down on bankrupt laws, and on all that thing. "O," you say, "that won't do. It 'll leave men without a dollar in the world." God bless you, I 've been there many a time myself. Many a time I did n't have a dollar in the world, and had a wife and four or five little children to feed. What 's the matter with you? Would you rather have a million dishonest dollars in your pocket than have an honest dollar? I would n't. If I handle money at all, let it be honest money!

I'll tell you another thing! Whenever a man who owes money can live in a fine house, and board with his wife, and be agent for his wife, he ought to have his name changed, and take his wife's name. Agent for his wife! I'd want to find my shroud and get in it before I could be agent for my wife. I'm never going to be agent for my wife or board with my wife; I'm going to have her board with me!

This question of honesty, brethren, must be brought down to plain, simple propositions. You speculators, if you run the price of bread and meat up, are taking the dollars and cents out of the pockets, and the food out of the stomachs, of the poor of this land, and if you run it down—then for you what? La, me, I can't pray, to save my soul, when one of you speculators gets gobbled up! I can't help looking on and saying, "Gone, thank God." I try my best to feel sorry for one of those fellows, but I never could get up any sympathy for 'em.

Right is right! Wrong is wrong! That's the truth about it! Honesty is the bed-rock on which we build, if we build at all! I know what I'm talking about, too. Righteousness! I do n't believe in your homestead or bankrupt laws. I've been to where I paid the last dollar I could pay at all; I still was a hundred dollars in debt, but I never took advantage of the homestead law or the bankrupt law. I 'll tell you another thing: when I started out on a poor circuit, preaching in Georgia, men who could have held me up said, "I could have more confidence in that fellow if he would pay his debts." Right then my precious wife, though raised far above that plane, was doing her own cooking,and ironing, and all her own housework, and I was cutting wood and doing every thing I could to help her, out of the poor, meager salary I was getting; and I saw at last my wife reach the point where she did n't have a good dress to wear, and I did n't have any thing to my name but an old coat, but I 'd pay two dollars and a half out on a note I owed, and, thank God, I paid the last dollar. You can pay, too, if you try; but, and under-derstand me, if you can pay, and do n't do it, God will put you in hell for it, and you need n't go mouthing around here on any other proposition either! If you can 't pay your debts, do your level best, and if you can 't pay a thousand dollars, pay a copper cent; do your best, pay every nickel you can, and God will bless you and take you to heaven yet, but he won't take these people to heaven in a day who can pay their debts and do n't do it. If you will just do your duty and live right, and pay your debts, God will look after your sort. God help you to make a start for glory to-night!

SERMON XXII.

PURITY OF HEART

"But the wisdom that is from above is first pure."—JAMES III, 17.

CHRISTIANITY proposes to do nothing less for us than to give us pure hearts. There is no such thing as a pure life emanating from any other source than a pure heart. About the hardest thing a man ever tried to do is to be a good man with a bad heart—to be a Christian without religion. Put old patches into new garments and they rend every time; put new wine in old bottles and they break every time. To be a good man without a good heart is the most up-hill work a man ever undertook in this world. I see a great many lives that are wrong, and I can see that the only hope of those lives is in the purity of heart given by the Gospel of Jesus Christ.

"Blessed are the pure in heart, for they shall see God." No corrupt tree can bring forth good fruit. No good tree can bring forth corrupt fruit. A salty fountain can not bring forth sweet water. O Lord, give me

"A heart in every thought renewed,
And full of love divine;
Perfect, and right, and pure, and good,
A copy, Lord, of thine.

"O, for a lowly, contrite heart,
Believing, true and clean,
Which neither life nor death can part
From him that dwells within."

Now, brother, has your heart been in the cleansing fountain?

"The wisdom that cometh from above is first pure." O, Lord, wash my heart, and I shall be whiter than the snow. Do you know what that means? A great many Churches do not put any stress upon what we call a pure heart, a clean heart; but I thank God that the grand old doctrine of Christian purity still lives in the world; that there is enough water in the river of love to wash the last speck of dirt out of the human soul. I thank God for that grand old Bible doctrine that still lives among men. Find me a Church that does n't accept it, and I 'll show you a first-class literary club—the Lord's crocheting society, or something of that sort. I 've seen Churches put on airs and strut around, and call themselves the Church of God, and they 've come up at last to be nothing but the Lord's crocheting society; and if they go to heaven with any material to work on they would n't be there three months until they 'd have all the angels hung full of lace. Crocheting society! O, they 'll get up the nicest little suppers for the Church, and little grab-bags, and they 'll have the nicest little entertainments in the world, and run the nicest little socials, and all that sort. But, when it comes to rolling up their sleeves and pitching in to rescue the perishing and save the fallen, "O, no," they say; "we never do that sort of work at all. But we had a nice little supper at the church last evening." The idea of a Church having a supper or an entertainment to raise money! It's a disgrace to God's cause on the earth. I don't blame you, good sisters—it's that or nothing with you—but I blame your stingy husbands.

A Church of purity! Purity! The wisdom, the religion that comes from above is first pure—a pure religion, a religion that is pure in thought, and pure in life, and pure in all manner of conversation. I recollect in one town where I was preaching, to illustrate the point, I met a young man on the street one day, and he said to me: "Mr. Jones, Mr. So-and-so is never going to hear you preach any more." I asked him, "Why?" "Because he says you are the vulgarest man he ever heard talk in his life in the pulpit." "And who is this man that says so?" I asked. And the young man said that "It is Mr. So-and-so, a bar-keeper down town." A bar-keeper! And do you notice, "To the pure all things are pure." I was preaching a very close sermon on the sins of society, and an old husband got up and walked out of the church with an angel clinging on his arm, and he said to her: "Wife, I would not have had you hear that batch of vulgarity for a thousand dollars." And she answered: "Why, I thought it was the sweetest sermon I ever heard in my life." To the pure all things are pure.

I wish some of the low-bred people that have called me vulgar in this city would get to be decent themselves, and then they would not hear the vulgarity in what I say. It is not what I say that is vulgar, but it is how they have been bred. "To the pure all things are pure." O, for pure society, and pure homes, and pure Churches, where all things are pure, and then it would never be necessary for such things to be discussed.

The religion that comes from above is, first, pure; for you get that sort in the Bible. Have you, brethren, got the religion that makes you pure in your heart, and pure in your life, and pure in all manner of conversation? That is the first thing to see to, and that is the grandest thing of all—a pure heart, and that heart the sovereign of all your life and actions. Have that, and it indeed shall make your life pure.

Religion is "first pure, then peaceable." That is the second point. I wish that we could see that we are often too quiet in this country. Jesus Christ said himself, "I came to send fire upon the earth. I came to put parents against children, and children against parents, and neighbor against neighbor." There can be nothing accomplished in this life without warfare—without fighting for it. Now, do n't understand me as wishing to make an incendiary speech, and ordering you to bring out pistols and guns. I have the utmost contempt for all that sort of thing. The fighting, the warfare, that I talk about is the fight of the forces of good against the forces of evil. And the strongest force is going to triumph every time.

Let me offer an illustration of what I mean by a pure and peaceable mind. Suppose that the devil

FARWELL HALL, CHICAGO,

WHERE MR. JONES'S NOONDAY MEETINGS WERE HELD.

were elected mayor of this city by an overwhelming majority; and suppose that the common council had been imported from pandemonium as aldermen and councilmen. Do you know of any other spot in town where they could put another bar-room? Have they not got them already just as thick as if the devil were actually running the town? Could you support any more if you had them? That is the way to look at it. I do n't think that the devil would try to open another even if he had his aldermen running it. They have got now all that they can look after. Do you reckon if the devil and his councilmen from pandemonium had a saloon-keeper brought before a judge of this city they would let him be fined for the offense charged against him less than five dollars? Come down to facts. Do you believe they would, brethren? Do you believe that lewdness in this city would be allowed to escape with less than a dollar fine? Do you believe, my hearers, that if the devil himself were having the thing done up for him in this city in person he could do it better than it is being done by his agents? We want warfare in this town. We want soldiers; not those that fight with the sword, but those who carry on a fight in which evil is overcome with good deeds. God make good men, efficient workers, and soldiers of the cross as thick in this city as bar-rooms are! and then we will take the initiative for Christ, and overcome evil with good. I tell you, my congregation, when we look out on this city, I do n't say my first prayer is, "God save and keep the city in holiness," but "God save her from herself!" She is cutting her own throat and committing suicide. You can not put the stabs of four thousand saloons in a city without doing any thing else but kill it. You can not sprinkle lewdness through the streets in this city, as God has sprinkled the heaven with stars, and do any thing else but commit suicide for your city.

"First pure, then peaceable." Now, I want peace, and I thank God for all the peace we have in the world. But, brothers and sisters, as long as you are peaceable, and things are as they are, you have not the religion that comes from above. For it says, first, pure, and then all other things follow it. When you are this, then you can proclaim a peace with God that shall smile upon you, and perpetuate itself forever. But we don't want any peace now. That would be just what the saloon-keeper would like you to do—to keep your peace; to keep your mouth shut, and create no stir about it. They cry, "Peace! peace! Don't raise any issue here."

Now, have you, my brethren, a clearly defined moral issue in this town, or have you only a moral question? Suppose all your ministers were to turn themselves loose in the discussion of the issue next Sunday morning, and were to throw into the enemy's camp the hot shell and canister of the Bible. Suppose the preachers were to turn upon any evil in this city. If they would, the walls of the fort would fall, and the white flag would be run up. O, me, how much are we to blame in this city for this state of things! In my town is a harness-maker, a good, plodding member of the Church. One day the Baptist pastor, Brother Hayden, called upon him, and he said to Brother Hayden: "The barrooms of Cartersville are prospering, and you preachers are to blame for it." "What do you mean?" indignantly asked Brother Hayden. "I mean what I say." "Explain yourself, sir." "Brother Hayden, you have got four hundred members in your Church; the Methodist preacher has four hundred, and the Presbyterian two hundred, and any man in Cartersville ought to have known that with those thousand members with you for the work of God, you could have raised an issue and got the evil out of Cartersville if you wanted to." Brother Hayden slipped away full of that brother's words, and he went to the Methodist parsonage, and he told his Methodist brother what the harness-maker had said to him, and they talked it over, and then he went to the Presbyterian brother and told him, and talked it over with him; and the very next Sunday the few pulpits of Cartersville turned loose on whisky shops, and when the next election came and went, the whisky was gone forever. Thank God, the pulpit has not lost its power! It has just lost its voice—that 's all. Now, my brethren, let us for twelve months, for twelve weeks, in this city, take up the big question, and let us pour in the hot grape and cannister on these things.

"First pure and then peaceable." Peaceable! Brethren, we do n't want any peace in any sense until we have rid ourselves of those things that are cursing our city and our neighbors. Let us have war, and carry our warfare on our knees through this city. Then let us carry the city to the mercy-seat of God, and then to heaven. Let us carry on the war until we get pure, and then peace shall reign.

Pure, peaceable, and gentle! I like gentle Christians and gentle horses. I wonder if that word does n't mean the same thing in both places, for there is not a more valuable thing than a gentle horse. He is not worth so much for his looks or his gait, but he is perfectly reliable. Could we only be as faithful in our place as a gentle horse is in its place! A gentle horse you can hitch to any thing in the world, and it is perfectly safe hitched up anywhere. But I will tell you an animal that I despise more than any other animal is a malicious horse. He won't work at any thing, excepting with one of those fancy-striped buggies, and then he will go. But hitch him to a wagon, and he won't pull even the traces tight. Many a man is like that horse. He never saw a prayer-meeting. If you hitched him to a prayer-meeting, he would run away with it. If you hitched him to a family prayer, it would take three wagons to take in the pieces after he got through with it. He never had a Christian's collar on, and yet he has professed to be on the Lord's side for years.

"First pure, then peaceable, gentle." Now, brothers, I want to ask you in all love, are you what God calls a gentle Christian. Are you a gentle Christian in the sense that you do the Lord's works, whatever he wants you to do, and whenever and wherever he wants you to do it? That is what we call a gentle Christian in the best sense of that word. When I say a gentle Christian I do n't mean any of those quiet fellows who never open their mouths. That is not the sort of gentleness the apostle means when he speaks about "gentle." Some of you are mighty gentle; so gentle that the devil has nothing to fear from you. You never said a word against him in all your life. You are silent when you ought to be talking, and talking when you ought to be silent.

The religion from above is first pure, then peaceable, gentle, and "easy to be entreated." I like that sort of religion that you do n't have to sit long with, and beg with, and plead with in order to get a few dollars or a few good works done. I like the Christianity that says to my call upon it: "Put my name down for any amount you need. Call upon me for what you want." That is "easy to be entreated;" that is easy to be induced to take the proper steps in any movement; that is willing to do any thing and any work that is for the good of others. If a preacher says: "I will tell you what I want you to do. I want you to take charge of such and such a thing," you want to say, "I will do any thing for the Lord and for the salvation of souls to God."

I was once riding along behind a man in the pine woods. His wagon was stuck in the mud and remained stock still. It was mired down, and when the driver got off and pried one wheel up, he had no one to drive the horses, and he was in a bad fix because his team had balked. But about the same time I got up with him, a gentleman came riding by on a mule, and he told the fellow to go again and pry up the wheel, saying, "I will drive your team for you." The gentleman then took a switch and went to the balky mule and whipped it until it stood firm against the traces, and then he licked the other mule until it leaned against the traces; and as each would drop back, he would make it stand against the collar, and as soon as he pulled at the heads of the mules they carried the wagon out of the deep mire as if it had been a thing of life. My brothers I want to see every man of you lean against the collar which is around your city, and if we do that we will carry the whole thing out of the mud, and carry this city to God. Why not? Now, some of you have probably got your dignity outraged by my talking about collars and horses in connection with yourselves. Let us talk about souls, and how to get them out of the mire of sin.

Now, in this lesson we draw about this picture as to what I must be like. First, I must be pure in my heart and life. I must be peaceable in my nature. I must in all my ways be gentle. I must be easily entreated, and must be all these things without partiality and without hypocrisy. I will tell you what some of us say we would like to have in our meetings. "I would like to have Colonel So-and-so, and Judge So-and-so, and Major So-and-so in this meeting." Now I do n't go much on these colonels and judges and majors, so far as I am concerned. What do you want with them? Brother, sister, this is where I stand, "without partiality and without hypocrisy." There is not a poor tramp begging his way through this town that I am not as glad to see coming to get his soul saved as I am to see the richest man in this city. His soul is worth just as much. The others are valuable. "They make us preachers work ourselves to death," said a preacher to me. "In a town I was in there was a rich old colonel, and he was not a member of the Church, and I said to myself, I will angle for him. And I angled for him for about three weeks, but I never got him. But I got about sixty other first-class sinners. And the next year I said again I would angle for him, and I did angle for him about four weeks, but I did n't get him, but I got forty converts; and the next year I was determined to get him, and I angled for him for four weeks, but could n't get him, but I got in seventy-five other sinners. And, Brother Jones, those two hundred souls would not have been brought to Christ if it had not been for Colonel So-and-so." Old colonels are good nest-eggs. They make preachers work themselves to death trying to get them. There has been many a poor fellow got into the fold of Christ in this way. I open the door of grace to every body; but if there is any body that I want to see come to God it is the poor fellow who never had any thing in the world, who never will have any thing, and who will die as poor as he has lived. The poor are the ones I want to get in. I want to tell you that it is the tramp and the poor men and the humble classes that need religion and they feel its influence the most when they get it. A young lady who belongs to one of the wealthy families of this city said, when she was invited to come to this meeting: "What do you want me to come to the meeting for? It is poor folks who get religion." She did not think it was for rich folks to have it. O, what a transition it must be from a four-story, marble-front mansion, down to the depths of damnation at one leap! O, what a fearful thing that is! And thousands such as she are making that leap every day. God help us to do what we can for them, as well as for the poor of this great city. Christ said himself, "The poor ye have always with you." Let us go among them and bring them to Christ!

Now, just one word and I am done. When I was in Louisville at one of the meetings, fifteen men were taken to the front pew and knelt there as penitents. There never had been fifteen such characters in that house of God in all its history. They were ragged and dirty. O, how degraded they were. One of them was a man named Harney, a son of the editor of the Louisville *Democrat.* He told me that he had been drunk thirty years. While I preached, the pastor talked with the poor fellows and prayed with them, and when he was about to dismiss the congregation, he said: "Brethren, you see these poor ragged and dirty men. They are seeking religion. It is just as necessary to put clothes on them and make them cleanly as it is to pray with them. Now I want these official men to take them to the bath-rooms and barber shops, and dress them up neatly." This was done, and the next day and night when they were at the meeting you would not have known them again. And these fifteen men were converted to God. Now, what was the result? I was there twelve months after that, and thirteen out of those fifteen men were as bright, useful Christians as any I met in that city. One of them had backslidden, another had died happy and gone home to heaven, and the pastor of the Church told me: "I have had no more active man than Mr. Harney has been." For five years he had been one of the principal clerks in the Louisville and New Albany depot, and now he was sound and well clothed and in his right mind.

That is the kind of religion we want in this town. This is the kind of religion we are going to give you Christians. We are going to tell you to go down if you want to go up. The way up is down. God help us to throw our arms around the perishing of this city. And let us work for the poor fellows; and when a poor fellow comes up here, let us take him to Christ. I have seen a whole community moved by one of those old colonels getting saved. I saw every body in the meeting crying, because the old colonel came to God. Let us cry over these poor fellows. Let us do our duty by them.

May God bless you in your home life, and may he crown you with everlasting life.

SERMON XXIII.

PRISONERS WITHOUT HOPE.

"Turn you to the stronghold, ye prisoners of hope; even to-day do I declare that I will render double unto thee."—ZECH. IX, 12.

BRETHREN, there are many words in this text we might dwell at length upon. They are rich in their meaning to us. But the special words we want to direct your attention to are these: "Ye prisoners of hope." And we stand squarely upon the word of God and upon the pages of that Book we have just laid down. If you say, "That is not the word of God," then, sir, I shake hands with you with an affectionate adieu at this point of the service. I have no Gospel to preach to you to-night if you deny that the word of God is the truth of God. I get this text from that book, "Prisoners of hope." This expression presupposes that there are prisoners without hope, and when I turn over the pages of the Book I have just laid down, I find there are three classes of prisoners without hope.

The first class we mention are the angels who sinned against God and kept not their first estate, but were cast down in chains of everlasting darkness to await the final judgment day; and while atonement was made for man, and offers of mercy and pardon were given to men, those angels cast down in their dark and doleful estate, this moment are still without a ray of hope or a spark of heavenly day. While the sweet songs of the Gospel make melody in our hearts, and while the Gospel of love and promise is offered to fallen man, we are assured by that Book that no glimmering light or ray of promise has ever pierced the dark dungeons of despair that hold in their chains these lost and damned spirits. But we know not how to sympathize with angels. Angels are unlike men; they know not and they have not gray hairs, and wrinkles, and old age, and graves, and death as we have. We never see an angel, we know not how to talk with an angel; but, brother, while they are in chains of everlasting darkness, let us look upon the picture and shudder and dread, lest it may be true that men from America will take up their eternal abode with those lost and damned spirits in hell forever.

There is another class of prisoners without hope, and that is men—men who lived here and died in this city amid its Gospel privileges, and have lived and died without hope and without God in the world. If that Book teaches any truth plainly and pointedly it is this: There is no knowledge, or device, or repentance in the grave whither we are all tending. This is a world of sowing—that of reaping. This is a world of character-building—that at the judgment a place of award and assignment. The good go to heaven, the bad go to hell. I believe all Bible-reading men believe in punishment, and the only point at which men who revere and read the Bible differ at all, is in the duration of the punishment. Some men say it is not eternal, and when you prove to my mind that punishment is not eternal, then with the same logic you prove that heaven is not eternal. The same adjectives that apply to hell apply to heaven. "These shall go away into everlasting punishment, these into eternal bliss." But, after all, brethren, I am not so much interested as to the duration of hell. I will answer your question as to the duration of hell, if you will answer me a question: "How long will sin last?" If you will tell me how long sin will last, then I will tell you how long hell will endure. When in the history of America, or in the history of eternity, will the lie you told yesterday be any thing else than a lie? When God can make things that ought not to have been, as they ought to have been, then I can tell you when sin shall be wiped out of the universe. And it is n't a question of eternal fire, but it is a question of eternal sin, of eternal remorse, and eternal regret!

If we are taught any thing plainly in the Scriptures, it is that what we do for eternity we must do for this life. Mother, look me in the face. Have you ever prayed for your wayward boy since he breathed his last? Have you ever knelt at his grave and said, "O, God, save my boy from hell and save him in heaven?" Wife, have you ever knelt at the foot of your husband's grave and prayed, "Gracious Father, forgive his sins to-day and take him to heaven?" Listen to me a moment. I care not what the record of your prayers may have been previous to his last breath, none of us have prayed for loved ones since they breathed their last. Mother does not pray for son, wife does not pray for husband, father does not pray for loved ones who are dead. No, the common sense of humanity teaches us that as the tree falleth it shall lie forever. There is nothing in eternity that can undo the evil deeds of time, and if you live and die impenitent you have settled the question, and settled an eternal issue that involves the loss of your soul.

"Prisoners without hope." The old couplet may be true, that

> "While the lamp holds out to burn,
> The vilest sinner may return."

But when fate snuffs the candle and it goes out, it is out forever. None of us looks to the fact that there is a chance beyond the grave. Brother, will you meet me in your thoughts at this point; all the time that I have to prepare for eternity is between this and my grave; between this and my shroud; between this and my last breath. The great issues of eternity that involve eternal happiness or eternal damnation are wrapped up in the few hours between me and my dying couch. Will you face that fact a few moments, and look in the face of that proposition, and will you settle your mind squarely on it while we discuss these fearful questions to-night?

Your heart in your bosom is but a drum beating your funeral march to the grave, and every heart-stroke is numbered, and, when numbered, is proof of the fact that your heart shall beat one time less in all this world before you. Brother, suppose you knew that clock that sits upon your mantel at home, ticking away each fleeting second, would stop before you got home to-night, and you were to know that if that clock stops while you are away that you will never see your home again, and you will be carried in a corpse. Brother, if that little pendulum in your bosom stops beating before I am through preaching, if you have come here impenitent, then you shall be a prisoner without hope forever. Is it true that the gasp or two of the last dying moments are the only things between me and that doleful state of everlasting despair—"a prisoner without hope?"

I have preached the Gospel in twenty different States, perhaps, in America, and I may preach it in every State in America. Thank God for open doors! I may preach the Gospel in China. If God were to call me there, I would go as willingly as I came to this city; but there is one place, brethren, I have never preached, and there is a spot on which I never intend to preach, and that is at the cemetery. I will never stand among the tombstones of earth and beg dead men to come to God and love. But God has spared you from among the dead and brought you to this hall to-night to hear the Gospel. Will you wisely consider, and well, the proposition; that gray-headed man sitting here, this gray-haired woman, this young man—will you consider to-night that just a few more passing days and the question of eternity with you will be settled forever? I notice in reading the papers that more than one man I have preached to earnestly has gone to eternity, and, young as I am in the ministry, I have preached the Gospel to thousands of men who have rejected it, and to-night they are prisoners without hope forever. O, sad thought! In Knoxville, Tenn., I pointed my finger one night at a man, without special aim, of course, and said, "It is now or never with you," and two weeks after I left the city I got a letter from a friend saying, "The man you dropped your finger on that night died last night, and he said, 'It was then or never with me, I saw, and I surrendered my heart to God,' and he died happy in the faith, and has gone home to heaven."

O, sir, trifle not with the extraordinary means of grace; trifle not with the truths that will bring thousands of souls to Jesus Christ; trifle not with the meeting where the sermons are repreached to almost a million of souls through those secular papers. God has brought to bear on you extraordinary means to save you from hell, and may you give yourselves to God before these extraordinary means leave you forever. God has thrown these services between you and your grave; God has put this gracious revival between you and your coffin, and will you overleap all these things and die a sinner and pass into eternity unsaved, a prisoner without hope, forever?

Brother, let's you and I say, "If there is but one man who goes to heaven out of this meeting, God helping me, I am going to try to be that man. If there are only a half dozen saved, I will, with God's mercy, be one of them." O, sir, rush into the open gate, and find mercy and peace while it is called to-day. You may trifle with me and the meeting, and the calls of mercy; you may trifle with the prayers of God's people; but while you trifle with us you are trifling with God, and, above all things, you are trifling with your immortality, and you can not afford that. Friends, may be this sermon and this service to-night are put between you and this eternal issue that shall settle the question forever. Will you take the time and meet the issue squarely to-night, and say: "Whatever other men do, I do not intend to die impenitent?" As the rabbis used to say, every man ought to get religion one day before he dies; and, for fear you die to-morrow, had n't you better seek religion to-day?

But there is another class of prisoners without hope. They are, thirdly, men and women who live, and walk, and talk to-day in this city that are just as certain to be damned as they walk and talk to-day. Do you know there are whole families in this town that not one—father, mother, son, or daughter—has ever been religious? This is the saddest thing you can say about any family God's sun ever shone upon. Neither father nor mother, son nor daughter—not one of them—ever made any pretensions to being religious! And I can tell you another thing: I could be irreligious four years as a husband, twenty years as a son, and twenty-four years, I say, as a brother or a sister; but I could not be irreligious twelve months with a precious child looking up in my face. When you talk to a man of sense about his children, if you do not arouse his conscience and probe his soul it is because he is dead already to every thing that is ennobling and promising.

There are noble citizens all around this town; they are men of prominence, men of means, men of influence, and there they are—prominent to-day on the side of the devil. I was asking to-day what Church Mr. So-and-so belonged to. "He does not belong to any, but he attends a certain one." "Well, what Church does his wife belong to?" "None at all." I can see how a man can be Christless and godless, but the profoundest enigma in the universe to me is a godless mother—a mother with innocent children hanging about her neck! O, mother, are you here to-night? If you are I pronounce you the most fearful monstrosity in all the moral universe of God.

Prisoners without hope! Whole families irreligious! And do you not know right here a father, and son, and grandson, not one of whom for three generations has ever been religious? Look at that picture. I will tell you another thing: If you will take a boy or a man whose grandfather and father never were religious, and who is himself irreligious, I would almost as soon preach the Gospel to a horse or to an ox as to preach to that grandson.

"The iniquities of the father shall be visited upon the children to the third and fourth generations." What a sad thought that is! Shut out heaven to your children and to your grandchildren! There are families in this town who, if this meeting were to be protracted in every church in this city, and in every theater, every rink, every hall, would never put their feet in those places. They have deliberately, not with their tongues, but in all the thoughts and acts of their mental and moral constitution, said, "For time and eternity I never intend to try to be religious!" Prisoners without hope! Why, sir, when I walk these streets and take the hand of a man, and feel in my heart, "There is a man that never intends to repent, who intends to die as he is, I would as soon shake hands with a dead man as to shake hands with him. He is already dead to all that is true, and noble, and good. He is dead to heaven, and dead to God, and dead to the blood of Christ, and dead to every thing except the excruciating pains of eternal damnation. O, what a thought, what a thought! A prisoner without hope! He may be walking on the street; may be sitting in the hall to-night. Will any man in this audience to-night say that every man here will be saved? If there is only one to be eternally damned, which one? I wonder which man it is sitting and looking at me to-night that is just as certain to be damned as he hears my voice this moment. O, sir, is it you? is it you? A prisoner without hope!

I praise God for preserving me through a wicked life up to twenty-four years of age. I praise him in time, I shall praise him in eternity, that he kept me alive until I found peace with him and felt that he was my Father and my Friend. I can look back over my past life at the flash of a pistol in my face, the dirk in some enemy's hand, the crash in some railroad accident; I can see where I just missed death by a hair's breadth. O, my God, if I had gone unprepared as I was then!

O, blessed Savior, I praise thee to-night that I found the

> "Fountain filled with blood
> Drawn from Immanuel's veins;
> And sinners plunged beneath that flood
> Lose all their guilty stains."

Thank God, I live to see the day when I can testify to the world that Jesus Christ hath power on earth to forgive sins. I will praise him forever.

A prisoner without hope! Will you go through to the benediction of this revival service and stand out as a monument of what indifference and recklessness and prayerlessness can do for a man? Will you do that? Can you afford to do that? Can you? If we live right and die right, even while our friends mourn around our dying bodies they rejoice. When Bishop Marvin, the grandest man the Church of the South ever had, returned from his tour around the world and came back home and died in his own quiet, peaceful home, and his wife gave up to God the best husband and father and preacher the South ever knew, she looked upon his pale corpse and clapped her hands together and said, "God is so good to me to let my husband go to heaven from his own quiet home." The very fact that he passed out into heaven was the source of infinite gratitude to his wife.

I heard Dr. Haygood say, "I stood by the deathbed of Bishop Pierce, our grand old Georgia bishop, but he did not die; I know he did not die. He talked to me up to the very edge of the grave, and I almost literally saw him sweeping out of this world into the arms of God." Die! No, sir; no, sir. If I had had any doubts of the immortality of the soul, they would have been removed in the first town I was a pastor at. Dr. Ingraham, a quiet, peaceful, good man, a kind neighbor, who loved God and loved all mankind, was stricken with that fearful disease, consumption. And finally he was taken down to his bed, and for three long months he was a hopeless invalid, and death came hour after hour and stripped his bones of their flesh and muscles. There he was, under the potsherd of death, until death had robbed him almost literally of every ounce of flesh. I believe he was the thinnest man I ever looked into the face of when death had done its worst upon him. The morning, when death walked into his room and drove the dagger to his heart, he pushed his bony arms behind him and raised himself up, and just as death struck him the last blow he said, "Life, eternal life!" and swept out of his body to go home to God. O, brother, the man that can meet the dagger of death and cry "eternal life" is proof to all mankind that we shall live beyond the dying moment. Ah, me, to live beyond that time, and not to die beyond that time!

A prisoner without hope! The lost soul! Lost! lost! lost! Brother, can you meet your dying minutes without making your peace with God? If you can, you are a braver man than ever I want to be in time or eternity. And to the poor wandering one to-night let me say just one word more. Turn to the stronghold. The gates of mercy are open. You need not die, you need not be lost. But turn to the stronghold. And what does God say? "Even to-day I will render double unto thee." And may God draw reluctant hearts to himself to-night and bring us all to heaven!

SAYINGS.

EVERYBODY ought to keep good company. There is not an angel in heaven that would not be corrupted by the company that some of you keep.

I LIVE here a prisoner of hope, but at last I shall overleap the circle of friends above my dying couch, and my spirit shall be free and mix with the freemen of heaven forever! As long as the star of hope shines over my pathway I am ready for every good work.

EVERY man in the world ought to be in the Church of God. When I see men out of the Church I want to save them. To you men who drink, swear, and break the Sabbath, let me say: I have a right to-day to get as drunk as any man in this city. I have just as much right to steal something to-day as anybody. Who gave you the right to get drunk and swear? Who gave you the right to tell lies? Who gave you the right to profane God's name? I have just as much right as you to do it. I won't do it; you ought not to do it, and you know it.

SERMON XXIV.

A Sermon to Commercial Travelers.

I THOUGHT ON MY WAYS.

"I thought on my ways, and turned my feet unto thy testimonies. I made haste, and delayed not to keep thy commandments."—PSA. CXIX, 59, 60.

THE commercial travelers of America, or perhaps the more refined name is "the angels of commerce," are unlike the angels of old. Their visits were "few and far between," but your visits are every day and everywhere. Your name is legion. I suppose you number three hundred thousand in the United States. What an army that is! What a power for good or evil in the morals of America! What a power for good or evil in the commercial interests of America!

If the Lord Jesus Christ had an army of three hundred thousand active agents—as active in preaching love, joy, peace, long-suffering, gentleness, goodness, and faith, as you are in pushing the sale of your goods, it would not take Christ long to bring America to his feet, and my greatest desire and earnest prayer to God is that the day may come when you will carry your "grip-sack" in one hand and your Bible in the other and do business for both worlds on every trip and everywhere.

I have been thrown a great deal with commercial

men. I am a sort of drummer myself. I lead a sort of drummer's life. I spend very little time at home. It 's a great sacrifice. My children see very little of me. My wife sees very little of me. God forbid that in my absence from my wife and children there should ever be any wandering away from them. I never want to see the day come in my life's history when my wife shall detect any difference, any impatience, any restlessness when I am at home.

The curse of a traveling man's life is this: You are from home so much that you can hardly be at home when you get home. How many of you have brought tears of blood, almost, to your wife's cheeks by your treatment of her, by your selfishness and indifference to your home? Home! Home! The sweetest place on earth!

> " Be it ever so humble, there 's no place like home."

My wife has a claim upon me, my children have a claim upon me. And as a commercial man in one sense I can talk to you commercial men, and say this to you: Not only would I spurn and scorn an act that is unfatherly and unhusbandly when I am at home—but, brother, when you go home show your wife that home is the sweetest spot on earth, and peace and joy will reign in that home.

Well, there 's another thing. The question comes up, " If you have never been a commercial man you do n't know how hard it is for a commercial man to be a Christian."

I have received one letter that I want to read

to you, before I go into the text. The writer says: "I am a New York 'drummer.' I believe in Jesus Christ, my Savior. For some years I thought I could not sell goods without drinking with my trade, but finding it a dishonor to my Lord, I wrote down in my order-book, 'No more drinks, of any kind, so help me God,' and God blessed me. And I did the same with smoking, and ever since I wrote that down I have never used tobacco in any form. Hallelujah! I want to offer you, my brother, my sympathy and help, for I know what a terrible struggle it is to quit tobacco; but God is not unrighteous, and he will give you more joy than tobacco ever gave. Just tell the drummers that God saved me and kept me from sin and tobacco, and his grace is sufficient for me."

You see how he puts it—"sin and tobacco." I rather like that. Now, he says after having given up sin and tobacco, "I sell as many goods, to the best trade, as any man on the road."

That's a great declaration, brother, and if it is necessary in order to be a successful drummer that a man must be a blackguard, and a dram-drinking, and a dirty story-telling one—if that's essential to be a first-class drummer, I would rather be a third-rate dog than a first-class drummer.

Now, brethren, I wanted to read this letter in the first place because, if I can establish the fact that there is just one pure, good man, there is a living, walking demonstration of the fact that we can all be religious—every one of us. When you find only one man in a calling who is good it is a demon-

THE TABERNACLE, CARTERSVILLE, GA.

BUILT BY SAM P. JONES.

stration that every man in that same calling can do that same thing and be good.

Now, we come to the text, "I thought on my ways." Brethren, inconsiderateness is the curse of the world. Men won't think about the right things. They will think about stocks, and bonds, and money, and trade, and about what they will do, and what they will wear, and what hotel they will put up at, and by which route they will go. They will think about every thing in all the enterprises of life, excepting about their ways, their manner of living, their acting, and where they are going to for time and eternity. And now if we can spend a few minutes in wise, candid, considerate, and conscientious thought on this matter we shall be benefited by this service.

"I thought on my ways." Are my ways the ways of a wise man? Would a sensible, wise, thoughtful man live as I am living? Would he go where I am going? Would he do as I am doing? Would he talk as I am talking? Would a wise, prudent, careful, sensible man run on the line that I am running? You know your lives, brethren. You know how you have been running during the past two months, during the past four months, during the past year, during the past ten years. You know how you have talked and acted on the road. Will you run your mind back and ask yourself the question: "Are my ways wise? Have I done the best I could? Have I lived the best life that I could? Have I been prudent in the selection of my comrades? Have I been wise in my conduct in the midst of their company? Am I wise at day-time and at night-time, and in all my ways? Does wisdom control me in my life, in my words? Does it control my character? Am I seeking always the best means for the best end?" That is wisdom. Knowledge is one thing, wisdom is another. Wisdom is the skillful application of knowledge; the employment of the best means to secure the best ends. Now, knowing that I can go to New York is one thing; and then wisdom steps up into the province of knowledge and selects the nearest route, the best route, the fastest train, the most expeditious way to reach it.

Now, here I am a moral being. I have been selling goods for thirty years, but I must quit that some time. I have to die; and when I quit selling goods, I want to be able to look back and say in the midst of my family, "I have never done any thing that dishonored God or degraded my own being." And no drummer, no commercial traveler, can expect any thing valuable in his latter life where he has previously resorted to bad means to reach his ends, I do n't care what sort of an end that may be. I have received letters that have brought questionable transactions and questionable ways to my notice on the part of commercial men. Some of you use the bottle, some of you play cards and gamble—that is, you say, you put up just enough to make it interesting. And some of you use means that I could talk very plainly to you about, if it were not for those innocent, pure faces with bonnets over them here to-day.

"I thought on my ways." Brethren, I have seen the day when I could be devilish, and mean, and do a heap of bad things, but I can say honestly this thing, that a man could never hire me to do mean things by the month. I never got that low down from God. I never was on the market for sale. I never propose to let myself out to do any one's dirty work. I always had as much of my own as I could stand. And I will tell you another thing—the man who would ask you to do those things that are wrong in themselves in order to push his trade, is the man that sooner or later will become your worst enemy, and he will never give a dollar to your wife and children after he has ruined and debauched and damned you. The man that does evil that good may come, is only going to do evil to you in the end, and bid you a final farewell when you cease to be useful to him; do n't you forget that. "Well," you say, "what are we to do." Well, I will tell you what I say to that. When there is no reputable, decent, honorable, upright employment in this country for me to get, I am going to emigrate to the poor-house and die there. I would rather be an honest, pure, and upright man dying in the poor-house, than be a man who has to make himself disreputable and be dishonest in his own eyes in order to make a living. I feel that, and no man can be reputable when he uses bad means to a good end. It's no matter how good the end is as long as the devil himself runs that way to earth. He wants you to push trade in that way. There is only one line of business that you can run that way properly, and that is the liquor traffic. If I were running for that sort of business I would run it pretty lively. Every town I came to I would get them all drunk. I would get my business well started in that way in every community I went into. I will tell you another thing. There is not enough money in this world to hire me to sell whisky and beer. And God Almighty will hold you responsible as a paid minion of those fellows who are trying to damn this country if you let yourself out for any such business. I tell you, that for all the drunkenness and the evil and the fearful misery and the wrecking of homes brought on by whisky in this country, the manufacturer of whisky, the wholesale dealer, the drummer who is hired by him, and the saloon-keeper who deals it out, are responsible. I am angry with whisky, but I am not angry with any man that ever drank it or ever sold it. I do n't get mad with men. I get mad with demijohns, bottles, and that sort of thing, and I get mad with every thing that will hold whisky.

"I thought on my ways." My life; what is it? Am I a wise man? Am I wise in the selection of my occupation? Am I wise in the carrying on of my occupation? Am I wise in the best sense of the word? And then we stop and ask ourselves this question: Am I an honest man of business? "An honest man is the noblest work of God." O, brother, an honest man is worth his weight in gold anywhere. And when you are so honest your employers will find you and they will double your wages. And how many of you have been turned off on that line? I will tell you there are just hundreds of firms waiting for some of you of that kind to be turned off. "I have thought on my ways." Am I honest and candid? If there is any miserable thing to do I would not be hired to do it. It won't pay. You will never get rich in misrepresenting things. You may go on for a while, but you will be like the farmers getting rich. Every pound they grow costs ten cents. They can not get eight for it. The only way they explain this style of doing things is to say they make so much off of it. If it were not for that they would be ruined.

Determine first, to work for none but an honest house. You drummers have the power in your hands to reform all the houses that do business through your agency. All that you have to do is to say to dishonest houses, "We won't get business for you, and when you employ a man that is willing to do your dirty work we will boycott you and advertise you as scoundrels everywhere we go." If you drummers took a stand like that what a grand thing it would be. You would say, "Such an agent shall not travel on the road. That house shall not be represented on the road. We won't have our fraternity degraded with any such concern. That is a good thing. My way is honest. I deal honestly. I do honestly."

Then again I stop and ask myself, Are my ways pure or impure? Purity is one of the greatest blessings that ever crowned a life. O, brother, about the dirtiest thing in this universe is a really dirty drummer—dirty in conversation, dirty in his thoughts, dirty in his life. O, brethren, let me say to you to-day, live as pure men. Never say a word anywhere that you could not say in the presence of a parlor full of ladies. And never go to a place that you do n't want your sister or wife to go to. And whatever you do let your love and vows to your wife be kept as sacred as the word of God is sacred. And I beg you, brethren, to preserve the integrity and purity of your characters and be pure men everywhere you go.

"I thought on my ways" to see whether they were pure or impure. I thought upon my ways as a father. There is many a commercial traveler in this country that is the father of a precious group of little ones at home. Father, what is your influence over these precious ones? What is your example to them? What is your light before your children? I have thought many a time of that father who, traveling through the snow, when he had got one hundred yards from his house heard his little son cry out, "May I go with you?" and he said, "Yes." The father walked on, but directly he turned and looked back and said to his child, "How are you getting along?" "Finely, papa; I am putting my feet in your tracks." And the little fellow was jumping from one track to another where his father's feet had been. The father was a wicked man. As he walked along in the snow with the voice of the little boy in his ears, repeating, "I am putting my feet in your tracks," he said to himself, "God helping me, I will straighten out my tracks. I will turn right about, and lead my boy in a purer, nobler, and better track all the rest of my days."

Now, father, let me tell you that your boys are putting their feet in your tracks. They will go to the same house that you go to. They will drink at the same place that you drink at. They will gamble with the same cards that you gamble with, and if you live long enough they will follow your track when they become men unless you so alter your life that you will be indeed a father to your children. When a man gets so that he does n't love his children, when he gets so that the pride of his heart is not with his children, then he is indeed beyond the reach of any thing that I can say to him.

Then, in addition to that, "I thought on my ways" as a husband. I have received a letter from a lady in this city. It was a long letter, a sad letter, a heart-ache letter, a letter that meant a great deal. God forbid that my wife should write of me and of my sins in that way. This lady says: "We lived happily together for more than ten years. In the last few years the growing indifference of my husband—he has been on the road so much—almost breaks my heart. I could not bear it if it were not for the love of God in my heart; and I pray every day that God will help me to bear it, and make me as good a wife as it is possible for me to be." A growing indifference! Now, I was head-over-heels in love with my wife when I married her, but I love her a hundred times better now. They circulated the story about me, in some town I was at that I had quitted my first wife. Well, I never had but one wife, and, God helping, I will never have but one. I am like the Irishman who said, "I hope I will never live to see my wife married again." Many a fellow in this State has lived to see that, and some of them have lived to marry them again themselves after being divorced from them. Somebody told me the other day that a judge granted a fellow a divorce six minutes after he walked into the court-room. That is a disgrace in any civilized country where such a thing is possible. I tell you that when you let up on your matrimonial relations, right then you let up on the very foundations of your life. There is not a doubt about that. Well, I happened myself to get a good wife, I do n't know how. But if I had got a bad one I would have stuck to her through thick and thin. I would not want to have her divorced from me and get her off upon some other fellow. Now, "I thought upon my ways" as a husband. I thought of the vows that I had taken that I would love and cherish and keep, and that I would always, even unto death, be true to her that I had plighted my vows to. I thought upon my ways as a husband.

And then "I thought upon my ways" as a citizen. Now, every man in this country is a good citizen or a bad citizen. You know what a bad citizen is? Now, suppose every body were like him, what sort of a country would we have here? Suppose every body drank whisky like him, what sort of a country would we have here? Suppose every body, you can say to yourself, told as many lies as I do, or was as unfaithful to his wife as I am, what sort of a country would we have? Brother, did you ever look at your duty as a citizen? Did you ever consider that you are either a blessing or a curse to your country? Did you ever consider you are a part of the body politic, and that it takes just one hundred thousand good citizens to make a city of one hundred thousand people a good city, and that it does n't take any more or any less?

Then "I thought on my ways" as a Christian. I thought of the vows I had taken to God. I thought of the promises I made to God. I thought over this whole question. Now, brother, let us come close to these thoughts. No matter how much you think or how little you think, God help you to think enough to do as David did when he said: "I made haste, and delayed not to keep thy commandments. I thought on my ways, and turned my feet unto thy testimonies." Brother, I want to say to you this: I am like the old lady, who, when a man asked her which is the way to heaven, answered: "Just turn to the right, and keep straight forward, and you will get there." Now, what we want you to do is to turn to the right, and make haste and delay not to keep the commandments of God; and, if you have seen that your ways are not right, turn. Do it at once. Just think of Alexander Stephens, of Georgia, who died a governor. "I made it the one great rule of my life," he said, "when I found I was in the wrong road, to turn right and keep there." If we are wrong, turn around and go right. If we are right, keep to the right, and keep straightforward, and keep so during the balance of our life, and take no more time to consider when you find you are wrong.

Make haste and delay not. But you say: "I want time to consider. I want to do this thing, and I want to do the other thing first." You do n't want to do any thing, except to quit your meanness and turn to God. There was one of the inquiry women-workers (I do n't know what you call them) who sat down before a penitent; and she said: "You need not be in a hurry. I was a year and one-half in getting religion, and you will be in good luck if you get it in a year and one-half." Now, the devil sent her in there. There are a good many doing that. How long a time does a man need to turn? It is done in a second. If you have not lived right there is but one course for you to take. Make haste and turn around. You have no time to waste.

"When I first sent letters of condolence," said the noble secretary of your institution, "to the wives and children of deceased drummers, it was merely mechanical. It was nothing but sounding brass and tinkling cymbals; but, thank God, Mr. Jones, I am on the side of Christ now, and right where I can pour out Christian sympathy and love into bereaved and sorrowing hearts." O, brother, that is a point. Some of you say: "I have been thinking of being a Christian, but I think I had better put it off. I do n't want to take any stand until about twelve months from now. They say I must not hurry about the thing." I reply, brother, run up the flag right where you are, and let the world see that you intend to do right. Turn around! Now, who wants to do right—to turn around, to go the other way? Can you? Ought you? Will you? Is it best to turn? You must haste to do it while you can. In a few more days some of you will be very near that point where no man ever did turn. A few more days in those depths, a few more days of that debauchery, a few more days of drunkenness, and cursing, and licentiousness, will put you where you can not turn, and that is the saddest thing ever said about any man—he can not turn! O, thank God, you can turn to-day! The grandest period in a man's life is when he walks up and gives himself to God.

Brother, I read yesterday in a commercial paper these words: "Feed your farm, and your farm will feed you." Now, what we want is to give ourselves to-day to God and his righteousness, and God will give himself to us; and then we will realize that it is more blessed to give than to receive.

Give all you are and all you get and you shall receive it back from God. Give yourselves to a better life; and may God's blessings rest upon the commercial travelers of this city and of America, and on your wives and widows and children, forever and ever.

SERMON XXV.

CONFESSION AND PARDON.

"Blessed is he whose transgression is forgiven, whose sin is covered. Blessed is the man unto whom the Lord imputeth not iniquity, and in whose spirit there is no guile."—PSA. XXXII, 1, 2.

DAVID surveyed the whole field of human conduct, and swept the horizon of thought as much as any man before him, or any man after him. He took in the whole situation, and he said, "If you want to be happy, if you want to be contented, if you want joy, if you want peace, secure the forgiveness of your transgressions. If you are a pardoned man you are a happy man. If you are unpardoned you are unhappy."

Really, brethren, as we get further into life, we find there is nothing really here to make a man happy. Lord Byron, with a capacity of earthly enjoyment that perhaps you and I know nothing of, was sitting quietly and meditatively on one occasion shortly before his death, and a friend said to him: "My lord, what are you thinking about so solemnly?" "I was just trying to recollect and count up the happy days of my life." "How many days did you count?" Said he, "I can count only eleven days of actual happiness; and I was just wondering if I would live long enough to make out one more happy day, and say that I have had twelve such days in my life." This was a man who had lived in wealth. There was not a cup of pleasure he had not drunk of. With a genius that gave life to every enjoyment, with an influence that swept along the social circle and moved all the intellectual features of the lives around him, and with an appetite for earthly things, he said, "I have had but eleven happy days." I reckon he must have seen these happy days before he was eleven years old; but he did n't tell when he had experienced them.

This old Epicurean theory, which is but modern science turned inside out, is to "eat, drink, and be merry, for to-morrow you die." There never was any thing in the universe, brother, more fatal and false, than to seek happiness from this old Epicurean theory, the most selfish in the world. Look at it—"eat, drink, and be merry." I am glad that in the kingdom of God we do not have to eat or drink. The Epicurean theory is the father of all gouts and drunkenness in the universe. Now, David teaches us a different philosophy. Here is happiness indeed, but it does not consist in what we eat or drink. A man may be happy whether he has little or much. St. Paul was happy in prison, and did not care what sort of bed he had to sleep on, or what he had for supper or breakfast, but he said, whatever was set before him, "To-day I will take dinner with God and the angels."

"Blessed is he whose transgression is forgiven;" not, Blessed is that man who lives in a four-story house; not, Blessed is that man who has a hundred thousand dollars to his credit in bank; not, Blessed is the man that owns the most railroad stock and government bonds. No, sir. If you are seeking happiness in that direction, it is like trying to satiate your thirst by drinking salt water—the more you drink the more you want, and when you get filled up, you will want water ten times more than you did before. If you want to be happy, you must obtain the favor of God. And the way to obtain it, is to seek God's pardon.

This strong ground and high ground David takes—happy is the man who is pardoned for all his past transgressions.

Then, "Blessed is the man unto whom the Lord imputeth not iniquity." Brother, my relations to God are determined by my loyalty to him—that 's the truth at last. If I know my boy is through and through loyal to his father, I do not walk around watching him all the time; if he is playing marbles or whistling, I ain't bothered about him. Now in the same way, the Lord does n't look so much at what a fellow does as at what makes him do it. He does n't look so much at how many times he has fallen, but how hard he has tried to get up. God does n't deal with us as to the exact words and deeds, but as to the motives, altogether. Do you believe that? If that is n't so, how could Jesus have said, "Whosoever hateth his brother is a murderer?" A great many people commit sin, and they say, "The Lord knows my motive was good, though." Yes, but the trouble is, you have n't got any motive.

"Blessed is the man unto whom the Lord imputeth not iniquity," and that's the man that God can trust. He does n't have to watch him. The Lord tells the servants of men not to be eye-servants, that require constant watching. Brethren, I just want to live so that the Lord does n't have to watch me every day as if he were doubtful of my integrity, so that he can say, "I know that you have been all right." Some of you look as though you would like very much for him not to look after you for a month at a time.

Brother, when there is a man in your employ and you never look over his accounts, you know that man is correct, and whatever the error may be you know you can not attribute it or trace it to that servant. God works on that plan, and let us live on it. God himself has confidence in you, and you know your motives are pure and your loyality is unchallenged.

Now, listen further. "In whose spirit there is no guile." Here you have the whole matter of uprightness pointed out to you. I like a guileless man. Just think of the guile of this world. I passed by a dentist's shop the other day, and he had an artificial set of teeth with plugs in all of them. I asked him, "What do you put those plugs into artificial teeth for?" He answered, "To make them look more natural." Think of that! Do you see the guile? And there is guile in every thing now. Now, let me tell you, if there is any thing in this world that I detest it is guile. Guile! A person that is one thing to-day and another thing to-morrow; who is one thing in one place and another thing in another place, I despise. If there is any thing that I admire about a thing it is that it is real on both sides, that it is real on the outside and on the inside. I want to know of a man that he would not make a different looking man in the sight of God than he does in the sight of his friend. I want to have a man pure at the top, pure in the center, pure at the bottom, and pure all over.

Brother, in the sight of God you are a transparent man. He can see through you. I have a contempt for a man who has any thing in him to hide. I believe in having no wrong side and no right side to a character. It should be all right. I like that. But poor old human nature is so made up that no man knows every thing. Some will say in their hearts, "If our pastor knew these things about me, what would he say? If our pastor found this out, what would he say? If our Church heard of this thing, what would they say?" O, listen; God hath already found it out. Be what you are through and through. Let the first half-inch of earth about you be just like every other half-inch clear down to the bottom. Some pieces of humanity are put up like some bales of cotton down South. They put the nice, white cotton outside, and in the center they put the dog-tail cotton—the worst cotton there is. And some humanity is put up on the same principle exactly. There is many a Methodist and many a Baptist in this town with the nicest part of his character on the outside, but he will bring the price in the market just in proportion to the depth you can reach into his character. Dealers have got a method of finding out what a bale of cotton is right through. And, brother, some of these days God will show you what you are through and through.

Now, I will tell you another thing. A guileless, transparent man will make a heap of enemies, because a heap of folks will misunderstand him. They think that if he is just like that on the outside he must be worse on the inside, and so they will think he is a bad fellow, because he does not look right to them on the outside, and they decide he must be terrible on the inside. Do n't judge people that way. A guileful man will say to you that every body has his price, that you can buy every body. Now, he is just telling his own experience, and putting himself in the market. He says to you, "Just give me a tolerably good price and I will sell myself." And that sort of a man can be bought. If you are in need of him you can buy him.

David tells us that he sinned against God, and kept silence, and would not confess; and that by reason of his refusal to confess his sins, "day and night the hand of God was heavy upon him, and his moisture was turned into the drought of Summer." O, what striking figures he uses here! And right along here we find in this territory the whole question on this point opened up to us. A man walks up in front and takes his seat in the penitents' chair; he walks into the inquiry room and says, "I confess to God and man that I am not right." He gives us his hand, and opens his heart to the love of God. He is confessing his sins in public. Brother, if you have sinned against God, go to God and confess it. "I kept silence," says David, "and my bones waxed old through my roaring all the day long; for day and night thy hand was heavy upon me." Listen to me now, you who have not had peace of mind for these ten days, for months. Days seem years when your mind is on yourself, because you are miserable. David told what his trouble was, what your trouble is; and he said because of it, "My moisture was turned into the drought of Summer." I have learned how a person feels by seeing how the fields are in a droughty season. Our garden is dried up, and every green thing droops, and the best land produces only about ten per cent of a crop. We have only ten per cent of a crop of grain. As I look out upon the orchard leaves and the corn I understand how drought has laid hold of this crop. The poor farmer suffers for it. Brother, a drought of this kind may only last for weeks, but a drought in the human heart may be one that will last forever. "My moisture is turned into the drought of Summer." O to see the drought of Summer upon the hearts and lives of professing Christians, and upon those out of the Church, and to see their spiritual nature droop, and wilt, and wither, and die under a drought that is brought upon them by their own voluntary conduct and action! Where is there a man that won't confess? We come to him to-night asking him to seek the Lord, and he says, "I do n't want to come up." What he means is, "I do n't want to confess ;" that is the trouble. When a fellow gets willing to confess he will go and do it before any thing else.

The Lord says, "He that confesseth shall find mercy." "If we confess our sins, he is faithful and just to forgive us our sins, and to cleanse us from all unrighteousness." Sin is a debt: "Forgive us our debts as we forgive our debtors." Now, we will start out with that proposition. If I owe a man a dollar, I have to meet that debt with a hundred cents, or with bankruptcy. I must do one or the other. Now, down South our farmers are furnished by merchants or warehousemen with money and provisions to last until they make their crops. The farmer comes to the merchant and mortgages his farm, his buildings, and horses, and stock, and crop, and draws money and provisions to use during the year. At the end of the year he goes into town and pays about sixty-six cents on the dollar, and when he has paid this amount he says to the merchant, "You must carry the other thirty-three cents over to the next year." The merchant holds the mortgage on his farm and stock, and carries him over to the next year. The next year the same thing is repeated, and he carries over another thirty-three per cent, making sixty-six per cent for the two years. And then he does the same thing the third year; there is another thirty-three per cent added to his indebtedness. The next year I see the sheriff with a paper in his hand, crying, "This plantation for sale." What does it mean! It means that the mortgage is due, and the officers of the court are selling the owner out to pay his debts.

Now, brother, I will say this much: to get into debt financially is about the worst thing that a man can do. A man had better die than get into debt, and I speak that with all the honesty of my nature. Death is better than debt. Spurgeon has declared as the three greatest evils, "Dirt, the devil, and debt." By the grace of God, I hope to conquer all the three, and make my way to heaven. Dirt, the devil, and debt! I do n't know which is the worst. Soap will do away with the first, and by prayer and faith you can get rid of the second; but the third one, debt, is a mighty hard thing to manage. Now, when you owe a dollar, you have got to pay out that dollar, or meet bankruptcy—one thing or the other. The best thing is never to get into debt. Do n't owe any body any thing. And I will tell you another thing. A man that will buy a luxury on a credit is a fool. And when a man will buy a luxury, when he at the same time owes an honest debt, he is a rascal. I know what I am talking about. I tell you that during the first years of my religious life, I grappled with debt until it almost took the last drop of blood out of my body. When I was preaching on a $600 a year salary, as soon as I got my quarterly dues, I paid every nickel that I could, though I knew that my wife did not have a single good dress. I paid money out, though I had hardly a coat on my back. And I will tell you another thing. I would have had no rest for that money I owed if I had bought myself a coat and my wife a dress, because people would have said, "You see Jones has money, but he won't pay it back to his creditors." The same God that said, "Thou shalt not steal," tells us "Owe no man any thing but to love one another." And yet a great many people think that they are all right when they do not pay their debts, and they simply say that they owe them. They think that it is not stealing, even though they are able to pay them. I believe that I would rather have a man steal from me when I am sleeping than have him steal from me when I am looking at him.

Now, brother, as sin is a debt, the best thing to do in the world is—do n't sin at all. That is best, and thank God it is possible. "Yes," but you say, "I can 't help sinning." You can help it just as well as you can keep from getting into debt—do you know that? Am I obliged to get into debt to-day or to-morrow? Which sin am I obliged to commit to-day or to-morrow? "You are not like me," you hear people say; "I can not live without sin." Whenever you hear a person say that, you may know he is falling into sin more deeply, and that he has made provision for it. Well, I say, the best thing in the world is, do n't do wrong. But if you do happen to slip and do wrong the best thing is to fall down and repent. Do n't let it get cold before you have repented of it. I believe it is a good idea if you sin on the sidewalk, to drop down on the sidewalk and repent then and there. A man ought to be able to repent and to pray anywhere that he can afford to sin. The best thing for you to do when you do wrong is to exclaim: "Now, Lord, I am sorry, but I repent right now."

That was one good thing about David. He got out of the right path and did wrong frequently; but as soon as Nathan would drop his finger upon him he would sink down and go to repenting with all his might and soul on the spot. That is the next best thing—to repent on the spot for the sin there committed. If you do n't do that then you will probably say, "God helping me, I won 't go to sleep any night until the day's unworthy transactions are repented of." That is the way that fellow on the plantation got bankrupt—putting off paying his debts and letting them run one year after another. Now, brother, here is a member of the Church, and he is letting his sins go on without repenting of them week after week and month after month, and year after year, until they are piled up mountain high; and he walks up to the preacher and tells him to take his name off the Church book, and the poor fellow goes into temporal and spiritual and eternal bankruptcy and gives it up forever. And do you know there are hundreds of just such cases as that?

"But," you say, "Mr. Jones, what are you going to do with the doctrine of final perseverance?" I tell you the doctrine of final perseverance won't hold good here. But that is the only exception, thank God, in the universe. The doctrine of final perseverance will hold true in every other instance. You know how a poor fellow in debt for money will get despondent and discouraged. And it is the same with a poor fellow whose sins are allowed to accumulate, and he makes no effort to get rid of them. Sin is a debt you have to meet at the mercy-seat of God with an honest, open confession, or you will have to meet it in the judgment with eternal bankruptcy of your soul. Now, which will you do? If you have sinned, brother, the best time for you to repent is just now. You can not afford to put it off any longer.

Brother, I do not want to do wrong at all, but if I do I want to repent at once—repent right now. And you would better not go to sleep to-night with a consciousness that you have unpardoned sins hanging over you. Whether you 've been in sin forty years or thirty years, brother, if you will not see yourself in the light of truth to-night, despair will take possession of your soul. If all of the sins you have committed were scattered out among the people in this city, there would be enough to damn them.

Now, brother, let 's you and I begin to look over ourselves. God helping me, I will have a receipt, written in the blood of Jesus Christ, that all my sins are forgiven. You would better trifle with anything of a temporal nature than with these debts; but confess them at once, and obtain pardon.

I 'll tell you another thing, brother: When you go to confession, go to the bottom. I 'll give you an instance, and what I shall say some of you, perhaps, will not like. In one of the Southern cities there was, perhaps, as respectable a woman as ever moved in the high circle to which she belonged.

She became interested in a revival going on, and gave her heart to God, and on the Saturday afternoon before she was to be received in the Church she sought one of the best women in that town and said to her:

"I 've come to talk with you. To-morrow morning I 'm going to join the Church—the Church you belong to; and I say to you I have given my heart to God, and have repented of my sins, but I shall be disgraced to-morrow when my name is read out to the people."

"Why," said the lady, "what do you mean?"

"I mean this: I have lived a false life; I am living a falsehood. You know my little son Willie, ten years old?"

"Yes," said the lady.

"Well, you know I am called Mrs. So-and-so. My name is not Mrs. So-and-so, but it is Miss So-and-so; and so it shall go on the register of God's Church. I will go to the bottom."

God pity us if there is any thing wrong, whatever it is; let us go down to the bottom, and out with it. That woman had to do it or be damned. You can not live a false life and be a Christian. Go down to bottom facts. Say, "I will go to the bottom if it disgraces me among men; but I 'll put myself right before God and his holy angels." That 's what that woman did. And, whenever you see a man or woman who would rather please God than to have all the cheers and honors this world can bestow upon him or her, you can thank God that there is one honest man, that there is one honest woman, who has come down to bottom facts.

O, brother, if we could just spend one honest hour before God! and every man of us ought to pray God on our knees in confessing these sins that are piled up upon us, and which will inevitably doom us in the end if we do not repent. That is what we want—confession. God will listen and save.

David said, "I acknowledged my sin unto thee, and mine iniquity have I not hid." There is the whole process of salvation in a single line: I have acknowledged my sins, I have confessed my transgressions unto God. I know only one chance for us poor mortal beings, and that is, an honest confession before God. Two brothers went to battle. One was shot down. The other exclaimed, "Thank God, my brother was ready, and had given himself to the Lord!" Brothers, sisters, let us so live and die, having our peace made with God, that it may be said of us, "Thank God, he was ready!" Let us, you and I, get ready, live ready, and die ready.

SAYINGS.

THERE are problems and questions in your home life that no one but God can settle wisely and correctly. If you will know God personally, and will adjust yourself fully toward God, then all the love and grace of his heart will be poured into your heart and life day by day.

THE back door of the Church ought to be opened once a year and give all who have not lived up to its rules an opportunity to pass out.

THEOLOGY is a good thing. It is a good thing to stuff with sawdust, like the skin of a fish, and put in a museum as a relic of antiquity.

WE see God all around us. The mountains are God's thoughts upheaved. The rivers are God's thoughts in motion. The oceans are God's thoughts imbedded. The dewdrops are God's thoughts in pearls.

THE difference between a backsliding Methodist and a lukewarm Cumberland is this: The Methodist knows he has lost his religion, and the Cumberland, since he can't lose his, knows he never had any to lose.

A MAN'S power to love determines his immortality. Then, if that be true, let us bottom character on affections. How will we do it? I'll tell you how. I believe I would put law supreme, then I would put conscience right under law, then I would give conscience a good grip on the will, and then I would let the will through conscience and law, subjugate the affections, until I love every thing that is good and hate every thing that is bad, and then I think I am getting in shape to be a man—a true man.

SERMON XXVI.

A NEW CREATURE IN CHRIST.

(*First Discourse.*)

"Therefore, if any man be in Christ, he is a new creature."—2 COR. v, 17.

I TRUST that the good Spirit to-day may give us his presence and his help in the discussion of this wonderful text. For, after all, brethren, if Christ Jesus be any other than the Son of God and the personal Savior of man, then our preaching is vain and our faith is vain, and we are still in our sins.

Whatever else may be said of us, I am glad that more men are asking, "Who is Christ?" "What is Christ?" to-day than in any day in this world's history. There have been more lives of Christ written since I was born than were ever written before. In the last three decades there have been more men trying to answer these two questions—and not only more men, but the most gifted men this world ever knew, are asking, "Who is Christ?" "What is Christ?" and I believe the most philosophical statement in answer to these questions is about this: Christ is the living personal embodiment of wisdom, of justice, of love, of mercy, of truth, of purity, and all the attributes and characteristics which make the character of God lovely.

Christ is not a sentiment, brother! He is not

simply an historical person, but Christ is a living presence. The creed of a Church is but a garment we put about Christ, and there is no more life in a creed than there is life in this coat I have on. I am glad that my salvation and your salvation does not depend upon our belief in this creed or in that creed. And I sometimes think we make an idol of our creed and our Church. Our creed! I have known ministers to spend more time in the defense of their creed than they did preaching Christ to dying men. I am sorry for any preacher that has a creed which needs a defense. I would much rather have a creed that all men who want to be religious can assent to.

It's not faith in a creed that saves. The Methodist creed can not be swallowed by a great many intelligent men. The Presbyterian creed has never gone down some very good, wise men. The Catholic creed does not suit others, nor will the other creeds suit others; and when we come to boil this question down to a sensible proposition, brethren, we find at last that God does not say, "Whosoever believes in the five points of Calvinism shall be saved." He never put salvation on that proposition. He did not say that "Whosoever believeth in falling from grace shall be saved," nor "Whosoever believeth in immersion shall be saved," nor "Whosoever believeth in sprinkling shall be saved," nor yet "Whosoever believeth in final perseverance shall be saved," nor "Whosoever believeth in the infallibility of the pope shall be saved," nor "Whosoever believeth in apostolic succession shall be saved:" but "Whosoever believeth on the Lord Jesus Christ shall be saved." And it's faith in a person, and not in a creed, that saves the soul.

It is very ridiculous to me to hear a Methodist preacher speaking on infant baptism and all the little babes in town asleep, and half of the grown people in town going to hell. I could never see where the wisdom of such a movement as that came in. I have sometimes been disgusted with seeing a Baptist preaching "much water," and a majority of his crowd going where they can not get a drop to cool their parched tongues; or seeing an Episcopalian minister ringing the changes on apostolic succession, while a great many of his flock ought to be looking out where they are going to, rather than where they came from.

That's a very serious question to me. I am not so much interested about whence I came as to whither I am going. That's it. The doctrine of a man preaching that "mine is the only Church, mine is the first Church," contains no saving power. A great many very nice people assemble together, and call themselves "our Church," and "the Church," and really they are nothing more or less than a religious crocheting society. They can do almost any little thing—get up nice suppers, or run a Church entertainment or fair, or any such thing. They are first-class on that line; but if we get after them about visiting the sick, rescuing the perishing, and saving the fallen, they say, "O, we never do any thing like that in our Church." I have thought sometimes that if the Lord were to take that crowd to heaven as they are, it would not be six months before they would have all the angels rigged out in lace. The Lord be merciful towards us, and help us to be truly good!

After all, brethren, what is my Methodism, and your Presbyterianism, and Episcopalianism, and Baptism? It is nothing more than a duster we put on over our cloth coat, to keep off some of the dust and dirt of earth, and when we get to the pearly gates, we will pull off our dusters and walk in with our dress coats—we will never carry our dusters in with us, you may put that down; and is it not absurd that we should quarrel over the color and quality of our dusters down here? O, for a Church universal, that loves God with all its heart, and soul, and power, and in which we can get along with one another in spite of the little difference of the color of the dusters! Would n't it be a good idea to have such a Church universal?

Here, my brother; when you come to this one single question of all questions, it is not faith in a creed, nor membership in a Church, but it is your relation to the Lord Jesus Christ that brings salvation. That 's it. Now, you will say, "Why, Mr. Jones, you make light of the Church." No, no, I do not any more than I make fun of my coat; but I put my coat in its right place. The crowned instrumentalities in religion are all sent from God, for our good, and are efficient means to bring us to God. But there is only one sufficiency, and that is faith in Jesus Christ. Let us meet that fact.

When a Church reaches the point where its services are all formal, where there is nothing but formality, then religion with it is nothing more than what you see represented in a watermelon patch—a scare-crow put up on a forked stick. But where Christ rules and reigns in the heart, there is love and life and movement.

Who is Christ? The living personal embodiment of truth. He is all wisdom, all mercy, and all forgiveness. Well now, brother, St. Paul said: "I am crucified with Christ; nevertheless, I live, yet not I, but Christ liveth in me." The same desire, purpose, and resolution that moved Christ himself should move me. The wisdom, justice, mercy, purity, and love of Christ have been imparted to me as a Christian, and now with wisdom, mercy, love, and truth, I manifest to the world what it is to be a Christian. That man is the best Christian who is the most like Christ. Perhaps you remember having heard of that heathen who came to America, and finally when he bade farewell and stepped on the ship at San Francisco that was returning him to his native country, he looked out, and said, "In all Christendom I have found no man like Christ." What a commentary on this Christian continent! "I have found no man like Christ."

Now, brother, if a Christian is any thing, he is wise. There is a great deal of difference between knowledge and wisdom. I have seen very knowing men who were very foolish men. Wisdom is the skillful application of knowledge—it is the right use of what you know, of what you have in hand. Wisdom is doing the best thing in the best way.

Now a Christian is wise in this; he will adapt the best means to the best ends always. The water of the river of life is as clear as crystal, and thank God, any body who drinks of it and has eyes to see, may see the spring from which it flows.

Wisdom! Do you live on a wise plane and plan? Do you in your heart mean to live as you profess, to deny yourself and take hold upon Christ? Are you wise in your religious profession and practices every day? Do you counsel your family in godly matters? Do you pray in your family, read your Bible, visit the sick, help the destitute and needy, comfort the afflicted?

Now look here, brother; are you really honest in proposing to get to heaven? Will you adopt every plank in your platform as a Christian that has helped others to be Christians indeed? If you are honest in your purpose to get to heaven you will adopt every such plank, and help to lead others to Christ and to hold Christianity up.

I said once, while preaching in a Southern city, that a man who would not pray in his family had no more religion than a horse. Some rose up in arms against me and were about to put me out. The next day I walked down to the store of a leading Methodist there. He accosted me, and said:

"Mr. Jones, did you say last night that a man who would n't pray in his family did n't have any more religion than a horse?"

I said, "Yes, I did."

"You 're mistaken, sir," said he. "I 've got as much religion as you have, and I do n't pray in my family." And he was about to jump on me; and if he had had much religion he would not have wanted to do that, would he?

I said, "Look here, do you know what religion is?"

"Well," he replied, "you say what it is."

Said I, "It is loyalty to God."

He said, "That 's so."

"Now," said I, "let us take a sensible view of it. Is not my loyalty to my duty a test of my loyalty to God?"

"Yes, that 's good logic."

"If I am disloyal to my duty, can I be loyal to God?"

"No."

"Can a disloyal man be religious?"

"I never looked at the thing in that way," said he; and when he went home that night, he said to his wife: "Wife, get down the family Bible, and let us have prayers, and, God helping me, we will always have them and try to do our whole duty."

There 's many a fellow in this country who thinks he has religion, when it is just something he has eaten. But religion is loyalty to God.

A preacher came to me once, and said: "Jones, you say that any man who has got religion will pray in public?"

"Yes," said I.

"Well, the best man I 've got in my Church won 't pray in public."

"Well," said I, "that man is either a hypocrite, or he has no pastor to instruct him."

That preacher went off as mad as a hornet with me.

Now, hear me, brethren, whenever the best means are brought to bear upon your conscience, you have got to adopt them or backslide, one or the other. You have to do what God demands, or violate his will. And wisdom says, I must adopt that plank in my platform. These people would do their duty much better if you put thumb-screws on them. We know that if a man is disloyal to a plain, distinct duty, he can not be loyal to God. Do n't you have these old sinners point their fingers at you at the judgment bar of God and say you were lacking in your duty. Take care, brethren, and do n't let it be said that your lack of duty damned any man. Talk to your people, tell them their duty, even if they choke you for it. This is the very essence of Christianity—loyalty to God.

I was pastor seven or eight years of my life, and my mind and memory run back to-day over the different men and women of the Churches I was pastor of, and I can almost put my finger on every one I expect to meet in heaven, if I get there. It is those men and women who were loyal to God. I tell you that is a serious question to think of.

Some folks do n't like the Methodist Church because it changes its preachers every three years. But when you stay ten or fifteen years at the same place, you ought to get scared and say: "I wonder if some other preacher could not do more than I could."

Well, Christianity means justice. A Christian

ought to be a just man. He ought to be just to his wife, just to his children, just to his neighbor, just to every body. O, how innocent we seem. We hear people say: "You would better be just before you are generous." It is ten thousand times easier to be generous than it is to be just. I can give a poor, old woman a ten dollar bill much easier than I can beg my friend's pardon for an injury I have done him. I can give a check for a hundred dollars for a charitable purpose, and it does n't hurt me; but when my little Bob runs into my study while I am busy writing or reading, and I say to him, "Go out of here, Bob; I told you not to come in here and bother me;" the little fellow goes out, and my conscience says, "You have been unjust to that boy," and I sit there feeling as mean as a dog. I go out and find him, and see him sitting on the porch-steps, crying. I take him up on my lap and kiss him and beg his pardon. It is hard to do, but I say: "Bob, papa was cross and rough to you just now, but you will forgive him, won't you?" And the dear little fellow clings to my neck and says, "Papa, you must forgive me, for mamma told me not to go in there." You see, wife had found out that there was an old bear in there, and was trying to keep her children out.

Justice! You all know how that is, do n't you, brethren? Justice! I will be just to my wife, and beg her pardon if I have been uncouth. I will be just to all. If I trample upon the feelings of a dog, I will pet and feed him, and show him I am sorry for it. Justice makes a fellow do the clean thing. A Christian must be a just man; not simply pay his debts and pay what he owes, but, brother, there are some debts men won't pay. Let me tell you that in simple love and justice you ought to meet every claim of humanity upon you.

A Christian ought to be just, and he ought to be a pure man. A great many people are very fastidious and have a great deal of mock-modesty among them, but are very impure people. I have found that out. I could stop right here and say some things that would burn like fire. I have no doubt in my mind there are people in this city who have criticized Sam Jones as being vulgar. Sam Jones may be plain and outspoken, coarse if you will, in his sermons, but, thank God, he is pure in his life. And if I am going to be vulgar anywhere, it 's going to be when I am handling that sort who say, "Unto the pure all things are pure." I preached at a famous watering-place once, and I got on the subject of dancing. I simply told the plain, naked truth; I said that if many a girl in Georgia could have gone to the rooms of the young men and listened to what they said about them after the dance they would never put their feet into a ball-room or dance again. What I said at that famous watering-place aroused a tumult. They called me vulgar, obscene, vicious, ill-bred, and all that, but they came back to the meeting, however. And the girl who had the lecherous arm around her waist, thought that all I had said was vulgar and ill-bred; but the girl who was pure indeed, said, " Mr. Jones, that sermon was a good one, and

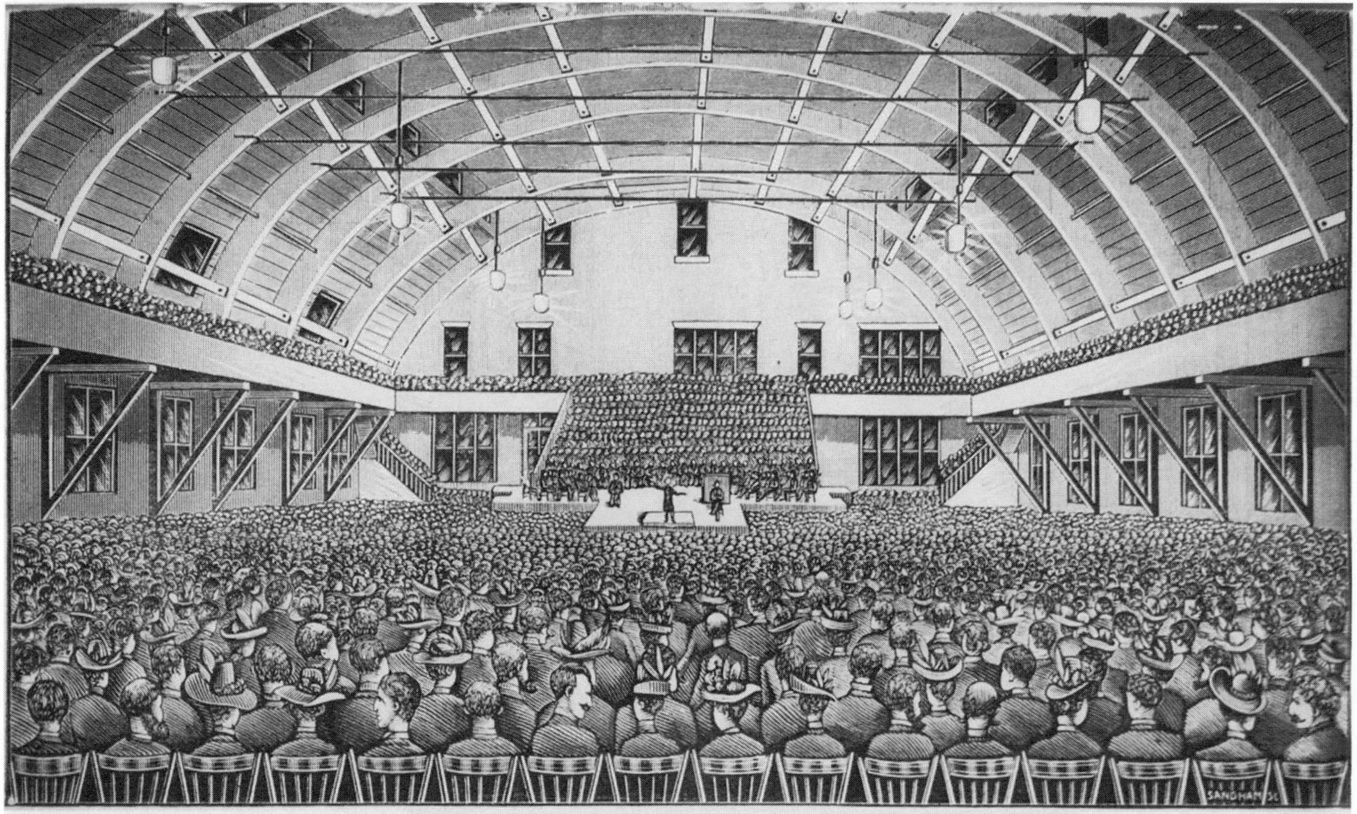

INTERIOR VIEW OF CALEDONIAN RINK, MUTUAL STREET, TORONTO, ONTARIO.

in perfect harmony with my ideas." "Unto the pure all things are pure." It is not so much who is the preacher, and what he is saying, as who is listening.

Purity! I know what it is to call a precious woman "mother!" I know what it is to call a precious woman "my wife!" I know what it is for my sweet, innocent daughters to put their arms around my neck and imprint the kisses of purity upon my cheek; and as God is my judge, in so far as mind and muscle goes, no man in America will stand to the death any more readily to defend the purity of the women of this country than the man now speaking to you. I would build, if necessary, a wall a mile high around the virtue of every girl this country has in it to-day. To those very persons who say, "he is vulgar and ill-bred," the day may come in their history when they will be sorry that such was ever said by them.

I will tell you another thing. If I had a company of ten thousand angels to preach to to-day, every word I uttered, in all of its applications and its etymological sense, should be as pure as heaven; but why preach thus to men? Our Savior himself preached to men, and I have thought a thousand times his sermon would not have had so much in it about adultery and a great many wicked things if he had been preaching to angels. God, keep me pure, and then keep me dead honest in dealing with souls, and help me to strike right straight out from the shoulder. I want to take a plumb-straight rest for my gun, and if I hit a fellow anywhere else but in heart or head, I will step up to him and apologize, and tell him I meant it to be a dead shot. And if you think I hit you by accident, you were never more mistaken in your life. The shot was sent with design to hit.

And the Christian must be a forgiving man. Thank God for the disposition of the heart I have to-day, through grace, that makes me utterly incapable of malice aforethought. I feel sorry for those Christians who are unforgiving in their nature. There are mothers and fathers who won't forgive their children, and sisters and brothers who won't forgive each other. God pity them. A lady once came to me, and said: "My mother won't speak to me. I wish you would say something about mothers whose unforgiving disposition will not let them even speak to their daughters." I said in my next sermon, "You mothers, who are unforgiving to your children, come with me to the zoölogical garden, and watch the lioness how she fondles her whelp; and you could see, if opportunity should arise, how she will give her very life for it. Watch the tigress as she stands over her cubs with guarding and loving eye. I will show you the house cat, how she tenderly carries her kittens about in her mouth; and when you have spent an hour in the zoölogical garden, then just look at yourself, and see what an old bear—or, rather, what an unnatural creature—your children have for a mother."

Ah me, what is it in heaven or earth that could prevent my speaking to one of my children? As Christians we are brothers and sisters—some, perhaps, step-brothers and sisters—but brothers and sisters, nevertheless.

Thank God for the power to forgive in the name of Christ. Jesus said that we must not bear malice towards our enemies, but "love your enemies, bless them that curse you, do good to them that hate you, and pray for them which despitefully use you and persecute you."

The first year I began preaching I had two or three fights. I did not have any better religious sense than to want to fight when a man did not treat me right. But I used to wonder if the Lord Jesus would want me to pray for and do good to and encourage a man in his meanness. If I could whip him, I thought, I would do him a great deal of good. But I found out at last that Jesus was not trying to protect the rascal, but was protecting me. Love your enemies.

The best way in the world to kill an enemy is to love him to death, and you do n't have to bury him and make a widow out of his wife.

O, what a stupendous fact this is,—what a pattern! If this world had had any response in it, Christ would have loved it to death long ago. He taught us how to love. When he was buffeted, he buffeted not again; when he was reviled, he reviled not again. Alexander the Great, Charlemagne, and Napoleon each gathered around himself great armies and marched them against their enemies, and attempted to conquer the world by force and blood, and each died a wretched death. When Jesus Christ wanted to conquer this world he went up on Calvary and suffered and died for it. Napoleon founded his kingdom and empire by force on that which perisheth, but Jesus founded his on love, and millions would die for it.

"Love your enemies, bless them that curse you, do good to them that hate you, and pray for them which despitefully use you and persecute you." That is the Christian spirit—doing good for evil, overcoming evil with good. The only principle in this world that will overcome evil is good. Evil with evil is a Kilkenny cat sort of business, and each will hurt the other equally. Overcome evil with good.

Thank God for a weapon that not only knocks my enemy down, but restores him to me as a friend. The best way in the world to get the advantage of a man is to love him. He that loves the most is the man who has the most immortal capital. God measures you off a lot in size and dimensions on the streets of the New Jerusalem by the amount of love which you have to pay for it. God gives us all enough love for a million-acre field in heaven, and we will have elbow room then. Love much, and God will give you plenty of room in heaven. Thank God, I have nothing to forgive any man. I am determined upon this much, never to get mad with any man until he treats me worse than I have treated my Lord.

Let us bear in mind that our hopes for time and eternity rest upon our acting upon those sweet words,—

"Simply to thy cross I cling,"

Or, better still,—

"Safe in the arms of Jesus."

God bless you all, and preserve you ever in his love!

BRIEF SAYINGS.

IN a Georgia town a number of girls married men to reform them, and now the town is full of little whippoorwill widows.

THE greatest rascals are those who are scrupulously honest. If I see a man walk across town to pay a nickel, I watch him.

A HORSE that will pull on a cold collar will do to depend on—and the best Christians are those who never need "warming up."

WHISKY is a good thing in its place, and that place is in hell. If I get there I will drink all I can get, but I won't do it here.

THE capacity of a woman for making every body about her uncomfortable can not be calculated by any known process of arithmetic.

THE Churches of Nashville furnish whisky to the surrounding country. Some of our wholesale liquor dealers belong to the Church.

THE matter of Church doctrine is an accident. If my mother and Brother Witherspoon's mother had swapped babies he might have been a Methodist preacher.

SERMON XXVII.

A NEW CREATURE IN CHRIST.

(Second Discourse.)

"Therefore, if any man be in Christ, he is a new creature."—2 Cor. v, 17.

CHRIST JESUS was a man, and in referring to his relation to our race, he spoke of himself as "the Son of man." "These works that I do demonstrate that I am divine. Now I would not have you forget that I am also the Son of man."

We have Christ in two manifestations, and I wish we had more of him in a third. We have Christ in his works, and we have him in his words. We have books written on the latter. Rudolph Stier, on the Words of the Lord Jesus, is, perhaps, one of the most valuable books in a preacher's library. I have been panting and hungry a long time for a book on the Thoughts of the Lord Jesus. Really when I look at his works, I wonder and say, "Behold!" Then, when I read his words, I say, "A man that could talk like that, of course could work like that;" and when I get into the great thoughts of Christ, then I say, "The words and works of Christ are the mere bubbles on the great ocean of his life. He who thought like Christ could surely work like Christ and talk like Christ."

Christ Jesus is a great deal more to us, brother, than we have ever realized. Really the wealth of the universe is hidden in Christ. Now I would not stand here and study Christ; I would not stand here with all the infirmities and difficulties that encompass me, with the seen things, and study the Lord Jesus, but I would go where Jesus is, and study the universe; and a man who stands where Jesus is understands things very differently from a man who stands here and studies them.

Jesus Christ is the great telescope to the Christian's eye. He not only brings the unseen things, which are afar off, down to where I may reach them, but he is also the great microscope to the Christian's eye, so that the things that are close to me I can see a thousand times better when I look through Christ.

Christ in his works and in his words, Christ in his thoughts, in the unfailing purity of his social life, his grandeur of intellectual life in the whole sum of his life, is an examplar for all men. O Jesus, thou art all in all, and from thee and through thee I may see all things in the light God sees them.

"If any man be in Christ, he is a new creature." I believe that Jesus Christ was born of the Virgin Mary. I believe that he was God. I believe that he was man. I believe we needed this God-Man. Jesus Christ is a mediator—one who works between two parties. I think it was Bishop Morris who put this in the strongest way. He said, "Jesus was the mediator, the one between the two, and Jesus was divine, and Jesus was human, and he laid the left hand of his humanity on the shoulder of man, and then, reaching up, caught the shoulder of God with the right hand of his divinity, and he brought God and man together." We needed Christ.

And I believe another thing, brother. I believe the Lord Jesus Christ not only came and lived among men, but he fared largely as other men did and do. Jesus Christ suffered and died for what he was and for what he said and for what he did. That 's true. And Jesus Christ died as naturally as St. Paul died, and St. Paul died a natural death. Do you want to know what I mean by this? I mean that in that day, in the fullness of the time, when Jesus came, it was death to any man to preach righteousness and live it before the people. And Jesus came and suffered the penalty of his righteous life and his righteous words. Now, on this question, I want to say, brethren, that Jesus Christ, the Son of God, the Savior of men, suffered the penalty of his words and his works. It was death to the God-man. It was death to those who loved this God-man, to talk and preach as he did. Then I see Jesus on that cross as he suffers and dies; and, listen, brother, on that cross I see the divinest, grandest manifestation of God's love to man. If you want to draw out from the deepest depth all that 's true in me, listen. You see Christ on that cross. I have heard men say that Jesus hung on the cross to satisfy the claims of divine justice. I have heard them say Jesus was hung on that cross to appease God's wrath against man; but I will tell you my conception of it, and this little bundle of paper, the Bible, which I hold in my hand, is with me. Jesus

Christ was not there to satisfy claims of divine justice. He was not there as a target of divine wrath. No. Would you make me believe that God was angry with humanity six thousand years ago, and that the only way to keep him from killing out the whole concern was to put his only Son on the cross and sacrifice him? I do not believe God suffered his Son to be crucified because he was mad with men, but that Jesus came and died because of God's love for man. "God so loved the world that he gave his only begotten Son, that whosoever believeth on him might not perish, but have everlasting life."

God does n't love me because Christ died for me, but Christ died for me because of God's unspeakable love for me. Now you are getting your theology right on this question, and you can knock all the infidelity out of this country by this great New Testament doctrine. Love! "Herein is love, not that we loved Him, but that he loved us, and sent his Son to be the propitiation for our sins." And this old idea we have, that God does not love any body but good people, won't do. Some people get this idea in their heads, and the first thing you know they think they have a corner on the grace of God, and are trying to run a monopoly on the love of heaven.

Hear, my brethren, God loves every man in this universe. I will take this view. The sun in mid-heaven shines on every thing alike. It shines on the verdant valleys, on the bold mountain peaks. It pours its vivifying rays on growing grain, fruits, and flowers, as well as on the stricken oak, or blasted tree, and sterile ground. It shines on all alike. Why? Because it is its nature to shine on every thing. God's name as well as nature is love, and God loves every thing that comes under the burning rays of his love. God loves all men. He loved me just as much before I was converted as he loves me now. If he had not, I never would have been converted. It is God's nature to love, and you can not make it out that God is mad with men. O thou infinite God of love and mercy, of long suffering and goodness, show us all that thou hast never dealt with us in anger, but always in love.

God loves us, brethren, and Jesus Christ was not hung on the cross as a target of divine justice, or to placate divine anger, but as the manifestation of God's love to dying men. That's it. I hope I am orthodox, brethren! I hope I am. If I am not, I will tell you this much, I can love God more with this view of the divine atonement than I can with any other; and you must let me have my way, because I can get along better on that than on any other ground. We won't quarrel about it. You may take the other view of it if you like, or mix the two together if you please, but I love Him because he first loved me. He is a loving Savior; a loving Savior, living; loving, dying; loving, going to the grave; loving, rising; always filled with love for me.

"Now, if any man be in Christ, he is a new creature." Jesus was emphatically a new creature in the world. There was none like him before, nor any like him since. Jesus prayed, "Father, as we are one, grant that these people may be all one with us." All are merged into one in Christ—one in purpose, one in desire, one in intention, one in love, one in purity, one in faith, one in forgiveness, one in pardon. It is a oneness in sentiment, purpose, virtue, desire, love, and purity.

You see two men walking along. You say these two men have the same purposes, the same interests, the same desires, every thing the same. When you hit one, you hit both. The bar-keepers in this city are all one. If you raise your voice against one of them, they will all rise up against you. You hit one of them in denouncing their traffic, and you hit them all. Their interests are identical. I wish I could say that when you hit one Christian in this town, you hit all; but, instead of that, when you hit one, the rest all say, "I am glad it was not me." Thank God, though we can not know like him, and can not have power like him, one thing we can do, and that is, love like God. And that is the grandest of his attributes—love.

Now, brother, being in Christ Jesus, presupposes a longing for Christ. I said before, Jesus Christ is not a sentiment. He is a divine person, and in the divinity of his person he embraces all wisdom, justice, mercy, love, and purity. Of all of these attributes Christ is the living embodiment, and he who is in Christ the most necessarily partakes most of these divine characteristics.

The Scriptural term for this longing is "hungering and thirsting after righteousness." That is a healthful and religious state. David said: "As the hart panteth after the water brooks, so panteth my soul after thee, O God." Hunger of the soul is a hunger for Christ. The sense of hunger and of thirst of the body, how intense it is. Did you ever locate the sense of physical hunger? A little boy once said to his father, "Papa, I feel so hungry." "Son," said the father, "how do you feel when you are hungry?" "I feel like chewing something," said the boy. So the organs of the appetite are where to look for physical hunger. Now where do I locate the sense of spiritual hunger? It is in the heart. My heart, my soul panteth after the living God. This longing, this intense burning desire, O Christ, nothing can satisfy but thyself.

See that baby boy; how he cries and kicks and screams! His nurse endeavors to pacify him by offering him his little toys and playthings, but he says: "I don't want my toys." She offers him marbles, but he cries, "I don't want any marbles." After she has exhausted all her resources to quiet him, and he still cries and refuses to be comforted, the little fellow's mother comes in. The instant his eyes light upon her his crying ceases; he rushes up and is caught in her loving arms. He "just wanted mamma." He did not want any thing else; and with her his soul was satisfied. And, brother, whenever a soul gets to the point in its childlike simplicity, that the devil, the world, and the flesh, with its cards, and dancing, and theaters, and all its other allurements can not satisfy it, and it says, "I don't want that, I want my Savior," he is sure to come and abide with that soul.

The way to get the fullness of Christ is to empty your heart of every thing that rejects Christ and his affinities. Always lean to those things that are Christ's. Let your prayer be, "Lord, help me to turn each idol out that dares to rival thee." How many can say now, "I would rather have Christ for my portion than all else besides?"

Being in Christ not only presupposes a longing for Christ, but a fleeing to Christ. O, blessed Christ, I will run upon the swiftest feet of faith to meet thee. O, dear Lord, I tried until I could try no more to remain away; my soul became impatient, and I could stay no longer; show me thy way. I will rush into thine arms of waiting love. Thank God for that purpose of my soul that makes me go out in search of my Lord. I will search for him. I am so glad that I never let the grass grow up in my pathway between my Lord and me. The devil shall never come between my Savior and myself.

I saw some time ago an illustration of how the devil works among his crowd, by an old colored preacher down South. He laid three objects on his Bible, and he said: "Now, brethren, I'm a-going to show how de debbil works de Christuon. Here's de Savior, here's de Christuon, and here's de debbil. Now when de Christuon move up to Christ, den de debbil he move off; de Christuon move nearer Christ, and de debbil he move furder off; den de Christuon sort o' back-slides, den de debbil move up; de Christuon gets furder and furder away from Christ, and de debbil moves up closer and closer to him, and de first thing you know, de debbil jump over him and get right between him and Christ; and when he gets over dar between you and Christ he's got you, and den he'll say, 'Now I's got you, sure.'" This is a living illustration. Never let the devil get between you and your Lord. Say to him, "Get thee behind me, Satan; you shall never come between me and my Lord."

Then running to Christ! Thank God for the privilege of going to Christ. Is there trouble any where? Take it to the Lord in prayer. What a Friend we have in Jesus! Thank God, brother! I have been at times in such tight places that I could not do a thing in the world but pray; and thank God that was all I needed to do. Just leave it all with the Lord. That's what we call rushing to the Lord in prayer.

O, my brother, if I wanted to divide the armies of Satan and put all perdition to flight, I would not order down a legion of angels and all the artillery of heaven; but I will tell you what I would do: I would fall on my knees in prayer to God.

"And Satan trembles when he sees
The weakest saint upon his knees."

A man can fall into no harm while he is on his knees praying. Did you ever hear of a man getting drunk on his knees? Did you ever hear of a man stealing while on his knees in prayer? I will tell you, your trouble is, you have not been on your knees enough.

Ah, me! how Satan has tempted me, how the passion for drink has come on and almost overwhelmed me;' but, thank God, I have found his grace sufficient to sustain me. Those people who say, I can not help drinking; or, I can not help doing this or that when tempted,—I know what the matter with them is: you do n't do enough of this knee-work I am talking about. I hear people say, "I 'm afraid to join the Church, I 'm afraid I can 't hold out, I 'm afraid I 'll swear or drink or do something wrong;" and I have said to them, "I never have been afraid of but one thing since I joined the Church, and that is, I am afraid I won't pray enough." I am omnipotent when leaning on the arm of God in prayer. If you want to whip the devil, just fall on your knees in prayer.

Being in Christ pre-supposes, again, submission to Christ. O, how we want our own way! How jealous we are of what we call our privileges! How we kick and rear if we can not have our own way, and how we rave, and pitch, and tear if we do n't get it! Why, we fall out with our preacher and abuse him like a pick-pocket if he attempts to abridge "our privileges." Ah, we are jealous of these "privileges." You touch them, and you get your foot into it. I sail into you on your dram-drinking, theater-going, card-playing, and dancing, and the town rises up in arms against me; but it is the hit dog that hollers, you may put that down. If you go and break a drunkard's jug, he 'll get mad, every time; but his wife won't. If we sail into these people who do these things I have the utmost pity and sympathy for them, and I do believe, my brethren, the poor people are so deluded and persuaded by the world, that they do n't see any harm in the things they are doing. Let us get them to reading books that have sense in them—I mean religious sense. If I have got but a little sense, good Lord, let it be religious sense.

I heard a man say once, "Myself and my wife never had a squabble in our lives—never had a quarrel—only when she wanted to have her own way." Well, who is n't lovable that way? The devil himself is agreeable enough when he has every thing his own way. Listen: I am sorry for Christian people who have reserved rights. Religion is like that pearl of great price, which, when found, the buyer sold all that he had and purchased. And, brother, thank God, from the day I gave up sin to this hour, I never had a reserved right. I say, "Lord, I will do any thing—every thing." I have invested my all in it. All that I have is in this Book, and if it does n't break I am a millionaire through all eternity. That 's the way to talk it.

Submission to Christ! Do as he tells you to do. You are a most humble member of your Church until your preacher says something that touches you, and off you fly, and say: "If I can 't live in peace here, I 'll go and join another Church." Or perhaps some good sister says, "My husband and I were talking about this the other night, and we ain't going to stand this sort of thing." Sister! God bless you; go over there, and have the best time you can while you are here.

A gentleman said to me that at a meeting of an official board of his Church, at which his wife and himself were present, rum was passed around, and every one present, members of the board, including the pastor of the Church, except the gentleman who told me and his wife, drank of it. A preacher who will indulge in such things, not only with his members, but privately, belongs to the devil from his hat to his heels. I know when I did that way I belonged to the devil, and I do n't care whether the man is a preacher or not, the test of his allegiance to Christ is how he lives.

Christ says, "Not every one that saith unto me, Lord, Lord, shall enter into the kingdom of heaven." Now you say, "Mr. Jones, you ought not to be so rough on the ministers." Well, I called no names, and I would not tell my preacher that "Jones is hitting at him." It 's an insult to tell him that he is being hit.

Then we say again, that being in Christ Jesus presupposes union with Christ. "I am the vine, and ye are the branches," says Christ. Did you ever go into a vineyard and examine the vines and branches? Did you ever see how closely in vital forces they were united? how the very vitality of the branch was determined by the vine? If united to Christ, he and myself are one, one in all things, in earnestness, in energy, in goodness, in mercy, in purity, in truth.

Being in Christ Jesus presupposes also all the affinities which control one's life — his likes, his looks, his thoughts, his tastes, his all. It is a religion, assimilation with the character of our Lord Jesus Christ, doing like him, thinking and being like him. Blessed Christ, give us a religion that makes us like thyself, and then we shall be Christians in the grandest sense. Our blessed Lord loved the sinners and died for them. Let us, brethren, imitate our divine Lord, and do the best we can for the sinning and erring ones around us.

BRIEF SAYINGS.

A CHRISTIAN who will do things in New York that he would not do at home is a very poor Christian.

IT takes less sense to criticise than to do any thing else. There are a great many critics in the asylum.

I DON'T think much of dignity. My observation is that the more dignity a man has, the nearer dead he is.

WHEN the doctor says you can't live but an hour you'll want just such a preacher as myself talking to you.

WHEN you find a man that is first-class for some one thing, you will find him pretty good for every thing else.

THERE is more religion in laughing than in crying. If religion consists in crying I have the best boy in the world.

IF any of you don't like the way these services are going, there are three doors—you are cordially asked to leave.

SERMON XXVIII.

WORKING TOGETHER FOR GOOD.

"And we know that all things work together for good to them that love God, to them who are the called according to his purpose."—ROM. VIII, 28.

WHY am I in this world? I had no choice as to the time or the circumstances of my coming into it. The question of environment is a question that was decided for me—that temptations should beset me; that difficulties, sometimes insurmountable, should present themselves; that obstacles, over which I might not go, should be in my way. After all, this question has aroused the imagination and escaped the lips of many a man—"Why am I in this world of so much sin and so much suffering? What am I doing here?" And the most patient man the world ever saw cursed the day he was born.

Brethren, if a man looks on the things that are seen, and not on the things that are unseen, it is not much trouble to get up a state of mind to curse the day when he was born; but a man who looks at the unseen and determines what the seen things are by the unseen things, then, thank God, he blesses the day he was born into a world of such providences and privileges. Ten thousand men, may be, had walked along the highway and had seen that block of marble. It had been gazed upon by thousands of eyes, but they saw simply a block of stone; but Michael Angelo came along and saw what they did not see. He saw an unseen something in it, and he sat down at that block with chisel and mallet in hand, and the first thing they knew, he had hewn out an angel, which, if God had breathed the breath of life into it, might have sat near the throne of God and adorned heaven with its beauties. He saw an angel there that others did not.

I tell you, brethren, when I simply look at rough-hewn nature, as I see it, I am astonished that I am here; but when I see God with the mallet and chisel of his goodness, as he begins to hunt for the angel that is in me, and I realize that if I lie still under the strokes of God's hammer, some of these days God will hew that angel out of me, then I realize that in this world it is possible to make an angel out of every such a being as I am.

After all, brethren, it is to the unseen that we must look. I walk into a great work-shop, and I see in there pieces of timber, boards, carpenter's tools, saws, planes, and machinery at work. I say, "What is all this? It's confusion and disorder to me. What do they mean?" The architect looks at me, and says, "Wait about three months, and I will show you what it all means." And I wait three months, and there is a palatial residence that grew out of the disorder in that work-shop. I did not know what it all meant, but the architect did. In this world of temptations and trials and griefs and tears, sick-beds and good-byes, we do not understand these things, but the great Architect, who

METROPOLITAN CHURCH, TORONTO.

is working out the problem of eternity, understands them all, and if we only stand still, he will show us the mansions "not made with hands, eternal in the heavens."

I wish we had faith to look on and see God at work.

And, brother, really, I believe I am willing to turn the matter over to the good Lord. I tried to run the thing according to my own notion twenty-four years, and I declare to you, I wound up in disgust. I said, I am willing to turn this thing over to any body. But I found nobody but God to take it off my hands in the condition I was in, and it is astonishing how he is working things into order out of chaos. The process in this world is to take from, and not to add to. Michael Angelo never added any thing to the marble block; he just cut it away and chipped it off, until finally there was an angel, sure enough. Now, brother, you lie still under fire, and let God chisel off the rough and rugged points and angles of your nature, and let grace work you down to where you ought to be, and you will be beautiful enough to charm heaven after a while.

Human nature wants something added, but God wants to take away all those things that damage you in time and in eternity, and if you let God hew off and take away all that ought to be taken off, he will see to it that eternal life, in all its purity and glory, is imparted to you. Let no one say the Lord does n't do any thing for him but hew off things from him, that God does n't put any thing on to him; for God imparts to man some things, and those things are all necessary for a pure and holy life, for time and for eternity.

I suppose our text is one, of all texts, the hardest to be understood. "All things work together for good to them that love God, to them who are the called according to his purpose." You see it is in the present tense; the work is going on now, and for all who love God. In order that we may the better understand it, let us notice some of the terms. "All things work together for good to them who love God." Good! What do you mean by good? There is no wonder you do not understand the text, you have interpreted it wrongly. If you have interpreted it wrongly, there is no sense in it. With a wrong interpretation, there is not a word of truth in it; but if you interpret it wisely, it is the divinest, grandest truth of all.

Suppose you interpret it this way: "All things work together for good to them who have riches." That would not be true, because many of the poorest people in the world are God's people, and they never have any thing; they live from hand to mouth day by day. And if that were true then religion would be something we could buy—"the rich would live, and the poor would die"—but it is not. I am so glad that it does n't take money to get religion, for I was bankrupted with all worlds, and I never would have gotten it if it required money to have it. It does n't take any thing to purchase religion, but it takes a good deal to keep up repairs after you have got it. Well, you can't get to New York quickly or easily, without a cent. You might foot it every step of the way and beg your bread, but that's a hard route; but you can't go on a Pullman sleeper, with all the conveniences and comforts at hand, without money. And that's the difference in the routes or manner of traveling. One is easy and restful, and the other is exhausting and uninviting.

Hear! There is not a man in the world who values the stated meetings of the Church and the work of the pastors more than I do. I was eight years a pastor myself. Thank God for every pastor and all Church organization in this country. Suppose there was nothing in this country but evangelists; you would be in a bad fix.

What is an evangelist? He is just an extra hand at the harvest, to throw the cradle. If you had not prepared the ground, sowed your seed, and protected the growing crop, you would have had no use for evangelists. Remember our Father saith, "One man soweth and another reapeth, and let him that soweth and him that reapeth rejoice together;" and "He hath given to some prophets, and to some evangelists, and to some pastors." It takes more patience, and courage, and fortitude to make an efficient pastor than it does to make a hundred evangelists. It's a nice thing to go around throwing your harvest cradle into somebody else's wheat.

No man values the work of a pastor more than I do; but, brother, I think our membership is very much like locomotive engines. An engineer told me once that after every trip the engine went into the shops; her machinery was overhauled, the bolts tightened; but, he said, about every four years she must go into the round-house and be taken all to pieces, overhauled, and made new again. So with our membership; every time they come to the house of God we overhaul their religious machinery and tighten the bolts of their purposes, but ever and anon these revival occasions are but the grand round-houses, where our membership are taken all to pieces and overhauled from head to foot. I said to the engineer, "How do you know when an engine needs this thorough overhauling?" He said, "When she gets so she can't make schedule time and carry the loads." So frequently our membership is run down in its love and faith and hope, to where it does n't make schedule time towards the good world, then it's time for a revival. This community now has many a Christian in it that can't make schedule time, and surely they need overhauling. The devil can run a mile while many of you are pulling on your boots, and revival meetings are almost useless unless you have perennial revivals, and they are things of beauty and joy forever.

An old brother once said, "God showed what he thought of money by the people he gave it to." That was death on those who strive after riches alone. "All things work together for the riches of God's people." That won't do, brother, for some of God's people are the poorest people.

Suppose we say then, that "all things work together for the health of God's people." That won't do either. The best people I have ever seen are those who have suffered the most. It is the bruised violet that sends forth the sweetest odor. The sweetest Christians are those most deeply afflicted.

It is a right good thing to be sick occasionally. It helps almost any man to shake him over a coffin for awhile and then turn him loose; and when he is turned loose he will hit the ground, running a mile a minute. But take a great, healthy, two hundred pound fellow, fat and saucy, and it's mighty hard to keep him straight—that's a fact. David said, "It is good for me that I have been afflicted." The best people I have ever met were the most afflicted people. And God never said that all things shall work together for the health of his people.

Well, there is another thing. Suppose we interpret this way: "All things shall work together for the happiness of God's people." He does n't say that. I have seen God's people under the most severe gloom and despondency, with the deepest and darkest clouds hanging over them. I have seen the purest and most loyal Christians I ever met with clouds of sorrow upon them that would have crushed my own heart, and, thank God, I can be just as good when I am miserable and despondent and gloomy, as when I am happy and joyous. It is not how you feel, but how you do that makes you a Christian.

Some people think they are backsliders when they get a little gloomy or a little unhappy about things. Brother, it's no sin to be tempted. You may feel divers temptations, but stand firm like a man, and fight them off. Some of the best fights I have ever made, when it looked as if God had withdrawn his presence from me, have been fights that I have won. Happiness is the normal state of a Christian, but when sorrow and gloom overtake him let him recollect Job, and say, "Though he slay me, yet will I trust in him."

Suppose we interpret the text to read, "All things shall work together for the honor of God's people." A great many of God's people in this world never received any honor; and there are women, pure, Christly women, who have never been seen in their works of charity and deeds of kindness; but, sister, when you get to heaven, God will announce to all worlds that, "here is one, who, in feeding the hungry, in relieving the thirsty, in clothing the naked, in visiting the prisoner, and in waiting on the sick, because she did it unto the least of my brethren, did it unto me."

There are many poor humble Christians in this world who never had any body to clasp their hands for them in welcome, but the angels in heaven will clap their hands as they watch their good works. Even while no man cries hosannas for you, you are working under the sympathy of God and the smiles of angels. Go on and do your duty, whether you meet the applause of men or not.

And after all, brethren, the difference between a great man here and great success, and a street car mule, is very little. They are very much alike in some things. You know a street car mule always walks and the crowd rides. You know whenever you see a man of much reputation, he is doing the pulling and the crowd is doing the riding. And there is another thing about them that is alike. Just as soon as the street car mule dies, the company gets another in his place that will do just as well. So it is with a man of much reputation; you work him to death and then put another right in his place.

At the close of our series of services in Cincinnati, a gentleman came into my room and said, "Mr. Jones, I come from men of business and men of means to say, that if you will stay here thirty days longer we will give you twenty thousand dollars." Said I, "Yes, that's just about enough to buy a solid silver casket to bury me in, and have my name engraved on it, and ship my body home to my wife. And you will meet and pass a set of resolutions a yard long, lauding my name and character, and publish it as a historical fact, that, 'Sam Jones preached his last sermon in our town.' Now wouldn't that be a joke on me?" "O, we'll do wonders for you if you'll stay."

Well, brother, listen; they will work a man to death, pass resolutions about him, ship his body home to his wife, and then publish it that, "he preached his last sermon to us." Brother, go on in your humble way in the service of God. I know it is a great thing to be like George Whitefield, to throw your blade into any and all of the harvest fields of the Lord; but, brother, go out into the harvest field with your little jack-knife, and say, "Good Lord, I am doing my best." And harvest time means a busy time. Every body is busy, the old gentleman, the old lady, and all doing something—all busy. And, brother, during a season of a revival of religion every Christian ought to be very busy, little and big, old and young. The harvest does n't last long, but work must be done. If you do n't cut the wheat, it will fall down. There is many an old sinner tottering on the verge of ruin, and if we do n't cut him down, he will fall into perdition forever. You 've got to be in a hurry about this, brother.

"And we know that all things shall work together for the honor of God's people"—that is n't it. We know God's people are not people of a great deal of honor, or fame, as the world looks upon it. I am glad of it, too. Why, a man never gets to a position of honor in this country until he is covered with mud from head to foot. You may take the case of any President in the White House. His term of service is four years, and it takes him the four years he is there to wash off the mud he got on him while on his way to that exalted station. I ain 't running much on that sort of honor. And if I ever told the truth in my life, I would rather be a humble, earnest, efficient preacher of the Gospel of Jesus Christ than to be the President of the United States in the White House with all his money, this minute. I would not swap places with him. "But," you say, "that won 't do; every body would like to be President." I do n't want to be. I may have done a heap of devilment in my life, and I do n't want it uncovered any more; but just as soon as I got to be President they would uncover it immediately—the game would n't pay for the powder and shot. And my wife is as foolish as I am. I saw in a newspaper where a reporter had been talking to her, and she said, "I had rather be the wife of Sam Jones than the wife of the President of the United States." Some of you sisters who are turning up your noses at Sam Jones, do n't you forget that.

"All things work together for the honor of God's people"—it does n't say that, brethren. But what does it say? There is but one word in this universe, and, thank God, it 's the grandest word that heaven ever gave to man. It covers all for all worlds—Listen:

"All things work together for the *salvation* of them who love God." This is what our text means. Thank God for this grand truth. Now I can understand; now I can see through it.

Brother, what is salvation? It is the good of heaven. It is the *summum bonum*. It is the all good, and of all worlds. There is nothing good on earth and in heaven that is not covered with that word, "salvation." "All things work together for the *salvation* of them who love God." Whatever there is in honor, happiness, riches, or health, thank God, if you lean on him in your ways and words, he promises salvation in it; and that is what we are all going for, brethren.

"All things work together for salvation to them who love God." I wish I had time to go into that thought thoroughly—the love of God to us—we could talk a month on it. Whenever I think of the love of God I am lost in wonder at his great compassion, until I cry out, "O my Father, how unbounded, how inconceivable is thy love to us."

"All things work together for good to them who love God." God makes all his forces work to and converge at that point, where they must bring salvation to you if you love him. God is an active God. I will tell you, my brother, as I look about me in this vast world and around me, I see how God has put his power and energy upon and into every thing. I see it in the cyclone and in the storm. He made the sun to shine by day and the moon to be a light by night, and the rivers to flow, and the flowers to bloom, and he made all nature to manifest his power and activity; and amid the rush of the world and the stillness of the stars, God looks down and says, "Why stand ye here idle? Look at all nature, how she rushes and stirs. What are you standing there for?" That's it. God is all activity, and he says, "All things work together for good to them who love him."

Many a time we wonder what good can there be in this or in that thing that happens, and say, "There certainly can not be any good in this;" but, brother, when you step up into the light of God's love, and look back, you will say, "Glory be to God, every thing worked together for my salvation." You can not understand it from the end you have been looking from, but when you get to heaven you will say, "I see it all now; I could not see it from the other end, but I see it now from this end."

"All things work together for good to them who love God." We will put it in this way: Let us go to our homes; doubtless each of us has a clock on his mantle. Well, I'll take my clock at home all to pieces, and when I endeavor to put it together again I find I have enough wheels left out for three clocks of the kind. I do n't understand it. That clock was made by a clock-maker, and it must be put together by a clock-maker, and he must put all the wheels in the right place, and there must be just a certain number of cogs in each wheel. There is one wheel in that clock that has sixty cogs, and if you put sixty-one or fifty-nine cogs in it you will never get it to keep time. God knows how many cogs to put in the wheels of our lives, does n't he? I take off the face of a clock and look in at it. I see one great wheel turning slowly, and another wheel turning faster, and one wheel turning backward and another forward, and I say, You can't tell me that this thing is keeping time, for, look! some of the wheels are turning backwards—this thing can't keep time; but I put the face on again, and I put my ear to it, and listen, and I hear it going, "tick, tick, tick," and I hear it strike the hours, then I say, "It does keep time, sure enough."

Now, look here, brother, God says, "All things work together for good to them who love God." You have lost the best wife a man ever had—that was one of those big wheels turning slowly. O the sadness of your heart and home. Adversity came, and swept away your fortune; that was the small wheel turning backwards, and you said, "O how can this work for my good?" God never said every one thing works, but "all things altogether work together for good to them who love God." God blesses you with prosperity—that's one of the little wheels going faster. One of your children died, and that's one of the little wheels going backward; but when God puts them all together with his own master hand, he sits in heaven rapt in the contemplation of his wonderful work well done. Now, brother, let the problems of life be worked out by our Father in heaven, and his blessings shall be upon you.

I am so glad God understands me and knows me and leads me, and I am so glad when God says, "All things are working together for your good." There is but one thing in the universe that is an exception to this rule, and that one thing is sin. God never made sin work for the good of any one. God himself can not make sin work for any body's good. Until God can make what ought not to have been, so that it ought to have been, he can not make sin work for good to any man.

I used to think, as a boy, when my father whipped me that I would ask him why he did it, but I found out before I was twenty-one years old that my father was trying to whip the devilment out of me.

Do n't resist God; take whatever he puts on you. Do n't run away or fight; just fold up your hands and lean towards God, and rush up to God, and may be he won't strike a lick.

Precious Father! thou art always right; thou

can'st not make a mistake; thou art all love; thou can'st work no hardship to me, and if I trust thee all will be well. Brother, let us get that sort of faith in God.

Now, then, on the score of gratitude and thanksgiving, let us start out on that line. The way to get more good is to thank God for that which you have. That was a grand old man, an old Presbyterian pastor, of whom I have read. He was the idol of his people and a blessing to his city. After years of faithful service, all at once he commenced bleeding from his lungs, and hemorrhage after hemorrhage followed. Every time he tried to preach it grew more violent, until finally his physician said to him, "It will cost you your life to attempt any further service. You must quit the pulpit now, and, perhaps, forever." That was sad news to him, and a few days after the leading elder of his Church came to him, and said: "The new pastor is coming in and you must vacate the parsonage; but the best place in my house is at your disposal, and you and yours shall be cherished in my wife's heart and in my own, and shall have a home as long as you all shall live." That was worthy of the elder, and in a few days he moved the old pastor and his family to his home. In a short time the old pastor's only child was taken suddenly ill, grew worse, and then died. What a stroke was that! A few days again, and the old pastor's wife was stricken with some eye trouble, and she became totally, hopelessly, blind. One day after this new affliction the pastor walked out in the pleasant evening, and when he returned to his room his wife heard his footsteps and hurried up to him, put her hands on his shoulders, and turned her sightless eyes up to his face, and with tears welling up, that would not have stained an angel's cheek, said, "Husband, I have gained a great victory since you left, and have made up my mind to submit to God." He said, "O precious wife, what great victory? Did you gain it understandingly?"

"Yes, yes," said the wife.

"Well, let us see; we have the best home here any body ever had."

"Yes," said the good woman.

"Wife, will you submit to that?"

"Yes, husband."

"Well, we have the best friends God ever gave any body."

"Yes, that is true."

"Will you submit to that?"

"Yes," she said.

"Well, we have a darling daughter in heaven, sitting now under the shade of the tree of life to be with God forever. Will you submit to that?"

"Yes, yes," she said.

"Then, wife, we have all the precious promises of God to be ours every day. Will you submit to that?"

"Yes, O yes."

"Well, God is going to come after a while to take us both to heaven to live and reign with Christ. Will you submit to that?"

"O, my husband, hush, hush; I'll never say

any thing more about submission as long as I live. I'll praise God the balance of my life."

And, brother, all we have to do is to submit to the will of God. Even with home and all gone, submit yourself to God without a word of murmur or a thought of reproach. "I will just praise God always." And in the direst extremities of life we can thank God for ten thousand blessings we receive from him.

I will tell you when we reflect upon the goodness of God to us we ought to be ashamed of ourselves to be talking about our "crosses and our losses." Let us have that kind of religion, even though we lose all that we have and love here; we can love God and submit with patience and gratitude to his will. God bless you, my brethren, and keep you according to his perfect will.

BRIEF SAYINGS.

I HAVE known women too poor to own a pair of shoes—but I never knew one to be too poor to own a looking glass.

I HAVE seen preachers who looked as sad and solemn as if their Father in heaven was dead and had n't left 'em a cent.

HEAVEN is the spiritual center of gravity for all things good; hell is the spiritual center of gravity for all things evil.

YOU do n't believe what you do n't understand? Do you understand why some cows have horns and some are muley?

SERMON XXIX.

PROFESSION AND PRACTICE.

"Many will say to me in that day, Lord, Lord, have we not prophesied in thy name? and in thy name have cast out devils? and in thy name done many wonderful works? And then will I profess unto them, I never knew you: depart from me, ye that work iniquity."—MATT. VII, 22, 23.

IT is not advantages, but disadvantages, that make a man. Many a time you hear a man say, "I 'm going to lay by something for my children; they shall never undergo the hardships that I underwent." But he does n't know, you see, that those very hardships that he underwent made him what he is, and that if he lays by and endows his children, the probability is, they won't have money enough to pay for their funerals, when the time comes to bury them. God save this country from an endowed Church, and the Church from an endowed member. The one will soon be a failure, the other will soon be in the cemetery, or *vice versa.* I have never known a prosperous endowed Church, and very few endowed sons. I say it is disadvantages that develop the man. It is hindrances, not help, that make success. Almost any body can come to a meeting on a fair Sunday, but earnest people only come out on stormy days.

I have been sitting here, brethren, revolving in my mind what is the best evil to run on this morn-

INTERIOR VIEW OF METROPOLITAN CHURCH, TORONTO, ONTARIO.

ing. What is the best thing to do? Now, I like expressions like this: "Bless the Lord, O my soul, and all that is within me, bless his holy name." "What shall I render unto the Lord for all his benefits towards me? I will take the cup of salvation and call upon the name of the Lord." "I will bless the Lord at all times; his praise shall be continually in my mouth." "My soul shall make her boast in the Lord." People are afraid to say much about their religion. They 're afraid somebody will consider them Pharisees.

Well, now, brother, I think you would do just as well to give over any such notion as this of being considered a Scriptural Pharisee. I do n't know any body here that is likely to be one. Do you know any body that fasts twice a week and gives one tenth of every thing he possesses to the Lord? So now, it is possible that you might be considered a Pharisee, but I do n't suppose you ever were within a thousand miles of being one. You have n't got that near yet. Do you know any who fast twice a week, and give abundantly to God? If there are any such persons, they 're coming along to where they might be considered Scriptural Pharisees. A great many things are worse than being a Pharisee. I believe that being afraid you will be called one, when you ain't worthy of being called one, is worse than actually being one. To say the least of it, there was a strong disposition in the minds of the Pharisees to tote fair with God; and I say to you, that 's our difficulty—toting fair with God; giving God such a portion of my time as he ought to have, such a portion of my money as he ought to have, and such a portion of my influence as he ought to have. Very few people will do that—very few.

Our Christianity, somehow or other, has been converted largely into a sort of begging arrangement—everlastingly receiving and holding on to what we get. I went to a good old woman's house once, and she put me up stairs in a room, and there was an old chest in the room—a large chest, the top of which was sprung up. I had a curiosity to know what the old soul had in there, and I just raised the lid and looked. It was about four dozen of the nicest counterpanes you ever saw in your life. But she did n't have a single one on any bed in the house that I saw at all; and I wondered in my soul why this old woman did n't put some of these on the beds. But I heard, after that, that another gentleman went in there—it was n't myself—and he dropped a coal of fire off a match, or a cigar, or a pipe, and set fire to the old lady's counterpanes and burned the whole business, and was like to have burned the house up. That was a natural consequence of keeping counterpanes packed up that way. I do n't say that in some great casement in your heart you have got a thousand good sermons, and good resolutions, and good purposes packed away, and the lid of the thing is springing up, it is so full; but you have n't got a single one on your tongues that you might speak words of cheer and kindness; on your feet, that you might walk in the paths of righteousness. Just say,

"Every sermon, instead of being packed away in the casement of my heart, I believe I will spread out on my tongue, and hands, and feet, and make it indeed not only an adornment to my life, but a blessing to my neighbor." Now we have been packing away sermons, and we are everlastingly intent on receiving.

Well, now, a man gets out of religion just in proportion as he puts into it. A man gets off his farm just in proportion as he puts into it. A man that 's everlastingly drawing off his farm and never putting any thing in, is headed to agricultural bankruptcy. A man that 's everlastingly drawing on his religion, and never putting any thing in it, is headed to spiritual bankruptcy. I believe that. Now, I infer that most of us here are professed Christians, and we are here to receive something. There appears to be a type of Christian in the world who has every pocket empty every time he comes to hear about God. He has every hand empty, and his mouth wide open, to get something. He is one of those receiving Christians, like an old pond with water draining in; the pond takes in every thing, but has no outlet in the world. You know a pond or a lake that has no outlet, only tends to breed miasma, mosquitoes, and tadpoles, and such like, and in religious life, when it catches every thing, and has no outlet, it breeds division in the Church and selfishness. I hear a great deal said about "self"—the worst and most miserable picture of hell. Hell is nothing but selfishness on fire. Brethren, it is not what we receive; it is what we give out, that keeps us spiritually alive. There was a good old woman who got up at the camp-meeting and said she was going to fly to heaven, and she jumped up, and gave a flop, and down she came. Every body laughed, and she jumped up, and brushed the straw off her dress, and said, "Well, ye need not be laughing; my trouble was I did not get the right flop." There is a good deal in the right "flop." Religion in a big meeting is not the best religion in the world. You can not fly to heaven from a revival. Revivals! revivals! A great many people think they are the best things in the world. Brother, in a sense, they may be very good, but they are not the best things in the world. A revival like this may be likened, in a sense, to a conversation I heard between a sewing machine agent and a merchant. A gentleman was talking sewing machines to the merchant, and he talked with a vengeance. I listened, and I said, "O, if I could only preach Christ as that fellow talks sewing machines." By and by, the merchant said, "I would take all the machines you have, if I could talk 'machines' as you can." The agent said, "When I sell a lady a machine, I say very little about it. All I do is to put the machine up, and show her how to thread the needle, and let her learn the rest from the book of instructions." At the revival we show you how to thread the needle, and here is the Book of Instructions to guide you in every thing to success in life. Revivals can only start you, but God says, "Continue patiently in well doing," and says, "Well done, thou good and faithful servant." Well finished! There is a heap in a good start. There is a great deal more in carrying a thing on well, but when it comes to "Well done, it is finished," you are right.

Now, brother, there is more real joy in giving a cup of cold water in the name of Christ than there is in receiving any thing at the hands of another. Sometimes we value a present, not so much by its intrinsic value as by the person who gives it to us. I have known a souvenir of some sort, a present not worth fifty cents if its associations are taken away; but a person would not take thousands for it. This was a gift of a precious mother, on her dying bed. This was the gift of the best friend you ever had. Brethren, God's gifts to his children are invaluable. This Bible was given me by God. You can not price such presents as that, and yet God is giving, and giving, and giving; and what have we shown in return? Lord, thou hast fed me this day upon thy bounty; and to show thee I am grateful for it, I am going to feed some other one.

The best way to get God to help you is for you to pitch in and help every person else that needs help. The Lord helps men that help somebody else. The Lord works on a contrary line to selfishness every time. You hear a fellow say, "I have about as much as I can do to get to heaven myself. I have no time to fool with other people." Take him now, and follow him up. It is the truth. He has all he can do to get himself to heaven. He has the biggest job of any man I know of.

Really I would rather run forty locomotives, direct twenty cyclones, and look after forty earthquakes, than look after two hundred pounds of the genuine selfishness that wears breeches, and looks like a man. It is about the toughest job a man could undertake, to rule a genuine, solid lump of pure concentrated selfishness. Do n't get shocked at any of these things. I am talking about natural history now. These animals live all about in these days. "You may not be familiar with them," as the old darkey says, "but they lie 'round as sure 's you live." Really, some of us are too decent to be religious, anyhow. That is the fact about it. There are plenty of people here in churches too decent to be religious.

I read a clause this morning in one of the papers, about what a preacher said in St. Paul. He is preaching to a fashionable church. They drove up in their carriages. At the meeting he said, "Brethren, if Jesus Christ were on earth, and followed the trade of a carpenter, as he did in his youth among men, there is not one of my members who would speak to him, and he could not come into the respectable society of this town until he got into a carriage to attend the divine service, and joined some town club." Do you believe that?

Now, Jesus Christ is represented in the person of every poor man in this town. Do you know that when Old Hickory Jackson, President of the United States, sent over to France to know by his representative, what France was going to do about the American claims, they treated his messenger with indignity, and when Old Hickory received the message, that they said they would not pay the claim, he shook his fist towards France, and said, "By the eternal, if they do n't pay it, I will make them do it." Do you get the idea? Whenever France, or any other country, so heaped an indignity upon the ministers of the United States, they heaped that indignity upon the government of the United States. When you meet some Christian people in this town, whom you do n't run with, and associate with, because they do n't happen to have as much as you have, you heap indignity upon Jesus Christ, and he will resent it with all the force of heaven, earth, and hell.

Why, we move in strata. Some of you good women know there is a certain stratum you run with. There may be thirty or forty ladies in the Metropolitan Church, about a dozen of whom you call upon, and about half a dozen you are really intimate with. Take the Metropolitan Church, with all her history, and if we were all called up to heaven to-morrow, it would take the angels two or three weeks to get you all introduced to each other. It would just keep the angels busy awhile. Now, what sort of religion do you call that? When two or three *bon ton* members get off to themselves, you might overhear something like this: "I can tell you why I never met her. She was cook with Mrs. So-and-so, and we never associate with this sort." Sister, what are you going to do in heaven? Won't you hate to run with your cook in glory? Is it not true that there are some too decent to be religious? The hopeful, brotherly, cheerful Christianity is unselfish. This is what we want in this world.

I was in Milledgeville, Georgia, preaching once, when I struck the idea of brotherly kindness. I used this illustration just as it happened to come upon my mind, and I said, "Here is Mrs. A. She lives in a beautiful, palatial home. She has the best servants in the town, the best husband, and every thing she could wish for. She gets sick, and I sit on a portico opposite the home. I say, 'What does it mean by all these ladies going in and out of that home?' And as I sit there for a few minutes, there comes an elegant waiter, covered with its linen towel, and I ask, 'What is the matter over there?' 'Well, Mrs. So-and-so is sick, and the neighbors are calling on her with their waiters, and nice things fixed for her.' I say, 'I declare, there are the cleverest people here I ever saw in my life. I have seen nothing comparable to that.' And the first thing I know the door bell is muffled. The doctor says she must not have company, and I call in for a few minutes to know how she is getting on. When the elegant waiters are going into her sick-room, I understand she said: 'Take them to the kitchen,' and I hear that when they went out to the kitchen, the servants had a good time over the waiters. They are sending in things, and that woman has a better cook in her place, and better things than any one else, and she does not need a thing in the world. But," said I, "there's old Sister Snipe, living down there on the hill side, in a little log cabin. She got sick three weeks ago, and I never saw any body going there to call on her, and she was a member of the same Church. And," said I, "I never heard the doctor tell her she 'd better not receive company for so many weeks, and I never saw the waiter going up to her house." Well, you 'll hardly believe it, but at the end of that service, an old lady came up to me, and said, "God bless you, Mr. Jones; you just gave them the truth. I have lain sick three weeks many a time, and no one of them ever came near me." "Why, what 's your name, sister?" I asked. "Snipe," she said; "I thought you knew me. I live up in the little log cabin on the hill side." Well, I never was more surprised in my life. Old Sister Snipe was there "bodaciously," as they say, and I just happened on the truth.

O brothers and sisters, do good to them that need it most. Thank God for the unselfish Christianity that makes me see in every man's face the beaming eyes of a brother, and that makes me see in every woman's face the countenance of a sister. Suppose we were brothers and sisters, indeed; would any man, could any creature upon this world do aught to spoil the life or the character of a sister or brother? There 's where the world has missed it. We won't be brothers and sisters. God wants us to be. And, brethren, the more unfortunate your brother is, the more kind, and the more faithful you should be to him. I want to see a religion that gives us something to do, and is n't everlastingly catching at something. Why, if your religion were like grapes, and would not keep but two or three months, why, bless your soul, what would become of you? 'T would all go off on your hands like the grapes. Just get up and get at work, and not let your religion decay on your hands. O brethren, religion not used is religion misused. I wish you could see that. "What shall I render unto the Lord for all his benefits toward me?" Some of you say, "I got a deal yesterday. I wonder how much more I shall get to-day." "What shall I render unto the Lord for all his benefits toward me?" Let's look around to-day, and say, each one of us, "As God is my judge, I am going to do something for God; I am going to do good to somebody to-day." I have gone home from a revival many a time very hungry, because passive religion is not the best religion in the world. When I got home, I would say to my wife, "How is poor old Aunt Ann up the hill?" She was a poor, old negro woman, dying from the cancer, and my wife had been feeding her from her table for months. My wife says, "She's a great deal worse." I often used to visit the old woman. She is in heaven to-day. "Well," said I, "then you get on your bonnet, and let's go up and see her." And we would go up the hill and see Aunt Ann, and we would sit by her bedside and sing hymns, and read the Scriptures, and pray to God; and when we went away, we did so feeling, sure enough, as if we had been to heaven. The last time I visited her, I left a dollar or two in her poor, withered hand, and she said, as she turned her shrunken eye on me, "Young master" (she always used to call me so), "when I get to heaven it won't be long before I'll tell the angels how good you have been to me," and the consciousness that I have done good to one poor, old negro woman is as much, and more, to me, as the biggest revival meeting I ever saw running under my ministry.

I tell you, brethren, good religion is n't in great big crowds, where they're preaching. It's over yonder, by the bedside of that sick woman, or by the side of a destitute friend, trying to soften his troubles with kindness. That's good religion. I meet a poor, old negro on the road, and stop him, and say, "Uncle, here's a half dollar piece for you." And as I go on, the old negro says, "Good Lord, bless dat man. He's jus' like an angel dropped down from heaven, to come right here, and gib me dis half dollar," and that night, when I go to bed, the eagle on the half dollar piece turns into a nightingale, and sings me to sleep. Have you ever been along there, brethren? I paid five dollars for a hat one day. It was n't a good one, and I never got any satisfaction out of that hat—never had any enjoyment from it. I gave half a dollar to an old negro, and got more enjoyment from that act than from all the hats in town. I wish we could see that religion would help us along. Blessing others! That's religion. I am just going to leave these thoughts with you for you to think over. I tell you, brethren, there is something in this line of things for every one of us to go home and think about. Ask yourself, "Who would think about me, if I were to die?" Let me give you an illustration I've given frequently. I was called to the bedside of a sick man one day. "Mr. Jones," he said, "I want to be honest with God." "You mean," I said, "you want me to pray for you to get well?" "Yes," he said. "But," I said, "I can't pray for you to get well. Suppose God should ask me why I wanted you to get well, what should I say? You know you ain't fit for a thing in this round world, that I've ever found out. You won't pray, you won't pay, and I know nothing to bank on, if I ask God to keep you alive." Well, brethren, it just scared him up. He said, "Brother Jones, do you need any corn?" I said, "I don't need any particularly, but I guess I could do with a little." "Well," he said, "I'll send you 'round a load or two in the morning."

I tell you, brethren, there's nothing like tapping a fellow when he's down. You can work on him then. Some of you, if you thought you were dying, would want your pastor to pray for you to get well, and if the pastor were to do as you wanted him to do, and the Lord were to ask him why he wanted you to get well, I wonder what answer he would be able to make the Lord. Some of you ain't fit for a thing in this round earth, but just to come up and get your rations. Think of a soldier that does nothing but come up and draw his rations! The poorest kind of a soldier is the fellow that never fired a gun, or went to the front, but is still drawing his rations. The Lord deliver us from that sort of soldiers! Let's take these things home, and fit them to our lives. I am not banking on the fact that I am a revivalist, or that I preach to men, and move them, but on the fact that God can use me for little things, and that my name is written there. That is the secret of a true Christian joy. The glorious fact is that the cheerful part of my religion is not seen by men, and that my name is written in the Lamb's book of life. What avails me if thousands are converted? It is said that Judas Iscariot was the most earnest preacher of the twelve. God help us to get the sort of religion that will bless other people. And the Lord wants us to have that sort. I can't do any thing for God, who is independent in himself. I can't aid him in any way, personally, to him. But, brother, I will tell you how you can do it. "Come, ye blessed." Master, why dost thou say to me, "Come, ye blessed?" Because—listen—"I was an hungered, and ye fed me; I was naked, and ye clothed me. I was sick, and ye visited me." "Lord, when did we ever see thee sick, and visited thee, or hungry, and fed thee, or naked, and clothed thee?" "Inasmuch as ye have done it unto one of the least of these, my brethren, ye have done it unto me." Brethren, if you want to help Christ, go and look for some poor folks that love Christ, or ought to love him. Jesus says; "A cup of cold water, given in my name, shall not lose its reward." That's it. There are a great many impostors. A great many people hang around revivals just for the loaves and fishes. So they did in the days of Christ. But I would rather help ninety-nine impostors, and one genuine case, than let one genuine case go unblest. The truth of the business is, organized charity is the only real charity in the world — that charity that thinks of, and thinks into the cases, and thinks out the difficulties of those who need help, and puts them where they can assist themselves. But, brother, let us bless the people of this town this week. Let us go into it with our sleeves rolled up, and our hearts on fire with love to God and man. That 's what you want.

We have had hardly enough conflict in this milling. We have n't had as much as usual of the "I do n't like this," and "I won't put up with that." They are firing on us from the towns surrounding. But have you ever noticed how a cannon sounds in a grave-yard? There 's a peculiar ring to it. When a fellow shoots a gun from the cemetery, it has a sort of guttural tone, and seems to have crept from the tomb. But I say, brother, I never was afraid of ghosts, or cannons, or any thing else inside of a cemetery. But now, when you come out with the living, there may be a battery, but do n't you be disturbed by the cannonading of a cemetery. It is just a sound, that 's all. I suppose some of you may see the point, and some may not; but I mean it. To see an old fellow poke up his head till he raises his tomb-stone, and say, "Be quiet there," and then pull his head back in, and let his tombstone down! Be quiet there, do, boys; you will make infidels. May the grave-yards be kept enclosed, and the inhabitants not let out on us. Think on these things as you go. Work and pray, and when the cemeteries shall give up their dead, let it not be said of us that we were dead before the breath left us, but that we lived while we did live, and died in peace, and at last went home and found the Lord.

SAYINGS.

THE speed, and momentum, and destination of a cannon ball are to be determined always by how much powder is behind it; and your speed and course to the good world will depend a great deal upon how you start.

TALK about reason and common sense; if you will just let your common sense and your reason run over the past to-night, and look upon you in the present, you 'll say, "Well, surely God has poured his blessings upon me, and I ought to give him the homage of my heart, and the fidelity of my life."

LET 's quit singing the "Sweet By and By," and sing the sweet now and now. In joy make home pleasant. Make home pleasant! A thing of joy is a thing of beauty forever, as well as a thing of beauty is a thing of joy forever. Try to be joyous and pleasant for a whole week. Keep your faces straight, and if they get out of shape, let it be with a great big smile as broad as the double doors on your parlor. I like a smile a mile long sometimes.

SERMON XXX.

DELIGHTING IN THE LORD.

"Delight thyself also in the Lord; and he shall give thee the desires of thy heart."—PSA. XXXVII, 4.

THERE are moral forces in the world, brethren, just as there are physical forces. About two years ago, I was walking on the railroad track just above my town, with the pastor of our Church. He was a younger man than myself. "Jones," he said, "we will have a cyclone this afternoon about two o'clock." I said, "Have you gotten out your almanac yet?" "No," he replied. "Well," I said, "if you have got so that you can predict storms and cyclones, you ought to get out one." "I am not joking," he said; "do n't you see how the wind has changed? Just now it was in our faces; now it 's at our backs; in another minute or two it will be on our right, and then on our left. You look out about two o'clock." Well, we went out and took dinner with my brother, and then he drove us into town in his buggy. We got home just about two o'clock. My brother was around at the back, and we heard him suddenly shout, "Look! look!" We ran out to the back door, and there was one of those fearful cyclones, carrying houses, and trees, and almost every thing, in its sweep. I stood watching it in its deathly course, and it passed just a mile

ST. PAUL CHURCH, CINCINNATI.

below us. It was just about four hundred yards wide, and looked like a thousand coal-burning engines chained together. "There's your cyclone," said I to the pastor. "I will tell you why it had to come," he said, "because conditions met. Whenever the proper conditions meet we shall have a cyclone."

Now, brethren, I just want to say that wherever conditions meet you will have a moral cyclone that will uproot the evil of the whole community, and lay bare the giants of sin in the land. We don't want a small whirlwind, or a little blow, but a grand spiritual cyclone. Let you and me go to work and get up conditions, and whenever they meet you will have a cyclone. I have seen a few of them. It is a grand sight to see a physical cyclone doing its work, but it is a grander sight to see a spiritual cyclone in operation. It is a grand sight to see the gray-headed old man, steeped in vice for seventy years, come to the stool of repentance, and throw himself on the mercy of God; and it is a grand sight to see a whole family gathered up and brought into the arms of the Church and Heaven. What a grand thing to see conditions meet so that God can bless people in a spiritual cyclone.

Now, brethren, I never tried to be heterodox in my life. I always tried to be orthodox, but never cared much about it. I have found out that every body that agrees with me is orthodox, and every body who does not agree with me is heterodox. How are we to get the standard of orthodoxy? Who is to tell us who is right and who is wrong?

But experience is worth a great deal. Sometimes theology gets very muddy. If my boy were called to preach, I would not send him to a school of theology, but to a school of manology. Our preachers know a good deal about God, but very little about men. Did you ever notice that? I will say again, and I want to be understood, there are two sides to the Gospel, just as there are two sides to farming. God's side of farming is raining and shining; and man's side to farming is plowing and hoeing, and planting. There 's many an old farmer, now, that would like to swap sides with God. He thinks it so much easier to rain and shine than to plow and hoe. And it 's much that way in religion. "O, Lord," says an old sinner, "if you will come down and quit uncleanness in me, I will do the blessing." I am so glad he won't do it—so glad he has fixed it so that you have to do the cleaning thing before he will bless you.

There are a great many things we would like to have changed in this world. That old fellow out there says: "Now, if God had fixed it so that there should have been no death, what a blessing it would have been!" Now, if some prophet here were to get up and announce to you all as the latest news from Heaven that nobody was to die in this city for a hundred years, I would just close up this meeting right off; what would be the use in carrying it on if none of you had to think any thing about dying? But just about ninety-five years from now if I were to come back this way I 'd be able to get up a great meeting, for you 'd be saying to yourselves, "I 've got to think about death now; I may die in five years' time; it is better to get ready." If death were abolished here for a hundred years the grass would grow up in front of every church in this town, and there's not a preacher here who would get fifty dollars salary next year. These environments around us were put here by God. Let us light on them as the honey-bee does on the flower, and with velvet tread let us walk as it does. Do n't mar the beauty, but extract the fragrance. You live in these environments, and use them well. God's love is abroad in the land, and he that believeth and liveth shall never die. The best way to get away from God is to run up toward God; and the best way to live is to die; and the best way to be happy is to get very miserable about your meanness. Conditions meet. Delight thyself in the Lord.

Now to-day we are trying to get up conditions. I like a cheerful, happy, bright-faced religion. I have seen very good people with sad countenances and solemn looks. I can remember when I was a little boy an old Methodist preacher used to come to our house and look solemn and dignified, and when he cocked his eye round and looked me in the face, I thought as how the devil would get me, sure, in about two minutes. I was afraid of him. Look here. If to be sad and unhappy, and solemn and droopy is religion, I never want to die without it, but I do n't want it until just the minute before I die. I would not be loaded with it from now until I die for any thing in the world. An unhappy, sad Christianity! I do n't blame young people for not catching on to religion of that sort. As the boys say: You will never get up a "mash" with the young folks on that line. Never! God is my Father. I am his child. He loves me; I love him. Brethren, I love my children. They call me "father," and I call them sons and daughters. Do you know, when they come around me with glad faces, I am happier than at any other time in the world? And whenever one of them comes up looking sad and droopy, I know he has done something mean or is sick, and I either brush him or give him a dose of medicine on the spot. It is perfectly unnatural for one of my children to go around droopy when he is all right.

Now, brethren, some of you do n't believe in enjoying yourselves and looking happy. Well, if I have paid my debts and done right all the week, on Sunday when I go to church, I want to wear a smile as broad as heaven. But if you have been making money by gouging a widow or in any other mean way, and telling lies and drinking whisky, you ought to be as solemn as a paid mourner. But if I have done my duty and gone along and done well, O, my Father in heaven, no angel shall outsmile me, or no angel outjoy me. Religion never was designed to make one pleasure less. I love a happy, cheerful Christianity. I am happy here; I will be there. I am happy on my journey. I thank God there is not only water enough in the river of life to wash the last speck of dirt out of a soul, but joy enough and over to keep every one happy on the way there. If God could not have made every one happy here

He would have knocked the devil in the head and boxed him up long ago.

Some people are never happy unless they are very miserable. They just know there is something wrong when they feel well. An old fellow said to me once: "I like to sing sometimes, to make myself feel humble." I said, "You old dunce! you do n't know the difference between feeling humble and feeling mean." It takes a metaphysician to tell the difference between the two. "Delight thyself in the Lord, and he will give thee the desires of thy heart." Delight yourself! Sister, suppose you had a servant, and every time you bade her go and do something she went off moping and growling; you would keep her about a week, and then say to your husband, "I am going to settle up with that girl; I do n't want her; I would rather do the work myself; she mopes and growls to do the least thing." I think sometimes, when the Lord tells us to do things and we go off to do them moping and growling, that he says to an angel: "Erase his name from among my servants. I would rather go down and do the work myself than have such a servant as that." Sister, once you had a happy, bright-faced servant, and when you would bid her do a thing she always did it with a smile. When you handed her a new dress one day your husband asked you if you were going to give her every thing. You say, "Well, she is so cheerful and happy I can 't refuse her any thing." I suppose sometimes one of the angels asks the Lord if he is going to give some people every thing, and he replies that they do his work so cheerfully and pleasantly that he can 't refuse them any thing. Down in Columbus, Georgia, one of the pastors, a happy, bright brother, walked into the post-office one morning and asked for his mail. The postmaster asked him inside. "Do you see these boots," he said, pointing to a handsome pair of new boots on his feet; "what do you think of them?" "They are very good." "Well," said the postmaster, "you go to such and such a place and let them take your measure. I want you to have a pair made just like them." The pastor said, "I do n't need any boots specially. What does it mean?" "Well, it 's not because I 've heard you preach so often, but because you 've put your head in at my window about 300 days during the year and given me a pleasant smile."

"Delight thyself in the Lord, and he will give thee the desires of thy heart." In Monticello, down where I was pastor, a carriage manufacturer called up his hands for a final settlement, and when he had paid them all off he called to a yellow-colored boy of about twenty, and said, "Harry, come here; here is a $20 gold piece for you." "What 's that for? you paid me," said Harry. "It 's because," said the master, "I called you up at all times of the day and night, and sent you off on all sorts of errands, and never saw you except with a smile on your face. This is for the way you did your work, not for what you did."

Motive has a good deal to do with all this thing. If I speak with the tongue of men and of angels, and do a thousand other things, and have not charity—a loving, gentle, submissive spirit—what does it amount to? If you will do gladly and cheerfully what the Lord gives you to do, he will not only pay full price for what you have done, but will pay you over again for the way you have done it. A cheerful man is to the world what oil is to the engines of a workshop. He keeps away friction and makes things run smooth. I believe if you do n't benefit a man's soul by preaching to him, you have done some good if you have improved his body. It is mighty hard for a man with a physical infirmity to be religious. Beecher said irreverently—and Beecher says many a good thing—that when his liver got out of fix the kingdom of heaven got out of fix for him. That is irreverent, but, as we say down South, "There 's gum in it." Before I commenced living and enjoying myself as I do now, I was thin and sallow, and look at me now. "Laugh and grow fat" on your way to glory. "Delight thyself in the Lord, and he will give thee the desires of thy heart." I believe in a happy, cheerful Christian. I believe that the happiest people in the world ought to be Christians, and that Christians ought to be the happiest people in the world, and enjoy themselves more than any people on earth.

Mope 'round here just as if your Father in heaven had died and left you nothing in his will and you are an eternal orphan! If some of my children looked as some of you people do sometimes, I would n't want to hear them call me "father" in company where any body could hear them. Let 's get the idea out of our head that a sad face means a clean heart, that a solemn look means purity of life, that dignity and usefulness are synonymous terms. When a man is full of sin he needs a good deal of dignity to hold him up. The more dignity a man needs and employs, the less he has of other things much better than dignity. I am going to be as dignified some day as any man in this crowd. It will be when I am laid out in my coffin. I will be as straight and composed then as any body. I never expect to be dignified until then. The more dignified a fellow is the nigher he is dead. Did you ever notice that? I said it—I mean it. What is dignity? It is the spread of a shroud. I fancy I hear some sister say about me, "He is so dreadfully out of propriety in every thing." Do you know what propriety means? See now. Did you ever see a fellow go right up to a thing straighter than I do? I have more propriety than any fellow you ever saw. Only you do n't know what propriety means. Your ignorance gets you into a heap of trouble. It does that. Your idea of propriety is this: You go down and look into a shop window, and see a hat bent and twisted and crooked until it will fit your foot as well as your head. That is your propriety. O, for a little more real dignity in the pulpit, and more propriety among our members! What is true dignity? To maintain with earnestness and fidelity the claims of God upon humanity; and true propriety is to go right up to a thing and strike at it without any circumbendibus.

Do you ever go to prayer-meeting on Wednesday nights? Some places in the United States you go in and you see the brothers and sisters drop in one by one until there are about seventeen of them sitting in seventeen different seats of the church. And one looks as if he came from China, and another as if he came from Africa, and a third as if he belonged to Greenland, and so on. By and by the preacher comes in, looking sad and solemn. "Brethren," he says in the solemnest of tones, "we are in the house of God, and it behooves us to be solemn." Then he solemnly announces a hymn, and solemnly kneels down in prayer. Then he will get up off his knees and read a chapter about the mountains trembling at His presence, and so on. You 've been along there. Then he 'll throw the meeting open for a talking meeting. One brother over there will get up and say, "It looks to me as if I 've had more temptations in the past week than ever before; it seems as if I must be getting along poorer in my religious life." Then another brother will look at another as much as to say, "It 's your turn now; I talked last week, and if you can 't do any better 'n I did you had better keep your seat." Then they all sit round and look solemn at one another; then they have another song and prayer, and then they call on old Brother A, and he gets on the bended knees of perishing humanity, and, if one may speak for all, they 've had a bad time of it. Then the brother dismisses the meeting, and tells them all to be sure and come back next Wednesday night. They all go away, and thank God they have been growing in grace. I 'd as lief try to make a shade tree out of the leg of that bench as to try to grow in grace on that line. Brethren, I want to go to the prayer service with joy in my heart. I want to be able to say, "I was glad when they said unto me, Let us go into the house of the Lord." I want to see the people of God go into the house of God with a rush, and conduct their meetings with a rush. Our Christianity is too slow. Half of us never get up with an old sinner until he is dying, or dead drunk, or too sick to move. Then we catch up with him. Nine out of ten of these nineteenth century sinners can run a mile while we are fastening ourselves. I have known a preacher who did n't expect to do any thing but worry the living and bury the dead. And that 's about all he did do. As soon as an old sinner got down to die, he 'd go and cry over him and talk about the Christian life, and at last perhaps he 'd get him to give to God the last remnants of a miserable life.

Brethren, have an aggressive, earnest, cheerful Christianity, full of life. Christianity is life or it 's nothing. Life! Life! And your words and works and actions and conduct are but the fruits which hang upon that tree which is your life. Be a cheerful, happy Christian. Go home and make home happy. Go home and make the wife happy. Go home and make the children happy. O, brethren, if there 's a place on earth that ought to be an Eden it is home. I hate to see a man who 'll stand behind the counter all day, and smile on every lady that comes in, and wait on her politely, and then will go home and look cross as a bear at his wife, and never say a word to her until bedtime, and then go off to bed having no more to say to her than if she had n't any existence at all. I never did like that kind of a fellow that was kind, and graceful, and polite to every woman but his own wife. Yes, and some of you 'll sit there now and look as innocent as if you never heard of such a thing. Sister, that 's a fact, is n't it? And to see a lady—I 've seen a few in America, polite and graceful to every gentleman she meets and yet she is n't cheerful and pleasant with her husband. Good Lord help me always to say it—if there 's one woman in this world that I 'll be polite and pleasant with, by the grace of God, it shall be my wife, and the mother of my children. If I do n't treat any but one family of children right, by the grace of God it shall be my own family of children. I tell you, brethren and sisters, the more religion you have, the better husband you are going to be, the better father you are going to be, the better mother you are going to be, the better children you are going to be. That is what we want to make our homes happy—Christianity in all its force and life and power. Delight yourself in the Lord. Let religion be your joy, and teach your children by your life and example that religion is not only designed to make you blessed, but it is the most blessed thing in the world.

Now, how can I get every thing I want? By delighting myself in the Lord—going along cheerfully and doing whatever the Lord tells me to do.

I dare say it, and I say it with a thankful heart and with all humility, I do n't believe there 's a brother here that has done as much work in quantity—a heap of you beat me in quality, but I yield the palm to any brother in this town on that—but I believe I have done more ministerial pulpit work than any living man within the past ten years. I have preached four times a day, an hour at a service, right along for weeks and months together. And if you ask me, How have you stood so much work? I can tell you that the only reason I know is that I have gone steadily and cheerfully and done the work God wanted me to do. An old brother will get up in the pulpit and say, Woe is me if I preach not the Gospel. God never called him to preach. It 's a lie! It 's a lie! Well, you say, St. Paul said: "Woe is me if I preach not the Gospel." St. Paul said: "Woe is me if I preach any thing else but the Gospel," but he never said: If God will let up on me, I 'll quit. He did n't. He said: "I count not my life dear unto myself. I count all things but loss for the excellency of the knowledge of Christ Jesus my Lord, and for the privilege of doing the work God gives me to do." But you get up in the pulpit and make out you 'll quit preaching if only the Lord will let you get to heaven without. You ain't fit to preach. A man that would rather do any thing else than preach is n't fit to preach. Brethren, the first time I preached there was trepidation and fear in my heart and quivering in my frame. For many months I was troubled because I feared I could not preach as God wanted me to preach, and the only fear or trouble I have ever had is, not that I have got to preach, but, Am I right in every thing I have got to say? I want to tell you that if in America there were a law passed to prohibit preaching, I would take the first steamship for some other country, where I could preach the Gospel of Jesus Christ. I would n't live anywhere I could n't preach, I like it that well. And when you get a fellow liking any thing it 's astonishing how much of it he can stand up to. It is that. To preach Christ twice a day is n't much of a job. But I have known a preacher used up preaching religion twice a week. After his two sermons on Sunday he would n't be fit for any thing next day with "the Mondays." I have, as true as you live. But I believe he could preach Christ twice a day and it would n't hurt him. A great big strapping preacher with the Mondays! He sits round the house a perfect nuisance all day Monday, and his wife says, "The Lord knows I hate to see Sunday coming around for I know Monday is coming too." The Lord deliver us from the Mondays! I never had a touch of them in my life. I thank God for the grace that delivered me from the Mondays all my religious life.

Brethren, if you want all that heart can desire, get along to be a happy, cheerful Christian, and God will give it to you. You need n't doubt that. Listen. "He will give thee the desire of thy heart." Give you every thing you want. Who is the happiest, richest man in the world? The man who has every thing he wants. Brethren, I believe I can say a truth, and I say it to the honor and glory of God. Listen: I have gone along cheerfully for weeks and weeks doing the will of God cheerfully, happily, in my work and I believe, if any time in any week you had asked me, What do you want? I could not have told you, to have saved my life. It did n't seem that I had a want in this universe.

> Thou, O Christ, art all I want:—
> More than all in thee I find.

O, brothers, there is the secret, the great secret of a happy life in Christ Jesus—I have found my all. And I may say another thing to you: You might make me the highest in the land, give me riches and honor, make me wholly blest in this world, give me a happy dying hour, and I might be taken to heaven, and as I walk down the golden streets arm in arm with my Father, and he walks into a magnificent mansion and shows me all its beauties adorned by angel's hands, and shows me into every apartment of that beautiful mansion in the skies, and when he has shown me all its apartments he turns to me and says:—Farewell forever, I will never see you more and you will never see me more, I would be an eternal orphan in heaven; heaven itself would be but the home of an orphan if God is gone forever. But if I have God on earth I have heaven here. There is nothing on earth that I desire but God, and heaven itself has nothing better than God. Brethren, have God in your heart here, have God for your heritage here, and then you have all. If a man has God in his heart, he is to him righteousness and peace and wealth and strength and life and hope and heaven. He is all of it.

I want to say to you that during the first years of my religious life, I did n't understand things. I was a very ignorant creature. I am ignorant yet; very ignorant—but it does n't become many of you to say so, because you do n't know as much as I do. I make an honest confession. I did n't understand a great many things. And I was sometimes unhappy because I did n't understand these things. I 'll tell you my life when I first started. For the first months and years of my religious life, when wife would get sick and suffer, I would say: "Well, surely God does n't love me. Just look how wife suffers." When one of my little children, would get sick and swing like the pendulum of a clock between life and death, I would say: "God does n't love me, or my precious child would n't suffer that way." Again, when a little prosperity would come I would say: "God loves me now; we 're all well, and have plenty to eat and wear." Then again, when adversity would come and as a poor preacher I would n't have a dollar in the world, I would say: "God can 't love me or I would n't be going round without a dollar." And so I was happy or miserable in proportion to the things I saw round me. Happiness is a distinct thing from joy. "Happiness" comes from the same word as "happen," so that "happiness" only "happens"—depends upon fortuitous circumstances and fortuitous circumstances alone may bring happiness. If things happen right, I am happy. But joy has its source from a different quarter. I have quit looking at the things seen and have taken to looking at the things unseen. When a man can get his eye on the things unseen he is a millionaire.

Let me give you an illustration. Here is an ocean steamer leaving New York for Liverpool. I get aboard. She weighs anchor and moves out. To-day is clear, the next day is cloudy; one day is calm, the next stormy; one day I am well, the next day I am sick; one day I can eat, the next day I can 't; one day I am cheerful conversing with my friends, the next day I am moping about. These are the things known and seen. But wait. What are the things unseen? Away down underneath that grand old ship is her mighty propeller pushing her right on to Liverpool, no matter whether I am sick or well, no matter whether it is clear or cloudy, no matter whether it is calm or stormy, no matter whether I am talking to friends or moping about, no matter whether I am happy or miserable, that grand old propeller is pushing the ship right on to Liverpool, and probably I have never seen the propeller from the time I left New York to the time I reach Liverpool. No matter if wife is well or sick, no matter if children live or die, no matter if they are sick or well, no matter if I am poor or rich, no matter if I am happy or miserable, I say—O, God, let me feel the everlasting arm underneath me, lifting me closer to thee every day and hour. And now my song is:—

Nearer, my God, to thee,
Nearer, to thee;

E'en tho' it be a cross
That raiseth me,
Still all my song shall be
Nearer, my God, to thee,
Nearer, my God, to thee,
Nearer to thee!

Thank God for the unseen arm that lifts a world to heaven. Brethren, get that arm underneath you, and be lifted up the balance of your life.

BRIEF SAYINGS.

RICHES are as much in the way of religion as poverty.

YOU must have eyes to see the sun, and you must keep your eyes open.

IF you will show me a praying pew, I will show you a powerful pulpit.

IT takes a first-class preacher and a first-class hearer to get up a first-class sermon.

IT 's as much your duty to get ready to hear, as it is my duty to get ready to preach.

YOU can 't lay down your religion to-day and take it up again to-morrow and go on with it.

BROTHER, God knows just each chord of your nature, and knows what one to play upon when he wants the sweetest music.

O, BROTHERS, let you and me realize that if we ever get to heaven there must be a process of making symmetrical and beautiful a character otherwise very unlovely indeed.

SERMON XXXI.

BORN OF GOD

"Whosoever is born of God doth not commit sin."—1 JOHN III, 9.

THIS is, perhaps, one of the most difficult texts in the Word of God. I know it gave me more trouble for years of my religious life than all the other verses of the Bible. The cold chills ran over me many a time when I read it. This verse for years of my religious life was a two-edged sword cutting to the dividing asunder of joints and marrow. But, thank God, these latter years this verse, which was once a sword, is now bread. A man's moral condition determines for him what the Gospel is to him. If there are swords in the Word of God you have made them so. God intends every word that proceedeth out of his mouth to be bread. I 'm not going to preach a sermon on sanctification. I believe in the doctrine of sanctification, but I am just going to talk good, old-fashioned religion to-night, without dividing it into the first and second blessing. There is one class of men—the first blessing did nothing for them—and that class need the second blessing bad. But to-night we are talking of good, old-fashioned religion.

"Whosoever is born of God doth not commit sin." If I were to say to you an honest man can not steal, a truthful man can not tell a lie, a sober man can not get drunk, every body would believe me. Well, I say, if an honest man as an honest man can 't steal, and a sober man as a sober man can 't get drunk, and a truthful man as a truthful man can 't tell a lie, then logic forces us to the conclusion that a Christian as a Christian can not commit sin.

Now, if this text is a climax, we can only get to this climax by going up a ladder to it. We must climb up with the context; and the first rung in the ladder is this: "Behold what manner of love the Father hath bestowed upon us." "Beloved, now are we the sons of God." I can explain the fact that you and I are here to-night on no other hypothesis except that God is our Father and we are his children. If I am the son of the Lord God Almighty, and he is my Father, then I belong to the noblest family of the world. It is worth something to a man to belong to a good family. I am not talking about what we call Bourbon blood in our country. I never saw a boy that was very proud of his father that the father was not ashamed of him. I am not talking about that kind of blood, understand. But still it is often a good thing for a young man that he belongs to a good family. Many a boy has drifted to the very verge of destruction in dissipation and wickedness, and in some thoughtful moment a kind friend walks up and takes him by the hand, and says, "Young man, I knew your father. He was a princely man. I knew your mother. She was a noble, true woman.

With such a father and such a mother, why do you behave as you do?" "It is true," replies the youth, "my father was a princely man; my mother was a noble, good woman; and by the grace of God I reform my life at this hour. I will never again, God helping me, do any thing to bring disgrace on the names of my noble father and mother." God pity a boy that will take the name of his precious, pure mother, and of his noble father, and smirch and disfigure it by a godless, dissipated life. Now, brethren, I am the son of God Almighty. I am not heir-apparent to a kingdom, but I am joint heir with Jesus Christ, and heir of all things. There is royal blood, glory be to God! And I will say another thing. When a man speaks out before the world and professes to be a son of the Lord God Almighty, this old world doffs its hat and says, "You have made a great profession. You say you are the son of God Almighty; now act like the son of a noble King. Act, and talk, and give, and go, and come, and be like one." Now see! This old world will not let us profess to be religious and then live just as they live without having a contempt for us. That is—old sinners are not satisfied with us unless we live better than they do. Did you ever notice that?

Now you hear a man say, "I can't live without sin." Yes, and if you'll watch him you'll catch him at it; he's made provision for it. Now, let's be sensible along here and look at it in a commonsense way. Suppose you go home to-night and make a list of the sins you can't help committing, and when you pray say: "O, Lord, save me from all other sins but these I have on my list. I know you can't save me from these. I'll go right on committing them; but, please, Lord, do save me from every other sin." You would n't do that. Let us look at this thing in a common-sense way. I'll suppose a case, and of course it's only a supposed case. Here is a good woman; her sin is tattling. On Monday morning she gets her house in order, then she says: "Here, children, you keep house for a while. Your mother is a poor sinner, and her sin is tattling, and she has to run over to the next neighbor's and tattle a little." How would you like that sort of logic? Coming down to plain facts, here's a brother whose sin is overreaching in trade. Suppose he were to say in the morning, "Well, wife, I'm off to business. I do n't know when I shall be home. I have to cheat somebody to-day, and I can't help it, to save my life." His wife and children would have an inquest on him to see if he ought n't to be sent to the lunatic asylum.

The idea of necessary sin is an absurdity to start with. A member of my Church said to me once: "Brother Jones, I have one trouble; I will curse when I get mad; I can't help it." I said, "Can't you help it sho' nuff?" "No, I can't." "Well," said I, "go right on. The Lord won't bother you about it, and I won't. You lam in whenever you get ready, and you cuss away, if you can't help it." "Well, but," he says, "I might help it." "Well," I said, "if you can help it the

Lord will put you in hell for it, and I 'll turn you out of my Church for it." And that 's the point I want to make on you. If you can 't help it, go on, go on! But if you can help it, you had better look out.

I overhauled my life about four years ago, and found I 'd quit every sin I wanted to quit, and those I did n't want to quit I was still running. A preacher in my State once said in the pulpit that a man could n't live without sin. If I 'd been there I 'd have felt inclined to jump up at that point and ask him to "name the sin a man could die committing and get to heaven, or take that back. I 'm not going to give you any such chance as that to inveigle my soul into hell." Do you believe me when I say every man of us has as much religion as we want? Do you believe that? Religion, what is it? It is a matter of choice, choice, choice! What does choice mean? It means to take this and reject that. It does n't mean desire. Now what is holiness? What is the purity talked about in this text? I 'll tell you. It is a hundred cents on the dollar, doing right every time you get half a chance and refusing to do wrong under any circumstances. It is n't doing right ninety-nine times out of a hundred. You can 't bank on a man like that, because you can 't tell to save your life when he is going to do wrong. I want a fellow to refuse to do wrong. I feel like an old woman who found fault with her husband about getting drunk, and he promised he would n't get drunk that day, but he came home drunk as a coot that night. She said: "Just look at you now, and after your promise too." "Well," he said, "I didn't go to get drunk." "But did you go not to get drunk." That is just the word. That is religion—to want to avoid the thing that's wrong and to do the thing that's right.

O, these little silly excuses you make for staying away from prayer-meeting, for not praying in your families, for not paying your debts. Brother! I want to be understood about that debt business. If you can't pay your debts and want to pay them you have the sympathy of God and the angels. But if you can pay your debts and won't, God will put you in hell for it. You can take that for what it's worth. The same God that says, "Thou shalt not steal," says "Owe no man any thing, but to love one another." I believe I'd rather a fellow would steal any thing I've got when I'm asleep than buy of me on credit and not pay me. Because, if he steals it when I'm asleep I say it's clear gone, and I don't know who took it, and I ain't meeting him every little while. But if it's the other way, he's sticking himself in my way and breaking up my religious enjoyment everywhere I go. I despise a fellow like that. I have known men get into debt that way, and the next thing you hear from them is, that they are agents for their wives. Think of a great big ship of a man towed round by his wife as her "agent!" I'll tell you. Brother! As God is my judge I'll never sign my name as agent for my wife. Understand that. I believe my wife loves me well enough and loves my character well enough that if she were worth $100,000 and I owed

$99,000, she would say: "Husband, take it and pay your debts; I would not have your honor stained for all the money in the world." And you fellows that are agents for your wives try to get your wives to settle up for you.

We can afford any thing else as a Church rather than to carry these men who are not clean in their business and practical life before the people. These old sinners—you preachers say these are in your way. You are lower down than ever I was if you let that sort get in your way. Do you hear that? A fellow can't be in your way unless he's ahead of you. And when a man gets low enough down for that sort to be ahead of him, I never would tell it again while I lived. If I were you, I'd shut my mouth and say no more about it. I would. Brethren, there's but one attitude toward sin for the Christian, and that's the attitude of abhorrence. Lord, Lord, teach us to know that every sin in this universe has the blood of Jesus Christ upon it, then every Christian when it is brought into his presence will cry: "Take it out of my presence. It has the blood of my precious Savior upon it. I loathe it. I hate it. I will not touch it." Brethren, I say that repentance precedes belief, and I believe repentance means I'm done, I've quit; and a man that hasn't quit those things has not only never been converted, but he has never repented. He is still in the bonds of iniquity. God, pity a man that has not got religion enough to keep him enjoying life without running into the sins of the world, the flesh, and the devil.

Every Christian should be as jealous of his purity as the little ermine is of his fur. The ermine is the most fastidious little animal in the world. He is as white, almost, as the driven snow. The only way they can capture it is, when it comes from its den, to sprinkle mud and dirt on its path, and when the little ermine comes back and sees the mud and dirt, it will lie down and subject itself to capture and death before it will surrender one of its little white hairs. O, brethren, we want Christians who will die before they will surrender their Christian character.

That is the line we want to get on. Because, brethren, sin is worse than death. There is nothing in death to harm a good man; sin damns soul and body for ever. Do you recollect that time when the devil had come from going to and fro in the earth and walking up and down upon it? God said, "Have you beheld my servant Job? I can bank on him; I can trust him." The devil looked up in the face of his Maker, and said, "Job is wealthy, and he is serving you for what he has got. Take away his property, and he'll curse you to your face." And God said, "Take every thing he has away from him, but don't lay your hand on him." And one messenger runs up to Job, and tells how his cattle have been destroyed, another how his sheep, and another how his camels were destroyed, and finally runs in a messenger and tells how every one of his children was destroyed. And when the last earthly prop had been swept away he stood there before God and said: "The Lord hath given, and the Lord hath taken away; blessed be the name of the Lord." And the devil stood aghast, and said, "Why, Adam fell the first lick I made at him; that innocent being that God had made, the first lick I made at him down he came. And here is Job, whose last earthly prop has been taken away, and he is as loyal to God as he was in all his wealth and glory." Then he said to the Lord: "If you 'll let me take his health away, he 'll curse you to your face." The Lord says: "I can bank on Job; I 'm sure of him. Take his health away, but leave the breath of life in him; do n't take away his life." And the devil set in on him. The next we hear of Job he is down on an ash-bank scraping himself with a potsherd. And his wife came to him and said, "Your breath is a stench in my nostrils; curse God and die." And Job answered: "Though he slay me, yet will I trust in him." And the devil stood aghast, and said: "Well, well, just look at that. I have done all I can do, and Job 's as loyal as in the days of his prosperity."

Then the devil went and got Job's friends, with Job's wife thrown in—and the devil makes a big jump on a fellow when he gets his wife—and he pitched in on him with his wife and his friends. They said to him, "It 's your character we 're after. You 've got nothing left but your character, and we 're going to take that from you. It 's your meanness; it 's your sins that have done this." Old Job heard them strike him, and he said, "I have maintained mine integrity. I have done the clean thing." And God came up and walked with Job, and he blessed him more in his latter days than in his former days.

O, brethren, be good so that God can bank on you, and you will be pure, and God's richest blessings will rest upon you. The Lord bless you preachers, and put you on a platform where God can bank on you everywhere and every day. My brethren, to-day I can say that if I am not loyal to God I do n't know it. Since I was converted I have not seen a minute that he could not command every drop of my blood, every minute of my time, every passion of my soul, every dollar of my money. O, come up higher; get where God can make something out of you. Then you will enjoy peace and prosperity, and you shall be a blessing to your native land. O, brethren, a Christian ought to be like the larks of Scotland. The sweetest-throated birds that ever warbled a song are said to be the larks of Scotland. They roost upon the grass of the fields, and early in the morning the Scottish farmer walks through the fields, and he flushes the larks, and they begin to rise, and circle as they rise, and sing as they circle, and it is said the highest note of the lark is its sweetest note, and, listening to its last sweet tone, it seems as though the heaven bent down and mingled its melody with the melody of the throat of the lark.

Brethren, let us get up, and circle as we rise, and sing as we circle. Let us sing a victory over sin and death and hell. Let us be loyal to God. Now every Church member of a Church in this house that will pray, "Lord, get me up to where you are;" every man in the Church or out that wants to have religion, and will have it if he gets it, I want you to stand up and join us in a short prayer. The Lord help you and bless you.

BRIEF SAYINGS.

THE wife either makes or unmakes her husband.

IT is the little things in this life that keep up the worry.

THERE are few men in this world better than their wives.

A CHRISTIAN girl runs a great risk when she marries a worldling.

LET 's make it fashionable to love God and keep his commandments.

GOD pity the woman that has no more sense than to marry a man that drinks.

WHEN you have spent all, it seems, so far as you are concerned, that nobody else has any thing.

GOD pity a mother that has to send her children to a dancing school to learn grace and manners.

GOD pity the mother that has raised up a lot of kicking animals—animals that bite and kick too.

A MAN wants a soul big enough for God and the angels and all men to come in and live with him.

THE girl that will marry a boy whose breath smells with whisky, is the biggest fool angels ever looked at.

SERMON XXXII.

CLEANNESS OF HEART.

"Create in me a clean heart, O God; and renew a right spirit within me. Cast me not away from thy presence; and take not thy Holy Spirit from me. Restore unto me the joy of thy salvation, and uphold me with thy free spirit. Then will I teach transgressors thy ways, and sinners shall be converted unto thee."—PSALM LI, 10–13.

"CREATE in me a clean heart, O God, and renew a right spirit within me." Then, and not till then, will I teach transgressors thy ways, and sinners shall be converted unto thee. Now if David, with all his authority as king of Israel, with all the advantages and facilities he could command, needed this in order that sinners might be converted, I reckon we are free to admit that we can do nothing until we get the thing he talked about. We have got no prestige, and very few facilities, and really we 're not much any way.

Now, let 's drop back a little and see what he wanted, in order that sinners might be converted unto God. He said, "Hide thy face from my sins and blot out mine iniquities." I think it very foolish for me to get down on my knees and ask the Lord to do something for another fellow he 's never done for me. I do really, brethren; it 's not only foolish but wicked for me to pray to God to save the sinners, when may be I am myself one of the biggest in town. And usually, people are converted on a dead level with the Christian people standing round them at the time of their conversion. You say some people have been powerfully converted. Well, if that be true, every body standing round at that time had been already powerfully converted. Let me illustrate what I mean, because I want to be understood. Suppose that down in the mountains of North-east Georgia, where people are very ignorant, a Methodist preacher in that territory will run a revival for two weeks and have fifty converts. I want to tell you a conversion in North-east Georgia does n't amount to nearly as much as it does in the enlightened settlements. It means that that minister has got fifty people to profess religion, and to come into the Church—who will pay twenty-five cents a year to the preacher and five cents a year for missions. Do n't you call that a tolerably low conversion, now, to say the least of it? One man will get religion, and shout a mile high; but another will say nothing about it, and come next day and give a thousand dollars for foreign missions. You can bank on that fellow. It does n't cost any thing to shout; it 's the cheapest exercise in religion of all—except singing. You can shout all night for a nickel. That 'll about pay for kerosene oil to keep the light up. I say, my brother, let you and me get up as high as God wants us to be, and then every soul that we bring to Christ will be on a level with us. Now, sister, if your girl were to come down this morning and get religion as you 've got it, would it do much for her?

Just bring facts where they belong. If your boy were to get religion and get it as you have it, would n't he be a sight? You know whom I 'm talking to. You can 't hurt a good man by talking that way. I 'm not talking to good men or women. I do n't call any names, but every one knows his own number, and just as soon as you strike it he knows it. Your converts in this meeting are going to be grand, and lofty, and glorious just in proportion as you who profess religion are yourselves upon a high plane. If you were a penitent, and a man came to you in whom you had no confidence he could do you no good at the altar. Many a penitent has been knocked cold and stiff at the altar, because somebody has approached him he had no confidence in, somebody he knew to be a hypocrite. There 's a sort of spiritual intercommunion, and a man that does n't live right has no power over a sinner. I can 't explain it, just as I can 't explain how a horse knows when his driver is afraid of him. But the horse knows it every time. I just know it; that 's all I can say about it.

Suppose you were to buy a house and lot and an elegant residence, pay the money and get the deeds, and the day you were to go in the gentleman said, "Here 's the key to eight rooms; I have reserved two rooms." "Did n't I buy the house?" "Yes." "Well, what do you mean?" "I want to keep four tigers in one room and the other I want to fill with reptiles. I want them to stay here." You say, "Well, my friend, if you mean what you say I would not have your house as a gracious gift. You want me to move my family into a house where one room is full of tigers and the other full of snakes." Many a time we turn over our whole heart to God, and when he comes in we have reserved some rooms for the wild beasts of pride and the hissing serpents of iniquity. Let me tell you, brethren, I won't ask God to come and live in a house that I won't let my family live in. Empty every room in the house, and then the heart is the center of gravity to Jesus Christ, and he will come in and live with you. How many people have ambition and pride in a sense in which God himself excuses it? I like to see a well-dressed woman, for instance—not a gaudy-dressed woman. I wish silk were cheaper than cotton, for I think it is much better. I wish every servant girl could wear silk all the time, because she looks better in it. I say I commend pride of character and pride of dress. I think I ought to dress so that nobody will notice what my clothing is at all. There are women in this town, you look at them from first to last, and all you see is their rig. If my daughter had only one dress, that should be a whole one. If it lacked any thing at all, I should cut it off at the bottom and never at the top.

Religion will make the floor clean and the pillowcase shine as bright as snow in its purity and whiteness. Cleanliness is next to godliness, and filth is next to perdition. Spurgeon said, "There are three enemies that I have fought all my life—dirt, debt, and the devil." A clean heart likes clean hands and clean words and a clean life. Let us look at our hearts this morning. Is there lurking in the cells any thing contrary to the Spirit of our divine Lord? Some of you holiness people have got a clean heart, but you have not got a right spirit. You 're clannish, and you do n't like a fellow if he does n't agree with you. Some of you will get up and go out of a church if the pastor does n't preach to suit you. Now, the more religion a man has, the more he loves the pastor and the Church of God, and the more he will do for them. If you get too much religion to love your pastor and do your duty to your Church, you may have a good deal of religion, but very little sense. Now, the Lord sees how a fool can find his way to heaven. The Lord has a side door that he lets some people in at. When I was on the train, I noticed some fellows that the conductor never asked for a ticket—little fellows, like that—and if some of us fellows will get right in, the Lord won't notice us because we are so little.

A clean heart is one thing; a right spirit is another thing. It is a kind spirit, a forgiving spirit, a gentle spirit. That 's it. Get a wrong spirit in you, and let it dominate your life, and you are a ruined man as certain as God reigns in heaven. I recollect once two of my brothers in my Church fell out. They were both stewards, I think. I could n't get them to settle their difficulty, all I could do. Then I tried to get them to fight it out, but they would n't fight. I did n't know what to do with them. Finally, when a revival broke out in the Church one morning I looked over, and they had each other in their arms hugging each other. I had a talk with one of them as soon as I could. I said, "You 've got sense; now I want to ask one question. How did you pray while you were feeling mad with that brother?" "Well," he said; "I 've acted the rascal, but I have n't acted the fool. I have n't been on my knees since I got mad." I 'll put up with a fellow acting the rascal, but when he gets to mixing things and acting the fool too, he 's getting in mighty bad shape then. I made this proposition at a woman's meeting once! Every body that 's mad with any body stand up, and before they thought, about twelve jumped right up. But they sat down again mighty quick. It was the impulse of their nature. I suppose if I were to put the same question here, about fifty of you would jump up. You would if you answered the impulses of your heart. Well, you say, you have been mad too. Mad about what? Well, I 've had a fight or two since I became a preacher. I thought it as much my duty to defend myself from assault since I became a preacher as before. I 've been mad enough to strike a man or two. The last fight I had I got in the fire, and the sparks flew right off me, and I thought, God will turn me into hell forever. I made a vow. I said, O Lord, I 'll never get mad again with any body, unless he treats me worse than I have treated you. See how God treats us. And the idea of a man that God has forgiven ten thousand talents jumping on another fellow about a nickel and beating him half to death is preposterous. That 's a poor business, is n't it?

And I 'll tell you another thing. This getting mad is the poorest business in the world. Do n't you know Jesus settled this question when he said, "If thine enemy hunger, feed him; if he thirst, give him drink." I said when I started in religion, if a man slandered me or injured me, Why does the Lord tell me to pray for him? I wish the Lord would let me go for him and whip him. He 'd stop then. But instead of letting me knock him down and stamp on him, I 'm to pray for him. I had n't gone very far when I found the Lord did n't want to protect the rascal that had injured me, but to protect me. Alexander tried to conquer the world, and died a conquered wretch himself; Napoleon tried to conquer the world, and died in exile. When Jesus wanted to conquer the world, he walked up on Calvary and died for his enemies, and thank God, Jesus will conquer this world yet, to a man. It is not simply the words you use, but the spirit of the man that uses the words that gives you influence with sinners. I 've had men say to me—I simply speak of this—"If I were to talk like you, Brother Jones, they 'd ride me out of town on a rail." I say to them, If I talked like myself with your spirit, they 'd ride me out. Somehow a fellow knows whether you like him or not. If a fellow thinks you like him, he 'll let you skin him from head to foot and take his hide to the tan-yard, and he 'll walk along with you all the way begging for his hide. If you know any man on the face of God's earth that I do n't love, bring him to me, and I will hug him till he hollers. If you know any woman I do n't love, I will send for my wife and let her hug her till she hollers. I felt for a long time just as the fellow said he felt when his sweetheart accepted him: "I felt just as if I had nothing against any body in the world." If I had an enemy in this town I would n't let the sun go down until I had hunted him up and settled the question.

Brotherly love and kindness! Where you find divisions and bickerings, you will find there that the Church of God will never thrive. A man once bought a farm, and the neighbors said, "You can 't live with your next door neighbor. He is a terror to the settlement. That 's what the other man sold out for. He will torment you to death." The new man said, "If he fools with me, I will kill him." Well, they told the bad neighbor this, and it made him worse than ever. He would cripple his stock, and throw rocks at his children. There was not a mean thing in the world he would n't do. The new neighbor would send him quarters of sheep, and care for his stock, and give his children apples and books, and kind words. One day the bad neighbor was coming home with a load and he got stalled on a big hill. The new neighbor came and helped him out and offered to do any thing he could for him. The man dropped to his knees and said, "You said you were going to kill me, and you have knocked me cold and dead; and I 'm going to make you the best neighbor you ever had in your life." You see, if you kill a fellow with love, you do n't have to bury him.

Get the right spirit toward Christians, and you will soon get the right spirit toward sinners. Talk about the Salvation Army beating drums and kicking up a noise. Show me the Church in this town that has reformed seventy-five poor drunkards in the last twelve months. See an old D. D. sitting on the banks of the river with a silver-tipped fishing-pole, and a silk line, and silver sinkers and a steel hook. You walk up to him and you say, "Brother, how many fish have you caught?" "O, I 've not caught any, but I 've got some mighty fine bites." Well, brother, bites won't make a breakfast. Well, that D. D., after a while, will take in his line and go a little way down the creek, and there 's a little fellow with a red shirt on, and "Salvation Army" on his cap. He 's fishing with a crooked stick, and a cotton line, and a rock sinker, and a pin hook. "Just look at that pole and that line! I would n't fish with that!" The little fellow puts his hand in the water and pulls out a fine string of fish an arm long, and says to the D. D., "Where 's YOUR fish?" "O, I hain't got any fish, but I 've got a heap more pole than you." Brother, it does not matter what you 're fishing with, but how many fish you have got; that 's it. Some people think God loves Christians better than sinners, but the fact is God loves sinners no less than he does Christians. The Lord loves sinners and hates sin.

SERMON XXXIII.

I KNOW THY WORKS.

"Unto the Angel of the Church of Ephesus, write: These things saith he that holdeth the seven stars in his right hand, who walketh in the midst of the seven golden candlesticks: I know thy works and thy labor and thy patience and how thou canst not bear them which are evil; and thou hast tried them which say they are apostles and are not, and hast found them liars; and hast borne, and hast patience, and for my name's sake hast labored and hast not fainted. Nevertheless I have somewhat against thee, because thou hast left thy first love. Remember, therefore, from whence thou art fallen, and repent and do the first works; or else I will come unto thee quickly and will remove thy candlestick out of his place, except thou repent.—REVELATION II, 1–5."

"I KNOW thy works." I believe all orthodox Christianity starts out with the proposition that there is a God, and that he is omniscient and omnipresent and omnipotent; and when I stand up here and read the words of this text, "I know thy works," that is enough to bring every man of us to his feet with a tremor in every fiber of his being. I believe it would be wise for every man to write upon the lintel and door-posts of his house, and upon every shelf of his store and business place, "Thou God seest me." He not only sees me, but he knows me. He knows who I am. He knows my name. He has numbered the very hair of my head, and tells me that not a sparrow that chirps in the thicket falls to the ground until he has signed its death warrant. There is this awful thought, that if I am unfaithful either in motive or life God knows it; and this blessed thought, every step I take to visit the sick or relieve the needy, God counts them all and says, "Be not weary in well doing, for in due season you shall reap if you faint not." Brother, I 'm so glad I 'm not to be judged by men or angels. This world can see my faults and my shortcomings. This world can see the frailties of my nature. But none but God, only God's eye, has seen how earnestly I pray and how I long to be like Christ. Thank God, he knows me from head to foot.

We very frequently misjudge each other, misunderstand each other, but, brother, God never made a mistake. He not only hears every word and sees every act, but he analyzes every motive of my life. I know you! I know you! O, brother! Let 's realize that all things are open and naked before the eyes of Him with whom we have to do. If you will only accept three facts: In the first place, God made me; therefore, in the second place, he knows me; and in the third place he loves me, then you will realize this further fact: I 'm brought in sympathy with the gracious Father who knows me, and knows which wheel of my make-up will break down.

The strength of a ship is in the weakest plank in its build; the strength of a chain is in its weakest link, and the strength of a character in its weakest point. Mr. Davis, the President of the Southern Confederacy, was imprisoned for months after the cruel war in the territory of what he considered his enemies. Relating his experience, he said it was hard to be away from wife and home; hard to be in prison; but that which was most unbearable in his prison life was that every conscious or unconscious moment, no matter what he was doing, no matter whether waking or sleeping, the burning eyes of a sentinel were fixed upon him. So if I do wrong or live wrong, the most terrible thing in my life is to feel that the burning eyes of God are upon me. If I go about to preach; if I kneel down to pray; if I sit down in my room; if I walk the streets, every moment the burning eyes of the Great I Am rest upon me; and when I am filled with this thought, I fall down and say, "God be merciful to me; my life won't bear such a scrutiny, my motives won't bear such a scrutiny, as that."

"I know thy works." I know what Church you belong to. I not only know what Church you belong to, but I know when you joined. I know what vows you took. I know whether you have been faithful to those vows or not. I know your relations to your pastor. I know your relations to the Church work. You shall be rewarded according to what you have done, whether it be good or evil. There 's this thought in connection with the judgment. Every time Christ prefigured the judgment, the man was condemned by something that he neglected to do. You know the man that did not have on the wedding garment, and they cast him out. What for? There was but one charge; he neglected to have on the white garment. You remember the poor fellow against whom his lord pronounced this doom: "Bind him, and cast him out." He had one talent given him. Did he steal the talent? No, he brought it back. What was he condemned for? Just because he did not get usury for it. Those five foolish virgins, why were they condemned? Was it because they had no lamps, because they were 'nt kind, good, hearty people? No; it was just because they neglected to have oil in their lamps. Brethren and sisters, let God tell us this morning, "I know thy works;" but do n't let him tell us, "I know your idleness, your indifference, your carelessness, your prayerlessness."

"Brethren, what are we doing now? We pay our preacher. That 's right. We give to missions. That 's right. We give to the poor. That 's right. But, brethren, the grand work of the Church of Jesus Christ in the world is to pitch in, roll up its sleeves, and bring the world to God. That 's it. God could convict every sinner in this city in the twinkling of an eye. Why does n't he do it? It is his mercy that keeps him from doing it. Suppose God struck every man in this town blind in an instant. We would grope through the streets, one saying, "Show me the way home," and another, "Why, I do n't know my own way home; I am in as bad a fix as you are." And if at twelve o'clock to-day every sinner in this town were convicted, there would n't be enough Christians here to show them the way to Christ; they would wander back into sin, and their last state would be worse than the first. God never goes outside of the Church to do any thing. Do you understand that? I am as much dependent on the Church to help me to win souls to Christ as I am dependent on God for the help of the Holy Ghost. How many converts did God have in China or Japan before the missionaries went there. I can not tell you why Christ has adjusted the means and method of grace as he has. But I know no man in America ever was brought to Christ, except directly or indirectly through the Church.

We had a great revival once in the lumber regions of Maine. There was a man there that had never been to church in his life, and would n't associate with Christian people. And the good Spirit permeated the community so it took hold upon this man, and he surrendered his heart to God, became religious, got up in the meeting, and told how God had saved him. He was called on to pray. He had never heard a public prayer in his life. He got down and said, "Good Lord, you have had such good luck on me, please try your hand on some of those other sinners." Was n't that a grand prayer? It was the first prayer he ever prayed, but it was a good one, was it not? "O, Lord, you have had such good luck on me, try your hand on some of these other poor sinners." Brother, there was an earnest and sensible putting of his feelings—a thousand times grander than those elegant prayers you frequently hear in public.

"I know thy works!" Listen, "She hath done what she could." He hath done what he could. There 's a commendation! Let me say right here—

I'll boil it down into one sentence — Heaven! Heaven is just the other side of where a fellow does his best. There's where heaven is if you want to know. I believe Christianity is nothing more or less than doing the best you can under the circumstances. I believe that will stand the test. I wish I could get people to see that heaven is the home of every man who has done his best on earth. Strait is the road and narrow the way that leadeth into life, and few there be that find it. Brother, resolve now, by the grace of God, if there be but two men saved on this earth that you will be one of them, and that you will get to heaven.

"I know thy works;" I know what you are doing. We have run Christianity on sentiment until it is about played out in some portions of the world. Sentiment! We have got lots of Sunday-go-to-meeting religion. I do n't know how many other things you have got in this city, but you have Sunday piety in this town. Now I never said you did n't have every-day piety, but I am satisfied you have a good deal of Sunday piety. I believe that. I'll tell you another thing. I believe your piety may be something like your residences—with all the beautiful brick, and windows in the front of the house, and when you get around to the rear they do n't look so well. Did you ever notice that you are like a system of underground railways? Did you ever hear any thing like that in this city? Thank God, the Lord has the surface railroad in this town, but the devil has a big long charter on the underground line, and a fellow can go almost anywhere he pleases here by the underground line. Do you know that? You can't take a surface railway in this city and ride to a lewd house, but you do n't have to go far on the underground to get to one. Lord God! awaken us and show us that this world ought to belong to God from the farthest star down to the very gates of hell! Show us that there is no room nor place for underground railways to be suffered by Christian people.

"I know thy works." I know how you go at it. It is perfectly natural for people to put their best foot foremost. Is n't it? Well, brother, if I can have religion only one day in the week, I am going to have it about Wednesday or Tuesday. You see, the whole lot of you can fall back and have Wednesday religion, and I won't miss you much on Sunday, because so many of you have religion on that day. Wednesday Christianity is n't any worse than any other sort. That's the truth. If we do n't get any Sunday Christianity out of these meetings we won't be heard of, but if we get a few Saturday or Wednesday Christians, we will do some good in the meetings. I know you! You're just as good in one place as you are in another; just as good or as bad on Friday as on Sunday! All right! I think of all times in the world we get less credit for being pious on a Sunday, because we can't do much else then. And, sisters, is n't it a fact that Sunday furnishes us a splendid day to show what the milliner's shop has done, and the hat-rack? Does n't it furnish us a splendid day to see and to be seen? And if it is new bonnets and dress on the part of my neighbors, the big thing is to see them, but if I have it on the big thing is to be seen.

I am not going out of my path this morning to talk about you, good sisters, but I 'll tell you where I got this joke on you. In Louisville there was a woman whose husband was a very pious man. God took him to heaven. He left his wife means to live comfortably. She rebelled against God, and did much that was contrary to his will. I was preaching in Louisville, and she was listening to me one night. She was convicted of her sins. She went home, and to her room, and knelt down by her bedside. I saw her next morning at nine o'clock. She came to the parsonage where I was staying. "Sir," she said, "I went home last night with all the horrors of the damned pressing on my soul. I knelt down and prayed until I heard the clock strike one, and then two, three, and four, and just as it was about to strike five, God came with the precious baptism of salvation on my soul. I have been so happy since that I do n't know whether I am in the body or out of it." Afterwards she said to me, "I have gone into Church many a time dressed from head to foot in all the latest fashions of our city, and while God's people were praying, I was looking around and wondering what the people thought of my dress, or cloak, or hat." You see woman-nature is everywhere mightily alike, and if you have n't done that yourself, why it 's because you got religion before you started in dressing well. There may be something in that. I 'll tell you the kind of woman I like—a woman who will walk down here, to one of your dry-goods stores and ask the price of some elegant piece of goods. "Four dollars a yard," says the shopman. "Four times twenty are eighty. That's a beautiful piece of goods. My husband gave me $100 this morning to invest in a new dress. This dress I have on has a few splotches on it, but I am going around to the Orphans' Home and shall give it that $100, and wear this dress all through the season. I don't care if every body who sees me laughs at me."

I could give you another incident. I was preaching in Atlanta, Georgia, in the interest of my Orphans' Home. I called for contributions and scattered cards through the audience. A gentleman at the back of the church filled one up for a good round sum. His wife cast her eyes over and saw what he was writing. He told me about it next day. He said: "Just a few days before you preached my wife asked me for a sealskin cloak. I told her I wished she'd make the one she had do for the present, as I was pretty close run, but next Fall I'd get her a fine one. She saw what I wrote on that card, and when we got out of the Church she said, 'Husband.' Then I knew something was a-coming." You can always tell whether your wife means business by what she calls you. Sometimes she says "husband," sometimes "honey," and sometimes plain "John." "She said, 'Do you recollect last week I asked you to get me a cloak?' 'Yes'm.' 'And what did you tell me?' 'I told you I was a little hard run, and I wished you'd wait till next

Fall, and I 'd get you a fine one.' 'Well,' she said, 'I 'd rather see you give that money to the Orphans' Home than have the finest cloak that was ever imported.' "

I wish we had more of that sort of women who do not live for themselves, but live for humanity. The proudest attitude I ever saw my wife in was when a poor creature was leaning upon her, and that poor creature would have fallen down if wife had n't supported her. How many people in this world are doing no more than toting their own skillet? People will say they do n't like such slang. The trouble is they do n't know what is slang, and I ain 't responsible for your ignorance. I want you to notice that. There is n't a purer word in the language than "tote." It 's a Saxon word and means a great deal, and a skillet is one of the most useful things I ever knew in the South. I knew a woman who fried her meat in the skillet and baked her bread in the skillet, and washed her dishes, and I understand that once she washed the baby in it; but I do n't know that—I've heard it. So you see I 'm keeping within the range not only of the pure but of the useful. The Lord deliver us from selfishness; it 'll ruin us sooner or later.

I hurry on; "And how thou hast tried them which say they are apostles and are not, and thou hast found them liars." Brethren, it is as much our duty to condemn the evil as it is to love the right. Now, we have a kind of an easy-going Christianity in this country that speaks well of every thing. Well, when you speak well of every thing you speak well of nothing. If you speak well of every body you speak well of nobody. If every body 's good, then nobody 's good. A man that gets drunk and whips his wife, and steals the money she 's been sewing for to buy bread for the children—if he 's good, then nobody 's good.

I am criticised for the hard manner in which I speak of Church members. I repeat what I have said many a time. The best men in the world are professed Christians, and the meanest men in the world are professed Christians. When I talk about mean men, if it does n't happen to stick you, I do n't mean you. I ain't talking about good members when I 'm talking about bad ones. You say I do n't give you credit for what you do. Well, the Lord's giving you credit, and he is the one that 's going to settle with you; but if I can tap you up along the line anywhere, won't that be good? If you 've got a lazy mule in your team anywhere, that 's the one to tap up. I visited a Church once, and just before I got there the pastor had arraigned his dancing and card-playing members, and turned out about twenty-five of his leading members. And they came down on him with a vengeance. Just about three weeks after the trial and expulsion of those godless members I came along by appointment with him. I preached about being "first pure, then peaceable." I just struck a bee line right along in there, and the first thing I knew those godless members of the Church commenced seeking for grace, and they would rush up in the Church and throw their arms round the pastor's neck and shout, and shout; and the pastor would holler and cry, and say, "Glory to God; if a man tries to please God, he will make even his enemies to be at peace with him." I wish I could see the Church thoroughly cleansed. There is not an old sinner in this city that some Church member has not acted the dog with him, and made him say, "If this is religion, I do n't want religion." Some member of the Church has cheated him or told him lies or done something. Now, let 's see to it that you and I are not the fellows that have done that. That 's the point.

Now, I am the last man to take up with these old sinners and try to excuse them in any way, and you know it, too; and you know that when I talk to irreligious people I talk to them as candidly as I talk to you. Let 's take up the dancer. I do n't know the rules of Methodism in Canada; but in the Methodist Church in the United States, when a member joins he has to promise that he will obey the rules of the Church, and we have a rule against worldly amusements; and when my Church members dance, and they come to me and say, "Mr. Jones, will you turn me out of your Church for dancing?" I say, "No! I will turn you out for lying, because you promised not to dance, and you have been dancing; and I 'll make out a case of lying against you." And in the States every member of the Methodist Church promises to support its institutions. I say to the stewards, "If you find a man or woman in the Church that does not support its institutions turn him out, not because he does n't support them, but because he has lied. He promised to pay, and if he does n't do it, he 's a great big walking liar wherever he goes." I believe in calling things by their right names. Lord! Lord! those little, trifling, no-account, shilly-shally, dilly-dally members of the Church that do that sort of thing, the sooner you take them out of the Church the better you are. What are you worth, anyhow? My! My! one good, solid, earnest Christian man or woman is worth a million of you! Or, in other words, the more of your sort we have, the worse off we are. Such a Church reminds me of old Dr. Reland. When somebody asked him, "Do n't you own five hundred acres of land?" "No, no," he said; "I 'm not so poor as that; I own only two hundred." Some people in our country own so much land that it keeps them poor to pay taxes on it, and a good many Christians are loaded down in the same way.

Here is a mother with ten children—one thirty, one twenty-eight, one twenty-six, one twenty-four, and so on down to the youngest, who is sixteen. Little fancy fellows they are, who have never grown an inch since they were a day old. There are three or four of them in a trundle bed, two or three more in her lap, one here and another there, and the rest of them in the big cradle. They 've never grown one bit. Would n't you be sorry for that poor old mother? All she can do is to trot from the cradle to the trundle-bed, to and fro, to and fro, with a spoon and a bottle of soothing syrup in her hands, and there 's many a preacher in this country that 's just dealing out loads of soothing syrup to his people. O, Lord, rid our Churches of trundle-bed trash. We have too much of it. Little, little fellows! You know babies can 't talk. Well, you can 't talk to the Lord—and babies can 't walk; you can 't walk half a mile without Christ. Babies can 't work. You have folded your hands ever since you joined the Church. How like a baby you are. One of the best characteristics of the baby is that he always sucks a bottle. I suspect you have very little dram drinking in the Church here. But I have smelt liquor around this platform since I have been here, and the smell came from persons, too, who looked like Church members. I do n't want any dram-drinking up at this meeting. If you will have your drams, do n't come round here pretending you are going to save souls; you 've never been saved yourself. How can I tell? When I was converted it cut me loose from dram-drinking, and a Christian can 't drink whisky—or beer either—in my judgment. Members of the Church can; members of the Church do.

Brethren, hear me to-day; I say the best preparation for a revival is not prayer, but clean out God's Church, so that he can come down and walk and talk in your midst. There are elements in this town you 'll never harmonize. Both are selfish elements, and selfishness antagonizes itself. But if every man who employs others were to say, "Those in my employ are my brothers, and I 'm going to treat them as such;" and if every one who works for another were to say, "My employer is my brother, and I 'm going to work for him as any brother," would n't we have a better and happier state of affairs? O, Lord, show us we are brothers. A great many of you act toward one another as if you were step-brothers, and that 's about all. If you have a member in the Church who has nothing but money, he is the worst curse your Church has got. If an old colonel worth fifty or a hundred thousand dollars comes up to the altar, you ought to see that preacher dance. I was preaching in Louisville, Kentucky, when Brother J. C. Morris was there—a most Christly man. When I called up the penitents, I noticed that he went direct to the ragged dingy sinners, and talked and prayed with them. I said, "Brother Morris, how is it you do n't seem to take any notice of a decent sinner; but if there 's a raggedest, triflingest looking man you can find, you go to him?" Said he, "Brother Jones, there is always plenty of people to look after the rich sinners; but I am so glad my precious Savior died for these poor, lost, ruined sinners." In the meetings in my own town I said, "I know some of you are poor, and you work every day for what you eat next day. I 've got five hundred dollars in the bank, and it is just for your sort, and you can have bread and meat as long as this meeting lasts." When the meeting was closed I did n't have a dollar in the bank; but God fed my family, and I got old Sam Jones out of that hole, I did that. Do you reckon I would take five hundred dollars for him? There are people that would be here this morning if they had clothes. You say they are of no account. Well, if your father should die to-morrow, you would be one of that class as soon as you have worn out the clothes you have got.

God help us to see there are some unfortunate in the world. I never invested a dollar for Christ in my life that I did n't get a rich reward for it. The only speculating I do is in poor whites and poor colored folks, and I 've made many a dollar off of them. I recollect one widow said to me, with tears in her eyes, that she had not a lump of coal for the Winter. I sent her up a third of a carload of coal. A day or two after that the president of a coal company wrote to my wife and said: "I ship you a carload of coal, and may it warm your house as your husband's sermons warmed my heart." I made two-thirds of a carload of coal clear off that old woman. Do you ever speculate on that plan? I have taken a poor fellow sometimes and bought him a suit of clothes, or a part of a suit, and but a day or two afterwards a tailor says to me, "Mr. Jones, step into my shop," and I go inside and he measures me for a suit of clothes worth three times as much as the suit I had given away, and I make thirty dollars off that one man. And you can do this all along. I just mention these things to encourage you. Recently, when I was in Baltimore, I went just outside the city to preach for a poor pastor whose Church paid him only four hundred dollars a year. Four hundred dollars a year! And they were paying a base ball pitcher five thousand dollars a year. I got mad. There was too much difference between the salary they paid this pastor and the salary they paid their base ball pitcher. I said to the audience to which I preached, "Let 's give this man something." "Now," said I; "I am going to speculate on him. Down goes my ten dollars. I will make money on him poor as he is." And just as the service ended, a gentleman handed me a note from a lady who was sick and never expected to get up from her bed again, and she wanted to see me. And I went with the gentleman to call on the lady, and I had n't gone a quarter of a mile before the gentleman said to me: "Mr. Jones, I put one hundred dollars in my pocket this morning to give away. I have given away only fifty dollars; will you take the other fifty dollars?" "Well," I said; "if it will accommodate you I do n't mind doing so," and I did so. And there! In less than an hour I had made a clear forty dollars on that poor pastor. Have you ever tried it? The Lord help us to see there is something in doing our duty.

Now, let us spend a few minutes over the last clause of the text, "Nevertheless, I have somewhat against thee, because thou hast left thy first love." Brother, what is the first love distinctive? Listen. Here is a lost ship wrecked among the icebergs of the Northern Ocean. A rescuing party comes near. They lower their boats and climb upon the wreck. They go from deck to deck, and as they go to each man they find him frozen stiff and cold. Finally, they find one man who shows signs of life, and they take him to the ship and try every means in their power to resuscitate him. They work away for two hours, and at last they see his lungs expand, and he draws in one breath of air. What do you suppose he says? "I am so glad you found me before I died?" No; no. What then? "I am so much obliged to you for rescuing me from such a death?" No; nothing of the kind. As he draws in that breath of air, he says, "There 's another man on board that may be saved!" And just as that man thinks of his friend with first returning life, so the mind of him who has truly entered into the Kingdom of Christ reverts at once to the others in the ship that he has left, that may yet be saved.

I was literally born again. I began preaching at once, and have been at it ever since. I hear men say that I have n't religious feeling, religious fervor, but, brethren, it is the consuming fire of my nature to go and save men from the devil and hell. I was converted in August, and I worked until November, when conference met. I did n't believe they 'd take me, but they did, and when I heard my name read out appointed to Van Wert Circuit, I was the happiest man this side of heaven. A friend said to me, "Do you know how much that circuit paid its preacher last year? They paid just sixty-five dollars." Well, I worked in that circuit that paid sixty-five dollars the year before, as hard as a poor fellow ever did for Christ. Nobody said then, Sam Jones is preaching for money. They did n't! They did n't! They did n't! Nobody said it then. I believe if every man knew the facts to-day they 'd say it no quicker now than they did then. When a lecture bureau in New York would send word to me, "We will go into indefinite time with you at five hundred dollars a night." Now, will a man refuse a lecture engagement as long as he likes at five hundred dollars a night and come here to preach the Gospel if he 's after money? I do n't know how much you are going to pay, and I do n't care. I can say this much, that every dollar that God gives me shall be used to his glory, if I know what his glory is. If I were after money, I would take the lecture platform.

You say, " Jones, that 's a mighty big tale you 're telling." O, well, a short time ago a gentleman telegraphed me, " What are your terms for a lecture?" I said five hundred dollars—I thought that would shut him off. He answered back, " Your terms are satisfactory." If a fellow were after money, would n't he run that line? But, brethren, I would rather spread the Gospel to poor, lost sinners for fifteen cents a day than take the lecture bureau at a thousand dollars a night. Glory to God, I am in line with my heart when I am talking to sinners. Some of you say, " Mr. Jones, I can 't believe that. Some people won't believe this is any thing but a lie." I can say this with a clear conscience. In all my correspondence everywhere, I have never demanded a dollar nor made a contract. I always carry enough money with me to pay my way back home. I tell Brother Small, " Do n't you ever start anywhere without a round-trip ticket, for you may have to walk back." I marched off there; but a great many people are idle and curious about some things, and I have n't a thing to hide from any man. I want the back of my house as elegantly finished as the front. I want my back yard as clean as my front yard. I want every room in my house as clean as my parlor. Plenty of women, if you came through the back yard into their house, would get mad. They would say, "Just look at that fool." Madame, if your back yard were as clean as your front yard what would you care? It 's just a question of dirt, do n't you see? "Thou hast left thy first love; I have somewhat against thee." Let 's get back to that hour we first believed. Let us bless others with kind words and sympathetic conduct. I wish every man to-day would select some soul and say, I am going to hunt up this soul and try to win it to Christ. I wish you would say, "I know a person that I think I can influence, and I am going to try." There 's nothing like getting something to stand on. Now, I 'll illustrate that. A good old presiding elder came home one day, and his wife said to him: "Husband, the cow is sick. It 's a good cow, and if it dies we can 't afford to buy another. I 've done every thing I can for her, but I think she 's going to die." Said the elder: "Have you prayed for her?" "No," she said; "do you think that would be any good?" "Well," said the old elder, "have you got any thing to stand on? Have you given away any of the cow's milk and butter?" "Yes," she said, "I've given a quart of milk to old Brother Scott every day, and butter when I could spare it." "Well," said her husband, "I guess you can stand on the butter and milk, and pray to the Lord and he 'll hear you." Next morning the cow was better. Her mistress had stood on the butter and milk, and prayed to the Lord. If you have any thing to stand on, the Lord will hear your prayer. Get something to stand on. The Lord help you to understand these things and to be useful in the world!

BRIEF SAYINGS.

THE poorest kind of a soldier is the fellow that never fired a gun or went to the front, but is still drawing his rations. The Lord deliver us from that sort of soldiers!

THERE are a great many impostors. A great many people hang around revivals just for the loaves and fishes. So they did in the days of Christ. But I would rather help ninety-nine impostors and one genuine case than let one genuine case go unblest.

I AM not banking on the fact that I am a revivalist or that I preach to men and move them, but on the fact that God can use me for little things, and that my name is written there. That is the secret of a true Christian joy. The glorious fact is, that the cheerful part of my religion is not seen by men, and that my name is written in the Lamb's Book of Life. What avails me if thousands are converted? It is said that Judas Iscariot was the most earnest preacher of the twelve. God help us to get the sort of religion that will bless other people.

SERMON XXXIV.

ONE HEART AND ONE WAY.

"And I will give them one heart, and one way, that they may fear me forever, for the good of them, and of their children after them."—JEREMIAH XXXII, 39.

I WANT to say, brethren, in the first place, that whatever trouble or difficulty or defeat I may have suffered in the past, arose either from my ignorance of God's law and God's way of doing things, or else I have known the way and would n't be guided by it. You may rest assured of this fact: that if God made man, and God loves man, and God proposes to advise man, then the only hope I have to escape all that may harm me here or hereafter is in the implicit following of the things the Lord says for me to follow. When the builders of a road lay the track for an engine, that engine's safety and its all depends on its staying on the track; and many a man has found out to his loss of life, and his loss of limb, that a locomotive engine when it quits the track is not only a very helpless thing as to its direction, but a fearful thing in danger. The Lord knows me and he knows what I ought to do, and when to do it, and how to do it.

And I tell you, my brethren, if you will run over your past life, you will see that all your trouble has arisen from one of these causes—either you did not know God's law, you I knew it and did not obey it. I know we have people that think they can run themselves, but I have overtaken a few of this sort, and I know just how they wind up. But there are people in this world that have sense enough to know they have n't got sense enough to run themselves successfully. This book ought to be our guide; and now let us hear these four or five lines to the good of our souls:

"I will give them one heart." The first thing that I want to say about the heart that the Lord proposes to give his people is that it is a pure heart. You can not be a good woman or a good man with a bad heart. The best thing you can say about any body in the world is to say that is a good-hearted person; and the meanest thing you ever said about any person is to say that he is bad-hearted. It is the heart which determines what your life is and what your conduct will be. "I will give them one heart;" and the heart that God gives his people is a heart pure, in every thought renewed.

Then it is a heart full of love. I have often wondered where God's great storehouse of music is, from which he supplies every vocal chord and from which the spheres may draw their charming melodies. But I need not wonder where God's great storehouse of love is. Glory to his name, it is the heart of God! There is the great reservoir of his love. I know not how to estimate God's love to me. Only I look around me and I see that mother. She has twined her heart-strings about the worst boy she has; she follows that boy with tears and prayers until he dies, guilty before God and man; and then she follows him to the grave, and she will go to that grave week after week. I say I can only know what this love of God is as I can see the love of a mother, the love of a wife, the love of a brother, the love of a sister; and when I see such undying devotion as manifested by wife and sister, I just say if that woman will stick to that man that way with just a little nature of God in her heart, how much must God's great heart love us! Wonderful fact! "I will give them one heart," but it shall be a pure heart, a heart full of love to one another and devotion, a heart full of sympathy for those who need sympathy.

I wish I had time, on occasions like this, just to give an hour to one feature of the text, and talk about that word "sympathy." Above all creatures in the world, women should sympathize with each other. I will tell you there is a work in this town to be done that none but women can do. None but women ought to do it, and if women don't do it, it will never be done. If it is not done there will be a loss of hundreds of souls. And that is the work of saving the poor lost women of this town. I say to you that Jesus Christ, as he stood in the presence of that multitude who accused the guilty woman, and looked at the multitude accusing, said, "You that are without sin cast the first stone." The multitude stood and looked, and he said, "All who have not done worse in the sight of God than this woman has done in the sight of God, you throw the stones at her." The whole crowd looked around, and Jesus looked at the woman with a heart full of sympathy, and said, "No man deems you a greater sinner than himself, and now I say unto you, go and sin no more." Let me tell you—and I will say this—the best way to get along with a sinner is not to measure that sinner by yourself. That is not a good plan, to measure a sinner by yourself. You say, "We can put up with that fellow, as he sins just like us;" and when he has done something you do n't do, you jump on him in a minute. I tell you, you want to get down to the humble point, where you can work things. You see a sin committed, and you say, "O, what a horrible sin!" But take yourself off to one side, and put a few questions like this to yourself: "Now, I have n't done like that fellow, but have n't I done something else just as bad in the sight of God as that person has done?" It is just as bad to tell a lie as it is to be guilty of uncleanness. And who has not told a lie?

We must realize this point, that all sins are great sins, and if you have committed a sin of any sort you are a sinner in the sight of God, and that is about all you can say of any body—sinners in the sight of God. I would like to see growing out of this work of Christ one hundred Christian women who will consecrate themselves to this work of redeeming every poor lost woman in this town. I would like to see that. I will tell you that work will never be done until you consecrate yourself to it. I knew in some of the larger towns and cities of the United States the best women I have ever met in my life were women who were consecrated to that work. Any man might be proud of calling such a woman his wife, and any community might well be glad to have such a woman.

I will give them not only one heart, but I will give them a pure heart—a heart full of sympathy. Sympathy is a grand thing. I went home one day and my wife was looking very sad, and I said, "Wife, what would you want?" She says, "I feel like I want sympathy." I said, "I will go down town, and if I can help you I will buy $100 worth of sympathy. You shall have what you want as long as I have a cent." That is a sad calamity, but you can't buy sympathy with money. You can buy horses and carriages if you have the money, but you can't buy sympathy. Sympathy comes through the cross, gushing into the hearts of Christian people. I will give you this little incident: When we were at Loveland camp-meeting, close to Cincinnati, I always regarded or looked towards Sam Small as my brother, and I have loved him as if he was my own born brother; but when I saw him at that camp-meeting with his arms around a poor drunken fellow, and walking along with him under the eyes of a thousand people, trying to hold him up, I felt prouder of Sam Small that moment than if he were preaching the grandest sermon I ever heard him preach in my life. It takes brains, may be, to preach a grand sermon, but it takes heart to make you put your arms around a poor drunken fellow with a thousand people looking at you while you are doing it. It does that. Lots of us might get around behind a house and help a poor drunken fellow; but who wants to be seen walking with him with a thousand people looking on? He is our brother. Look after him, brother.

I will tell you, my sisters, this Christly spirit will make you rescue the perishing and save the fallen. It will help us Christian people, and give us something to do. A man told me—I was riding with him in a carriage yesterday—"I do n't go to prayer-meetings, and am seldom at church Sunday." I said, "What are you doing?" He replied, "I am working for Christ all over the town on Sunday." My, my! how many people here in this city never have any thing to do with religion but to put on a bonnet and race right over to church. Sympathy! All before the looking-glass, and that is the only idea they have of the world of religion. I reckon, sister, if a religious idea struck you at midnight, you would get up and go to church. I never have a religious idea until I start to meeting. Lord be merciful to us with such a religion as that—always receiving and never giving out any thing.

"I will give them one heart." I want to say a word about that word "one." Do you know that whenever God comes down and we let him have his way, we have one heart in common? Suppose every body in this church had one heart about prayer-meeting, do n't you see how things would go? Suppose every body had one heart about family prayer and duty. How the prayers would go up from every Methodist family in the town! One heart; one heart!

And then God comes right along with the other proposition, I will give one heart, but it shall be a pure heart, a consecrated heart, a sympathetic heart; and not only will I give them one heart, with love for all that is good and hatred for all that is bad, but he says I will give them "one way." What's the matter here in this city? I do n't know but one thing, and that is the members of the Church have about twenty different ways of trying to get to heaven. There's old Sister Fashion. She's trying to get to heaven by the millinery-shop, and she thinks she's on the road to glory with her whole family rigged out in lace. Then there's old Sister Worldliness. She's running through ball-rooms and dancing and cards. There's a brother who says, "I am going through trashy literature," and another, "I am going the way of avarice. I want to make money till I am the richest man in town." Down in my own town, a few days ago, I said, "Friends and neighbors, you all know me. I was raised among you. There's a whole lot of us in town trying to get to heaven—about nine-tenths of us. But I am going to fall out of the whole business, because you have got so many routes. God says he will give us one way, and you have got about twenty in this town. Let us come together. All you dancing Methodists and Presbyterians and Baptists, I want you to meet us next Wednesday night, and I want you all to be ready to testify. If you say dancing is conducive to piety, and you enjoy religion more the night after a dance than before, testify to that and we'll all adopt dancing, and we'll have movable benches in the church, and instead of prayer-meeting we'll have a dance every Wednesday night. If it 's a good thing let 's adopt it and have one way. If progressive euchre conduces to piety and makes us love God and our neighbors more, get up and testify so and we 'll all adopt it. There 's another crowd over there that say, 'I do n't see any harm in having wines on my table.' Do you feel more pious when you 're drunk? If you do, testify to it and we 'll all adopt wine-drinking and put a bar-room in the house of every Church member in town. If it 's a good thing, the more of it the better. Will you testify?"

How many dancing members in this town would go up inside of the judgment bar of God and say dancing is conducive to piety? Who would say that in progressive euchre, with the prize up and the game going on, you could give thoughts to heaven and find out your union with God? Let 's come to an understanding. Which is the best way to run the thing? Let 's all agree on one way. Some of you are going to miss; some of you are going to get left right along on the way you 're going. And I 'll tell you how I feel. Whenever a man gets up to talk, he gets my ear every time. That old man is talking about his experience. He says, "Family prayer has been the stay of my soul since I entered into wedlock." I think to myself, I need a stay, and I will adopt family prayer as one of the planks in my platform. Another old churchman says, "Three times a day I pray in secret and call upon God, and it has been a help and strength to me." Then I say, "I need strength and help, and not less than three times a day will I get on my knees before God and pray for strength and grace to help me in my life." Another Christian says, "I read the Bible, it is the man of my counsel, and its precepts guide me, and I never make a mistake when I trust it." I say, "I want to be saved from mistakes; I want to be a Bible Christian; the Bible shall be the man of my counsel." Another says, "The weekly prayer-meetings have been a stay to my soul." I say, "I want a stay too; I will adopt that, and I will never be away from weekly prayer-meeting without sending my pastor a certificate from the physician that I was not able to be out." I wish we had religion on that line. If some of you were to drop off the pier and wake up in heaven, you would say, "What, I in heaven—I 'm astonished, for I had no idea I would ever get here." No, you won't get astonished. Nobody ever went to heaven by accident. Nobody ever went to sleep indifferent in religion and waked up in heaven.

"I will give them one heart and one way." I will show that not only can they love God and love each other, but I will show that Christian people fall into line with each other, all marching hand in hand, without quarreling and going wild. Some people may say that there is no harm in dancing. Some think there is. Some think there is no harm in playing cards. Some think there is. Some think there is no harm in a little brandy. Some think there is. Some think they can go to church, and can be religious, and do this, that, and the other. I will tell you, my brethren, if any thing in this world were needed here it is this coming together. Let us get together on these grand Gospel propositions and say, if we can not agree let us divide up, each squad agreeing. Would that not be a good idea? Suppose the progressive euchre party should withdraw and build a church to be called the progressive euchre Church. I would like to be at one of their revivals. I reckon they would have a sockdologing time at their revivals. I wish they would get me to run it for them. About the first three days you would see more hides on a pole than ever you saw at one meeting-house in three days. Then the dancing crowd will have to go over and set up for themselves and hire their preacher. And when revival time comes the dancing crowd is going to have a revival of religion. Would it not be a grand sight to go over and look at them? La, me! there is only one way to get things. Every man should help, and go his one way to righteousness and holiness.

"I will give them one heart and one way." We will have one way of doing things. Men have divisions in the Churches, and sometimes nearly split the Church open with these divisions. I tell you the closer we get to one view on every question pertaining to God and righteousness the better. That is what we want. "I will give them one heart, one way, that they may fear me forever." There is but one way we can fear God and keep his commandments. Then those who get in that way walk in that way. Then, good sisters, you are fearing him forever, for your good and for your children's good.

Now, I am going to say a word or two in conclusion on this last proposition—for your good, for your children's good. I believe, brethren, as parents, before doing any thing we should stop right still and say: "Is this best for me?" and the next question we should ask is: "What effect will this have upon my children?" Good father, do n't you know soon you are going to lie down and die? Do n't you know in a few more days you have to shake hands with your children and bid them good-bye forever? Think before each act and each word comes up. Stop and say: "Is this the best for my precious children? Will it be best for them when I am dead and gone?" That is the way to talk it. There are some parents who are listening to my voice right now. It is time for you to halt and begin to think something about your children. You have run your selfishness and your own ideas of things, and perhaps that child of yours is ruined by it. And now it is time for us to bring up, halt, and see exactly how the thing lies. For your good, for your children's good, listen. It will be for your good, as for all of us, to have one heart and one way, and let us all face into line. That is the best thing for you, and then whatever is best for you is best for your children. It will be for your good, and for your children's good. Our children step on our corns, it is said, when they are young, but they get up in our hearts when they get older; and I tell you, as I look upon my children at home, the all-absorbing thought with me is: "My God, what will become of my children when I am dead and gone?"

I can not put my hands on little Bob's head and say, "This little boy will be safe in heaven." I can not put my hands on Paul's head and say, "This boy will never die drunk." I can not, to save my life. I would give all things in this world if I could throw my arms around my children to-day, and say for a certainty that these children are all as sure to be safe in heaven as that they live and breathe at home. I believe I would shout the balance of my hours in this world if I could just settle that fact.

"What is going to become of my children?" I tell you you won't be here much longer with them, and they are going to quote you and talk about you after you are dead and gone. I have seen children, and filled their hearts and heads with Gospel, and brought them down to, "What will you decide?" and they have stated boldly, "Mr. Jones, my father was as good a man as ever lived, and he did not object to dancing, and this, that, and the other thing." Not only have you thus set a bad example to them here, but you have locked and barred the gates of heaven in their faces forever. Now, sir, my children may quote me in a thousand things, but they shall not, never one of them, go astray in worldliness and say, "My father thought there was no harm in it." I am going to denounce now and forever every thing that can lead a soul away from good, or debauch a human being. Just for the sake of a giddy, foolish hour you're subjecting your children to the perils of eternal damnation. Here, look at that. What is there in a game of cards? What is there in having a dance? What is there in going to a theater? What is there in it, sister? You will find out that you have sold out yourself and your family too cheap. Here is a man sitting on the pinnacle or cone of a five-story building. He sits there whittling with a little penknife which cost only fifty cents, but it is a beautiful little knife, and all at once the knife slips out of his hands and slides down to the edge of the building and stops. He sits and looks at that knife and says: "I am sorry I let that knife slip out of my hand; I believe I'll go down and get it." "But you might slip and fall off; it's very near the edge." "I know that, but people have gone that near the edge and not fallen. It is true the knife is worth only fifty cents, and it is risking a good deal; but I think I can get it and not fall off." "But if you fall, it is death." "Well, I know, but I am going to be careful." And he crawls down to the edge and grasps the knife, and just as he grasps his knife, his hold loosens and he falls and is crushed to jelly on the rocks. But he got the knife.

I say to a woman, "Don't go to that dance, sister; it might be the cause of the first downward step of your daughters." "But," she says, "other people have had dances, and their children have come out all right." "Yes, but it might be the downfall of your daughters, and their damnation." "Well, that is true, but I am not afraid of my daughters." So she has the dance, and every one of her children wakes up in hell at last. But they had a dance at the house last night. God keep us from going to hell without a particle of reason for it. For one champagne supper a drunkard has been started to hell. It was just one little drink of champagne; and while the warning voice said, "Do n't drink it, do n't drink it," he did drink it, and woke up in hell at last. But he got the drink of champagne. Is n't that consolation for a fellow? Suppose you send your daughter to a dancing-school, and she gets to be the nicest dancer in town. Then suppose she wants to find a place as music-teacher. Why do you want to add something to her education that will bar her out of every honest job that she would apply for? I advertise for a teacher in my family; and if I had a young lady recommended by every governor of every State in the Union, and by the President of the United States, and by all the preachers in the country testifying to her culture and goodness; and if they just added this postscript, "She 's a first-class dancer," the whole concern might go. I would n't bring such a one into my house to train and educate my children.

I hope you will think over this matter. It is time you are beginning to think. I will do it for my good and for my children's good. Let 's "right about" in these things, and say, "I want that one heart and one way, for my good and for my children's good."

E. O. EXCELL,

Singing Companion of Mr. Jones

SERMON XXXV.

THE BEST THINGS LAST.

"But thou hast kept the good wine until now."—JOHN II, 10.

THERE are two questions which come up naturally, legitimately, and inevitably between the employer and the employe. There can be no such thing as an intelligent contract for labor to be performed without the asking and answering of these questions. If you seek to employ a man to-morrow the first thing he will ask is, "What sort of work do you want me to do?" And when he has got a satisfactory answer to this question he says, "And what will you pay me?" These two questions are at the basis of all contract labor.

There are a great many people here to-night, perhaps, who boast that they were never in the employment of any body, but there is a very important sense in which every one of us here is a servant. We shall all get wages, and pay-day is coming. I say it is a fact that all men must recognize that we are servants, that we are all serving masters. And I suppose the first thing each of us ought to do is to settle the question—Whose servant am I? Listen: "No man can serve two masters; ye can not serve God and mammon." And again, "He that is not with me is against me." And even that was not strong enough, and He said again, "He that gathereth not with me scattereth abroad." I am on one side or the other. I am either the servant of the Lord God or the servant of the devil. There 's no neutral ground. You would be astonished at the number of men in this city who say they are neither on one side nor the other; who claim that they are not serving either God or the devil. I tell you one thing. If you say that, it argues that you are scarcely responsible for your actions; you may get into heaven after all on the plea of *non est factum*, as the old lawyer said. What a moral monstrosity is such a man as that!

How can I determine whether I am serving the Lord or not? "Have you given your heart to God?" "No." "Have you kept God's commandments?" "No." Then you are not serving God. And as soon as you settle the question that you are not the servant of the Lord, you determine that you are the servant of the devil. And now I want to ask you, What sort of work does he want you to do? He 's got a way of making you work for him, without telling you what he wants you to do for him. I 'll tell what work he has for you—to profane the name of God, to lead a licentious life, to break the Sabbath day, to do those things that are wrong and degrading to soul and body, to make your wife weep tears of blood, to give a bad example to your children, to make your neighbor think less of you, to dishonor God, and finally to doom your soul. Is n't that the work? Ask every staggering drunkard, every miserable liar, every poor, licentious wretch that walks the streets of this town, and they 'll tell you it is. And I need n't go out and hunt up the rakes and offscourings of the town. I can take you, and you 'll say: "Yes, sir; that 's the sort of work the devil wants me to do." And not only that, but he pays you for it.

Now, if I must do such disreputable, dishonoring work as that I must have good wages. Now, what wages does the devil pay? Listen! An aching conscience, a wretched life, and damnation in the end. Those are the wages the devil pays. Just before I was coming away from my room this evening a gentleman—and he was a gentleman born and bred—came to me with tears running down his face, and told me how anxious he was to see me. "Mr. Jones," he said, "is there any way in the universe out of my difficulties? I came near going into my room, just before starting out to see you, and I thought of blowing my brains out. I have stood it as long as I can." He told me that he would be here this evening, and he may be within the sound of my voice now. Now, what 's the matter with that man? The devil has his foot on him, and is stamping on him. "The wages of sin is death." O, how many men I 've had to rush around to my room, sometimes at midnight, and at one hour or other, and with trembling and despair say to me, "O, sir, I know you have seen hundreds and thousands saved, but was there ever a man delivered standing where I am?" Glory to God! I believe Jesus Christ takes the greatest pleasure of all in saving the most lost man in the world, and so gaining the greatest victory of all over the devil. I used to doubt God's ability to save sometimes, but after the Lord came down, fourteen years ago, and saved me, I have been believing in the omnipotent grace of God from that day to this. If I get to heaven—and I 'm making my calculations to get there—you need n't come up with any excuses that you were too bad to be saved. "The wages of sin is death." Pay-day is coming. If you serve the devil you shall have your wages in the eternal despair of devils.

But let 's turn the picture a little. Thank God, there 's a heaven as well as a hell; there 's a Savior as well as a tempter. Am I the servant of the Lord God Almighty? What does he want me to do for him? To love mercy and to do justly; to walk humbly before him; to cultivate the fruits of the Spirit—love, joy, peace, long-suffering, gentleness, goodness, faith; to do those things that will make my neighbor and my wife and my children think more of me than ever; to honor Christ's name and bless the world. "Why, Master," you say, "if I do such works as that I do n't want any pay." But the Master says, "If you do those things, you shall not only have cash enough to last you as long as you live, but when you die I 'll take you into my own home and you shall live there with me forever and ever."

Now, can any body controvert any single proposition that I have made here? I have stated nothing but the simple truth, and if it is the truth, how is it that the devil has a servant in this universe? Look here; would you work for the devil and board yourself—at least, I was going to say board yourselves—but some of you let your wives and mothers board you. Do you tell me a man in his right mind will jump with booted feet upon his wife's breast, and crush the heart's blood out of her? Will a man in his right senses debauch his body with liquor, when already the fumes of damnation have been ignited in it? If a poor wretch cuts his throat or blows his brains out, you say, "He's crazy;" but if he takes a weapon of the devil and stabs himself to the soul day after day, you think nothing of it. You crazy dunce! Can't you see the devil is n't paying you properly? Quit him, quit him, quit him, and come over with me! These goody-goody fellows that do n't serve God and do n't serve the devil, as they claim, but try to stick on the fence all the time, with their hands in their pockets, are too mean for any thing. They 're beneath the contempt of the devil, and he just does n't care to give them any thing to do. If I were going to hunt out the smallest character in God's universe I 'd catch such a one as this, if I could get a hook small enough for him to swallow.

You 're a mighty small animal in God's universe if you 're not for the devil and won't serve God. You 've met the sort of man I 'm talking of. This is it: "Here 's Mr. So-and-so, who belongs to the Church and won't pay his debts; and here 's Mr. So-and-so, who does n't belong to any Church, and he pays his debts. I think I 'd rather be Mr. So-and-so, and not belong to any Church." Have n't you heard somebody say that? Have n't you thought that way yourself? If I know myself, I 'll be on one side or the other. How mad St. Paul must have been when he was going down to Damascus to persecute the Christians. He fought with all his might against the Church, and then turned right over to the other side, and fought on the side of the Church until the day of his death, and was able to say at the close of his life, "I have fought a good fight." O, I hate a man on the fence! You get up the question of prohibition in this town, and he 'll say, "I won't vote at all; I do n't know which would be the best thing. I have n't made up my mind." I have ten times as much respect for the loud-mouthed anti-prohibitionist as for the man who says he won't take either side. Listen! Rally around your aldermen that stand for good order and the right, and until you get a vote on prohibition—it may be a year or two before you get that—you hit the snake a lick on the tail until you can hit it on the head. Let 's have some fun out of it while it 's going on. Be on one side or the other. Have an opinion of your own, even if you get your head broken in consequence. Be a man with a cracked head. What if you should get your head cracked! It 's not the first that 's been broke, by many a head. Be on one side or the other. If it 's a good thing go in for it heart and soul, and help it on, and if it 's a bad thing fight it with all your might. I respect you when you go that way. But these little fellows in the moral universe who have no courage and no nothing, I have no patience with. God help you to wake yourselves up and convict you on the eternal question as to which master you are serving.

The text is a simple illustration of the thought I want to impress on you. It is an illustration of the Lord's economy. The Lord gives the worst things first and the best things last, and he gives you better and better all through the days of eternity; and the devil gives you the best things first, and then gives you worse and worse until there 's nothing left but damnation. Put yourselves now and forever on God's side. Though saturated with sin, attracted with its seductive charms, and led astray by it, let the Spirit of God teach you to loathe it, and your loathing will be followed by the calm of justification and the certain hope of salvation!

BRIEF SAYINGS.

THE trouble with humanity is, men dislike so much to give themselves to God just as they are; and the point of all salvation is, turn yourself over to God just as you are, and let him make out of you what you ought to be. That is the secret of giving yourself to God.

THE lines of my orthodoxy are the steel rails that I have got out of the Bible and laid down; and I have either got to keep the tracks or go over the rails. I might as soon run off the tracks of a railroad as to run out of God's order of things.

SERMON XXXVI.

BEING IN CHRIST JESUS.

"There is therefore now no condemnation to them which are in Christ Jesus, who walk not after the flesh, but after the Spirit."—ROM. VIII, 1.

THE words to which we direct your special attention this afternoon are the words, "In Christ Jesus." I might refer you for a moment to the context. "For we know that the law is spiritual; but I am carnal, sold under sin. For that which I do I allow not; for what I would, that do I not; but what I hate, that do I. If then I do that which I would not, I consent unto the law that it is good. Now, then, it is no more I that do it, but sin that dwelleth in me. For I know that in me (that is, in my flesh) dwelleth no good thing; for to will is present with me, but how to perform that which is good I find not. For the good that I would, I do not; but the evil which I would not, that I do. Now if I do that I would not, it is no more I that do it, but sin that dwelleth in me. I find then a law, that when I would do good, evil is present with me. For I delight in the law of God after the inward man. But I see another law in my members warring against the law of my mind, and bringing me into captivity to the law of sin which is in my members. O, wretched man that I am! who shall deliver me from the body of this death? I thank God through Jesus Christ our Lord. So then with the mind I myself serve the law of God, but with the flesh the law of sin." Now follows the first verse of the eighth chapter, and I say, brethren, I believe very much in the sentiment of the old preacher who said if we do not get out of the seventh chapter of Romans into the eighth the devil will get us.

There is a good deal of force in the comment of that old brother. I believe we have lots and lots of people all over in this nineteenth century who have put up and camped out in this seventh chapter of Romans. I do n't believe it is a good locality to live in. I know that a much more fertile and glorious locality may be found in the eighth chapter of Romans. Now, St. Paul in these verses I read gives us a very exact logical analysis of the law of God and its bearing upon conscience and conduct. One of the strongest expressions here is, "For the good that I would I do not; but the evil which I would not, that I do. Now if I do that which I would not, it is no more I that do it, but sin that dwelleth in me." I believe St. Paul here was giving expression to the feelings of an unsaved man. I know this was my experience exactly before I found the cross. I am satisfied in my own mind that a great many other brothers who have found the cross thought themselves right in this latitude.

Now, brother, there is no such thing in this universe as necessitated sin. If you are obliged to do a thing there is no sin in it. There is no sin in a thing you can not keep from doing. In all laws and courts that I know any thing about, I have learned that the will must go with the deed, and to kill a man is not murder unless it can be proved that it was done with "malice aforethought"—unless the intention to kill can be proved. There is a great deal of difference between saying "I have not sinned in five years," and saying, as the psalmist did, "I have not willingly, or willfully, departed from thy law." Now, when I come face to face with the law of God, I find that law is nothing but a mirror into which I can look and read the reflection of my image just as I am. I can hold a mirror up before me, and I can see the specks and spots on my face; but if I want to wash them off, I have to hunt something else besides a mirror. There is nothing in a mirror to take them off. The law of God shows me how imperfect I am, and it shows me the splotches and blotches on my character, but if I want to remove these splotches and blotches I must hunt up something else besides the law to do it. It is powerless, but God sent his Son, through whom we may be saved.

And now, St. Paul wound up these fearful verses with these words: "O, wretched man that I am; who shall deliver me from the body of this death?" I have heard preachers say the literal translation of that means simply "a dead body chained to you." O, what a load to carry about, and how offensive that load must be! Thank God for that cross where I first saw the light, and the burden of my heart was rolled away by faith. Thank God for those precious words, and they are true to every one that trusts in the Word of God. Now, it is Christ, not the law. I believe in keeping the law there is great reward. I believe in preaching the Ten Commandments, and it is a mighty poor Christian that does n't live up to a dead level with the Ten Commandments. I believe in keeping the law of God, and I believe it is possible for us to walk by God's law.

"There is now no condemnation to them that are in Christ Jesus." Who is Christ? What is Christ? Where is Christ? In answer to the first question, we might say intelligently that Jesus Christ is the living personal embodiment of wisdom, and justice, and love, and truth, and mercy, and forgiveness, and all the attributes that make the character of God lovely. A great many of us regard Christ as a sentiment. You know what a sentiment is. We have what we call religious sentiment. When you say a man has religion, what do you mean? If you mean when you say "I have got religion," that "I have opened the door of my heart, and let the Savior come in," you mean a great deal; but if you mean you have opened your heart to a religious sentiment, got happy at meeting one day, I do n't know whether you mean much or not. I have seen fellows shout the whole day and night when they joined the Church, but somehow or other I think they shouted it all out on the spot. The steam in the boiler of a locomotive engine either means noise or it means power. If you lift the safety valve and let the steam blow out that way it is a nuisance; if you let it work out through the cylinders and steam-chest, you have got power to move a train of cars a mile. Well, now, if I have got a religion of sentiment, and let it out through my mouth, there is not much in that; but if I make it go through my feet and fingers, there is something in it.

There is one kind of an engine that's always a nuisance to me, and that 's these little switching engines down here by the station. They run up and down side-tracks, shoving cars, and that 's all they do from week to week and from month to month. They 're always getting in the way of wagons and scaring horses. But when I see a grand locomotive start to the sea-coast cities, there is music in her whistle. There is something that says she is determined to land her passengers at their destination on time. There 's a great deal in that. There are a great many of us Christians that are just switching backwards and forwards on side-tracks. There 's many a one that you preachers will never see again until the next big meeting—everlastingly switching along big meetings and going nowhere. There 's many an old lady here, who is mighty feeble, but she 's been going to these meetings ever since I came here.

I say religion is not a sentiment. It 's not a gush. It 's not being baptized, or joining the Church. But religion, Bible religion, is opening the heart, taking in Christ. "But as many as received him, to them he gave power to become the sons of God." That 's what religion does for us—introduces us into the sonship and family of God. Now, when I say I have Christ I mean by this, if

Christ is the living personal embodiment of wisdom and justice, love, mercy, truth, and forgiveness, and all those blessed attributes, then, when I get Christ, glory to his name, I get all these things—wisdom, justice, love, truth, mercy, forgiveness. In the first place, then, a Christian ought to be a wise person. Do you know what wisdom is in its true sense? It is the skillful use of the knowledge at hand. It is doing the right thing at the right time. It is doing the best thing under the best circumstances that life affords. In other words, religion will make me take those things in any religious life that will help me to God, and eliminate those things that will hinder and retard my religious growth. There is a fellow trying to get to heaven without family prayer. He thinks he goes through this world just like a fellow trying to steal a march on Providence, and get into heaven and make God out a liar. "At last I am in heaven, and I never did so and so." I would hate to sneak into heaven in that way. I won't say a fellow can not get to heaven without praying in his family, but I will say you will never get there without saying you wished you had done it. Here is a fellow there who thinks the big road is not good enough, and he goes through the woods to get a better road. He strikes out through the woods, and before he gets to where he is going he comes back on the big road, with his clothes all torn and wet where he has jumped over holes and swum rivers, and he comes back on the road with his clothes and hide all torn, and says, "How I wish I would have come all the way by the big road, I would have saved myself so many hardships with which I have met." Brethren, you can not take a nigh cut on a straight road to save your life. You can put this down.

I use family prayer, secret prayer, and every sort of prayer, just as a bird does its wings. I use it just like the engine with its wheels—to roll on. That is it. They are wheels for me to roll on. The difference between a stationary engine and a locomotive engine is just a question of the one having wheels and the other not. There is many a little old stationary Christian in this country. Did you ever see a saw-mill run by a stationary engine? It runs a saw. It can not go anywhere. It can not do a thing but run a wheel for somebody else. The truth is, many of you Christians are running a saw-mill somewhere instead of being a grand locomotive on the highway to heaven. You are a little stationary engine, set down on the roadside somewhere for infidels and scoffers to laugh at. Up and get your wheels of duty under you, and roll on them forever. Wisdom and knowledge, then, are two very different things. I have seen a great many people who knew a great deal, but they have as little wisdom as all the fools I ever saw in my life. An educated fool is a most ridiculous fool. Many a fellow who is a graduate of the highest college in this country has not got sense enough to preserve him. He is in an awfully bad fix, is n't he? He is really a first-class doctor. He is intimate with anatomy and medicine, but he has no more sense about him or wisdom about him than to pour into his throat a fluid that will burn the vital parts of his being, as when he pours whisky down his throat. I say I have seen a poor old negro down South that could not read or write, but he would pray and sing night and morning with his wife and children, and when I go to his house the first thing he would think about after supper would be to say to me, "I wish you would read a few chapters in the Bible. We can pray and sing, but we can not read the Bible." I have looked at that poor old colored man and thought, If you can not read, you have more genuine wisdom about you than nine-tenths of the members of the Church who can read. And that is the truth. Yes, it is.

Then we should all possess the spirit of forgiveness. Above all creatures in the world, I feel sorriest for the people who bear malice in their hearts. Listen: when Christ was reviled, he reviled not again. If you do not forgive in person it hurts you more than any body else. Christians must possess the spirit of love and the spirit of forgiveness, the spirit of peace and the spirit of joy. If I have Christ in my heart, there is not an element in his character that I may not bring in with him. Christ Jesus is the living, personal embodiment of wisdom and justice. Where is Christ? Glory to his name, he lives in the hearts of his people; he lives in the hearts of his people. I tell you I am sick of this idea of worshiping a Christ of eighteen hundred years ago, or worshiping one that is going to come a little later. I believe they call this coming the Second Advent. I tell you, my brother,

Christ is not only the Christ that did come, but the Christ that is coming; and he is the personal, indwelling Christ in my soul, and I do n't have to wait for the Second Advent. Thank God, it has already come; that Christ came once, and he came to stay, and will stay with you always, until the end of the world. And have you Christ dwelling in your heart of faith? I do n't like that old doctrine, "If you seek it you can 't find it; if you find it you have n't got it; if you 've got it you can 't lose it; and if you lose it you never had it." I like the Methodist doctrine that says, "If you seek it you will find it; if you find it you 've got it; if you 've got it you 'll know it; if you know it you need n't lose it, and if you lose it you had it." Lord help us this afternoon to take Christ as he is and as he has promised himself to be.

Being in Christ Jesus presupposes a longing for Christ. In Scripture it is called hungering and thirsting after righteousness, with the promise, "They shall be filled." My heart panteth for the living God, as the hart panteth for the water-brooks. Brother, there is no more healthy religious feeling than that which hungers after God, holiness, and right. Longing for Christ—I love to see a soul hungering for Christ. I love to see a soul looking up to heaven and saying, "O Christ, I long for thee. Come into my soul." And when other suitors press us, when pleasures call us, wave them off. Jesus never comes to the soul until the soul says, "I do not want any thing but thee; nothing but thee will satisfy my heart." And I love to see a soul looking up to Christ, and when wine suppers and cards and dances are offered, saying, "I do n't want them; I want Christ. My soul perishes without him."

Being in Jesus presupposes another thing. It presupposes running to Christ. Christ meets you half-way. The cross is just half-way between heaven and hell. I like that song, "We 'll all go out to meet him when he comes." I want to know, whenever danger comes, that Christ is my refuge, and I can run to him. In olden times, when a man had violated the law, the first thing he thought about was a city of refuge. He thought, "If I can just reach that, there is no power on earth that can hurt me." Many a time when danger assails and temptations unite against me, the first thing I think of is Christ, my refuge, and I run there with all my might. Brother, do you know how to reach Christ? The way of prayer is the way to Christ. I will tell you another thing. Whenever you start to Christ in time, he will meet you half-way. Sometimes Jesus does n't, may be, look upon us when things are going along smoothly; but when you get into trouble Christ will see your trouble or danger, and he will help you out. Always run to Christ for refuge.

Being in Christ presupposes submission to Christ. Being in Christ also presupposes union with Christ. I wish every body would take Christ into copartnership with him. Suppose every business man were to say, "The Lord is the senior partner in this business, and if I do any thing wrong the Lord will dissolve the partnership and ruin me." I wish they would. I wish all of us preachers would take the Lord into partnership and say, "Lord, if I do any thing little or selfish, turn me out." My, my! there would be a heap of us bankrupted, brethren. O, for an unselfish man that wants the Lord to have his way! It takes a great deal of religion to see one Church getting forty new members out of a meeting, and you getting only one and being able to enjoy it. Enjoy it, I mean. Of course we have got religion enough to suffer it, but I'm talking about enjoyment. My, my! how much religion it takes right along there. I know it, because a preacher told me so once. But, brethren, Methodism in this city, for instance, is a unity, and if forty members join our brother's Church, Methodism is forty members stronger than it was before. Let us work for one another's interest. I can not help God and humanity without helping myself.

There are a great many preachers in this town that are waiting for the second advent. I saw yesterday that Mr. Talmage prophesied that it will come in sixty years. But there won't be one of the old sinners of to-day living in sixty years. There never was, and there never will be, a grander day or a grander time in this world's history to save sinners than the day we are occupying now. I heard a fellow say he wished he had lived a hundred years ago. I do n't, because I would be getting old now, and would have to die in a few days. I am glad I was born just in the year that I was. I am in my prime in the very noontide place in this world's history. I like that. I want to stay here just as long as I can. I do n't believe there is an angel in heaven who would not rather be down here now winning souls to Christ, if he had the opportunity. Union with Christ—that is it. "I am the vine, ye are the branches." There is union between the stem of the vine and the branches. Union with Christ, my brethren, is just the same as the relation between the vine and the branches. Are we united to Christ in the great love of humanity and the great effort to save humanity? Brother, to-day God calls upon humanity to help him to help suffering humanity.

And, lastly, we might talk a little about having affinity for Christ Jesus. Christ said, "Blessed are the pure in heart." I believe I may be so intimate with Christ, blessed be his name, that I can talk over the characteristics of his divine character and his divine person. Did you ever visit the Central Park, New York? When they were surveying that Park the engineers got to an immense heap of rock in the Park. They stood and thought. They did not know what to do with these rocks. It would cost thousands of dollars to move them. They were standing one day discussing the matter when a lady walked up; and hearing the conversation, she said: "I will tell you what to do with these rocks. Plant honeysuckles and other vines about them, and they will climb up and shade them." The engineers thought this was the very thing, and they planted honeysuckles and other vines around these rocks and now the most lovely and fragrant place in Central Park is where these rocks stood. Take the characteristics of Christ, that blessed Christ, we have been talking about, and plant them around this ugly and jagged nature of yours and blend them into your heart, and your character will grow like the grand character of the Lord Jesus Christ.

BRIEF SAYINGS.

LOVE is not only the divinest and sublimest, but the most omnipotent power in the world.

SELF-DEDICATORY love is the very bed-rock and foundation upon which you can build a happy married life.

I WANT to see a religion that gives us something to do, and isn't everlastingly catching at something.

IF your husband loves whisky better than he loves you, you had better get away from him—the sooner the better.

IF you want to help Christ, go and look for some poor folks that love Christ, or ought to love him. Jesus says: "A cup of cold water given in my name shall not lose its reward."

ORGANIZED charity is the only real charity in the world—that charity that thinks of and thinks into the cases, and thinks out the difficulties of those who need help, and puts them where they can assist themselves.

SERMON XXXVII.

CONFESSION AND FORGIVENESS.

"If we confess our sins, he is faithful and just to forgive us our sins and to cleanse us from all unrighteousness."—1 JOHN I, 9.

THIS text is the whole of the human side of the Gospel. I have nothing to do with the other side. God explains himself. God is his own interpreter, and whatever of the Gospel is on the human side of this question it is mine to talk about and yours to heed and obey.

"If we confess." Let us interpret this word, without any injury to the text, "If we repent of our sins," etc. Repentance to a man in this world on his way to a better world is just what the alphabet is to a man of learning. When a little boy I sat on mother's knee, and she taught me A, B, C, and so on down to Z. Finally she said, "Now, you know your letters perfectly, you may go to spelling," and I turned the alphabet pages over and said, "Good-bye, old A, B, C; I'm done with you now." But when I turned over on the next page I saw a-b, ab, i-b, ib, and so on, and found that I could not spell even the smallest of words without the alphabet. And so I went on until I got to my grammar and arithmetic, and still found that I could not do any thing without the alphabet. Then in the Latin language every progressive step was made through the alphabet; and so with Greek; and the man who goes through college finds that his very last step is through the alphabet; and when they give him his diploma they can 't give it to him without using the alphabet from first to last. Then the man takes the profession of law, and he finds the pages of Blackstone and Greenleaf and Story covered with the letters of the alphabet, and the further he goes on the more he uses the alphabet.

And so I repeat, What the alphabet is to a man of learning, repentance is to a man going to heaven. The first good thing I ever did was to go down on my knees and repent; and I have been repenting ever since. The last thing I want to do in this world is to go into a hearty repentance before God, and then go right on to heaven on the grace given me in repentance. David was a man after God's own heart. David was a great sinner, but he was a first-class repenter. He could sin with a vengeance, and then repent with a vengeance. The question is not how many times you fell down, but how hard you tried to get up after you had fallen; and I believe, after all, there is not much harm in a fall if you do it like an India-rubber ball, bounce higher than you were before. Simon Peter fell once, but, bless your life, he bounced higher than ever before.

Now, brother, we will drop back on the word of the text; we want to be so plain that any little girl or boy in the house can understand it. I want to say that when you talk sense in a practical way, you catch the understanding of every body from the premier to the child, from the shrewdest lawyer to the A, B, C scholar at school. That is, if you talk plain facts and truth. I do n't believe my business is to prove any thing is true that is true, but to set forth truth in a practical, sensible aspect. And I believe that is about the biggest job on a preacher's hands to-day. God does n't want any body to prove any thing that is true. An old brother said to me one day, "I can 't get 'em to come and hear me preach. They won't come." "Well," I said; "if you had a drove of hogs and you call 'em up a few times and pour a bucket or two of water over them and send them off, why, when you call 'em again they 'll just say, 'Boo! I won't come.' But if you give them a bucket of slop every time you call them, they 'll soon get so they 'll just stay there and wait for you." Well, sir, that old fellow 's mad with me to this day. He said I compared human beings with hogs. But sometimes a fellow is n't mad about what he 's mad about. Did you ever notice that? Let 's get truth so that we can hold to it.

Now, taking a practical and common sense view of this whole business, we may say that if a man does confess his sins, that is proof he is quit of them, for a man will not confess before he is quit. I 'll show you. You get that red-nosed gentleman at the back there and ask him, does he drink whisky? He 'll tell you "No," because he does n't know one thing from another. I want to see one man who drinks whisky and never told his wife a lie about it. I 'll give you a ten-dollar bill for him, but you'll have to get somebody to prove your veracity. I made a proposition once at a meeting that any man who drank whisky and never told his wife a lie about it should stand up, and one man jumped up. I said, "Old fellow, you 're a bachelor, I 'll lay my life." And so he was. Well, you take that man who has been drinking whisky to excess, and make him quit it and give his heart to God, and then, every time he gets up in public service, he says, "Brethren, I was the worst drunkard you ever saw. I drank and debauched myself till I was a disgrace to my family and to the community." He has quit now. How do you know? Because he confesses. Whenever a man goes to confessing, that 's the best proof he has quit. Take that old man there. He 's a gambler and a blackleg. Ask him, "Do you gamble?" He says, "I do n't know one card from another." Let him get religion and then he 'll say, "Brother, I was the worst gambler in this city. I used to play cards and gamble on Sunday evenings." You see, when he has quit, he 'll confess it; when he has not quit, he 'll die before he 'll confess it. A man's reformation never goes deeper than his confession.

Confession—that is, repentance—means "I 've quit; I have done." A good many people think repenting means to mourn, to cry, and to weep. There 's no particle of mourning or sorrow or weeping in repentance. Will some brother quote me a passage of Scripture that denies the proposition? One fellow wants to quote, "a godly sorrow that worketh repentance." Well, when a thing works a thing that is n't the thing, is it? Sorrow is no more a part of repentance than my coat is part of Sam Jones. I 'm glad I got one, but it is n't me. I 'm glad I have one, but I 'd be as much Sam Jones without it as with it. Here 's a boy twenty-one years old. His father has $100,000 in different sorts of bonds that he wants to give him. Now, that boy is getting drunk and carousing, and living a blackguard's wicked life, and every night he goes home and blubbers and blubbers, and says, "Father, I 'm sorry I got drunk again to-night." Finally his father says to him, "Look here, you 've got either to quit drinking or to quit blubbering. I can 't stand both." Next evening the boy comes home, cool, sober. He says, "Father, I 've drunk my last drop. I 'll do as you want me to do in the future." "Give me your hand, son," the father says. "You have reformed, and now you need n't blubber at all. All the blubbering in the world did n't do you any good so long as you kept on getting drunk." It is n't blubbering; it 's quitting.

One of your book-dealers has a book, he tells me, of mine on "Quit Your Meanness." I do n't know what the book is worth, but I know that the title is worth a fortune to a man who will do as it tells him to do. In one of the States where we were preaching, they said: "Brother Jones and Brother Small are not preaching any thing but reformation." Well, do you know any thing this country needs as badly as that? It is my business to preach reformation; God's business to preach regeneration. You see a little man racking around this country preaching "You must be born again!" That 's about half he preaches. Poor little fellow! He 's running on the profoundest question of God's side. I am trying to do as my Savior did. He knew what was best. He touched on it but once, and then it was at midnight, and when there was but one man to hear him, and that man one of the most learned and intelligent of his day; and when Jesus mentioned it to him, Nicodemus said: "How can this thing be?" And Jesus waved him off with a simple illustration, seemingly sorry he had mentioned it at all. I preach repentance, and God preaches regeneration.

O, how tired I get sometimes listening to a little fellow trying to explain the unexplainable! When I see a man dive out into that water, if he has n't got gourds under each arm, I say, "Good-bye, you are gone; you are gone." I say, brothers, little boats should keep near the shore; the large ones can venture further. I do know what repentance means; I do n't know what regeneration means, so that I can tell you about it. But God knows, and God is his own interpreter, and he will make it plain. Now, you 'll go away from here, some of you, and say, "Jones does n't believe in regeneration." If you do say that, you 'll tell a great big lie, sure 's you 're born. I do believe in it, when God made me a new creature in Christ just fourteen years ago. I do believe in regeneration, but I let God preach that side of the Gospel. I shall stay on our side. There 's fish there, and I like to fish where there is fish. Brethren, the Lord, I say, touched this question but once, and then at midnight, when but one man was present, though he had opportunities to preach it to great masses; and we have no evidences at all that he ever touched it again. But when he touched it, it was as the key-note of eternal life. Let 's you and I, then, get them to repent, and God will do the rest. That 's the division.

If we repent of our sins—that is, "confess" our sins—"he is faithful and just to forgive us." What is my part? To repent. Listen! The heart that is empty of sin is as the center of gravity to Jesus Christ. He always comes to it; and repentance is the means by which you can empty the heart of every sin of your life. Some folks think—and that is one of the objections I have to a Gospel only half told—some folks think the Lord will do every thing, and that the Lord will quit all your sins for you. If you 've been telling lies, you 've got to quit telling lies. The Lord won't quit your telling lies for you; and he won't quit your drinking whisky for you. If you 've been swindling your neighbor, you must straighten it out with him, and quit; you must not expect God to straighten out your meanness with your neighbor. It is your part to quit your meanness, and God's part to cleanse you and forgive you. Just so here. Is there any thing in the grace or promises of God that can keep a man sober with a half gallon of whisky in him all the time? That brings the thing home. Is there any thing in God's grace or mercy to make a man truthful, when the man won't give over lying? Talk about this little imputed righteousness business. Brethren, it is a sort of gum-elastic cloak that you are trying to stretch over bar-rooms and ball-rooms, and every thing else in the universe. I believe this idea of imputed righteousness is a scheme of the devil to win you away from your own purity, and expect God to be good for you, when you know you are not good. If this is what you mean by imputed righteousness, I do n't believe a word of it. Eternal righteousness comes through Jesus Christ. If you sit down and wait for God to quit drinking whisky for you, and to quit telling lies for you, when all the time your neighbor can 't rely on a word you say, you are making a mistake so long as eternity.

There are a great many people in this world who think that sin is off in a wilderness, and that it is a very difficult matter to get to heaven from there. Brethren, there is but one road in God's moral universe, and every man in the world is in that road. Heaven is at one end of it and hell at the other. The question is n't, Which road are you on? but, Which way are you going? Heaven and hell are the antipodes of each other in this road. Every sinner who has his back turned on heaven is going to hell, and every Christian has his back turned on hell and is going to heaven, walking for the celestial city. And, brethren, all that any sinner in this house has to do is to turn around in the road he 's in. What does convert mean? "Con," altogether, and "verto," I turn. Conversion is my part of the work, regeneration God's part. You convert yourself, and when you convert yourself God regenerates you. "Converto," I turn altogether. I turn my back on sin and the devil, and make for God. That 's it. I wish you could see that.

Brother George Smith down in our State—a fine preacher, but a metaphysician—was preaching one day on repentance, and was splitting hairs a mile long between evangelical repentance and some other sort of repentance, and an old pastor in the audience — a fine preacher himself, and uncle of George Smith—could not stand it at last; so he said, "George, you sit down, and let me tell these people what repentance means." "Of course I will, Uncle John," replied George; "I 'll sit down any time to hear you." Uncle John was lame, and he got down from his seat to go up to the pulpit. As he was going up the aisle he said, "I 'll tell them just what it means;" and he kept on saying on his way up the aisle, "I 'm going to hell; I 'm going to hell; I 'm going to hell," until he got to the top of the aisle. Then he turned right round and retraced his steps down the aisle, saying, as he did so, "I 'm going to heaven; I 'm going to heaven; I 'm going to heaven; I 'm going to heaven." Then he got into his seat again and said, "Now, George, I have told them what repentance means, and you can go on with your sermon."

O, how tired I get when a metaphysician gets hold of the Gospel of Jesus Christ. I want to do just as Uncle John did. I want to tell you. I was seeking religion a whole week, and never made any progress at all. I had just scattered the sins I could get along best without, and at the end of the week I seemed further from God that at the first. All at once I saw the futility of doing as I was, and I gathered up all my sins and threw them from me and turned my back on them and walked off; and I walked over the river of resolution, and I set fire to the bridge, and as the last expiring sin dropped into the water, I said, "Heaven or nothing," and as soon as I had passed over the river, I was in the arms of God and a saved man.

"If we repent of our sins he is faithful and just to forgive us." Brothers, do you want any thing stronger and better than that to bank on? It is like the platforms over the pools on the stock-farms out West. Here is a blessed promise of the river of life. Many of those sinners who try to climb up some other way than the right say there is no river of life there, but, glory to God! the pressure of my weight of sin on the platform forces the water right out into my lips, and, glory to God! I need never be thirsty again. Here 's the promise, "If we confess our sins," etc. There 's many a man pardoned and does n't know it because he does n't feel it. I tell you there 's mighty little about feeling in the Book. It is not a question of feeling. I 'll tell you how to get feeling. You just get up out of your wicked life, and go and do the things God tells you to do, and you 'll get feeling. What is feeling? Moral perspiration. What 's physical feeling? Physical perspiration. If you get up and throw down your sins, the moral perspiration will break out on you from head to foot. That 's what we call feeling.

I 'll tell you another thing. Sin not only makes a man a rascal, but it makes him a fool. I take a man by the hand, and ask him to give himself to God. "Mr. Jones," he says, "I 'd do it if I had feeling." "You fool!" I say, "what 's the matter with you? It 's not feeling you want. Your idea of feeling is something to blubber over. It 's repentance you want." When you say "feeling," what do you mean? There 's only one sensible answer, "Serious thought about my soul." If you have that, then you have all the feeling necessary to make you a Christian man and to take you to heaven.

"If we confess our sins." Now, brethren, what is faith? Faith is just taking God at his word. One of the grandest old men I ever heard tell his experience said, "Brethren, I started in this new life to be just what the Lord in his grace should make me. I said I am going to pray over my whole nature in sections. Lord, I want to be sincere from head to foot. And the Lord, came to me with the grace of sincerity and since that time I have been sincere to God and to man. The next thing I did was to pray, Lord, help me to believe thy word. I can 't believe it as I would. And all at once it seemed as if the Lord came right down on me and said, 'I heard you asking me to help you believe my word. What do you mean? I am the Lord, and can not lie. Get up and take me at my word, and I will bless you every day of your life.'" Well, now, ain't you a pretty fellow, asking the Lord to help you believe his word? I'll tell you what you remind me of. "Bob," I say to my little fellow, "you go and get me a drink of water, and I'll give you a dime." But Bob comes up around me, feeling to see if I've got the dime, and he never thinks of the drink of water. Many a time I've seen the promise hanging over your head, if you will do so-and-so while you are standing around wondering if the Lord meant what he said. The Lord pity us and help us to go out and do what he means us to do! Brother, you can bank on this promise.

Down in Tennessee, in one of the principal cities there, I saw a leading judge at my meeting every night, and I said to him, "You are are a sensible man; what are you trying to do here every night—trying to get religion?" "Yes," he says. "Have you confessed your sins?" I asked him. "Yes," he says. "Then you are a pardoned man," I told him. "How do you know?" he asked me. "Because," said I, "God says, 'If we confess our sins, he is faithful and just to forgive us our sins.' Have you confessed?" "Yes." "Well then, you are pardoned." Afterwards, at the close of the meeting, I said, "Every pardoned sinner come up here," and the judge, with a face all radiant with joy, came up and said, "I take God at his word. I just would not believe what God had said."

But if you just pardon an old sinner and leave him there, it's like washing a hog and leaving him to wallow in the mud again. The old sinner if left to himself would be as bad again inside a month. Brethren, let me give you this fact: It is your business to repent and God's business to pardon you. "If we confess our sins, he is faithful and just to forgive us." There is something better than that. After I was converted and pardoned I used to be troubled nearly to death how I could ever hold up my head in heaven. The Lord has seen all my meanness, and how can I ever walk the golden streets with my head up? But I read on and found that he will not only pardon our sins, but will separate them from us as far as the east is from the west. What a glorious thing it is to get so far from sin! And on another day I read, "He will blot out our sins from the book, and remember them no more forever." Is n't that precious? But I never understood what he meant until I was preaching at Louisville, one day, at the church of Brother Morris. He had been converted seventeen years before that, and up to that time had been a wicked, dissipated, carousing, wretched youth. But at the time I met him he was the most saintly man I ever saw in my life. One night he told the people how he used to gamble and drink and fight, and when the service was over old Sister Morris, his mother, came up to him and said, "What made you say that, Jimmy? You never did any thing of that sort in your life." And I learned that the precious mother had forgotten all about his past life. He had been seventeen years good, and the precious mother had blotted his wrong-doings out of her memory. I have cursed and swore and drunk and done a thousand mean things; but, brother, I will walk the golden streets as if I never done a mean thing in my life, and if any body says such a thing to me, I shall just refer them to the Lord.

BRIEF SAYINGS.

A WORKING girl is just as good as the girl who does n't do any thing in the world but let her mother wait on her.

IF there is a thing in this world I have the profoundest contempt for, it 's the infernal dancing-master going through the land despoiling the young people of our country.

ELECTION.—"Whosoever will, let him take of the water of life freely." I like that grand "whosoever" there. I have read a great deal about election, but I think I have found out from God's Word what is meant by election. The "elect" are the "whosoever-wills," and the "non-elect" are the "whosoever-won'ts."

THE JUDGMENT.—When God says "Depart," the sentence is written, and shall sparkle forever upon the tablets of eternity. And the issues being eternal, and there being no after jurisdiction or revisionary control, no higher court to which we can appeal, we say God will not hurry matters on that occasion. God will give every soul ample time and opportunity to bring out all the "pros" and "cons" on that occasion.

SAMUEL W. SMALL.

DELIVERANCE FROM BONDAGE.

A Temperance Sermon

BY

SAMUEL W. SMALL.

I HOPE you will give me your prayerful attention to-night. What I shall say shall be based on the sixteenth verse of the third chapter of Acts:

"And his name, through faith in his name, hath made this man strong, whom ye see and know; yea, the faith which is by him hath given him this perfect soundness in the presence of you all."

On one occasion there came into the market-place of a far Eastern city an aged, decrepit, and travel-stained man, who was a stranger to them all. He wandered through the vast bazaar without seeming to regard or take notice of the vast stores of merchandise, wealth, and accumulated wondrous handicraft of the people. Aimlessly he threaded his way about in that multitude until he attracted the attention of the people. Suddenly he stopped before one of the booths, where hung gilded cages, in which had been imprisoned birds of precious plumage and sweetest song. They were fluttering their little wings against the bars of their prison, and he listened intently that he might haply catch some note of their song; but they, thus imprisoned, refused to give forth any of the melody of their throats, but struggled and struggled impatiently and ineffectually against their imprisonment.

Suddenly the old man put his hands in the folds of his garment, and drew therefrom coin of a strange realm. He asked the price of a cage. He bought it, and, opening the door, he turned the feathered songster loose, and it fluttered its wings, so long untried, and for a little while balanced its slight body in mid-air, until nature restored its powers of equilibrium, and then it mounted up, and up, and up, and with a glad song of joy circled above the heads of the multitude, until it caught sight of the distant cloud-capped mountain, where its home had been, and then, with its precious melody flowing from its soul, it winged its way into the far and ethereal distance, and was lost to sight. Thus one by one he bought these little birds, and thus one by one he loosed them, and they repeated the glad notes of surprise, and took the same course back to their native mountain fastnesses. He seemed to take a greater pleasure and a sweeter joy as each little prisoner regained its liberty, and the tears streamed down his travel-stained and dust-covered face.

Those who stood by said to him, "Why dost thou do these strange things?" He said to them in reply, with a look of charity and joy indescribable on his face, "I was once a prisoner myself, and I know something of the sweets of liberty."

I, brethren, was once a prisoner myself, and now I have tasted something of the sweets of liberty in Christ, and with the precious coinage of his mercies and his promises I would stand before this multitude to-night and purchase from the willing hearts of men the liberty of their souls from a bondage more despicable and deadly, and more repressive of the natural melody of men's souls, than were these gilded cages to the birds of this far Eastern mart.

I have been under the bondage of sin, a bondage that was galling every moment almost; a bondage from which there was eliminated every element of joy, and from which there seemed to be at times no avenue of escape.

If you will pardon me, I will refer to myself. I will tell you something of my experience, because I would have my young compatriots know it, and know it to the good of their souls. I would have my fellow-men who are in middle life, with families, hear it. I would have these veteran fathers of this community hear it.

I was well born. I was given by kindly parents all the true and the religious culture that a boy could have in a loving home. I was instructed in right speaking; I was encouraged in right doing; I was inspirited at times to consider myself a child of God, and to recognize in my youth my responsibility to him.

And when I had left my mother's side, and had left my father's counsel, and left the old hearth tree and the family altar, and gone out into the avenues of the world, seeking, first, an education, and afterward position and prosperity, I fell into evil ways. With the strong and lusty passions of youth, with those whom I mingled I found there were courses and ways, there were allurements and temptations, that were strange to me; and I stood reliant only upon myself, forgetting the prayers and teachings of mother and father, and I was eager for a place, eager for the pleasures of this world, eager for the happiness and the enjoyments that I saw about me. And thus I easily fell in allurements, thus easily fell from virtuous thoughts and virtuous acts, and from the virtuous course of my life.

The great bane, as I look back over my life, and conjure up the recollections of my past—the great bane of all my sinfulness, the great moving cause of all the moral iniquities I committed—was nothing more nor less than this great gorgon-headed evil that is devouring so many of the people of this land, and sowing broadcast sin and sorrow in this chosen nation of ours—the sin of intemperance.

I thought that it would be manly to do as nearly every man I saw about me did. I thought there would be some addition to my pleasure and experience by going with them into their drinking places and indulging with them. I felt all the time that I had strength of will enough, that I had force of character enough, to protect me from the excesses that I could see other men had fallen into. I believed that when I reached a dangerous point, if I ever did, I could put on the brakes of my nature and stop.

I went away to college, and there again fell into evil courses. I struggled at times with the innate manhood that was in me, and attempted to throw off the growing appetite for these things. When I came away, after I had graduated, and began to enter among men and their pursuits, and endeavored to acquire a profession, I thought still that I must mingle with my fellow-men; have some participations in their customs and in their habits; that I must bring myself into some sort of agreement and harmony with their ideas of social enjoyments, and I yielded again and again to the temptations thus presented, and again and again I fell from my rectitude, and away from ideas that lingered with me of what was right and proper. And thus, day after day, these passions grew stronger and stronger within me.

I could feel and see that I was falling, falling, falling all the time. I saw that there would not be left in me strength enough to save me, and I was unconscious at times of the fearful length to which I had fallen; but I would not look at the picture I knew I was presenting to others. I went on and on. I went until I brought tears from the eyes of my precious mother, until I brought fearful lines to her face, until I brought gray streaks into her beautiful hair, until I had brought the lines of care about her loving eyes; and until I knew I was dragging, drop by drop the life-blood from her devoted heart. I knew that my strong and manly father was suffering on my account tortures that he would not, in his courage, let the world know were gnawing at his heart and at his soul.

I knew how it went out to me; how it followed me abroad in other lands, and I knew that the failing of his step, and the silvering of his hair, and the deepening of the lines of grief about his mouth, that had so often spoken golden words of counsel, were due to the course and ways into which I had fallen, and to the apparent hopelessness of my ever coming out of them, and being reformed and being renewed in mind and in body.

O, I shall never feel satisfied short of the ability in heaven to make obeisance at their feet and crave their pardon, which I know has long since been granted me, and which I shall ever see beam on their angelic faces until I am in my grave.

I married a lovable woman. I married one who was proud of disposition; one who had high and noble traits of character; one who had quick and responsive sensibilities; one to whom the very taint of any thing that was disreputable was like a knife-stab to her heart; but I disregarded the love and devotion of that precious wife. I went on and on, unheeding her counsel, disregarding her prayers, and from day to day getting grosser and grosser in my appetites, and getting more brutal in my insensibility to her pleadings and her prayers. And when children came to bless my home, even the sight of them in their little cradles, unconscious in the first moments of their life, and with the smiles of God drawing responsive smiles from them, I found it impossible for me to know that I was doing that which would sooner or later bring shame and sorrow and degradation upon those innocent babes; and as they grew from year to year their voices came, and they prattled about me; it was only at distant intervals that I began to regard the future that was stretching far off in the distance before them, and which I must make either one of peace and pleasure, or one of despair and wretchedness.

And year after year I went on and on in this course of sin and wickedness, and the light of my home went out. The love of my wife gave way, but the process of murder of affection could not last forever; and I saw at last, it seemed to me, that she had returned it to the sepulcher in which she had laid it away in its tear-bedewed cerements forever. I could see that the love and affection of my children were turning from me daily, seemingly by intuition. They saw I was not he who was appointed to be their father in the manifestations of fatherhood that I made to them. I could know, and know with a treble emphasis, that drove unutterable horrors into my soul, but it seemed only to drive me further and further into despair, that they would, at my coming, flee from my presence far away into the darkest and remotest parts of the house, for fear of the consequences of meeting their father.

I had friends, friends in position, friends high in authority, friends who were true and steadfast to me; but they, too, were unable to paint to me any picture that would allure me from the one I was painting with my own hand in the horrible colors of hell itself. They would point me to a goal that my bleared and confused vision would not see. They would endeavor to lift me up on plains of hope and sensibilities of ambition that I had ceased to be sensible of, as being worthy of achievement.

They would endeavor to control my appetite, and find it as useless as to bind with a cotton-woven string the raging lion of the arid and tempest-swept desert.

I had at times my lucid intervals, when there would come memories of mother's prayer, of father's counsel, of wife's tears, and of children's mute and helpless look; and I would say to myself, "I will summon to my aid all the powers of my soul and manhood, and I will put under foot this monster of hideous mien that is dragging me down into degradation, into social ruin, and taking a fast hold upon my soul, and which sooner or later will drag it a trophy into hell. I would summon all my powers, only to find that I was weaker than a babe in the arms of so strong a passion as I had awakened.

I would go to physicians, and ask them in the name of my family and future to do something for me, if indeed there had been found medicines on earth to minister to a mind diseased and an appetite debauched, and they would exhaust their knowledge and their skill, and hundreds and thousands of dollars did I spend in the endeavor to reinforce will, manhood, and my own powers of repression, but all in vain.

There were antidotes that were published abroad in the world, and with the use of which cures are guaranteed, but all, all in vain. I spent hundreds and thousands of dollars, and hours and days of time, and I purchased advertised efficient and warranted cures for drunkenness, and I was as faithful in the application of them as ever human being was; but it was all in vain! in vain!! in vain!!!

There was no medicament in them to cure my aroused passion and appetite.

I went so far that my wife, under the laws then existing in Georgia, had written by the judge of the court in which I was the official short-hand reporter, a legal notice, couched in the language of the law, and had this notice served upon every dealer in liquors in the city of Atlanta, warning them, under penalty of the law, not to let me have their damning fluid over their counters; and yet, outlaws as they were, disregarding my interest, disregarding my wife's pleadings and the tears of my children, and disregarding the very law of the land, they still continued to supply me with the horrible draught for which my inmost nature seemed craving with insatiety.

I even employed attendants and detectives, who followed me as I went about on my business in the streets of my city, and they followed me with the purpose, and were employed for the purpose, of keeping these men who would not keep the law themselves from furnishing me with whisky; and yet I, in conjunction with them, was able to hoodwink and defy detectives and law.

Further and further, deeper and deeper, I was sinking; I was getting hopeless for business; hopeless for all social standing; hopeless for all the temporal interests of this world; hopeless for eternity; and, in the very madness of my disordered brain, and in my very soul, there seemed at times no avenue of escape at all from this self-imposed bondage, except through insanity on the one hand, and through suicide on the other.

I saw that my wife and children had given up all hope; they did not know, from day to day, how I would come home to them. They had seen me brought there, day after day, time after time, insensible and unable to recognize them, from the influence of this deadly and poisonous drug. They had seen me when I was brought in and laid on my bed covered with blood, and it seemed as though my days were indeed numbered, and that I would soon fall in the midst of my iniquity. They had seen me when I was brought home with the wounds of the knife and pistol on my body, and they had heard the rumors from the streets and dives of the dangers with which I had been constantly surrounded of late. To them it seemed as though there was no avenue, no loophole, of escape for me from a terrible death. There was not the sign of hope or spirit beaming out from their beautiful faces. They knew not, from day to day, whether I would live to greet them another day. They knew not whether, if my life was prolonged, they would be able to procure the very necessities of life from day to day.

They knew not at what hour the very shelter that shielded them from the storm and from the heat would be removed from over their head, and they removed from under its shelter. There were visions of uncertainty, of the sheriff to dispossess, of the heartless landlord to distrain for rent, of the debtor to come and take all. There was no future ahead of them, except a future of impenetrable gloom, through which seemed to come nothing but warnings of deeper woe and agonies yet to come. O, Lord, how good thou wast to me! thou hast given me relief from that bondage at my seeking.

At last there came a time when I seemed to have reached the limit. Something strange impelled me to take my little children, as a loving act, an act, it seemed to me, of reparation for neglects of weeks preceding, and go upon the train to Cartersville, where Brother Jones was preaching to immense audiences, and from which the report had come that there were many and many hundreds, and even thousands, who were coming back into harmony with God. And as I sat upon the platform, endeavoring to take in stenography the words as they fell from his lips, it seemed to me that God had inspired him to preach upon one certain line. He preached it with that faith which is his alone; he preached it with that fidelity which is his distinguishing characteristic; he preached with the earnestness and with the conviction that broke down the casements of my heart and went home to it. When he had finished those words of Conscience! Conscience! Conscience! and of Record! Record! Record! of God, the infinite, the all-seeing and the ever-judging God, came home to me.

I went away from there troubled in mind and soul. I went home, and back into the devious ways, back into the bar-room, back into the open highways, back to the maddening pool, in order to get away from the torments I was suffering from an awakened conscience. But they would not leave me. I could find no solace where I had often found insensibility. I could find no relief in potations where I had often found indifference and capability to take on a cool exterior. There was nothing there to give me surcease from the sorrow in my bosom; and I went on and on until the second day, on Tuesday, at noon, I went into my library-room, fell upon my knees, buried my face in my hands, and I pleaded with Christ that he would let me cling to his cross, lay down all my burdens and sins there, and be rescued and saved by his compassion; that I might be washed in his blood, and that my sins, though they were scarlet, might be white as snow.

I wrestled for four long hours, in as much agony as I ever suffered. At the end of that time, when I had reached a conclusion, when I had come to understand that there was nothing of earth that could avail me, least of all with Christ, then I gave myself entirely to him, made an unconditional surrender, and that moment he seized my soul. He dipped it in the stream which was white and pure, and the light of heaven shone in upon me.

In my new-found joy, I rushed into the presence ot wife and children. I proclaimed the glad tidings to their astonished ears, and they could hardly believe it, though they saw that some great revolution had taken place. They knew not whether it was a surrender to Christ, or whether it had been a surrender to madness.

But when I went out that evening, I had three thousand circulars printed and distributed all over Atlanta, telling the people I had found my Savior; I had made peace with God, and that I would live a life of righteousness ever after, and desired to make a proclamation for once and irrevocable. They gathered at seven o'clock upon the public streets that night, and there before them I proclaimed the fact, and, blessed be God, I have been proclaiming it ever since with increased joy, and with the certainty that my salvation is complete.

Returning home, I could see that Jesus had knocked at the tomb of my wife's life, as it did at that of Lazarus, and had called it forth in all its pristine strength and beauty, and its bloom and blossom has been my pathway ever since. I could see that my children had found tongue to sing the joy and praise, and their hearts had been set attuned, as they never had been before, to the melody of childhood, singing to the ears of fatherhood. I could see that there was gladness, wherever I went, upon the faces of friends and acquaintances; and, when the news had gone abroad in the land, they who had known me abroad sent me their glad congratulations and their encouragement.

Blessed be God that, from the day he reached down and lifted me up from the horrible pit and the miry clay, and established my feet upon the rock of Christ that is higher than we, I have been going on from joy to joy, a bird of liberty, singing the praises of my Redeemer.

And so, having been thus saved and thus healed,

I would call you who are in that terrible bondage to seek relief of the same great Physician, and to draw your medicine from the same infallible spring.

What are we doing with ourselves? O, how, when we look abroad in this land, we can see how intemperance is becoming the great national vice, and how it is becoming the fell destroyer of so many thousands and thousands of our loved ones. What are we doing with these bodies of ours? "What, know ye not that your body is the temple of the Holy Ghost which is in you, which ye have of God, and ye are not your own?" Fellow-men, fellow-men, let me bring you to the contemplation of the fact that these bodies of ours are the temples of the Holy Ghost, and that they were fashioned after the architecture of his great brains, by the great Being who is the architect of the universe.

These bodies he made of the dust of the earth, and these bones of his rock; he made us with veins and with arteries, and filled them with the blood from the seas of his providence; he gave us breath, which, like the wind, cometh and goeth and scattereth; which cometh we know not whence, goeth we know not where; he gave us sight for all the beauties and grandeurs of the world, and inflamed it with fire from the center of his storehouse of fire; he gave us thoughts, like the clouds, for, like them, they move, and as they play in the sunlight of righteousness, are transformed into beauty, whether it be the beauty of the dawn, presaging what is to come.

or the beauty of the sunset, presaging the glorious death toward which we tend.

And we can make these minds of ours reflect the light of heaven, or they can have the light of heaven withdrawn, and be dark and dismal and foreboding as the storm-clouds, from which the mutterings of heaven come and roll the thunders of agony that spread destruction and death upon us. And in these temples he has placed the Holy Ghost in spirit for us, and we are its custodians, the priests of these temples; and when we degrade and defile them, we are degrading and defiling the architecture of God and his chosen resting-place in us.

O, what a touching instance it was when the favorite son of Tertullian died! His companions were bearing his corpse to the cemetery upon their shoulders, and as they went along, occupied with their thoughts of sorrow and grief, they stumbled by the way, when the grief-stricken father, noticing it, called out to them: "Young men, beware how you walk; you bear upon your shoulders the temple of the Holy Ghost."

So with us. We go about bearing with us the temple of the Holy Ghost, and we are recreant to our own creation, recreant to our own destiny, recreant to the great God who fashioned us, recreant to the great God who made us his temples, when we defile these bodies of ours, and ruin them with the licenses of our baser natures and our depraved appetites.

One time Diogenes saw a young man going to a place of revelry, where drinking was the custom, and from which men who went in sober and rational beings emerged besotted, and not knowing their way. He seized upon the young man, carried him to his friends, and informed them that he had rescued their precious boy from a great and awful danger. So it would be well if we had friends who would thus rescue us. But there are times when friends, as I told you, can have no influence, and no Diogenes, however wise, however honest, however mindful of his neighbor, could restrain us from going into these places.

But how many Diogeneses it would take to seize upon those that night after night and day after day are going into these places of danger and ultimate death in the city of Cincinnati! O, let us seek to save ourselves through the only influence, the only medicament, and the only Physician that this universe affords us!

What is intemperance doing? It is not necessary to marshal here before you the figures; you can see it all about you.

Young man, you know that you started in your intemperate habits just as I did. You know what influences have led you; you know what ambitions you thought you could cultivate by listening to them; you know how you have run out and gone into these places with like ideas of strength and ability to control yourselves just as I had. And now you are buoyant in the consciousness that you think that at any time you can slap on the brakes of your nature, and save yourselves from degradation that you see upon the planes just below us.

Beware, beware of that fatal cup. There are fathers, middle-aged; they know what intemperance will do. They are listening to me to-night, and they started on that road just as I started; but if they have not reached the same length to which I went, they are on the high road to it. They can already know that they are not received where once they were welcome guests; they know that they are passed every day on the streets of Cincinnati by men who formerly regarded them with esteem and claimed them as friends. They know that avenues were once open to them of usefulness, and which are now closed upon them forever on account of their habits, their companionship, and their places of resort. They know that the happiness of their families, once complete, is now gone, apparently forever. They know that the blanched cheek of that wife, that the constant redness of eye when they enter home, that the fleeing children, are all evidences of the steady growth of the evil; and they have grown just in proportion as they have gone deeper and deeper into this besotted condition.

There are old men here to-night who have led a long life, it seemed, of moderation, and who thought that they were exemplifying the ability of a man to drink and drink and drink, and yet preserve his manhood and his honest position; but they can see that their excesses are not only sapping the foundations of their health; they can feel that they are untimely gray; they can feel that they have diseases in them that they would not have had but for their intemperance; and they can see before them no life that is leading them on and brightening their way as they go. But they are seeing, upon the other hand—and if they are honest with themselves, they will confess it to their souls—that they are losing the powers, and that sooner or later they, too, must sink into the lowest depths of degradation, and be untimely cut off, and go to hell to everlasting death.

Families and individuals — cities — prostrated. There is nothing that is so glaring about them as intemperance, which sweeps over them like the storm over a forest, day after day and night after night. Thank God that my city of Atlanta has redeemed herself under the white banner of temperance, with the cross of Christ on it! Thank God, she will shine as a city set upon a hill, giving a light to this nation! Ohio to-day is giving full liberty to the whisky dealers to debauch and damn the most precious sons of your loins and your household.

God can not bless a people who are thus recreant to themselves and thus recreant to their duties, both to humanity and to God. Thank God that old Georgia is rapidly redeeming herself, and that after a while she will still be lying in the very apron of this nation, a redeemed State from the tyrany of alcohol, and that she will raise her banner and commend it in its purity to every State in this nation, as it blazons with the legend of Wisdom, Justice, and Moderation, under the broad and glittering arch of the Constitution.

Nearly twenty-five years ago misguided men in the South fired the first shot upon Fort Sumter that awakened this entire nation, and led to reform, and led to liberties, and led to the release of slaves from bondage, led to what no man had contemplated as being capable of realization. It marshaled the most impregnable arms of this continent, and that shot reverberated all through civilization. I tell you that whatever were the disasters of war, it struck the shackles from six million slaves; but to-day, in a holier and grander cause, by the approving smile of God, old Georgia has fired a gun upon the Sumters of sin and intemperance in this country that will arouse this whole nation; and we will batter down these forts of intemperance, whether they are in Cincinnati, Chicago, or New York.

The army of God in this nation is on the march. And you may listen here; and if you have not the courage and the Christian zeal, we will come and break down the barriers; we will pound down the forts of the demon of alcohol, and we will release you from this terrible bondage.

In the midst of influences like this, with these facts staring them in the face, statesmen of this country are too cowardly to seize upon this great question, and make it a question of public policy for the Christian people. Politicians go wandering about among the lower classes, and talk and rant about personal liberty and sumptuary laws, as though they had a right to give laws to these people, when these smiling scoundrels are only seeking popularity and applause from the foolish and depraved.

Scientists are disputing and debating, when all history and all true science have demonstrated that no curse is greater upon a people than to have the saloons and the dissemination of these deadly compounds in the community. These whisky dealers are outlaws; they are against the law; they are anomalous creatures, and the anarchists of the nineteenth century. If they would disobey and disregard the laws in my case, they will do it in yours, and they will do it in the case of every precious son you have got, of every living father you have got, of every devoted husband you have got in this country.

Churches meet in conventions, meet in conferences, meet in assemblies, meet in synods, and pass resolutions on the subject of temperance, and yet the very ministers, it seems, in places, are unwilling to enforce the declarations and laws of their own Churches against their own members, notwithstanding that right here in Cincinnati ministers of the Gospel have been disrobed through its influences, and Churches have been debauched.

And thus our very rulers, law-makers, public men, and public teachers are thus indifferent or cowardly in the face of an evil like that, while the red-winged and fiery-eyed Zamael of these distillers and brewers of the country is sweeping over this land and laying low in horrible death the first-born of American homes, as the angel did at the command of God in the land of Pharaoh centuries ago. And every man and every woman, especially in America, has a direct personal interest in seeing the banner of Christ triumph over the sign of the beer barrel and the whisky worm.

Is there any thing needed to arouse the humanity and the patriotism of you people to the iniquities that are being thus committed in your midst, and the sad havoc that is being made in your homes? If I to-night were to call around me a staff of bailiffs and furnish them with subpœnas, I could send them into the streets, and into the back-yards, and into the slums and alleys and tenement districts of Cincinnati, and I could send to Walnut Hills, and to Mount Auburn, and Avondale, and Mount Adams, and other of your respectable and high-toned suburbs of Cincinnati, and from the palaces of your richest down to the humblest huts and dens of your poorest, and examine the widows and the orphans that whisky has made, and array them here in grand mass by the thousands, with their weeping eyes, with their dismal recollection, with their mourning, with their hearts crushed and bleeding, and they would say to you, "If you are men, in the name of God and humanity, rise in your might and drive this monster out before he destroys and ruins your homes too."

If we but heed these witnesses, and are true to ourselves, to our children, to humanity, and to God, we can destroy this flaming monster, and soon be able to sing out to men and angels that our people are redeemed, regenerated, and disenthralled from the fatal powers of the dragon. Then we will be blessed by our Father in heaven with a posterity given to paths of righteousness and lives of Christian endeavor and achievement.

Our sons shall grow up in strength and honor,

and wear the Christian armor. Their feet will be shod with the preparation of the Gospel, their loins be girded about with truth, their bodies guarded by the breast-plate of faith, their shield be righteousness, their manly, sun-lit brows be crowned with the helmet of salvation, and their good right arms will wield the trenchant, victorious sword of the Spirit, which is the Word of God.

Our daughters will grow up in beauty and comeliness of Christian graces. Their feet will be sandaled with truth and faith; their limbs be clothed with robes of purity, on which, in silver and gold and prismatic hues, will be embroidered the record of their good deeds; their waists will be encircled with the golden girdle of strengthening prayer; their bosoms shielded by the bodice of innocence covering the virtuous heart, on which burn vestal fires of love; from their shoulders will drop the mantle of humility, and their hands will dispense the golden showers of charity upon the one side and of mercy upon the other; their throats will be wrapped with the pearls of precious words; their lips will give forth sweet songs of praise to God; their eyes will ever turn in trust to the great white throne, whose radiance will glint in the folds of their tresses, and presage the crown of immortal life that shall press their brows in Paradise.

And these two shall dwell in the splendors and happiness of the palace of purity, that rears its walls and dome around and over every true and consecrated Christian heart. They will go up to it over the broad white flag-stones of perfect desires;

they will climb up its great steps of geometrically and systematically fashioned purposes and ambitions; they will pass between the grand columns of strength and wisdom that stand before the Gate Beautiful, with its golden welcome, "All that is pure may enter in;" and in the hall of consecration they will put on the insignia of their heaven-given prerogatives, and pass on into the rotunda of a righteous life, and up into the throne-seats of honor in the East. From that exalted place, they may contemplate with rapture the idealized tableaux of the virtues of their lives. Here the picture of Truth—a fair maiden drawing from her exhaustless well the waters of sincerity that are poured out for the ennobling and refreshing of all people, and over her the glittering legend: *"Magna est Veritas et prevalebit."* There is the tableau of Faith, clinging to the rock-rooted cross that towers heavenward, and around which the wild waves of worldliness, woe, and passion surge unavailing, their highest spray not touching even the hem of her garments.

Yonder is seen the fair form of Virtue, her beautiful feet standing amid the treasures of the upturned cornucopia of fortune, her hands folded in peacefulness across her lovely bosom, and her golden hair blown into a halo about her head by the breezes that are born in the hills of happiness. Here again is figured the faultless goddess of Justice, standing upon the uppermost pole of the earth, holding the scales of God's earthly impartiality, and weighing out the dues of men in harmony with eternal truth. Over her the constellations gather and glitter in the edict of Jehovah: "*Fiat justitia, ruat cœlum!*" There again is the sweet face of Charity, swift-paced to carry succor and life to the hovel of the poor, the cots of the sick and cells of the wretched. And next comes the picture of gentle and tender-hearted Mercy, soothing the cares, relieving the burdens, reconciling the hearts, and ministering to the redemption of all the souls of God's children. And here is the grand portrait of the strong, manly apostle of Temperance, the embodiment of health, vigor, energy, and philanthropy; a giant in all good works, and approved servant of heaven.

Over in the West is the grand horologe of Time, counting out the moments of life in a monotone pæan of patience and labor, while its great pendulum swings through an arc that reaches from the cradle to the tomb.

In the center is the Christian's altar, on which praises and prayers turn to worshiping incense and pervade the place with heavenly odors.

Up in the high center of the vast dome blazes the Sun of righteousness, that lightens forever the splendid scene. Looking into it, the eye of faith, strengthened like the young eaglet's, can discern the transfigured cross of Calvary, pointing the soul to its home and rest around the throne of God in heaven.

Who are these that thus reign and rejoice? They are the Prince Christian and Princess Christiana of the kingdom of God on earth. They are the heirs apparent to everlasting life and the imperishable possessions of the King of kings! God direct us with his wisdom to so live and use our lives as to endow our children with these titles and these palaces of purity on earth—these inheritances of the meek, and pure, and temperate, and dutiful, in "the city whose builder and maker is God."

THE END.